MW01004380

Globe Law
and Business

The Rule of Law in the 21st Century

A Worldwide Perspective
Second Edition

Consulting Editors **Professor Robert A Stein**,
Justice Richard J Goldstone and **Homer E Moyer, Jr**

Consulting editors
Professor Robert A Stein, Justice Richard J Goldstone and Homer E Moyer, Jr

Managing director
Sian O'Neill

The Rule of Law in the 21st Century: A Worldwide Perspective, Second Edition
is published by

Globe Law and Business Ltd
3 Mylor Close
Horsell
Woking
Surrey GU21 4DD
United Kingdom
Tel: +44 20 3745 4770
www.globelawandbusiness.com

Printed and bound by CPI Group (UK) Ltd, Croydon CR0 4YY, United Kingdom

The Rule of Law in the 21st Century: A Worldwide Perspective, Second Edition

ISBN 9781787427952
EPUB ISBN 9781787427969
Adobe PDF ISBN 9781787427976

Table of contents

Foreword to the First Edition

Ruth Bader Ginsburg
Justice of the Supreme Court of the United States

Publication of *The Rule of Law in the 21st Century* coincides with celebrations of the 800th anniversary of Magna Carta. That foundational document, the editors of this volume observe, identified twin pillars of the rule of law: the supremacy of the law over the will of the king; and an independent, incorruptible judiciary, sworn to render judgments in accord with the law of the land. Those mainstays of the rule of law continue to guide and inspire judges and lawyers of goodwill the world over.

What does the rule of law mean today? That question is extensively explored in this volume by Robert Stein and Richard Goldstone, rule of law proponents held in high regard for their knowledge, experience and wisdom. Stein and Goldstone have enlisted as contributors to their enterprise lawyers, law professors and judges prominent in their fields – jurists well qualified to address aspects of the rule of law. They have produced a book designed to engage and enlighten readers at home and abroad.

Essential to the rule of law in any land, I have repeatedly commented, is an independent judiciary – ie, judges not under the thumb of other branches of government, and therefore equipped to administer the law impartially. As experience in the United States and elsewhere confirms, however, judicial independence is vulnerable to assault; it can be shattered if the society that law exists to serve does not take care to ensure its preservation. That key reality, recognised by Stein and Goldstone, is one I would emphasise in all arenas where the rule of law is discussed.

I have had the good fortune to take part in diverse efforts to advance the rule of law nationally and internationally. I appreciate what US jurists can bring to the table, for the legal system of the United States gives prime place to judicial review for constitutionality. US courts have measured ordinary laws and executive actions for conformity with the fundamental instrument of government for well over two centuries. At the same time, I recognise that, in the years following World War II, many other nations have installed constitutional review by courts as one safeguard against oppressive government and stirred-up majorities. Yes, we in the United States have rule of law experience to impart. But we can also learn from other nations seeking to preserve liberty and safeguard human rights in trying times. And if we do not listen to, and learn from, our global neighbours, we will diminish our own ability to promote the rule of law elsewhere.

As my colleague, Justice Anthony Kennedy, explained: "It does not lessen our fidelity to the [US] Constitution" to recognise "the express affirmation of certain fundamental rights by other nations and peoples."[1] Recall that in the first rights-declaring document of the United States, namely the Declaration of Independence, that nation's founders expressed "a decent respect to the opinions of mankind". I anticipate that the US Supreme Court will continue to accord a decent respect to the opinions of humankind as a matter of comity and in a spirit of humility. Comity, because projects vital to our well-being – combating international terrorism being a prime example – require the trust and cooperation of nations the world over. And humility because, in Justice Sandra Day O'Connor's words: "Other legal systems continue to innovate, to experiment, and to find ... solutions to the new legal problems that arise each day, [solutions] from which we can learn and benefit."[2] Openness to laws enacted and judicial decisions rendered abroad aids our comprehension of the values to be preserved by the rule of law. It also helps to ensure that the rule of law that the courts enforce rests on principled ground.

Installing and preserving the rule of law is no easy task. And no nation in today's world can go it alone. This book aims to arm individuals with the theoretical and practical instruction needed to play a meaningful part in advancing the rule of law. It is a mission that Stein and Goldstone have admirably accomplished.

---

1   *Roper v Simmons*, 543 US 551, 578 (2005).
2   Sandra Day O'Connor. "Broadening Our Horizons: Why American Lawyers Must Learn About Foreign Law", 45 *Federal Lawyer* (1998) 20, 20.

Introduction

Richard J Goldstone
Retired justice of the Constitutional Court of South Africa
Homer E Moyer, Jr
Miller & Chevalier
Robert A Stein
University of Minnesota Law School

A comprehensive description of the rule of law has eluded generations of judges, lawyers and scholars. It has sometimes been defined as 'no person is above the law'. However, it is clearly more than that. It is now widely accepted that it incorporates several concepts, including, at a minimum, the separation of powers, protection of human rights and, in particular, an independent judiciary. The question that is discussed in this book is: What does the rule of law mean in the context of 21st-century issues and challenges?

The contributors to this book examine the concept of the rule of law from a variety of perspectives. What is the rule of law? What is judicial independence? Is there an international rule of law? How can we overcome the major threat to the rule of law in the form of corruption? How should society address ultimate violations of the rule of law, such as war crimes and genocide? How can the rule of law be of assistance in reducing inequality in society? The book includes chapters describing law reform programmes that have strengthened the rule of law around the world during the past two decades.

In addressing these questions and others, we have been joined by an array of internationally distinguished leaders of the legal profession from North America, Europe, Africa and the Middle East. In addition to the editors of this second edition, chapter authors include Mark Ellis, executive director of the International Bar Association; Elizabeth Andersen, executive director of the World Justice Project; Essam Al Tamimi, chairman of Al Tamimi & Company in the United Arab Emirates; Michael Maya, director of the North American office of the International Bar Association; Allison Whelan, Sharswood Fellow, University of Pennsylvania Carey Law School and associate fellow, Leonard Davis Institute of Health Economics, University of Pennsylvania; Mariah Lindsay, PhD candidate, Department of Sociology, University of Wisconsin-Madison; and Kathryn Cameron Atkinson, chair of Miller & Chevalier in Washington DC.

We would like to express our appreciation to the late Justice Ruth Bader Ginsburg of the US Supreme Court – a tireless advocate for the rule of law – who authored the Foreword to the first edition of this publication.

The rule of law is humankind's best hope for freedom and justice. It is our hope that this second edition of *The Rule of Law in the 21st Century: A Worldwide Perspective* will give you a better understanding of this important concept in the world today.

Chapter 1. What is the rule of law?[1]

Robert A Stein
University of Minnesota Law School

1. Introduction

In the words of former US Supreme Court Justice Anthony Kennedy, "the term [r]ule of [l]aw is often invoked yet seldom defined".[2] Since the time of Aristotle, scholars, judges and legal practitioners have struggled to clearly articulate the meaning of the phrase.

A multitude of voices throughout the world express support for the rule of law. Frequently the phrase is a shorthand expression to encourage support for 'whatever happens to be the political agenda of the speaker'. When that happens, the phrase is chameleon-like – taking on whatever meaning best fits the speaker's purpose. Without a clear definition, the rule of law is in danger of coming to mean virtually everything, so that it may in fact come to mean nothing at all.

In fact, the phrase has been invoked so often that one commentator has written that the phrase "has become meaningless thanks to ideological abuse and general over-use".[3] I disagree. Because of the potential of the phrase to inspire individual actors and inform political and social change, it is important to rigorously identify the meaning of the rule of law. To the extent we can more clearly identify the principles of the rule of law, we can more effectively support the legal and political reforms that will advance it.

Although the concept of the rule of law can be traced back at least to ancient Greece, it has become much more widely discussed in the last 25 years.[4] Former US Supreme Court Justice Anthony Kennedy has stated that he does not recall the term being used often when he was in law school in the 1950s.[5] That was also my experience as a law student at about the same time.

---

1   An earlier version of this chapter was published as "What Exactly Is the Rule of Law?" 57 *Houston L Rev* 185 (2019). Permission to republish is gratefully acknowledged.
2   Anthony M Kennedy, 20th Sultan Azlan Shah Law Lecture: "Written Constitutions and the Common Law Tradition" (10 August 2006) (on file with the author).
3   Judith N Shklar, "Political Theory and the Rule of Law", in AC Hutchinson and P Monahan (eds), *The Rule of Law: Ideal or Ideology* (1987) 1: "It would not be very difficult to show that the phrase 'the Rule of Law' has become meaningless thanks to ideological abuse and general over-use. It may well have become just another one of those self-congratulatory rhetorical devices that grace the public utterances of Anglo-American politicians. No intellectual effort need therefore be wasted on this bit of ruling-class chatter."
4   FA Hayek, *The Constitution of Liberty* (2011) 232 n.1, 239–240.
5   Kennedy, footnote 2 above: "Although I cannot recall hearing the phrase in common usage when attending college and law school a half century ago, it has deep roots."

As a result of the fall of the Berlin Wall and the end of the Soviet Union, new democracies emerged in Central and Eastern Europe in the early nineties, and this development raised greater interest in the concept. As more people on the planet began to live under a democratic form of government, it became clear that democracy alone could not ensure liberty and freedom. The concept of the rule of law and its relationship to the realisation of important goals of political reform began to receive much more attention.

2. The meaning of the rule of law

2.1 Origins of the rule of law

The essence of the rule of law, originally attributed to Aristotle, is a "government by laws and not by men".[6] Scholars, judges and lawyers in various countries, particularly in recent years, have laboured to define in greater detail the meaning of this concept.[7] There is widespread agreement that the concept is difficult to define in a way that captures all of its meaning.[8]

A good starting point in examining the concept is the definition of the rule of law set forth in the 2004 Report of the Secretary General of the United Nations, entitled *The Rule of Law and Transitional Justice in Conflict and Post-Conflict Societies*:

> [The rule of law] refers to a principle of governance in which all persons, institutions and entities, public and private, including the State itself, are accountable to laws that are publicly promulgated, equally enforced and independently adjudicated, and which are consistent with international human rights norms and standards. It requires, as well, measures to ensure adherence to the principles of supremacy of law, equality before the law, accountability to the law, fairness in the application of the law, separation of powers, participation in decision-making, legal certainty, avoidance of arbitrariness and procedural and legal transparency.[9]

The principles constituting the rule of law identified in this definition are both procedural and substantive.

Rule of law principles are procedural, for example, in that the government must be subject to law, and that the laws are publicly promulgated, equally enforced and adjudicated by an independent judiciary. Additional procedural rules require that the laws must be fairly and equally applied, and that separation of powers must be observed in the enactment and adjudicative processes.

---

6   Hayek, footnote 4 above, at 243.
7   See, eg, AV Dicey, *Introduction to the Study of the Law of the Constitution* (7th edn, 1908) 179–201; Robert Stein, "Symposium, Rule of Law: What Does It Mean?" 18 *Minn J Int'l L* (2009) 293; T Bingham, *The Rule of Law* (2010) 3–5, 8.
8   See Kennedy, footnote 2 above; Dicey, note 7 above, at 182–184, 189–191; Bingham, footnote 7 above, at 5–7.
9   UN Secretary-General, *The Rule of Law and Transitional Justice in Conflict and Post-Conflict Societies: Report of the Secretary-General*, UN Doc S/2004/616 (23 August 2004) p6.

The principles of the rule of law are also substantive, in that the laws must be just and consistent with the norms and standards of international human rights law. Also, the rule of law requires the avoidance of arbitrariness in the law.

Two seminal writings on the rule of law – one in the late 19th century and another in the mid-20th century – have helped modern scholars and judges in their efforts to define the concept.

British lawyer and professor AV Dicey wrote in 1897 that the rule of law in England included at least three concepts:

It means, in the first place, the absolute supremacy or predominance of regular law as opposed to the influence of arbitrary power, and excludes the existence of arbitrariness, of prerogative, or even of wide discretionary authority on the part of the government . . .

It means, again, equality before the law, or the equal subjection of all classes to the ordinary law of the land administered by the ordinary Law Courts; the 'rule of law' in this sense excludes the idea of any exemption of officials or others from the duty of obedience to the law which governs other citizens or from the jurisdiction of the ordinary tribunals . . .

The 'rule of law,' lastly, may be used as a formula for expressing the fact that with us [in England] the law of the constitution, the rules which in foreign countries naturally form part of a constitutional code, are not the source but the consequence of the rights of individuals, as defined and enforced by the Courts; . . . thus the constitution is the result of the ordinary law of the land.[10]

Sixty years later, Austrian Nobel Prize-winning economist and political theorist, FA Hayek, wrote in *The Constitution of Liberty* about the history and meaning of the concept. Hayek traced the idea and development of the rule of law from its origins in the writings of ancient Greek and Roman philosophers to its refinement in English constitutional history.[11] The founders of the American Constitution were influenced by many British writings, particularly those of John Locke,[12] and embedded those ideals in the American Constitution in 1787.

More recently, many current and former justices of the US Supreme Court have written and spoken in support of and explaining the rule of law. Former Justice Anthony Kennedy addressed the subject of the rule of law in an address to the American Bar Association in 2006 and again in an unpublished Lecture

---

10   Dicey, footnote 7 above, at 198–199.
11   See Hayek, footnote 4 above, at 240–251.
12   John Locke, *Second Treatise of Government*, CB Macpherson (ed), (Hackett Publ Co 1980) (1690) 32: "[T]he end of law is not to abolish or restrain, but to preserve and enlarge freedom: for in all the states of created beings capable of laws, where there is no law, there is no freedom: for liberty is, to be free from restraint and violence from others; which cannot be, where there is no law: but freedom is not, as we are told, a liberty for every man to do what he lists: (for who could be free, when every other man's humour might domineer over him?) but a liberty to dispose, and order as he lists, his person, actions, possessions, and his whole property, within the allowance of those laws under which he is, and therein not to be subject to the arbitrary will of another, but freely follow his own."

in Kuala Lumpur, Malaysia also in 2006.[13] Justice Kennedy identified several ideas constituting the rule of law which have had a great influence on my thinking and the principles set forth in this chapter. Justice Kennedy compared the rule of law to the phrase, '*Per Legem Terrae*, or Law of the Land', dating back to Magna Carta: "It was an appeal to a general civic understanding that principles of fairness and justice must be respected."[14]

Former US Supreme Court Justice Sandra Day O'Connor, who was active for many years in promoting reforms to advance the rule of law in Central and Eastern Europe, has also written and spoken frequently on the rule of law.[15] "Broadly speaking," Justice O'Connor has written, "the [r]ule of [l]aw requires that legal rules be publicly known, consistently enforced, and even-handedly applied."[16] She attributed to Aristotle the idea that the rule of law is "'nothing less than the rule of reason' balanced by considerations of equity so that just results may be achieved in particular cases".[17] Justice O'Connor emphasised that judicial independence was essential to the rule of law.[18]

Another US Supreme Court Justice, Ruth Bader Ginsburg, in several speeches and articles made clear the importance of judicial independence to the rule of law. Justice Ginsburg has written: "Essential to the rule of law in any land is an independent judiciary, judges not under the thumb of other branches of Government, and therefore equipped to administer the law impartially."[19] Justice Ginsburg described the essence of an independent judiciary by quoting former Chief Justice William Rehnquist:

> [The role of a judge is similar] to that of a referee in a basketball game who is obliged to call a foul against a member of the home team at a critical moment in the game: he will be soundly booed, but he is nonetheless obliged to call it as he saw it, not as the home crowd wants him to call it.[20]

Chief Justice John Roberts[21] and Justice Stephen Breyer[22] have also spoken

---

13 Kennedy, footnote 2 above; Anthony Kennedy, Keynote Address at the American Bar Association Annual Meeting (5 August 2006), available at www.c-span.org/video/?193757-1/justice-kennedy-address.

14 Kennedy, footnote 2 above, at 257–259.

15 See, eg, Sandra Day O'Connor, Remarks at the CEELI Institute Dedication (June 2007), excerpted at *CEELI Institute Newsletter* (June 2007) 2; Ruth V McGregor, "A Tribute to Justice Sandra Day O'Connor", 119 *Harv L Rev* (2006) 1245, 1246: describing Justice O'Connor's advocacy for the rule of law and service on the Executive Board of the American Bar Association's Central and Eastern European Law Initiative.

16 Sandra Day O'Connor, "Vindicating the Rule of Law: The Role of the Judiciary", 2 *Chinese J Int'l L* (2003) 1, 1.

17 *Ibid* (quoting Judith N Shklar, "Political Theory and the Rule of Law", in AC Hutchinson and P Monahan (eds), *The Rule of Law: Ideal or Ideology* (1987) 1).

18 *Ibid* at 2–5.

19 Ruth Bader Ginsburg, "Judicial Independence: The Situation of the U.S. Federal Judiciary", 85 *Neb L Rev* (2006) 1, 1.

20 *Ibid* (quoting William H Rehnquist, "Act Well Your Part: Therein All Honor Lies", 7 *Pepp L Rev* (1980) 227, 229–230).

21 See, eg, John G Roberts, Jr, "Thirty-First Annual Pepperdine University School of Law Dinner: Keynote Address", in 37 *Pepp L Rev* (*Special Issue*) (2009) 1, 6; John G Roberts, Jr, "William H Rehnquist: A Remembrance, Address at Middlebury College (October 24 2006)", in 31 *Vt L Rev* (2007) 431, 436–437; John G Roberts, Jr, "Remarks at Fair and Independent Courts: A Conference on the State of the Judiciary (28 September 2006)", available at www.c-span.org/video/?194520-3/judicial-independence&start=1288.

22 See, eg, Stephen Breyer, "Judicial Independence", 95 *Geo LJ* (2007) 903; Stephen G Breyer, "Judicial Independence in the United States", 40 *St Louis U LJ* (1996) 989.

and written to establish greater meaning and understanding of the rule of law and judicial independence.

On the British side of the Atlantic, a thoughtful and significant book on the rule of law was written by the late Senior Law Lord Thomas Bingham in 2010.[23] The core of the rule of law, Bingham wrote, is:

> [T]hat all persons and authorities within the state, whether public or private, should be bound by and entitled to the benefit of laws publicly made, taking effect (generally) in the future and publicly administered in the courts.[24]

Bingham expanded on this definition of the rule of law by advancing eight subsidiary principles that give more detailed meaning to this definition of the rule of law.[25] Bingham's eight subsidiary principles raised issues with regard to the rule of law that will be explored later in this chapter.

Another widely-read definition of the rule of law has been set forth by the World Justice Project, which is an "independent, multidisciplinary organisation working to advance the rule of law worldwide".[26] Originally established by the American Bar Association, the World Justice Project is now an independent multinational, multidisciplinary organisation that publishes annual evaluations and rankings on the extent to which the rule of law is observed in more than 100 countries throughout the world.[27] The evaluations in each country are based on a thousand household and expert surveys in that country.[28] The World Justice Project definition of the rule of law is based on four universal principles:

1. *Accountability – The government as well as private actors are accountable under the law.*

2. *Just Laws – The laws are clear, publicized, stable, and just; are applied evenly; and protect fundamental rights, including the security of persons, contract and property rights, and certain core human rights.*

3. *Open Government – The processes by which the laws are enacted, administered, and enforced are accessible, fair, and efficient.*

4. *Accessible & Impartial Dispute Resolution – Justice is delivered timely by competent, ethical, and independent representatives and neutrals who are accessible, have adequate resources, and reflect the makeup of the communities they serve.*[29]

The International Bar Association (IBA) is another organisation that has identified characteristics of the rule of law. Because of the difficulty of satisfactorily and comprehensively defining the rule of law, the IBA has instead

---

23   See Bingham, footnote 7 above.
24   *Ibid* at 8.
25   *Ibid* at 37.
26   World Justice Project, "About Us", available at https://worldjusticeproject.org/about-us.
27   See World Justice Project, "Rule of Law Index" (2019) 6–9 (cataloging the countries involved in the index and explaining the study), available at https://worldjusticeproject.org/sites/default/files/documents/ WJP-ROLI-2019-Single%20Page%20View-Reduced_0.pdf.
28   *Ibid* at 7–8.
29   *Ibid* at 9.

adopted "an authoritative statement on behalf of the world-wide legal profession [that] ... sets out some of the essential characteristics of the Rule of Law ...".[30] These characteristics include:

> *An independent, impartial judiciary; the presumption of innocence; the right to a fair and public trial without undue delay; a rational and proportionate approach to punishment; a strong and independent legal profession; strict protection of confidential communications between lawyer and client; equality of all before the law ...*[31]

2.2 Core principles of the rule of law

Through this historical record, organisational definitions and modern scholarship and speeches, several principles that are central to the meaning of the rule of law, have emerged. They include at least the following ideas.

(a) *Superiority of the law*

The law must be superior. All persons are subject to the law whatever their station in life.

This first principle states the essence of the rule of law dating back to Aristotle: The rule of law is a "government by laws and not by men".[32] In *Politics*, Aristotle wrote that "it is more proper that law should govern than any one of the citizens ...".[33] American Bar Association president, Chesterfield Smith, summarised this principle in the following way in 1973 in discussing the Watergate controversy and the role of President Richard Nixon: "[N]o person is above the law."[34] The law applies to everyone in society whatever their station in life.

(b) *Separation of powers*

There must be a separation of powers in the government. The lawmakers should enact the law in general terms. The lawmakers should not be the body that decides on the application of the law to specific situations. The executive applies the law to specific situations. The judicial branch rules on disputes regarding the application of the law to specific situations.

This second principle ensures that an enacted law will be applied generally to everyone in society and will not be enacted to criminalise the acts of only selected persons. Laws must be general, prospective and must apply to all persons. The ancient Greek writers were particularly concerned about the separation of power between the law-making body and the law-applying body.[35]

---

30   Francis Neate, "Commentary on the IBA Council 'Rule of Law' Resolution of September 2005", *Int'l Bar Ass'n* (October 2009), available at https://perma.cc/QNP9-ESPY.
31   Int'l Bar Ass'n, "Rule of Law Resolution" (2005), available at https://perma.cc/6WSY-NVAU.
32   Hayek, footnote 4 above, at 166.
33   *The Politics of Aristotle: A Treatise on Government*, William Ellis (trans) (2009) 117.
34   Chesterfield Smith, "President's Page", 59 *ABA J* (1973) 1347, 1347.

In *Rhetoric*, Aristotle wrote that "the decision of the lawgiver is not particular but prospective and general, whereas members of the assembly and the jury find it their duty to decide on definite cases brought before them".[36]

William Paley described the necessity of separation of powers in this way:

The first maxim of a free state is, that the laws be made by one set of men, and administered by another; in other words, that the legislative and judicial characters be kept separate. When these offices are united in the same person or assembly, particular laws are made for particular cases, springing oftentimes from partial motives, and directed to private ends ...[37]

(c)   Known and predictable

The law must be known and predictable so that persons will know the consequences of their actions. The law must be sufficiently defined and government discretion sufficiently limited to ensure the law is applied in a non-arbitrary manner.

Through the centuries, scholars and philosophers have greatly distrusted government discretion. Decisions by individual persons, it has been argued, cannot be trusted because there is a strong possibility they will be arbitrary.[38] Dicey, writing in the late 19th century, called for the elimination of discretion in government actions.[39]

As expressed above, this third principle of the rule of law recognises the need for some discretion by government officials in the modern administrative state, but requires that discretion be minimised. Arbitrariness is the danger to be avoided. The principle expresses the idea that discretion, while not forbidden, should be "sufficiently defined and ... sufficiently limited to ensure the law is applied in a nonarbitrary manner".[40]

(d)   Equal application

The law must be applied equally to all persons in like circumstances.

The principle of equality is a central idea in the rule of law. The Greeks had another word – *isonomia* – that more fully expressed the idea of equality of all under the law, whatever their position in society.[41] For some ancient Greek writers, *isonomia* represented an even higher ideal than *democracia*.[42] In a

---

35   See Aristotle, "Aristotle's Rhetoric and Poetics", W Rhys Roberts and Ingram Bywater (trans) (1954) 20–21.

36   *Ibid* at 20.

37   William Paley, "Of the Administration of Justice", in *The Works of William Paley, DD*, (1833) 123, 123.

38   See Aristotle, "The Politics", in S Everson (ed), *The Politics and the Constitution of Athens* (1996) 9, 87–88; Cicero, "On the Commonwealth and On the Laws", JEG Zetzel (ed), (Cambridge University Press, 1999) 173: "[T]here is nothing more unjust than [laws made by individual persons], since it is the essence of law to be a decision or order applying to all."

39   Dicey, footnote 7 above, at 183–184.

40   *Ibid*.

41   See Hayek, footnote 4 above, at 239–242; see also Gregory Vlastos, "Isonomia", 74 *Am J Philology* (1953) 337, 366.

42   See Hayek, footnote 4 above, at 240–241; see also Vlastos, footnote 41 above, at 348: explaining that *isonomia* does not mean "equality of distribution" but rather the "equality of law".

democracy, the majority might persecute a minority. *Isonomia*, however, requires a society to treat all of its citizens equally. As expressed above, this fourth principle recognises that the law may treat classes of persons differently, but requires that the different treatment have a rational basis. This idea is captured in the statement of the fourth principle by requiring the law must be applied equally to all persons "in like circumstances".

(e) **Just laws**

The law must be just and must protect the fundamental human rights of all persons in society.

This fifth principle embodies a substantive rather than a procedural guarantee of the rule of law, and expresses the idea that the laws in a society that honour the rule of law must be just. This substantive requirement is intended to distinguish a government under the rule of law from a government operating with a rule by law. In Nazi Germany, for example, some of the elements of the rule of law might have been present, but, unless the laws are just, the society is not governed by the rule of law.

One difficulty with incorporating the principle of substantive justice into the concept of the rule of law is identifying what universally constitutes 'just' laws. Laws considered morally repulsive in some societies – for example, capital punishment – are the accepted law of other jurisdictions that purport to uphold the rule of law. British Senior Law Lord, Thomas Bingham, in his book *The Rule of Law*, addressed this difficulty by observing that although there may be ambiguity around the outer borders of this concept, there is general agreement about the core of substantive justice.[43] I believe the problem is more difficult than Lord Bingham suggests.

I suggest the important sources for identifying the substantive justice principles of the rule of law are the basic human rights documents of the United Nations. These documents – the Universal Declaration of Human Rights[44] and the International Covenant on Civil and Political Rights[45] – set forth principles that the nations of the world have agreed constitute the basic human rights of all persons.

Dr Mark Ellis, executive director of the International Bar Association, has taken this idea one step further and has proposed that the definition of the substantive justice principle of the rule of law be based upon the non-derogable rights codified in the Covenant of Civil and Political Rights.[46] These rights are those human rights that cannot be abrogated by a government, even in times

---

43 Bingham, footnote 7 above, at 66–84.
44 GA Res 217 (III) A, Universal Declaration of Human Rights (10 December 1948).
45 GA Res 2200 (XXI) A, International Covenant on Civil and Political Rights (16 December 1966).
46 Mark Ellis, "Toward a Common Ground Definition of the Rule of Law Incorporating Substantive Principles of Justice", *72 U Pitt L Rev* (2010) 191, 199–201, 200 n.47.

of crisis.[47] Such rights, he argues, can constitute the core elements of the substantive justice principle required under the rule of law.[48]

A distinction has been drawn in some recent writings between a 'thin' rule of law and a 'thick' rule of law.[49] A thin rule of law describes governance in a society in which many of the procedural principles of the rule of law are observed, but not the elements of substantive justice and protection of human rights.[50] An example would be a society that has a system of laws governing all of its citizens and an efficient court system to enforce those laws, but the system does not include a robust protection of human rights. A thick rule of law, by contrast, is governance under a rule of law that includes all of the principles of the rule of law, including those related to substantive justice and enforcement of human rights protections.

(f)   Robust and accessible enforcement
Legal processes must be sufficiently robust and accessible to ensure the enforcement of the just laws and human rights protections.

This sixth principle expresses the idea that the laws must be enforceable. In the United States, it has long been established that a right without a remedy is not a right at all. In *Marbury v Madison*, Chief Justice John Marshall wrote for the Supreme Court in 1803: "The government of the United States has been emphatically termed a government of laws, and not of men. It will certainly cease to deserve this high appellation, if the laws furnish no remedy for the violation of a vested legal right."[51] 'Access to justice' is an essential element of the rule of law, and must afford persons remedies to enforce their rights and the ability to access the courts to pursue those remedies.

(g)   Independent judiciary
Judicial power enforcing those just laws and human rights protections must be exercised independently of either the executive or legislative bodies, and individual judges must base their decisions solely on the laws and the facts of individual cases.

The principle that the rule of law requires an independent judiciary has been described by Justice O'Connor as the 'foundation' of the rule of law.[52] Alexander Hamilton, writing in *The Federalist* in 1776 in support of approval of the US Constitution, described the importance of judicial independence in this manner: "No man can be sure that he may not be tomorrow the victim of a spirit of injustice, by which he may be a gainer today."[53] If governance is to be

---

47   *Ibid* at 200.
48   *Ibid*.
49   See, eg, Brian Z Tamanaha, "A Concise Guide to the Rule of Law", in N Walker and G Palombella (eds), *Relocating the Rule of Law* (2009) 3, 3–4.
50   See *ibid*.
51   *Marbury v Madison*, 5 US (1 Cranch) 137, 163 (1803).
52   O'Connor, footnote 16 above, at 2.
53   Alexander Hamilton, *The Federalist*, No 78, ed by Terrence Ball (2003), at 382.

by law and not by people, it requires an application of the laws in an unbiased, even-handed manner by an independent judiciary.

As expressed, this seventh principle includes the ideas of both 'institutional' and 'decisional' independence. Institutional independence describes the independence of the judicial branch from the executive and legislative branches of government.[54] Decisional independence is the requirement that a judge must decide a particular case only on the basis of the law and the facts presented to the judge in the case.[55] Both institutional and decisional independence are essential to governance under the rule of law.

(h)   Right to participate

Members of society must have the right to participate in the creation and refinement of laws that regulate their behaviour.

This principle, included in the UN Secretary General's definition of the rule of law, suggests that a democratic form of government is a requirement of the rule of law.[56] Lord Bingham, in his treatise on the rule of law in the United Kingdom, also suggests that this principle is part of the rule of law.[57] There is not universal agreement with the idea that the rule of law exists only in democratic societies.[58] It is, perhaps, theoretically possible for a benevolent dictatorship to include most, if not all, of the other elements of the rule of law and not have a democratic form of government. While theoretically possible, it is difficult, if not impossible, to find an example of such a non-democratic benevolent dictatorship under the rule of law.

There is considerable authority, noted above, that these eight principles are central to the meaning of the rule of law. The next part discusses other principles that might also be considered to be important aspects of the rule of law.

3.   Additional principles that might be added to the definition of the rule of law

Issues raised by scholars and the various definitions of the rule of law that have been advanced suggest that these additional principles might be added to the list of principles that define the rule of law.

3.1   Protection of persons and property

Should the following 'law and order' principle be part of the definition of the rule of law?: *The law must protect the security of persons and property.*

---

54   O'Connor, footnote 16 above, at 2–3.
55   See *ibid* at 3–4: explaining that "decisional independence" is also referred to as "individual" judicial independence.
56   See footnote 9 above and accompanying text.
57   Bingham, footnote 7 above, at 66–67.
58   See Tamanaha, footnote 49 above, at 18: explaining that "the rule of law does not, in itself, require democracy".

A thoughtful scholar writing about the rule of law has argued that maintenance of law and order and the protection of persons and property should be one of the principles constituting the rule of law. Rachel Kleinfeld Belton has written:

> Law and order is central to the popular understanding of the rule of law. Most citizens within weak states see law and order as perhaps the main good of the rule of law. Law and order is essential to protecting the lives and property of citizens – in fact, it is a prime way of protecting the human rights of the poor and marginalized, who often face the greatest threat from a lack of security. In this end goal, the rule of law is often contrasted with either anarchy or with a form of self-justice in which citizens do not trust in the state to punish wrongdoers and to right wrongs but instead take justice into their own hands and use violence to enforce the social order.[59]

Supporting this view is the World Justice Project definition of the rule of law quoted above, which provides in its second universal principle that the 'fundamental rights' protected by the rule of law include protection of persons and property.[60]

While this argument has considerable merit, the danger in including *law and order* as one of the principles constituting the rule of law is that maintenance of security is oftentimes accomplished by laws and actions that violate human rights of the people.[61] For this reason, this principle is not invariably set forth as part of the rule of law.

3.2 Understandable by ordinary persons

The following might also be added to the principles of the rule of law: *The law must be written in a way that can be understood by ordinary persons in society.*

As noted above, Lord Bingham added to his definition of the rule of law, quoted above, eight subsidiary principles to further explain the concept.[62] Bingham's first subsidiary principle, "The law must be accessible and so far as possible intelligible, clear and predictable",[63] expresses the idea of the third principle in this chapter that the law be "known and predictable". Bingham adds a further dimension and meaning to this principle by asserting that the law must be written in a way that can be understood by ordinary persons in society.[64] That is, statutes and judicial opinions should use words that can be understood by the average person.[65] A related point expressed by Bingham is

59   Rachel Kleinfeld Belton, "Competing Definitions of the Rule of Law: Implications for Practitioners", 55 *Carnegie Papers* (January 2005) 11 (internal citations omitted).
60   World Justice Project, footnote 27 above, at 9.
61   See generally, for example, Shirin Sinnar, "Procedural Experimentation and National Security in the Courts", 106 *Cal L Rev* (2018) 991: investigating the procedural safeguards that accompany national security authority and the potential for insufficient safeguards to allow violations of civil liberties.
62   Bingham, footnote 7 above, at 37.
63   *Ibid.*
64   *Ibid* at 39.
65   *Ibid.*

that these sources of law should not be unnecessarily lengthy and complex so as to make it difficult for the public to understand them.[66]

3.3 Resolving disputes without excessive cost and delay

The sixth principle of the rule of law might be expanded to add: *Means must be provided for resolving disputes without prohibitive cost or inordinate delay.*[67]

This idea is advanced in Bingham's sixth subsidiary principle.[68] It may be assumed in the sixth principle about enforceability of legal rights, but it is an important idea that may require expression as a separate principle. Over 100 years ago, Roscoe Pound asserted that "[j]ustice delayed is justice denied".[69] The assertion was true in 1906 and it is even more true today with the greater expense and delay built into the civil justice system.

3.4 Independent legal profession

A very strong argument can be made that the seventh principle of the rule of law requiring an independent judiciary should be expanded to also provide: *An independent legal profession to enforce just laws and human rights protections is essential to the rule of law.*

Without an independent legal profession there is no assurance that the just laws and human rights protections will be enforced. An independent judiciary cannot accomplish this by itself. Indeed, it might be argued that an independent judiciary will not exist without an independent bar.

The fourth universal principle of the World Justice Project definition of the rule of law[70] goes a step further. It extends the requirement of independence to all who 'deliver' justice, and that would include, for example, law enforcement officials, such as prosecutors, in addition to attorneys and judges.[71]

3.5 Emerging international rule of law

Another of Bingham's subsidiary principles is an eighth principle that provides:

---

66   See *ibid* at 39.
67   *Ibid* at 85: "Means must be provided for resolving, without prohibitive cost or inordinate delay, bona fide civil disputes which the parties themselves are unable to resolve."
68   *Ibid.*
69   Tania Sourdin and Naomi Burstyner, "Justice Delayed is Justice Denied", 4 *Victoria U L & Just J* (2014) 46, 46 n.1: explaining that while William Gladstone famously stated that "justice delayed is justice denied", the meaning of the phrase can be traced back to biblical writings and the Magna Carta. The concept is expressed, but not in the exact wording, in Roscoe Pound, "The Causes of Popular Dissatisfaction with the Administration of Justice, Address Before the Am Bar Ass'n (August 29 1906)", in *ABA Reports* (1906) 395, 395, reprinted in *Am Bar Ass'n, National Conference on the Causes of Popular Dissatisfaction with the Administration of Justice* (1976) 3. See also Robert A Stein, "Causes of Popular Dissatisfaction with the Administration of Justice in the Twenty-First Century", 30 *Hamline L Rev* (2007) 499, 503: describing the historical complaint of delayed justice.
70   World Justice Project, footnote 27 above, at 9.
71   See *ibid*: "Justice is delivered timely by competent, ethical, and independent representatives and neutrals who are accessible, have adequate resources, and reflect the makeup of the communities they serve."

"The rule of law requires compliance by the state with its obligations in international law as in national law."[72]

This idea raises the issue of whether there is an international rule of law. The principles set forth in this chapter are directed at the existence of the rule of law in a particular country. They set out the obligations of a government to the citizens of its country to maintain and promote the rule of law in that nation. Bingham draws our attention to the issue of whether the rule of law exists in an international context.[73] He raises the question whether nation states have a duty to other nation states to obey the international obligations agreed to by the community of nation states.[74] I agree with Bingham's eighth subsidiary principle and believe that an emerging international rule of law is developing and will continue to develop over the coming years.[75]

4.   The rule of law is an ideal

It is unlikely that all of these principles will be robustly present in any society. This does not compel the conclusion that the rule of law is not present in such a society.

The rule of law, I suggest, is an ideal, a goal, something to be strived for. As an ideal, it is never fully achieved. Its presence or absence, therefore, should be judged in relative terms; what is possible in highly developed western democracies may simply not be achievable in a developing country.

No country can claim perfect adherence to these principles. The rule of law, then, is a lodestar to which we can turn for guidance now and in the future. It is our best hope for freedom and justice.

---

72   Bingham, footnote 7 above, at 110.
73   *Ibid* at 110–112.
74   *Ibid* at 112.
75   Compare Thomas M Franck, "Democracy, Legitimacy and the Rule of Law: Linkages", *Pub Law and Legal Theory Working Paper Series, Working Paper No 2* (1999): arguing that international governance norms will become increasingly uniform and standardised.

Chapter 2. Independence of the judiciary[1]

Richard J Goldstone
Retired justice of the Constitutional Court of South Africa

1.   Introduction

In democracies, human rights are nowadays almost invariably to be found in a bill of rights. They are enforceable only if those whose rights are violated are aware of their rights and their ability to enforce them before independent and impartial courts or tribunals. Primarily for this reason it has become axiomatic that there can be no rule of law without an independent judiciary.

The equal treatment of all under the law is not possible without independent and unbiased judges to interpret and apply the law. This self-evident truth was recognised in 1945 in Article 10 of the Universal Declaration of Human Rights. It is provided there that:

> *Everyone is entitled in full equality to a fair and public hearing by an independent and impartial tribunal, in the determination of his rights and obligations and of any criminal charge against him.*

Similar provisions are to be found in regional human rights conventions.[2]

In 1985, the General Assembly of the United Nations endorsed the Basic Principles on the Independence of the Judiciary. Article 1 provided:

> *The independence of the judiciary shall be guaranteed by the State and enshrined in the Constitution or the law of the country. It is the duty of all governmental and other institutions to respect and observe the independence of the judiciary.*[3]

So much is likely to be common cause for democratic lawyers and politicians.

2.   Appointment of judges

It should also go without saying that the manner in which judges are appointed is crucial to their independence and impartiality, both actual and perceived. Yet there is no generally accepted procedure by which judges in democracies are appointed. No method has been devised that succeeds in making appointments

---

1   In this chapter I have drawn on an address delivered by Professor Sir Jeffrey Jowell QC at a symposium held in Johannesburg on 16 May 2012 under the auspices of the Helen Suzman Foundation.

2   European Convention on Human Rights, Art 6; African Charter on Human and Peoples' Rights, Arts 7 and 26.

3   Basic Principles of the Independence of the Judiciary, adopted by the Seventh United Nations Congress, UN Congress on the Prevention of Crime and the Treatment of Offenders and endorsed by the General Assembly by Resolutions 40/32 of 29 November 1985 and 40/146 of 13 December 1985.

solely on competence and judicial excellence. There is a political dimension to the appointment of judges that cannot be ignored or avoided. This is especially marked in jurisdictions in which the courts have the power of review. Members of the legislative branch do not accept with equanimity the power of a small number of unelected judges to declare unconstitutional legislation that reflects the will of the majority of the electorate. For this reason, the legislative branch tends to do all within its power to have a say in the appointment of judges. And, of course, they have a legitimate interest in ensuring that the judges will act in an independent and impartial manner. I hasten to add that this in no way at all justifies the appointment of judges who will represent the interests of a political party. In the following analysis of some of the methods of appointment of judges, these unavoidable tensions will become apparent.

Israel and South Africa were among the first countries to adopt the judicial appointments commission model. In Israel there are nine members of the commission. They comprise the following members:

- the justice minister – chair;
- another member of the cabinet appointed by the cabinet;
- two Knesset members, appointed by the Knesset (usually one from the governing coalition and one from the opposition); and
- the chief justice and two other judges of the Supreme Court.[4]

The Israeli system has been strongly criticised for a number of years by some leading politicians and especially those from right-wing parties. The critics claim that judges with right-wing leanings are not appointed. To date, efforts to change the system of appointment have failed.

The South African Judicial Service Commission (JSC) consists of:

- one judge-president (provincial chief judge) designated by the judges-president;
- the justice minister;
- two practising advocates (barristers) nominated by the South African Bar;
- two practising attorneys (solicitors) nominated by the attorney's profession;
- one teacher of law designated by the teachers of law at South African universities;
- six persons designated by the National Assembly from among its members, at least three of whom must be members of the opposition;
- four persons designated by the National Council of Provinces (the Upper House of Parliament); and
- four persons designated by the president of South Africa.[5]

---

4   Judges Act 1953.
5   The South African Constitution 1996, s 178(1).

The JSC has come under scrutiny and complaints have been made that only eight of its 23 members are lawyers while 15 are representatives of political parties or appointees of the president. The effect, so it is alleged, is that there is political domination of the commission.

Professor Sir Jeffrey Jowell, the inaugural Director of the Bingham Centre for the Rule of Law, London, made the following trenchant remarks concerning the JSC:

> *In some ways the JSC system has been a massive success. Its judges in the highest courts have been models of rigorous legal analysis, and have promoted transition and social change within the constraints of limited authority. The judiciary is being transformed into better representing the composition of the population. Initially even those appointed for their political attachments avoided the conferment of political patronage. The interests of the ANC were subjugated to the interests of judicial independence and the rule of law. The conduct of the JSC has begun to place the publicly perceived independence of the judiciary in issue. The remedy lies with the JSC.*
>
> *That degree of tolerance seems to have been abandoned. Some rejected for judicial office are lawyers of the highest ability in respect of their analytical skills, wider qualities, and commitment to equality and human dignity. Their rejection has been viewed internationally with disbelief. If their rejection was due to their political affiliations or their independence, then the loss for South Africa is beyond calculation.[6]*

In more recent years the JSC has been justifiably criticised for failing to consider expeditiously serious ethical complaints levelled at judges and especially the judge-president of the Western Cape. Some of those charges were submitted to the JSC more than a decade ago. More recently, other serious charges have been submitted to the JSC against the same senior judge. Unfortunately, the present split within the ruling African National Congress (the governing party) is very much a part of the issues concerning the judge president.

Traditionally, judges in the United Kingdom were appointed by the Lord Chancellor, who used criteria and procedures that were not made public. As the 20th century came to an end, this process fell into disrepute and especially as it was perceived, with some justification, that judicial appointments were restricted to an elite who attended certain schools and universities. In 2005 the United Kingdom abandoned its traditional model and replaced it with a system of appointments recommended by an independent Judicial Appointments Commission. There are 15 members of the commission, who are appointed through open competition save for three judicial members who are selected by

---

6   Helen Suzman Foundation, *Delivering Justice: The Appointment and Accountability of Justices*, 5, available at http://hsf.org.za/resource-centre/justice-symposium-series/JustSymp3rdweb.pdf.

the Judges' Council. The members are drawn from the judiciary, the legal profession, the magistracy and the public.[7]

In 2011 the Council of Europe recommended the judicial appointments commission model for the new democracies that emerged from the former Soviet Union. It opted further for such commissions to consist of a majority of lawyers and with no politician members. That model has also been incorporated in other modern constitutions.

In the United States, federal judges are nominated by the president and require the assent of a majority of the Senate. As is widely known and criticised, the US system is blatantly political and, I would suggest, weakens the regard in which the federal judiciary is held in that country and abroad. What is more important, it places at issue both the fact and perception of impartiality in cases that have a political connotation. These tensions came to the fore in the litigation that followed the 2020 presidential elections. The many attempts by President Trump to question the outcome of the elections in some states were all swiftly rejected by state and federal courts. Some of the judges who rejected the cases presented on behalf of President Trump had been appointed by him during his term of office. There can be little doubt that security of tenure and the trust of the electorate played important roles in ensuring that the decisions were made impartially.

In most of the individual states in the United States, judges are elected by the people of the state. This has introduced many concerns about the impartiality of the elected state judges. Impartiality may be compromised by election promises made by a judicial candidate, or by large campaign contributions made by special interests or by future litigants.

I would also draw attention to the problem that has emerged with regard to the appointment of international and transnational judges. This will be discussed in the next chapter.

In summary, there is no fail-safe method by which judges are appointed only on merit and without regard to their political affiliations or loyalties. The more public the method of appointment, the less the likelihood political appointments will be made. Most judicial appointment commissions provide for the public nomination of judges and for the questioning of the nominees at a public hearing. The Supreme Court of Appeal in South Africa has held that unsuccessful nominees for judicial appointment are constitutionally entitled to be furnished with the reasons for the JSC failing to nominate them.

3.   Court procedures that reinforce judicial independence

In order to further the rule of law and judicial independence it is important that, save in exceptional circumstances, court proceedings are held in public

---

7   Constitutional Reform Act 2005.

and are open to the public. This includes the argument presented by counsel and the reasons for a decision.

Judges are not formally accountable save to higher courts. They are, however, accountable to the public that they are appointed to serve. That judges are required to furnish full reasons for their decisions is an important element in the protection of their independence. If a decision is the result of partiality or bias, that partiality or bias is likely to emerge from even a cursory analysis of the reasons furnished for that decision. Cases in which important legal principles or public interest are raised invariably receive full consideration and criticism from academia. Any indication or even suspicion of political or other bias is likely to be a topic of discussion. These are elements of independence that are often taken for granted. But they are very real. In extreme cases of misconduct, judges are also subject to removal, usually by impeachment proceedings in the legislature. In some jurisdictions judges are subject to discipline by a statutory body for misconduct that does not justify dismissal. It is crucial to the independence of the judiciary that disciplinary proceedings, in fact and perception, must be free from even the suggestion of political motivation.

In increasingly more jurisdictions, judges are allowing proceedings in their courts to be televised. With regard to trial as distinct from appellate proceedings, there are some legitimate objections to this trend, based on privacy and dignity concerns. Witnesses are frequently compelled to testify and there is no warrant for having their faces broadcast far and wide in a manner that might turn them into well-recognised personalities. That is of even greater concern for victims and especially in gender-related cases.

Confidence in the quality and impartiality of the judges is essential for respect of the law. If that respect is lost or diminished, an inevitable consequence is the lack of the effectiveness of the whole judicial system, both criminal and civil. This is well illustrated by the effect of the oppressive and racist laws applied during the Apartheid era in South Africa. The laws were made by a white minority and many of them were designed to oppress the black majority. The laws were justifiably considered to be unfair and the judges partial. Imprisonment, far from resulting in social stigma, often became a badge of honour. The whole substratum and foundation of criminal law became corroded and the crime rate soared. In civil cases, judges who were not well versed in commercial law were considered by the business community ill equipped to preside over civil disputes. The consequence was that members of the business community chose to resort to arbitration rather than placing their trust and confidence in incompetent judges. Small wonder that the Apartheid justice system failed, notwithstanding that the judges were in effect independent and many of them competent. This all goes to illustrate the fragility of judicial independence. If trust and confidence in the judiciary is eroded, it can cause permanent harm to the bench and to the system of justice.

4.   Independence of the legal profession

The independence of the legal profession is directly linked to the independence of the judiciary. In common law jurisdictions, judges are chosen from the ranks of private legal practitioners. Their careers will have inculcated a mindset of independence and the acceptance that there are duties to the public and the courts that, in some circumstances, might transcend the interests of a client. For example, if the lawyer becomes aware that a client proposes to embark upon criminal conduct, there is no duty of confidentiality and, if the contemplated criminal conduct is sufficiently serious, a duty will arise to report it to the prosecuting authorities.

5.   The relationship between the judiciary and government

It is essential to the rule of law that judges are free from political pressure and especially that they are independent of the government. They must feel absolutely free to rule against government and to censure government where it violates the law. There might well be room for actual invasion of judicial independence when government is in a position to punish the judicial branch by limiting judicial salaries or facilities.

Clearly, the resources for the efficient functioning of the judicial branch must be voted by the legislature. In some democracies the judges have control of their budget and in others that control rests in the executive. Whichever system is adopted, it is essential for the operation of the rule of law that control of the purse is not used in any way to interfere with the independence of the judges. In order to function efficiently, judges require appropriate facilities and any threat to diminish those facilities can impact negatively on their independence.

It is also important that the conditions of judicial service are sufficient and conducive to attracting the best practitioners to judicial office. Judicial salaries can never compete with the income of successful private practitioners. The attraction of the bench is usually the quality of life and the public respect that goes with judicial office. If those are compromised, the quality of the judiciary will suffer irreparably.

6.   Security of tenure

One of the most important safeguards of judicial independence is security of tenure. If judges are subject to having their tenure cut short by government, they are deprived of the reality and perception of independence. For the rule of law to operate there cannot be allowed any suspicion that judges might decide disputes in a manner designed to please the government of the day.

A sad illustration is provided by laws passed by the Parliament of Hungary in 2011. The mandatory retiring age of judges was 70 years; the effect of the new legislation was to reduce that to 62 years. The consequence was the compulsory retirement of some 270 judges. There was no question that the then recently elected government objected to the political views of many of those judges and this method was used to get rid of them. In a matter of months, more than 100 new judges were appointed to replace some of those forced to retire.

On 16 July 2012, the Hungarian Constitutional Court found that the lowering of the retirement age for judges was unconstitutional. It held that it violated the security of tenure of the judges. The egregious legislation was then compounded when, following the judgment, Prime Minister Orban said that "the system is here to stay". This reflects a policy under which the government would not respect the decisions of its highest court. More recently, the Orban Government has sought to set up new administrative courts that will be subordinate to the executive. The harmful effect of these developments to the rule of law in Hungary speaks for itself.

7.   The weakest branch of government

The judiciary is the weakest branch of government. It has no power over the public purse and it has to rely on the executive branch to implement its orders. For this reason, in particular, it is crucial to the operation of the rule of law for the courts and the judiciary to be respected by the other two branches of government. Court orders must be scrupulously carried out and criticism of judgments and judges by political leaders should be based on issues of principle and policy and not directed at particular judges or courts. Of course, the effects of judgments are open to criticism and, if done constitutionally, the legislature is free to change the law. This is not an infrequent occurrence in some democracies where the rule of law is respected.

8.   Conclusion

At the High-Level Meeting of the 67th Session of the General Assembly of the United Nations, held in September 2012, a Declaration was issued that stated:

We are convinced that the independence of the judicial system, together with its impartiality and integrity, is an essential prerequisite for upholding the rule of law and ensuring that there is no discrimination in the administration of justice.

That the independence of the judiciary and the legal profession lies at the heart of the rule of law cannot be questioned.

Chapter 3. Internationalisation of the rule of law

Richard J Goldstone
Retired justice of the Constitutional Court of South Africa

1.   Introduction

In his report of 23 August 2004 to the Security Council, the then UN secretary general, Kofi Annan, referred to the rule of law as being at the very heart of the organisation's mission. He said:

> *It refers to a principle of governance in which all persons, institutions and entities, public and private*, including the State itself, *are accountable to laws that are publicly promulgated, equally enforced and independently adjudicated, and which are consistent with international human rights norms and standards. It requires, as well, measures to ensure adherence to the principles of law, equality before the law, accountability to the law, fairness in the application of the law, separation of powers, participation in decision-making, legal certainty, avoidance of arbitrariness and procedural and legal transparency.*[1] (emphasis added)

The former secretary general was conflating the rule of law as a protection of the rights of individual citizens, on the one hand, and the relationship of states *inter se*, on the other. I will be suggesting that both analogies are useful.

2.   The rule of law in the domestic arena

Many books, articles and discussions have been devoted to the meaning of the rule of law in the domestic arena. It emerges from them that there is general agreement that the core principles for democratic government are the separation of powers between the legislature, the executive and the judiciary, the independence of the judiciary, an independent legal profession, equality before the law and due process.

For many, an important ingredient of democracy is regular, fair elections. Democracy does indeed depend on the will of the people being reflected in the choice of government – both legislative and executive.

However, that is by no means sufficient. It should not be forgotten that Hitler, Milosevic, Mugabe and Erdogan either came to power or retained power as a result of elections that were held to be free and fair. It was the subsequent

---

1   UN secretary general, *The Rule of Law and Transitional Justice in Conflict and Post-Conflict Societies*, UN doc S/2004/616 (23 August 2004) 4.

subversion of the rule of law that enabled their oppressive regimes. They used their majority support to achieve their nefarious ends. The history of democracy has taught us that if any of the core principles of the rule of law is compromised, the consequences are usually devastating and destructive.

One of the essential ingredients of democracy that is too frequently overlooked is the protection of minorities and fringe or marginalised groups. In too many new democracies and even in some older ones, the constitution is regarded as a document to empower the government rather than as a brake on the misuse of majority rule.

Nelson Mandela had an instinctive grasp of the essence of constitutional democracy. The first case heard in 1995 by the then new Constitutional Court of South Africa was on the constitutionality of the death sentence. This was the only issue on which the drafters of the Interim Constitution could not agree. They decided to omit any reference to it in the new Bill of Rights and to leave it to the Constitutional Court to decide the question in light of the provisions that were incorporated into the Bill of Rights. The court unanimously held that this extreme punishment was indeed inconsistent with the right to life and the right to human dignity and that it constituted a cruel and inhuman punishment. On the day that the decision on the death sentence was announced, the former Apartheid president and, at the time, deputy president of South Africa, FW de Klerk, made a public statement to the effect that while he accepted the decision of the court, he believed that a majority of South Africans, black and white, supported the death penalty. He suggested a referendum on the question and that if he was correct, the Bill of Rights should be amended to expressly sanction the death penalty. That same evening, in a televised address, President Mandela expressed surprise at the suggestion of rule by referendum. He said he had thought that all the major political parties had agreed to South Africa being a constitutional democracy and not government by whatever standards the majority of South Africans might wish. He viewed the Bill of Rights as having been designed to restrain the will of the majority. However, if we were to be governed by referenda, he suggested the first one should contain two questions. The first, he said, should relate to the death sentence and that if the majority of South Africans, black and white, wished to reintroduce it, the Constitution should be amended accordingly. The second question, he said, that should be posed in such a referendum was whether the majority of South Africans, black and white, wished white South Africans to keep the property they had acquired during the preceding 350 years of racial oppression. If the majority of South Africans, black and white, thought that they should not, then the provisions in the Bill of Rights prohibiting the confiscation of private property should be removed. It should come as no surprise that there has not been another call for a referendum! President Mandela appreciated that the Bill of Rights was there to protect minorities from the whims of the majority and not simply to entrench power in the hands of the government.

It follows that if the provisions in a constitution designed to protect minorities and marginalised members of society are to be meaningful and effective, there has to be an independent judiciary and its decisions have to be respected and carried out by the legislative and executive branches. By the same token, the executive must be obliged to carry out the terms of legislation consistent with the constitution.

The International Bar Association (IBA) encountered a thorny rule of law problem at its annual meeting held in Singapore in 2007. The annual meeting attracts more than 4,000 lawyers from over 120 countries. In recent years the last day of the week of meetings has been devoted to the rule of law and is open to members of the public. The IBA was informed some months prior to the meeting that in order to allow members of the public to attend any meeting in Singapore a police permit was required. The IBA decided with some reluctance to make an application for such a permit. Ten days prior to the meeting the police permit had not been issued. After much debate it was decided to cancel the rule of law day if it could not be opened to the public. The permit was issued the following day. A decision to call off the rule of law day would have garnered wide support from the constituent bars.

Subsequent to the meeting the IBA published a report critical of Singapore for its failure to respect the rule of law and especially freedom of speech. *The Wall Street Journal* published an editorial supporting the criticisms contained in the report. Within days the Singapore Government commenced legal proceedings claiming substantial damages for libel from *The Wall Street Journal*. This was swift and compelling confirmation of the findings of the IBA. I would suggest that those few Asian leaders who claim that the rule of law is a Western ideal are usually the very people who violate the human rights of their own people.

It can safely be said that the rule of law today is by and large respected by all true democracies on all continents. Apart from the older democracies in Western Europe and North America, I would include Japan, a number of Commonwealth nations and a number of African nations, including South Africa.

I have attempted, albeit briefly, to demonstrate the essential and universal nature of the rule of law in its domestic setting.

3.   The rule of law in the international arena

I turn now to consider the international context. Does the rule of law apply at all? Is it a relevant concept? It is certainly not an easy fit. The first and most obvious distinction is that there is no international legislature and no international executive.

There is, however, a fast-growing international judiciary. Is this a paradox? Not really. Although there is no international legislature, there are certainly international laws. Their sources are to be found primarily in international treaties and customary international law. They are based upon the voluntary agreement of sovereign nations.

As originally conceived, the United Nations, and even its General Assembly, was not designed to be a legislative body. However, nowadays most international treaties are a consequence of action taken by the United Nations. This capacity developed in the first place through the work of the International Law Commission (ILC). It was established in 1948 by the General Assembly acting in terms of the provisions of Article 13 of the Charter of the United Nations. Article 13(1) provides:

The General Assembly shall initiate studies and make recommendations for the purpose of

(a) promoting international cooperation in the political field and encouraging the progressive development of international law and its codification;

(b) promoting international cooperation in the economic, social, cultural, educational and health fields, and assisting in the realization of human rights and fundamental freedoms for all without distinction as to race, sex, language and religion.

The ILC included in its work the drafting of international treaties for submission to the General Assembly.[2] Treaties may be adopted by the General Assembly itself through a special conference of plenipotentiaries convened by it. By its nature it is a highly political procedure.

There are organs of the United Nations that initiate treaty-making. Firstly, there is the Economic and Social Council, also established by the charter.[3] Then there is the United Nations Committee on Peaceful Uses of Outer Space.[4] Finally, the United Nations Commission on International Trade has been responsible for a number of treaties.[5] The General Assembly has sometimes convened a special conference to consider and adopt a new international treaty.[6]

---

2   Examples of treaties that originated in the ILC are the Vienna Convention on Diplomatic Relations (1961), the Vienna Convention on the Law of Treaties (1969) and the draft statute for the International Criminal Court (1994). More recently it has drafted a Treaty on the Prevention and Punishment of Crimes Against Humanity.

3   It was in that body that United Nations human rights treaties originated, including the International Convention of Civil and Political Rights (1966), the International Convention of Social, Economic and Cultural Rights (1966), the International Convention on the Eradication of Discrimination against Women (1979), the Torture Convention (1984) and the International Convention on the Rights of the Child (1989).

4   This committee was responsible for the Treaty on Principles Governing the Activities of States in the Exploration and Use of Outer Space, including the Moon and other Celestial Bodies (the Outer Space Treaty) (1967), the Agreement on the Rescue of Astronauts, the Return of Astronauts and the Return of Objects Launched into Outer Space (the Rescue Agreement) (1968), the Convention on International Liability for Damage Caused by Space Objects (the Liability Convention) (1972), the Convention on the Registration of Objects Launched into Outer Space (the Registration Convention) (1975) and the Agreement Governing the Activities of States on the Moon and Other Celestial Bodies (the Moon Treaty) (1979).

5   These include the Convention of the Limitation Period in the International Sale of Goods (1974), the United Nations Convention on the Carriage of Goods by Sea (1978), the United Nations Convention on International Bills of Exchange and International Promissory Notes (1988) and the United Nations Convention for the International Carriage of Goods Wholly or Partly by Sea (2008).

6   This procedure resulted in the United Nations Convention on the Law of the Sea (1982) and the Rome Statute on the International Criminal Court (1998).

In more recent years, the Security Council has embarked on what are clearly law-making exercises, especially by using its peremptory powers under Chapter VII of the UN Charter. The most prominent illustration is the establishment of the *ad hoc* international criminal tribunals for the former Yugoslavia and Rwanda.

These are all obviously cumbersome procedures. There is no alternative having regard to the absence of an international legislature, the sovereignty of states and their right to join or decline to join an international treaty.

Notwithstanding these differences and difficulties, there is certainly no shortage of international laws that touch on many aspects of our lives. These laws are universally respected and applied. There are the laws that control civil aviation over-flying national air space, laws relating to post and telecommunications, the law of the sea and international trade. And, of course, there is the rapid growth of literally hundreds of treaties on international criminal law, drug trafficking, trafficking in people, extradition, refugees, war crimes and terrorism. Courts have been established at a growing rate to implement these laws: the Law of the Sea Tribunal, the International Criminal Court, the *ad hoc* tribunals for the former Yugoslavia and Rwanda, and the mixed tribunals for Sierra Leone, Cambodia and Lebanon. Then there are regional courts such as the European Court of Justice, the European Court of Human Rights, the African Court of Justice and the African Union Court of Human and Peoples' Rights, and the Inter-American Court of Human Rights. There are too many sub-regional courts to mention.

The call for additional international criminal courts has not ceased. A Boston-based non-governmental organisation, Integrity Initiatives International (III),[7] is campaigning for an International Anti-Corruption Court (IACC). The United Nations Convention Against Corruption (UNCAC) is one of the most widely ratified international conventions – 187 parties as at February last year. UNCAC requires member states to enact domestic anti-corruption laws. Those laws are required to prohibit extortion, bribery and money-laundering. A majority of the states parties have done so. Those laws have hardly deterred grand corruption or kleptocracy – corruption at the level of the highest officials of state. The reason is not difficult to locate – UNCAC is government-driven and relies on governments to implement the Convention and the laws promulgated pursuant thereto. The kleptocrats are invariably in control of their own governments.

UNCAC says very little about the mechanisms for enforcement of the provisions of the Convention or the domestic laws that it requires. Its provisions against political corruption, not surprisingly, are weak. The consequence is that every year corruption has diverted trillions of dollars from

---

7   See www.integrityinitiatives.org.

public resources such as healthcare, education and economic opportunity. Indeed, the COVID-19 pandemic has resulted in enormous corruption by public officials in many countries.

Kleptocrats operate with impunity. They steal vast sums and, in most cases, launder their ill-gotten gains in safe havens such as Switzerland, Singapore, the Cayman Islands and elsewhere. The conclusion, unfortunately, is that we must recognise that UNCAC has substantially failed to curb or deter grand corruption. The criminals are protected by their control of their own criminal justice systems. They control the police and prosecuting authorities and, sometimes, the courts themselves.

The solution can only lie in an international mechanism with authority and power to freeze the laundered money, and to investigate and punish the kleptocrats, namely, an International Anti-Corruption Court (IACC). It would be staffed by experienced judges and prosecutors and have authority to enforce relevant domestic laws as well as crimes of corruption defined in its founding statute. It would operate on the basis of complementarity; that is, its jurisdiction would be triggered only if the domestic authorities of the state of the kleptocrat were unable or unwilling to investigate the crimes. An important benefit of complementarity is that it would encourage domestic investigations and prosecutions. Whether or not there are domestic prosecutions, the IACC would be empowered to order the disgorgement and restitution of illicit assets for the benefit of the victims. The IACC could also be partly funded by the proceeds of stolen assets. If the IACC is able to attract the membership of 20–25 countries, some of which are financial centres in which kleptocrats launder their money, it would have the capacity to prosecute kleptocrats from non-party states.

In January 2020, the president of the UN General Assembly and the president of the Economic and Social Council established the High Level Panel on International Financial Accountability, Transparency and Integrity for Achieving the 2030 Agenda (FACTI). Its report was published on 25 February 2021. It provides for increased governmental enforcement of laws designed to prevent corruption but no international mechanism to enforce the provisions of UNCAC. Autocratic governments will thus continue to remain outside the purview of international criminal or civil justice. I would suggest that this is unfortunately a missed opportunity.

In the first edition of this book, I included in the list of international courts the Appellate Body of the World Trade Organisation (WTO). I referred also to its success as an international court that had grown exponentially. It was being used most frequently by the large trading nations and, in particular, the United States, the European Union and Canada. Some Asian and Latin American states were also referring disputes to the Appellate Body. So, too, with increasing frequency, was China. There had been substantial compliance with the rulings issued by the Appellate Body. I recognised that the use of the WTO trade disputes mechanism was driven by the self-interest of nations. The more a nation trades, the more it wishes the terms of its trade agreements to be respected and implemented. Today, this is no longer the position. The Trump Administration, in effect, put an end to the Appellate Body by vetoing the appointment of judges to fill vacancies. It has lacked a quorum since December 2019 and there is no longer a mechanism to rule on disputed decisions made by panels appointed by the Dispute Settlement Body of the WTO.

This is not the place to discuss the WTO in any detail. Suffice it to say that the organisation requires reform not only at the level of the Appellate Body but with regard to the whole Dispute Settlement system. I would be so bold to suggest that globalisation is here to stay and that the overwhelming number of states recognise that the rule of law and states adhering to their agreements is in the interests of all members of the global community. It seems likely that the Biden Administration will ensure that the Appellate Body is resuscitated.

I also stated in the earlier edition that: "Today the international rule of law is increasingly being recognised as a doctrine that operates in the commercial interests of states." Since I wrote those words, nationalism and populism and the assault by the Trump Administration on the rules-based international system has caused substantial harm to the recognition and application of the rule of law in the international arena. In the field of international trade, it has been replaced to a large degree by a system of trade tariffs and the consequent domination by powerful states. The Trump Administration also preferred bi-lateral rather than multilateral trade agreements.

As a result of the proliferation of international and multinational courts, there are hundreds of full-time international judges serving on international and transnational courts. They are issuing increasing numbers of opinions and orders. What is important is that the majority of them are honoured – either complied with or enforced by the government to which they are directed. I need hardly add that the legal profession has responded to what has become a growth industry.

The absence of an international executive power can be troublesome. It makes the implementation of some international laws more difficult as their enforcement is subject to the goodwill and cooperation of governments. However, as the world contracts, governments recognise more frequently the importance of reciprocity with regard to international law and order. For this reason, compliance and cooperation is likely to grow.

The rapid development of international law makes it both timely and apposite to consider the rule of law at this supranational level. Is the international justice system fair and unbiased? Is the international judiciary truly independent? How are international judges appointed? Is equality before the law implemented by these courts? Is due process recognised and implemented in trials and hearings before these courts? Is there an independent international bar?

There have been allegations of political bias directed at some of the international criminal courts. At the inception of the International Criminal Tribunal for the former Yugoslavia (ICTY), the government of Serbia alleged that it was anti-Serb and represented an act of discrimination against its people. This complaint by the Serb leadership came to my attention soon after my appointment as the first chief prosecutor of the ICTY. I decided that it was appropriate to pay a courtesy visit to the three major capitals of the former Yugoslavia: Belgrade, Zagreb and Sarajevo. My first meeting was with the Serb Minister of Justice. He expressed his government's strongest objection to the tribunal and criticised what he called the biased role of the United States in having the Security Council establish it. He pointed out that the United Nations had not considered setting up a criminal tribunal in the face of the awful crimes committed in Asia, the Middle East and elsewhere in Europe. He referred in that regard to atrocities committed by the regimes of Pol Pot and Saddam Hussein. "Why was the first such tribunal established to put Serbs on trial?" This was, he asserted, an unacceptable act of discrimination and partiality.

Of course, he had a point. The only response I could make (with more confidence than I felt) was that if the ICTY was the first and last such criminal tribunal then that would indeed be unacceptable. It would be treating the former Yugoslavia as an exceptional case. But, if others were to follow, then Serbia had no good reason to complain because it happened to be the first. Little did I know that scarcely more than a year later the Security Council would establish a second *ad hoc* tribunal, the International Criminal Tribunal for Rwanda; and that mixed domestic/international criminal tribunals would follow for Cambodia, Sierra Leone and Lebanon. Most important of all, the International Criminal Court (ICC) followed not many years later. In retrospect, then, my response to the Serb Minister of Justice was vindicated. The ICTY was not selective punishment, but instead the very beginning of a new era in the history of international criminal law.

With regard to the ICC, for some years there were allegations of it being anti-African by the African Union and some of its members. Of course, it is everyone's right to criticise the ICC and decisions taken by it. However, if that is to be done, it is only fair and appropriate this should be done on the basis of the correct facts. At one point, the eight situations before the ICC related to African nations. However, of those eight situations only two had resulted from an initiative of the ICC itself. Five of them – those relating to Uganda, the Democratic Republic of the Congo, the Central African Republic, Mali and Ivory Coast – were referred directly by their own governments. Two situations, one in respect of Sudan and one in respect of Libya, were referred to the ICC by the Security Council. Only the situations in Kenya, the Ivory Coast and Burundi came before the ICC as a consequence of the exercise by the prosecutor of his or her own powers. At the time of writing, there are 12 situations before the court. Four of them are not in Africa, namely Afghanistan, Bangladesh/ Myanmar, Georgia and Palestine.

The important question is whether in the situations that have been referred to the ICC serious war crimes have been committed. We should also ask whether the ICC should rather have become involved in other situations that are open to its jurisdiction. Of course, the ICC should have investigated possible war crimes in Sri Lanka and in Syria. But it can hardly be blamed in those cases – it has no jurisdiction, and permanent members of the Security Council veto or threaten to veto their being referred to the ICC. We should also ask whether the cases presently before the ICC should rather be coming before the domestic courts of the countries concerned. That would be the first prize and consistent with the ICC system of complementarity. But I would suggest that in none of the countries concerned could the persons accused be given a fair trial. That partly explains why five of the African governments requested the ICC to investigate their situations. It explains also why the ICC arrest warrants against Kenyan political leaders were a consequence of Kenya's parliament failing to investigate the crimes arising from the violence that accompanied the country's 2007 elections.

These complaints, in essence, are little different from those I received from the Serb Minister of Justice. They should teach a lesson on the important elements of a just system of criminal law. The rule of law must apply also in the international community. In order for any system of justice, whether domestic or international, to earn credibility and to gain acceptance, there has to be both the fact and the perception that the system is fair and equal in its application and that it is not driven by political rather than moral concerns.

There will remain unfairness in the ICC system for as long as powerful nations remain outside it. I refer in particular to China, India, Russia and the United States. They protect not only themselves from the jurisdiction of the court but also weaker nations they wish to shield. Thus Libya is referred to the ICC but not Syria. You have Sudan referred to the ICC but not Sri Lanka. The analogous situation in a domestic situation would be criminal laws applying only to the poor and weak and not to the wealthy and strong.

It follows that there is a strong case for the operation of the rule of law in international criminal justice. However, that ideal will not be realised until there has been universal ratification of the Rome Statute. Until that occurs, the global community will have to console itself on the basis that some justice is better than none at all. The withdrawal of immunity for war criminals that now obtains with regard to the 123 nations that have ratified the Rome Statute is a far cry from the pre-1992 world in which there was effective immunity for all war criminals.

It is comforting if not a little surprising that there have been very few allegations of bias or lack of independence on the part of international judges. The main reason for this is that they are invariably selected by a public and transparent process. There is the additional consideration that the governments that nominate them would not wish to have their nominees criticised for what would be perceived as unprofessionalism – whether in their appointment or in their work. Having said that, there remain some wrinkles in the appointment process.

In the first place the rule of law assumes that there should be actual and perceived fairness and due process. I would question in this context judges being eligible for more than one term of office. A judge who seeks a second term will often be perceived as having rendered decisions designed to curry favour with his government. The judges of the UN *ad hoc* tribunals were eligible for appointment for two terms of four years each. Judges of the European Court of Justice are similarly eligible for appointment for two terms of six years each. Until 2010 the same system applied in the European Court of Human Rights. Since 10 June of that year, under Protocol 14, judges are now appointed for a single non-renewable term of nine years. The same holds for the ICC. There is a move away from renewable terms. No doubt this is to remove any sense of (or actual) currying favour to which I have referred.

Every three years, six of the 18 judges of the ICC are elected by a two-thirds majority of all the states parties (known as the Assembly of States Parties). The threshold is thus a high one. Nominees for election must possess competence in criminal law and procedure or in relevant areas of international law. They are required to be persons of high moral character, impartiality and integrity who are eligible for appointment to the highest judicial office in their own country. The Assembly of States Parties, in electing the judges, is obliged to have regard to the representation of the principal legal systems of the world, equitable geographical representation, and a fair representation of female and male judges. Only in 2012 did the Assembly of States Parties establish an Advisory Committee on the Nomination of Judges. Its mandate is to independently scrutinise the nominees and rule on their qualifications for appointment.

However, the problems have not been eliminated. During 2020, this author chaired the Independent Expert Review Committee (IER) established by the Assembly of States Parties of the International Criminal Court.[8] One of our findings was that some of problems being experienced by the court might be, in part, the result of the standard of some of the Judges, some of whom have not been judges or jurists of the highest calibre sought by the court.[9] We stated

---

8   See the final report of the IER at https://asp.icc-cpi.int/iccdocs/asp_docs/ASP19/IER-Final-Report-ENG.pdf.
9   *Ibid*, para 961.

that "it is disturbing to discover that the practice of trading votes out of political self-interest, unrelated to the calibre of the candidate for election to a leading, international judicial post, is so well-entrenched that some States Parties still to this day find it politically expedient and acceptable to adhere to it".[10] The IER made a number of recommendations. To avoid political trading of votes regardless of the calibre of the candidate, we recommended that "States Parties should accord utmost respect to the assessments in the ACN report and should not cast their votes in a way that is inconsistent with any aspect of an assessment".[11] We recommended that the appearance of candidates for interview by the Advisory Committee on Nominations should be made obligatory, save in exceptional circumstances.[12] Further, that the Advisory Committee, at the candidate interview, should endeavour to assess the ability of the candidate to manage and conduct complex international criminal trials fairly and expeditiously and their suitability as a presiding judge.[13]

It follows that the method of appointing international judges is in a state of change and moving towards the incorporation of more transparent procedures and closer compliance with an international rule of law. The role of civil society and its organisations has been impressive in bringing about or hastening these changes.

By and large, international judges have insisted on just procedures in their courts and they have held trials deemed by the overwhelming majority of academic and professional observers to be fair and just. Their decisions are easily accessible on the internet and they are frequently the subject of academic comment and criticism in reputable law journals and other legal publications. The judges have been supported by an active and independent bar, with lawyers from many countries and diverse jurisdictions.

On 24 September 2012, a High-Level Meeting of the 67th Session of the General Assembly of the United Nations was held on the rule of law at the national and international level. A long declaration was issued that dealt holistically with the rule of law at both the domestic and international level. In the preamble, it was agreed that the collective response of the global community:

> to the challenge and opportunities arising from the many complex political, social and economic transformations before us must be guided by the rule of law, as it is the foundation of friendly and equitable relations between States, and the basis on which just and fair societies are built.

In paragraph 2, it was recognised that the rule of law:

> applies to all States equally, and to international organizations, including the

---

10   *Ibid*, para 963.
11   *Ibid*, Recommendation 378.
12   *Ibid*, Recommendation 371.
13   *Ibid*, Recommendation 374.

United Nations and its principal organs, and that the respect for and promotion of the rule of law and justice should guide all of their activities.

The High-Level Meeting also agreed that the rule of law and development are strongly interrelated and mutually reinforcing. They acknowledged that the independence of the judicial system is essential for upholding the rule of law.

It becomes apparent that an international rule of law has indeed developed and that it is a growing phenomenon. It bears a clear relationship to the domestic rule of law. However, there are differences compelled by the sovereignty of nations and especially by the absence of means to compel compliance with the orders of international courts save through the cooperation of governments. In an increasingly globalised world, international and transnational courts rely on reciprocity and the self-interest of governments.

Chapter 4. Rule of law initiatives: CEELI – its genesis and milestones[1]

Homer E Moyer, Jr
Miller & Chevalier

The story of CEELI (the Central European and Eurasian Law Initiative[2]) is a story written by literally thousands of lawyers, judges and legal scholars who participated as *pro bono* volunteers in assisting more than 25 countries emerging from a generation or more of communist rule. Unpaid, but energised to be involved in that seismic historic transition, CEELI volunteers worked with law reformers seeking to establish legal systems that would allow them to enjoy the freedoms, dignity and prosperity that can come with the rule of law. At a CEELI luncheon held during an annual meeting of the American Bar Association (ABA), Justice Sandra Day O'Connor shared with the large audience her view that we "should be justifiably proud of these splendid, dedicated, talented, and selfless lawyers who have interrupted their lives and careers to make a difference in the world in which we live". Together with a small, dedicated staff, these volunteers were the engine of CEELI.

1. The genesis

Launching CEELI, the ABA's Central and East European Law Initiative, entailed developing the concept, identifying a potential executive director, travelling to Eastern Europe to test interest in the idea, obtaining approvals from the board of governors of the American Bar Association (ABA) and the US Department of State, and getting funding. The process took nearly a year.

The Berlin Wall fell on 9 November 1989. Three weeks later, I met with Sandy D'Alemberte for lunch in Washington DC. Sandy, whom I knew from both ABA and Florida connections, was then the president-elect designate of the ABA, and I was the chair-elect of the ABA's Section of International Law. We wanted to discuss whether there might be opportunities for the ABA to support countries emerging from Soviet domination in light of the historic fall of the

---

1   This chapter is an abridged version of Chapter 1, by Homer E Moyer, in *Building the Rule of Law: Firsthand Accounts from a Thirty-Year Global Campaign*, edited by James R Silkenat and Gerold W Libby. © 2021 American Bar Association. All rights reserved. Reproduced with kind permission.
2   CEELI, originally the Central and East European Law Initiative, became the Central European and Eurasian Law Initiative in its second decade after expanding into the former Soviet Union. The acronym remained unchanged.

Berlin Wall, Mikhail Gorbachev's policies of *perestroika* and *glasnost*, and the emergence of newly independent states in Eastern Europe. Both Sandy and I brought points of reference for our open-ended lunch agenda, and each of us had in mind involving the other (a skill I have sought to develop based on Sandy's example).

Sandy told me that the US Agency for International Development was funding some rule of law projects, including the Caribbean Law Institute (CLI), a 1988 initiative that Florida State University (where Sandy had been dean of the law school) had jointly undertaken with the University of the West Indies in Barbados. This nascent law reform project was designed to "clarify the laws affecting trade, commerce and investment in the region, while at the same time respecting the unique needs of local jurisdictions".

I told him about the Moscow Conference on Law and Bilateral Economic Relations, a joint project of the ABA's International Law Section and People to People, that was planned for the autumn of 1990. Having outlined the conference, I touted the luminaries on the US and Soviet Organising Committees who had agreed to participate, and suggested that he, as the ABA's president-elect, may want to participate.

Although the word 'Institute' was to get us into some difficulty when we later sought ABA approval, the precedents of other US-funded law reform projects and a large conference in the Kremlin discussing fundamental freedoms and other law reforms, further inspired the notion of CEELI.

In 1990, the Moscow Conference became a reality. Seven hundred American lawyers, judges, government officials and legal scholars attended, along with 2,000 Soviet counterparts. Sandy participated, as did two former Secretaries of State, a former Attorney General, the general counsel of the CIA and the National Security Agency (the first time the general counsel of either agency had been on Soviet soil), a number of federal judges, several past and future ABA presidents, and an array of eminent private practitioners. Law reform topics were openly discussed (some for the first time in Russia) in 32 diverse panels scattered about the Kremlin. A one-hour break in the schedule for Rosh Hashana mystified our Russian hosts, but during that break American delegates filled the historic Moscow Synagogue near the Kremlin to capacity and spilled out into the street.

The dialogue and debate on reforms and openness then underway in the Soviet Union brought out candour in both discussions and presentations. At the closing plenary, Sandy gave a memorable speech noting that the original US Constitution was flawed as it sanctioned slavery, limited voting to "white men of property", and allowed states to ignore the Bill of Rights. Former Attorney General, Nick Katzenbach, related that when working on his Oxford thesis, "Different Conceptions of Democracy", he studied Marx, read the full works of Lenin, and concluded that the early conceptions of our two systems "had much in common as well as serious differences". Noting that he had not publicly acknowledged his past studies while serving as US Attorney General, he stated that "today we are all Marxists to one degree or another". The Chief Justice of the Supreme Court of the USSR told the assembled plenary that the operation of the Soviet judicial system had become "intolerable to society" and that impartial justice required that Soviet courts have "absolute independence".

At the final banquet upstairs in the Palace of Congresses, Mikhail Gorbachev, weary from a long day of debates at the Duma, gave lengthy extemporaneous remarks to a mesmerised audience. Dancing followed dinner, reportedly a first in the Palace of Congresses. The after-dinner entertainment featured a blues singer from New Orleans in a blue-tasselled dress, with a booming voice and tassels flying, who performed directly in front of Mr Gorbachev – without question a first for the Palace of Congresses.

In many respects, the Moscow Conference captured the euphoria over potential reforms, the hopes for change, and the obstacles to change across the Soviet Union. And the far-reaching discussions foreshadowed the timeless issues that CEELI volunteers were to encounter throughout Central Europe as newly independent countries debated constitutional revisions and democratic reforms, quests that continue to this day.

2. Testing the water

The ABA International Law Section was then chaired by my predecessor, Jim Silkenat, a future president of the ABA. In early 1990, with Jim's enthusiastic support, the Section authorised and funded two trips to the region to explore whether there would be interest in an American offer of technical legal assistance as those countries reimagined and restructured their legal systems. Sandy and I, together with future CEELI executive director, Mark Ellis, and two representatives of the US Agency for International Development, USAID deputy general counsel John Mullen and Jerry Hyman, chief of USAID's Democracy Pluralism Initiative, formed two three-person teams to visit six countries. Among our questions were:

- Would East Europeans welcome a project such as CEELI?
- Would it be seen as presumptuous on our part?
- Was it needed?
- Was it irrelevant because it was American?

Those trips and our meetings with exuberant counterparts – many young, some clad in bluejeans, brimming with excitement – dispelled any doubts about our welcome. Worn by years of oppressive government, hungry for reform and euphoric about the opportunity of regaining long-lost freedoms, they encouraged us and reinforced our resolve. Some provided early insights – discussing political reforms in Poland, for example, a newly minted Minister of Justice advised me that "without economic reforms, there will be no political reforms". Throughout the region there was, with few exceptions, intense interest in learning more about the experiences of America and American democracy. Their objective was not to replicate American laws and institutions, but rather to learn and benefit from US experiences, successes and missteps.

Our discussions also revealed that when it came to the rule of law, the United States was widely perceived as the gold standard. And our affiliation with the American Bar Association generated instant credibility and respect, allowing us later to advise future ABA presidents, a bit tongue-in-cheek, that in Eastern Europe the ABA seemed to be held in even higher regard than in the United States.

The organisational steps that followed proved to be more challenging. We obviously needed the blessings of the ABA to launch CEELI. As a practical matter, we also needed US government approval, since a regional US law reform project such as CEELI would require coordination and support from US ambassadors and embassies in numerous countries. To get funding, certainly from the US government, we would need both ABA and State Department approval. And we would need some organisational structure to direct and administer such an audacious idea.

State Department officials were initially sceptical. Among their doubts was a concern that a flood of American lawyers would go into the region, hustle business and provide extra-diplomatic advice that would not be aligned with US national interests and diplomatic goals. Happily, however, some in government, including John Mullen, Gerry Hyman, others at USAID, Ken Juster, Deputy Secretary of State Larry Eagleburger's Special Assistant and Walt Raymond of the US Information Agency (USIA) supported the idea from the outset. Mark Ellis also consulted then with Alberto Mora, the general counsel at USIA who, more than 25 years later, would become the executive director of the ABA's Rule of Law Initiative (ROLI), the successor entity of CEELI. And with strong support from Florida Senator Bob Graham, the idea of CEELI was generating bipartisan support on the Hill as more and more members of Congress got word of the potential initiative. Following numerous meetings and explanations of CEELI's law reform objectives and *pro bono* ground rules, State Department officials ultimately agreed, probably with lingering reservations.

The ABA presented different challenges. Sections of the ABA other than the International Law Section felt that they were the rightful homes for CEELI (some saw the creation of stock exchanges and securities laws as the most needed and promising reform). And other Sections with legitimate interests in law reform in Eastern Europe also spoke up. Having funded the needs assessment trips for a project that it viewed as inherently international, the International Law Section unsurprisingly believed that CEELI already had its rightful home. But approval and final decisions had to come from the ABA's board of governors.

To that end, in April 1990 Sandy and I travelled to Point Clear, Alabama, where Sandy was scheduled to present the idea to the ABA board of governors. With some board members unsure of a project to assist what they regarded as 'communist countries', the board referred the issue to a committee headed by Judge Sylvia Bacon to consider the proposal and any needed stipulations.

After some weeks, Judge Bacon's committee recommended that the board approve the project, but subject to several explicit conditions. CEELI could receive no general revenue funding from the ABA. It must be an Association-wide project, not the project of any single Section. The project must be overseen by an ABA 'special committee'. The president of the ABA would name a 15-member board of advisers for the project. The name should not include the word 'Institute', which suggested an overseas presence, and, correspondingly, the establishment of any overseas office would require approval of the ABA's board of governors. With active support from Bill Ide, Jim Silkenat and others, the board, with some trepidation, gave CEELI the go-ahead.

3.   Getting off the ground

In the meantime, we had determined that CEELI's executive director should be Mark Ellis. Sandy knew and recommended Mark, an FSU law school graduate who had studied in Yugoslavia on a Fulbright Scholarship, but was back practising law in Washington DC. Sandy's recommendation of Mark, which proved to be another of Sandy's invaluable contributions to CEELI, was one of our most important early decisions. For the next decade, Mark Ellis, as executive director, skilfully directed the development and growth of CEELI. Mark, who later became executive director of the International Bar Association, navigated ABA political perils and personified CEELI's commitment to being purely a *pro bono*, public service undertaking.

Operating as a *pro bono* project was one of three core principles we developed at the outset. First, those who participated as *pro bono* CEELI volunteers would not be compensated beyond reimbursement of their expenses, and they were required to comply with strict conflict of interest guidelines which forbade volunteers who came from law firms from engaging in any business development activities for their firms while working with CEELI. Second, CEELI would go only to countries to which we were invited – not necessarily by the national government, but an invitation by some governmental entity, court or bar association. Third, the assistance provided by CEELI volunteers must be neutral. We would come without an agenda and without promoting American-style solutions. While CEELI legal experts would share experience and insights, the countries we visited would design their own reforms. These three foundational principles served us well.

As for an ABA special committee, our private view was that this was an inelegant label, not well-suited to attract the type of high-profile individuals we thought might add credibility to our fledgling project. Our solution was for the

ABA to have its special committee listed in its directory, and for us to recruit an 'Executive Board' which became the parlance in all CEELI pronouncements. We brainstormed ambitiously about a board. Sandy mentioned the new Supreme Court Justice, Sandra Day O'Connor. Since her husband, John, had joined Miller & Chevalier, my law firm, I said that I had met her and maybe knew her well enough to ask.

I did not then divulge that my principal social interaction with Justice O'Connor had been at a dinner-birthday party she hosted for her first law clerk to which my wife Beret and I were the last to arrive. Provided with a gin and tonic, I was seated in a Spanish-style chair positioned at a right angle to the overstuffed chair in which Justice O'Connor was sitting. As she stood to say she needed to "check on the chicken", there was room for her to pass between my chair and hers. Nonetheless, as a courteous gesture, I slid my chair back slightly, only to hear the sound of cracking wood as the back leg of my chair broke, causing me – in an unimaginable spectacle – to summersault backwards onto the floor, gin and tonic flying. John O'Connor rushed over to me, leaned down and said, "Not a problem, Homer. Just sign right here". When we later finished dinner, Sandra stood and asked, "Well, shall we go back out into the living room and break up some more furniture?"

Nonetheless, when I called Justice O'Connor and described CEELI and our plan for an executive board, she listened and finally said – I remember the words exactly – "I think that's something I would like to do". The next day, John queried me: "She doesn't volunteer for things; what did you say?" But CEELI presented a unique opportunity that appealed to her, to our great benefit. We were elated, but did not then fully appreciate how much credibility we would gain from her involvement and what an important role she would play – providing support and clear-eyed guidance, attending every board meeting over a 10-year period, encouraging and inspiring CEELI volunteers, and being a widely admired face of the project.

Recruiting for a board on which Justice Sandra Day O'Connor had agreed to serve made populating the board easier. We happily recruited Abner Mikva, the former Chief Judge of the US Court of Appeals for the DC Circuit. Ab Mikva was one of the few people to have served in all three branches of government, having also been a Democratic member of Congress from Illinois and, later, White House counsel under President Bill Clinton. A CEELI footnote is that Ab, known to be a quite liberal congressman, became acquainted through CEELI with Tom Griffith, who had been counsel to the Republican-controlled Senate and someone with a distinctly more conservative orientation. But Ab and Tom became great friends, and Ab was one of Tom's strongest supporters when he was nominated to become a judge, as Ab had been, on the US Court of Appeals for the District of Columbia. Their friendship typified the non-partisan *esprit de cours* of the CEELI board and the bipartisan support it enjoyed in Congress.

We also were able to enlist Max Kampelman, Ronald Reagan's nuclear arms negotiator and former Ambassador to the Conference on Security and Cooperation in Europe. Soft-spoken and elegant, Max was a valuable board member with broad global experience and thoughtful insights. While Sandra Day O'Connor was the most widely known and celebrated member of our board in the many countries we visited, it was Max Kampelman for whom many of those countries sent a separate car. He was widely admired and, in countries with which he had worked, welcomed as the knowledgeable and respected gentleman that he was.

Sandy knew and sought out former New York Congressman Matt McHugh, who later became counsellor to the president of the World Bank. Matt became the fourth person recruited to the original executive board, on which he served with distinction for more than a decade.

We were also able to attract others who, like Sandra, Ab, Max and Matt, were wonderful board members and mentors for CEELI. We welcomed Lloyd Cutler, one of Washington's most distinguished lawyers and former White House counsel for President Carter. After his ABA presidency, Sandy D'Alemberte became a member of the board. Others who later became CEELI board members included Senator Nancy Kassebaum, ABA presidents Jerry Shestack and Martha Barnett, Judge Charles Renfrew and Soviet expert Steve Walther. Judge Patricia Wald, former Chief Judge of the US Court of Appeals for the District of Columbia, was both an executive board member and an indefatigable CEELI volunteer, participating in numerous workshops throughout Central Europe and Eurasia.

As chairman of that illustrious executive board, it was for me easy – unavoidable, really – to be quite humble.

The greatest asset of CEELI, however, was its ability to turn and reach into the vast membership rolls of the ABA to find exceptional legal expertise on almost any subject, as well as an eagerness to participate in CEELI's mission. Early on we decided to avoid press coverage, to select volunteers on the basis of expertise only, and to listen and learn from the dedicated, determined, excited lawyers, judges, officials and law reformers with whom we worked throughout the region. Many graciously thanked us and praised the effective, public-spirited assistance that CEELI volunteers provided. At the same time, for most CEELI volunteers their own experiences were educational, eye-opening and exhilarating. In some instances, they were life-changing. Volunteers involved in constitutional revisions often found themselves engaged in heady discussions of fundamental issues not unlike those debated during our own constitutional convention, 200 years before. Occasionally we had to ask ourselves some of the same questions we were being asked.

4.   Little did we know...

At the outset we never foresaw what was later to come: more than 500 lawyers of all ages and backgrounds serving as unpaid, in-country liaisons and legal specialists in the field for up to a year or more; the expansion of CEELI from Eastern Europe to all of the former Soviet Union; a total of more than 5,000 lawyers ultimately participating as CEELI volunteers; the growth of CEELI to become the largest *pro bono* lawyer project ever undertaken by the ABA; the creation of the CEELI Institute as a Prague-based institution dedicated to advancing the rule of law; CEELI luncheons at ABA annual meetings honouring heads of state and attracting more than a thousand ABA members; the creation of CEELI-like projects in other parts of the world; or the ultimate evolution of ABA CEELI into ABA ROLI, the ABA's Rule of Law Initiative, a global project that today promotes the rule of law in scores of countries around the world.

Through the CEELI years, we also realised that fundamentally changing constitutions, laws, legal institutions, legal traditions and public expectations is not a two- or three-year undertaking, but a generational one. Nor is progress linear – some reform efforts will succeed, some will fail, some will lapse and rebound. We also now better appreciate that realising the noble ideals that the rule of law embodies is a continuing challenge for countries, our own included. Most importantly, we have come to appreciate that the rule of law, if we honour it, enables and nourishes freedom, justice and individual dignity and that it holds extraordinary promise for the future.

5.   CEELI milestones

5.1   The first wave

Quietly beginning a somewhat controversial project with a limited but welcome initial budget (thanks to the National Endowment for Democracy and its president, Carl Gershman) and a staff of one, in a windowless basement office, CEELI focused on six countries of Central Europe – the Czech and Slovak Federal Republic, Poland, Hungary, Bulgaria, Romania and Albania. Almost immediately, these countries began sending requests – requests focused primarily on assistance in rewriting constitutions, reviewing new draft laws and judicial reform. CEELI's first workshop on the duties and organisation of prosecutors, investigators and judges was held in Prague the week of 12 November 1990.

Workshops on constitutional revisions, reviews of draft laws ('Legal Assessments'), and the Sister Law School programme got off to an exceptionally fast start. Soon thereafter followed Technical Assistance Workshops and Legal Training Seminars on specific issues or substantive areas. Through representatives of 23 different Sections of the ABA, CEELI was able to identify lawyers with deep experience in all the areas for which requests were received.

The lawyers contacted were all eager to volunteer and help with the historic changes underway.

A few months later, the CEELI executive board, to ensure continuity and in-country coordination, authorised the creation of in-country CEELI 'liaisons', and in early September 1991, Bill Meyer, a lawyer from Boulder, Colorado, landed with his wife, Jane, in Bulgaria as CEELI's first liaison. By the end of that year, CEELI had conducted 27 Technical Assistance Workshops, four Legal Training Seminars, placed 21 long-term liaisons and 22 short-term 'legal specialists', coordinated the visits of 41 law school deans to 120 US law schools, and assessed over 120 draft laws. CEELI volunteers not only came from all 50 states, but they also included some Canadian and European lawyers. These lawyers, surprised at being invited to be a part of this American initiative, were welcomed by East European countries with civil law traditions and enhanced CEELI's credibility.

In hindsight, and in light of the scholarship on 'the rule of law' that has blossomed in the last decade or two, it is appropriate to recall a comment I made during the CEELI years that Jim Silkenat preserved in a 2014 SMU law review article. Although the fall of the Berlin Wall triggered a determination throughout Central and Eastern Europe and the former Soviet Union to design governments based on 'the rule of law', that term, which was not new, had not been popularised or definitionally scrutinised as it has been since. Rather, as recalled by Jim, I noted that the widespread reforms in the early 1990s were driven by what was seen as an absence of the rule of law, by a converse, not affirmative, definition:

I know it when I don't see it. That is, we could identify the absence of the rule of law more easily than we could affirmatively define the rule of law. This allowed many communist and other repressive, authoritarian regimes to be classified as lacking the 'rule of law' or, more simplistically, as countries ruled by men, not laws.

Even today, with the emergence of sophisticated definitions and exegeses of the term, it is the absence of core principles of the rule of law – limits to the power of government, independence of the judiciary, equal treatment before the law, free press, etc – that are the most obvious and unambiguous benchmarks.

5.2 Judicial reform

From the outset, judicial reform was one of CEELI's core areas of emphasis. Given that an independent, fair-minded, incorruptible judiciary is an essential cornerstone of the rule of law, this was one of CEELI's first callings. In CEELI's first four years, judicial reform projects included helping establish judicial training centres in Bulgaria, Estonia and Latvia; a regional conference for judges from 14 different countries on 'judicial education and training: creative approaches to institution-building'; workshops in the region and in the United States on trial procedure, the appellate process, comparative constitutional principles, judicial independence and separation of powers, commercial law, CLE programmes for judges, judicial ethics and court administration; and assistance in establishing judges' associations, journals and newsletters for judges, law libraries for judges, and computer systems for national courts.

5.3   Sister Law School programme

Led by former law school dean, Sandy D'Alemberte, with support and expert guidance from Jim White, the ABA's Consultant on Legal Education, CEELI's Sister Law School programme blossomed quickly. More than 120 American law schools agreed to partner with 41 European law schools and host deans and faculty visits and exchanges. The programme began with the deans from the 41 European law schools each visiting three different American law schools. The paired law schools then continued to develop their own relationships further with a variety of collaborations, exchanges and other programmes.

Among the Sister Law School programmes was the Balkan Law School Initiative, which paired five law schools in Bosnia-Herzegovina, Kosovo, Macedonia and Montenegro with five American law schools. They conducted joint workshops, annual mutual visits and exchanges of law professors, and month-long exchanges of two law students from each of the 10 participating law schools.

5.4   Secretary of State James Baker's offer to Albania

On 23 June 1991, Secretary of State James Baker and his wife, Susan, made a stop in Albania, the first visit by a US Secretary of State to that country. A throng of 300,000 people jammed Skanderbeg Square to welcome Secretary Baker, swarming his motorcade, throwing flowers, kissing his car, chanting "USA, USA, USA" and "Baker, Baker, Baker", waving flags, and holding signs. "I've been in politics now for 14 years, and I don't ever recall seeing something like that," Secretary Baker later said. Speaking to the joyous, friendly crowd of a country that had suffered under dictatorial rule for four decades, the Secretary welcomed them "to the company of free men and women everywhere", reassured them that "freedom works", and assured them that "you are with us and we are with you".

In Washington, Mark Ellis and Homer Moyer, reviewing press accounts of the remarkable visit together, read, to their surprise, that Secretary Baker had assured the crowd that the American Bar Association would provide technical legal assistance and help them develop a new constitution. Almost immediately thereafter Homer found himself on a plane to Tirana, where he met with Bill Ryerson, America's new ambassador to Albania, communicated back through Ambassador Ryerson's fax machine which rested on boards across the sink in his room at the Hotel Dajti, and joined the ambassador each evening greeting enthusiastic Albanians out enjoying the xhiro, the traditional, social evening stroll. Within a year, CEELI had conducted four technical legal assistance workshops in Albania, two on the country's new constitution.

5.5   CEELI liaisons

CEELI 'liaisons', residing in-country for a year or more, were the in-the-field linchpins to CEELI's success. Working entirely *pro bono*, liaisons typically lived in a single country, coordinating the various CEELI programmes and activities with local partners, and providing long-term continuity. With liaisons in place, it became easier to conduct effective Technical Assistance Workshops and Legal Training Seminars on specific issues or substantive areas. By the end of 1991, CEELI's 21 liaisons populated 15 different countries, from Estonia to Kazakhstan, from Belarus to Albania. Adventuresome and resourceful, these volunteers were on the ground and were breaking new ground across a diverse range of emerging independent states.

In the end, more than 500 American lawyers lived and worked as liaisons and legal specialists in more than 25 countries, responding to local priorities, building relationships, collaborating in historic transitions, and, in almost all cases, improvising as necessary. Some re-enlisted for a second tour in a different country. Mary Noel Pepys, the record holder, ultimately served as a CEELI liaison or legal specialist in six different countries over the course of five years. CEELI's liaisons and legal specialists, whose contributions and whose sacrifices were remarkable, were CEELI's stars.

5.6   Central and Eastern Europe and the former Soviet Union

On 26 December 1991, the Supreme Soviet voted to dissolve the USSR pursuant to the Belavezha Accords reached earlier that month. This presented CEELI, still a young project, with the obvious question whether it should offer the newly independent states of the former Soviet Union technical legal assistance as it had done in Central and Eastern Europe. Recognising that doing so would be no small step, the CEELI executive board nonetheless promptly authorised CEELI to broaden its mandate, a decision that US government funders approved.

The former republics of the Soviet Union, unlike countries in Eastern Europe that had come under Soviet influence and control after World War II, presented special challenges. In most of the countries of Central and Eastern Europe, there was still an older generation that had lived before Soviet dominion. Although many of those countries had been civil law countries, their older generations knew their former legal traditions and culture. By contrast, in former Soviet republics there was no older generation that had lived under a different system; communism was the only governing system they had known. As they became independent countries, the old guard – former communist leaders – often retained power, sometimes creating greater obstacles to adopting democratic, rule of law reforms.

Some years later, well after the State Department had reorganised and re-labelled some of its own constituent parts and had urged CEELI to do the same, the ABA agreed that its 'Central and East European Law Initiative' would become its 'Central European and Eurasian Law Initiative'. Essential to this compromise decision was agreement that the acronym 'CEELI', which had by then become a recognised and respected brand throughout Central Europe and Central Asia, would remain unchanged as the word changes did not change the acronym.

5.7   Annual CEELI liaison meetings

To an engaged and knowledgeable board, it was a natural idea to meet from time to time on the ground in one of the countries where CEELI volunteers were working. The advent of in-country liaisons reinforced the idea, as including liaisons allowed the board to get first-hand reports from the on-the-ground liaisons from all of the countries, as well as from officials of the country where the meeting was to be held. The first such meeting, small and hastily arranged, was the only one not held in a country where CEELI volunteers were working. Executive board member Lloyd Cutler offered to host the first liaison meeting at the Salzburg Seminar, on whose board he also served. For that first small meeting we had only a handful of liaisons, but that gathering set the stage for meeting the following summer in Vilnius, Lithuania, and, thereafter, increasingly large summer meetings in various countries in Eastern Europe or Central Asia where CEELI was operating.

Hearing directly from the liaisons who came from countries throughout the region proved to be uniquely informative – and inspiring – to the board. First-hand accounts of the experiences, successes, challenges and setbacks of liaisons helped guide the project and the development of its programmes. The work that liaisons were doing was invariably impressive. Working long hours on issues of potentially profound importance, liaisons were faced with challenging, but heady, opportunities.

Meetings with board members were also a welcome and invigorating departure from the daily experiences of liaisons in the field. Most came from countries in which intense, and sometimes difficult, reform efforts were underway. While their work was legally and culturally fascinating, they were typically living solitary, often spartan, lives. To have discussions and meals with prominent board members who were serving or had served in senior government positions, was an abrupt and exhilarating change of pace. (We instructed board members to sit during meals with liaisons, not with other board members.) Most liaisons who had conversations with Justice O'Connor vividly remember, as do we all, how she focused her gaze, laser-like, and gave her unbroken attention to the one person with whom she was speaking.

5.8 CEELI honours heads of state, US rule of law champions

Beginning in 1994, CEELI initiated a series of annual awards to courageous heads of state from countries that were making impressive progress in establishing the rule of law. These presentations were made at annual CEELI luncheons held during the summer annual meetings of the ABA. In most instances, but not all, the reforms of those honoured were lasting and continued the process of transitioning from authoritarian regimes to democratic, rule of law-based societies. In 1994, ABA president Bill Ide presented the first CEELI Award to President Kiro Gligorov of Macedonia. This initial award was followed by CEELI Awards to President Michal Kovac of the Slovak Republic (1995), President Leonid Kuchma of Ukraine (1996), President Guntis Ulmanis of Latvia (1997), President Petar Stoyanov of Bulgaria (1998), His Excellency Emil Constantinescu of Romania (1999), and President Vaclav Havel of the Czech Republic (2001).

Several of the annual CEELI luncheons also featured rule of law champions as keynote speakers. Ambassador Max Kampelman, counsel to President Abner Mikva, South African Constitutional Court Justice Richard Goldstone, US Secretary of State Madeleine Albright, and Supreme Court Justice Sandra Day O'Connor all delivered keynote addresses at CEELI luncheons. With both inspiring foreign heads of state and marquee keynote speakers, these annual luncheons grew to become the largest ticketed event at the ABA's annual meeting, with 1,300 ABA members attending the 1997 presentation of the CEELI Award to President Guntis Ulmanis, President of Latvia, and keynote speech by Justice Sandra Day O'Connor.

5.9 Establishing the new Constitutional Court for Bosnia-Herzegovina

In 1994, following the genocidal war that engulfed Bosnia, the new Federation adopted the Constitution of the Federation of Bosnia and Herzegovina, which provided for the creation of a new Constitutional Court of Bosnia-Herzegovina. Reminiscent of earlier days when Sarajevo was a peaceful, multi-ethnic city, the six ordinary lawyers named to the court, without fanfare, were two Serbs, two Croats, and two Bosniaks.

Before the court had ever met in session or heard a case, CEELI executive director Mark Ellis asked to meet with the six judges. The judges of the court were not well known. Nor did they all know one another. The fratricidal Bosnian war had devastated each of them, and killed children of two of the six. But in meeting with this group of subdued judges, Mark sensed a shared belief in the potential of law to bring justice. To discuss their new Constitution with the US experts who had drafted it, however, they would have to travel to the

United States, something they could not do from Sarajevo. Although the war in Sarajevo continued, the judges unanimously agreed to go forward.

They made that trip. Leaving after midnight, walking through the half-mile muddy tunnel Bosnians had dug under the destroyed Sarajevo airport, crossing Mt Igman, then hitching a ride with a military vehicle driving without lights to avoid snipers, they arrived at the coast of Croatia 30 hours after they began. In Washington, CEELI had arranged meetings with the drafters of their Constitution. After 10 long days of intense discussions, questions and answers, the six judges returned to Sarajevo by the same route they had come. Thereafter, CEELI provided the court with assessments of its draft procedural rules and held a final workshop for the justices in Sarajevo the day before the court's inauguration.

Although creation of the Constitutional Court had attracted little attention, CEELI helped with preparations for a formal swearing-in, on which the judges had insisted. Mark Ellis, Homer Moyer and Bob Stein travelled to Sarajevo for the occasion, flying on a Russian military plane from Zagreb to Sarajevo, the departure of which was delayed by "reports of anti-aircraft fire in the area". Once in Sarajevo, Mark and Homer met with the Minister of Justice in his office, a meeting that was briefly interrupted by the explosion of a mortar shell that we later learned had been fired at a Sarajevo tram, one of the last breaches of the existing ceasefire that ended the war.

As news of the swearing-in spread, interest grew. Bosnia's only television stations decided to broadcast the ceremony across the nation. The event was scheduled to take place in a majestic old building in the style of the Austrian-Hungarian empire, one of the few buildings not destroyed by the war. Three international judges from Belgium, Nigeria and Syria, had been assigned as members of the court through the Dayton Accords, an addition that the Nigerian judge described as "not just innovative; it is unheard of".

One unresolved detail of the ceremony was whether the judges would wear the robes that Mark Ellis had acquired for the occasion and brought to Sarajevo as a gift from CEELI. One judge objected to wearing a robe, something he thought would be seen as pretentious. Ultimately persuaded by the other judges, including the three international judges who had brought their own robes, the reluctant judge finally donned his robe.

Inside the reception hall for the investiture were hundreds of people, filling all the seats and standing 10 deep at the back. When the judges entered wearing elegant black judicial robes, an uncommon sight in the Balkans, there was a hush in the audience, which row-by-row silently rose to their feet. Nearby, in the audience, Bosnians, young and old, had tears running down their faces. The acts of these six courageous jurists gave a nation desperate to look past its devastating war a moment of hope.

Federation President Kresimir Zubak presided over the swearing-in and welcomed CEELI's representatives as "both our guests and our hosts". Court

President Omer Ibrahimagic, whose nine-year old son was killed during the war while playing in his front yard, welcomed all present and voiced the hope that through the court "the power of weapons in this war will be replaced by the power of argument, justice and law". US Ambassador John Menzies expressed his heartfelt appreciation to CEELI and reminded us that the rule of law is "a prerequisite to civil society". For a multi-ethnic country that was emerging from a horrific war, it was a remarkable occasion.

After the swearing-in ceremony had ended, the judge who had balked at wearing a black judicial robe appeared at the reception following the swearing-in, still wearing his robe, an unconventional confirmation of the historic importance of the occasion.

5.10 After five years

In its first five years, CEELI sent 220 liaisons and legal specialists abroad, conducted over 250 workshops and training seminars, and assessed over 255 draft laws and constitutions in 25 countries in Central and Eastern Europe and the newly independent states of the former Soviet Union. CEELI volunteers increasingly worked to help establish and strengthen indigenous institutions that were critically important to the law reform process. Among the examples of such institutions are:

- PIOR, the Bulgarian Legal Initiative for Training and Development, which conducted seminars on a wide range of subjects and which continues to operate today;
- the Latvian Judicial Training Center, an NGO that disseminated needed information to Latvia's judges and conducted a variety of training programmes;
- the Library Center for Legal Information (LCLI) in Bishkek, Kyrgyzstan, which became the premier legal research facility in Central Asia and which provided legal professionals with legal texts, periodicals, various databases, and legal materials from a variety of countries;
- the Saratov Legal Reform Project in the Saratov region of Russia, which established its own fully indigenous CLE programme and offered substantive training courses in commercial and criminal law; and
- the Moldovan Judicial Training Center, the first comprehensive judicial training centre in the former Soviet Union which, in cooperation with the Ministry of Justice, conducted a month-long CLE course for every judge in the country over a three-year period.

5.11 CEELI asked to assist Yugoslav War Crimes Tribunal

In 1995, Secretary of State Madeleine Albright asked if CEELI would assist the new International Criminal Tribunal for the former Yugoslavia (ICTY) in The Hague, which was launching investigations into war crimes in the former

Yugoslavia, a test of accountability under the rule of law. CEELI responded affirmatively, and Mark Ellis went to meet with Justice Richard Goldstone, the chief prosecutor of the war crimes tribunal. Assuming that the tribunal and its staff could benefit from more resources to prepare prosecutions, Mark was surprised when Justice Goldstone asked if CEELI could assist the defence team in the upcoming Tadic trial. Concerned that the defence team did not have adequate resources, Justice Goldstone explained that the credibility of the tribunal would depend not on whether or not Mr Tadic was convicted, but on whether the public perceived the trial to be fair. In his memoirs, Justice Goldstone stated his view that because of CEELI's assistance, the Tadic trial was deemed to have achieved that goal.

CEELI then sent a liaison, Alain Norman, to the tribunal to assist in what became an expanded role, which included providing assistance on such issues as provisional detention of suspects and witnesses, assignment of defence counsel, protection of witnesses, service of process, and discovery. CEELI led an effort to establish the Coalition for International Justice (CIJ), which not only provided technical legal assistance to the tribunal, but also helped increase public awareness and helped educate the press, opinion leaders and congressional committees about the role of the ICTY and its sister tribunal, the International War Crimes Tribunal for Rwanda.

In 1997, CEELI and the CIJ sent four teams of prosecutors to review files on suspected war criminals that authorities in Bosnia-Herzegovina had forwarded in accordance with the Rules of the Road agreement to the parties of the Dayton Peace Accords. Using press and NGO reports, the CIJ published a list of the locations of 37 indicted criminals who had not been apprehended.

5.12 USAID audit and evaluation of CEELI

In 1998, USAID conducted a comprehensive audit and evaluation of CEELI's programmes, many of which it had funded. The results were overwhelmingly positive, confirming that CEELI had made significant contributions to legal reform throughout Central and Eastern Europe and the former Soviet Union. The audit noted in particular CEELI's initiatives in judicial reform, bar reform, legal education, commercial law and assessments of draft laws.

AID evaluators reported that "partners and clients consistently praised CEELI's contribution for being responsive, entrepreneurial, effective, and appropriate". They also noted CEELI's cost efficiency, finding that "CEELI has a consistently positive record of leveraging funds from other resources and for operating frugally". USAID went on to recommend that CEELI be used for more long-term development projects, including the creation of judicial training centres, that CEELI expand its work in commercial law, and that CEELI and USAID enter into a multi-year funding agreement rather than the current series of one-year agreements.

5.13   CEELI's Ambassador Award

The work of CEELI liaisons and volunteers was often facilitated by the leadership and initiatives of US ambassadors in countries in which CEELI volunteers worked. Among these heroic figures who worked to promote the rule of law in Central and Eastern Europe and the former Soviet Union were four ambassadors to whom CEELI presented its Ambassador Award at awards dinners in Washington DC. In 1997, CEELI presented its first Ambassador Awards to Ambassador Bill Montgomery, who was US Ambassador in Bulgaria and then Croatia, and Ambassador John Menzies, the former Ambassador to Bosnia-Herzegovina. The following year, the Award was presented to Ambassador Victor Jackovich, who had served as US Ambassador to Bosnia-Herzegovina and then to Slovenia, and Ambassador James Swihart, who was US Ambassador to Lithuania where he was at the forefront of formulating and implementing US policies supporting and strengthening Lithuania's independence and sovereignty.

Cooperation between CEELI and its volunteers and American ambassadors, diplomats, and foreign service personnel greatly enhanced CEELI programmes and the partnerships CEELI volunteers built with those committed to law reform and strengthening the rule of law.

5.14   Creation of the CEELI Institute in Prague

A visit to the American University in Bulgaria in 1994 during an annual liaison meeting prompted the question whether CEELI's effectiveness might be enhanced by having a permanent presence in the region for training and conferences. As that idea continued to percolate, Mark Ellis and Homer Moyer explored the feasibility of sites in several different countries. Many were unsuitable: in the former Yugoslavia, armed conflict persisted; some locations presented logistical obstacles; and some possibilities were available only at ambitiously unrealistic prices.

In the late 1990s, Vojtech Cepl, a former Justice on the Constitutional Court of Czechoslovakia, took Homer to see an abandoned, run-down villa that he thought might be available. Prague put out a request for proposals. There then followed a protracted RFP process in which CEELI's proposal competed against a plan to convert the dilapidated villa into a discotheque and another plan for a casino. Prague, the owner of the building, offered an award of 10,000 Czech crowns for the winner of the bidding process. After all the bids were submitted and considered, authorities announced that there was no winner, and thus no monetary award, but that CEELI's proposal had come in second and CEELI had therefore earned the right to negotiate a lease. That led to the negotiation of a long-term lease for what was to become the CEELI Institute.

A summary of the development of the CEELI Institute appears in the next chapter of this book.

5.15   War Crimes documentation project

In April 1999, at the request of the US Department of State, CEELI began interviewing Kosovar refugees who had flooded into Albania, Macedonia, and a temporary refugee site set up at Ft Dix, New Jersey. After the conflict in Yugoslavia ended in June 1999, CEELI continued its work with the Kosovars in their native Kosovo. To assist investigations and potential prosecutions of war crimes, CEELI and its partner organisations in 1999 and 2000 collected testimony from some 2,500 Kosovar Albanians, both at Ft Dix and in the region. Though not admissible evidence, the interviews were collected in a database that was made available to the ICTY to help its investigations and to help identify potential witnesses.

The information collected was published in *Political Killings in Kosova/Kosovo, March–June 1999*, which was released in October 2000. This publication, which was a cooperative endeavour of CEELI, the American Association for the Advancement of Science, Human Rights Watch and The Center for Peace Through Justice, an Albanian NGO, addressed the number of ethnic Albanians killed in Kosovo and whether they were inadvertent casualties of the conflict between Serbian forces and the Kosovo Liberation Army or targets of a campaign of systematic ethnic cleansing. Based on the interviews and information gathered, the report found that approximately 10,500 Kosovar Albanians were killed over the course of the conflict in patterns that suggested that the killings were the result of a systematic campaign targeted at ethnic Albanians, conclusions relevant to possible violations of international humanitarian law.

5.16   CEELI honoured at ABA memorial to the Magna Carta, Runnymede, England

In the summer of 2000, in conjunction with its annual meeting in London, the American Bar Association rededicated its memorial to the Magna Carta, which is in Runnymede, England. It took this occasion to honour CEELI and the work that CEELI volunteers had done over the past decade in advancing the rule of law in the world, one of the American Bar Association's institutional goals. The special award was accepted by Homer Moyer and Sandy D'Alemberte and witnessed by a number of CEELI lawyers who had travelled to Runnymede from Sarajevo, where more than 100 CEELI volunteers had gathered for CEELI's annual summer meeting.

On a beautiful day in the meadow at Runnymede, US Ambassador to the United Kingdom Philip Lader welcomed those in attendance. Speaking on behalf of CEELI and its thousands of volunteers were Justice Sandra Day O'Connor and CEELI co-founders Sandy D'Alemberte and Homer Moyer.

Sandy D'Alemberte stated on that occasion that through CEELI "we American lawyers who had railed so long in thousands of Law Day speeches ...

stepped forward to redeem our rhetoric with real action ... Our hope today is that we will be found worthy of the opportunity presented us, that we will not fail those who heed our exhortations to build a just society based on the rule of law and that we will live up to the standards set ... by the splendid group of lawyers who ... have declared by their action that they will not let this moment of history pass without contributing what they can to that grand ideal, the rule of law".[3]

Homer Moyer reported that in Sarajevo, "we were inspired by the dedication of unpaid CEELI lawyers living in Minsk, Bishkek, Pristina, and more than 20 other cities, ... humbled by the courage of two young Central European lawyers maintaining a CEELI office in Serbia, where CEELI lawyers cannot now reside, ... and moved by the determination of CEELI's local partners who strive to give life to the ideal of the rule of law in countries where it has had no life for a generation, or longer". Every CEELI volunteer is "proud to be identified with the ideal we commemorate today" and "grateful that our profession has enabled us to share in ... this historic endeavour".

5.17 Elections in Ukraine

Throughout 2004, during the run-up to the Ukrainian presidential election, CEELI focused on judicial training and Ukraine's presidential election law. Using five Ukrainian Supreme Court judges as trainers, CEELI trained other judges of the Supreme Court and 700 lower court judges throughout Ukraine. With a Ukrainian elections lawyer on CEELI's staff and a member of the Central Election Commission, CEELI developed a detailed judicial bench book for judges on the adjudication of election disputes. That bench book, edited by the deputy chairman of the Supreme Court, was distributed to every court in Ukraine. CEELI also helped devise and then publish 2,900 copies of the *Commentary on the Election Law*, written by five election law experts, which was widely viewed as the authoritative treatment of the election law. Working with other organisations and funders, CEELI also established Election Consultation Centers, trained 16 legal clinics that conducted approximately 100 public education seminars at academic institutions, and organised a nationwide, toll-free hotline for election-related complaints.

In proceedings broadcast on local and national television, the Supreme Court issued an historic decision overturning the results of the presidential election. The court found massive, systematic violations of the presidential election law, unlawful actions of the Central Election Commission, including illegitimate interference in the electoral process by the executive branch,

3   CEELI's 2000 Annual Report.

violations in the compilation of voter lists, and violations in the use of absentee ballots. The court then ordered a new run-off election.

Ten days before the new runoff election, *The Wall Street Journal Online* described the impact of the court decision: "Two weeks ago, Ukrainians felt the earth move beneath their feet. By invalidating the disputed presidential runoff election and scheduling a new vote for Dec. 26, Ukraine's Supreme Court ... displayed the kind of independence that many demonstrating on the streets of Kiev doubted the judiciary possessed. But those familiar with the efforts of the American Bar Association's Central European and Eurasian Law Initiative (or 'CEELI') might have seen it coming." The *Journal* quoted CEELI Deputy Director Michael Maya: "Politicians and the elite who observed the bold and independent behavior of Ukrainian judges ... may begin to properly fear the courts as a true and independent arbiter of justice, and not just another institution that can be bought, corrupted or intimidated" (*The Wall Street Journal Online*, 16 December 2004).

A few days later, the *New York Times* reported that "The Central European and Eurasian Law Initiative of the American Bar Association, which trains lawyers and judges across the region ... conduct[ed] a series of sessions tutoring Ukraine's judges in election law ... 'This is the most dramatic example of judicial independence that we've seen in the developing countries of Eastern Europe', Homer E Moyer, Jr., a senior partner in the law firm Miller & Chevalier in Washington and a co-founder of the association's program, said in a telephone interview ..." (*New York Times*, 22 December 2004).

The new election of 26 December 2004 resulted in the election of opposition leader Viktor Yushchenko as Ukraine's new President.

5.18   The legacy of CEELI volunteers

The CEELI concept of relying on volunteer assistance from legal experts, ABA members and others continued far beyond the heady days and excitement of the early 1990s. That vibrant public-service, volunteer ethic not only drove the CEELI project, but also remains as an admirable attribute of most American lawyers. The various characterisations of CEELI as a 'legal Peace Corps', a 'mini-Marshall Plan' and 'the crown jewel of the ABA' are all tributes to the selfless dedication of CEELI volunteers.

Not surprisingly, former CEELI liaisons and volunteers have gone on to many other public service roles, among them senior positions in the US State Department and the United Nations, Deputy Counsel to the President, the diplomatic post of United States Ambassador to India, and the cabinet position of United States Trade Representative.

Chapter 5. Rule of law initiatives: the CEELI Institute – advancing the rule of law[1]

Homer E Moyer, Jr
Miller & Chevalier

Returning to Sofia after having visited the American University in Bulgaria during a summer CEELI (Central European and Eurasian Law Initiative) liaison meeting, a few of us on a bus filled with ABA (American Bar Association) CEELI liaisons and board members discussed whether it might make sense for CEELI to have a permanent training facility in the region. Those musings on that mountain road in Bulgaria were the germ of an idea that was to become, five years later, the CEELI Institute.

1. The realisation of an institute

Over the ensuing five years, the idea persisted, raising questions about possible locations, necessary approvals, funding possibilities, substantive focus and where to find trainers. At that time, no one anticipated that 25 years later the idea might lead to a postgraduate institution in a historic villa in Prague where lawyers and judges from more than 45 different countries would come for training on issues of building and preserving the rule of law.

As with CEELI itself, the creation and development of the CEELI Institute was the work of many hands.

1.1 But where?

Several countries in Central and Eastern Europe seemed possible locations for a regional training centre. Half-a-dozen countries still involved in, or adjacent to, continuing conflict were ruled out, even though some US ambassadors, seeing the value of the Institute, pushed for their countries. Searching in other countries from time to time, Mark Ellis and I failed to locate suitable, affordable possibilities. But in Prague, we were introduced to the Green Tree building, a historic structure owned by the Prague Jewish community in Prague's Old Town, parts of which dated back to the 13th century. An intriguing possibility, this ancient structure also presented a host of issues.

1   This chapter is an abridged version of Chapter 8, by Homer E Moyer, in *Building the Rule of Law: Firsthand Accounts from a Thirty-Year Global Campaign*, edited by James R Silkenat and Gerold W Libby. © 2021 American Bar Association. All rights reserved. Reproduced with kind permission.

While discussions concerning Green Tree were underway, Bill Meyer, who had been CEELI's first in-country liaison in Bulgaria nearly a decade before, was about to earn another sabbatical from his progressive Boulder, Colorado, law firm. Bill agreed to be the first executive director of this yet-to-be-established training centre. Bill and his wife, Jane, then travelled to Prague, rented a flat in the Old Town and, once again, sailed into uncharted waters. Ultimately, the needs of the Jewish community, which had been decimated during World War II, to bolster their finances and CEELI's near total lack of resources made clear that the Green Tree building was not the solution.

During a visit to Prague the following winter, however, Vojtech Cepl, a former judge on Czechoslovakia's Constitutional Court and outspoken advocate of law reform whom we had met on our first visit to Prague, said "Homer, I have a place to show you". Bundled up for the elements, Vojtech, Bill and I took the metro two stops to Prague 2 (Prague's districts are numbered) and walked up the hill to Havlíčkovy sady, a 35-acre public park in the centre of which sat Villa Grebovka, a large, rundown structure that had been built in the 19th century by Moritz Grobe, a Czech industrialist as his Italian Neo-Renaissance style villa. Owned by the city since the early 1900s, the building had variously been abandoned, dedicated to neighbourhood use, used by Hitler Youth during the Nazi occupation, taken over by The Pioneers, a communist youth group, and abandoned again. Its only use at the time of our visit was for neighbourhood ballet classes for young girls in one corner of the first floor of the abandoned building.

Believing that we could make a ramshackle villa work for us, we floated the idea, and the ABA, pleased with CEELI's track record, relaxed its 1990 prohibition on any CEELI offices overseas and gave us the go-ahead to pursue the idea. Shortly thereafter, we learned from US Ambassador John Shattuck that he had arranged for Secretary of State Madeleine Albright to be in Brno in April 2000 to dedicate a research facility at the Czech Supreme Court that the US Supreme Court, through Justice Sandra Day O'Connor, had helped create. Secretary Albright, a strong supporter of CEELI, agreed to announce on that occasion the plan of CEELI and the ABA to establish a rule of law centre in Prague, to be known as the CEELI Institute.

For the occasion, Bill Meyer and I travelled to Brno in April 2000. Bill, who was directly involved in the planning, recalls that Secretary Albright cut just one ribbon (for the new research centre), but also announced that ABA CEELI planned to establish a regional training centre in Prague. My recollection, not to be trusted, is that we had brought both scissors and a ribbon of our own. If we did, they would have been the Institute's only assets. In any event, Secretary Albright performed her other duties, announced our plan, and cut at least one ribbon. With that, the virtual flag of 'the CEELI Institute' was formally planted.

Our brief ceremony completed, Bill returned to Boulder, Colorado, as his sabbatical ended. Importantly, Bill's tenure in Prague had also included developing the curricula of judicial training programmes that continue to be key elements of the Institute's core curriculum and, following the end of negotiations on the Green Tree building, conducting a quest throughout the city, scouting alternative sites for the Institute. With Villa Grebovka identified as a potential site for the Institute, foundational courses for the curriculum in hand, and a prominent US public figure having announced that a future ABA legal training centre was coming, the prospect of the Institute began to seem real. Once again, Bill Meyer, with ingenuity and persistence, was at the forefront of a new CEELI enterprise, just as he had been the first of what became a 500-strong network of CEELI liaisons and legal specialists a decade earlier.

It is ironic that the path to a home for the Institute led us back to Prague. When Mark Ellis and I were in Prague early in CEELI's history, we were offered a large building just off the Old Town Square for CEELI. At that time, soon after Czechoslovakia's independence, there was intense interest in attracting foreign organisations and investors, and we were offered this substantial building at no cost. Friends in the State Department advised us, however, that this would be a bad idea since the law reform process in Central Europe would not take very long and CEELI would likely be gone in a couple of years.

1.2   Virtual beginnings

Bill Meyer was succeeded for several months as the Institute's executive director by Frank Cooksey, a former CEELI liaison from Texas. Frank's tenure included initial training programmes that we conducted in borrowed space in Prague. Indeed, for two years, the CEELI Institute had no facility of its own, but depended on the good offices and facilities of New York University and the University of Michigan, which had a graduate programme in economics in Prague. During that period, the Institute was able to conduct important trainings and programmes, including a human rights training course in which more than half of all of the lawyers in Kosovo participated.

Frank Cooksey was succeeded by Joel Martin, who served as the Institute's executive director for more than four years, including one or two return stints during later transitions. A tall, deep-voiced lawyer from Maine, Joel had been a CEELI liaison in Moldova. Having given an elegant toast in response to a toast by Justice O'Connor at one of our summer liaison meetings, Joel proved to be a steady hand on the Institute's tiller, providing thoughtful, knowledgeable leadership as executive director.

A primary focus for Joel was the request for proposals (RFP) that Prague 2 issued for tenders for the use of Villa Grebovka. The process had begun in the autumn of 1999 when Prague 2 invited ideas for use of the villa and park, offering a financial prize of 100,000 Czech crowns to the first-place winner. One idea was to convert the villa to a discotheque, another proposed making it a casino. On 12 January 2000, CEELI submitted its idea, suggesting a post-graduate centre for training lawyers and judges on aspects of the rule of law. When the process concluded on 29 May 2000, Prague announced, first, that there had been no first-place winner and thus no 100,000 Kc prize (a modest setback for transparency) but, second, that CEELI was the second-place finisher and thus entitled to a modest prize, which we contributed to the ballet school holding classes in a first-floor corner of the abandoned villa. After submitting a formal tender to Prague 2, our prospective landlord, our proposal was accepted, and within a month we negotiated a 50-year lease with Prague 2, signing the lease agreement on 24 June 2001.

In his recollections of his time in Prague, Joel Martin recounts the last resistance to Prague's leasing the villa to American law reformers. It came at Prague's City Hall where a group of very young, quite adorable, tutu-clad ballet dancers gathered to register their disapproval of the city's decision, which would effectively displace them from the abandoned villa, which had become their improvised dance studio. Touched, but resolute, we pushed ahead.

The initial lease for Villa Grebovka covered the 80-room villa itself and its terrace overlooking a vineyard below and a vista beyond, the Pavilion, an adjacent U-shaped structure with both a courtyard in the centre and a grass terrace in front, and the Landhaus, a building at the foot of the hill near an entrance to the park that contains six flats. Because Prague was eager to have the historic villa refurbished, our principal obligation under the lease was to renovate the building in accordance with the standards of Prague's historical preservation authorities. The lease required that the restoration process be completed within five years and that the Institute partially subsidise restoration of the park in which the villa sits. Beyond that, however, the monthly rental fee was nominal, and the 25-year term of the lease is renewable at the sole discretion of the tenant on the same terms.

The front-loaded financial obligations of the lease required us to raise funds to cover the cost of renovations. The once-handsome structure of which we took possession was striking, but the restoration process was daunting. The building was thoroughly dilapidated from decades of neglect and still had ageing symbols of the prior occupations of both the Nazis and the Communists. A further structural distinction was that the villa ironically suffered damage in World War II during an air raid when an Allied pilot, mistakenly believing he was over Dresden, dropped a bomb that pierced the roof and set the villa on fire. Though that damage had been repaired, there was an odd symmetry in the restoration of the building now being undertaken by Americans.

Joel and his wife, Joyce, lived across the street in an upstairs flat overlooking Havlíčkovy sady and the busy construction site that was the Institute. From there, they had a bird's-eye view of the work underway under the careful supervision of architect Michal Hron, who, with his wife, Hedvika Hronova, skilfully guided us through the renovation process. The restoration work was done by SKANSKA, a well-known, highly regarded European general contracting firm. To meet the strict standards of Czech historical preservation authorities, SKANSKA did meticulous work, transforming the building into the imposing, and highly functional, building that it is today. Once historical frescoes were discovered on the walls of the abandoned Pavilion, the restoration of which would have far exceeded our budget, the Institute returned the Pavilion to Prague 2, removing it from our lease. At the same time, however, it became clear that we could make 34 hillside rooms below the first-floor guest suites, enabling the Institute to have residential capacity for its programme participants.

Restorations proceeded floor-by-floor and dollar-by-dollar, as we sought to raise funds to cover renovation costs. As the value of the dollar dipped significantly at points during construction, costs increased. Our fund-raising, often a step ahead of our payment obligations, focused first on the ground floor, which once completed, would allow us to begin training in the villa itself. First-floor renovations were completed in October 2003, and dedicated two weeks later, utilised within a month for training of a delegation from the Fergana Valley, a region that marks the confluence of Uzbekistan, Kyrgyzstan and Tajikistan. To celebrate our second ribbon-cutting, Czech President Vaclav Havel attended and addressed the crowd, and our friend, Michal Basch, the Mayor of Prague 2, and Institute board member Jirina Novakova did the ceremonial honours by cutting the ribbon. Former Secretary of State Madeleine Albright, who had hoped to attend this event in her home country, sent a gracious letter, describing CEELI as "the most effective voluntary legal assistance initiative in history", which we read aloud at the event. The dedication of the villa, she added, "begins another chapter in an epic and uplifting tale".

Throughout the CEELI Institute's first six years, fundraising was both a priority and a necessity. The cost of renovation, which ultimately ran well into seven figures, created stress throughout the renovation phase and, as discussed below, thereafter. Without the great generosity of supporters in what became a public-private partnership (predominantly private), the CEELI Institute could have become a short-lived venture ending in a half-restored building. But as renovations progressed, the possibility of default on our lease became unthinkable to us, even as it may have begun to strike some denizens of Prague 2 as possibly a fortuitous outcome.

The many friends and supporters of the CEELI Institute, and the scores of volunteers named in its annual reports, are too numerous to name. For those who signed on early, their offers of help were leaps of faith. Not all of those involved were convinced that a CEELI Institute could survive. But the project attracted the interest and enthusiasm of many, and that made the difference. The result was the type of public-private partnership that USAID typically hopes to ignite with seed money, but that does not always materialise.

The Institute was welcomed and encouraged by friends in the Czech Republic. Vojtech Cepl, a former judge of the Czech Constitutional Court and outspoken advocate of law reform, not only led us to Villa Grebovka, but also was, up until his death in 2009, a staunch friend and board member of the Institute. His friend and colleague, Jiri Musil, a Czech sociologist and recognised European intellectual who had spent time in a concentration camp during World War II, was a strong booster of the Institute. Recalling that Prague was once an intellectual hub of Europe, Jiri believed that Prague was an appropriate home for the CEELI Institute. Eliska Wagnerova, the chief justice of the Czech Supreme Court, and Judge Vladana Woratschova were early members of the Institute board. Jirina Novakova, a historian, Jewish community leader, former council member of one of Prague's districts, and friend has been a steadfast supporter and is still today a valued board member.

Another special friend was Michal Basch, the Mayor of Prague 2. With a quiet, understated manner and gentle good humour, he guided and supported the Institute's executive directors and board members. It was appropriate that he and Jirina Novakova cut the ribbon when we christened the renovated first floor of the Institute. Most celebrated of our Czech supporters was Czech President and national hero, Vaclav Havel. An honouree who was presented with the CEELI Award at one of ABA CEELI's Award Luncheons, President Vaclav came to the Institute on more than one occasion, encouraging our efforts and the Institute's rule of law mission, noting the challenges we faced, and celebrating with us some of the Institute's early baby steps forward.

1.3 Iraqi judges

With the 24 June 2006 deadline for completing renovations on Villa Grebovka still some way off, and with restoration of the main floor completed, on-site training programmes proceeded simultaneously with continuing construction. Funded by both ILAC (the International Legal Assistance Consortium) and the UK's Department for International Development, the Institute committed to train 200 of the approximately 860 judges in Iraq, a country marked by conflict and violence following the end of Sadam Hussein's 24-year rule, which ended in May 2003.

This multi-month training programme began quietly in September 2004 with the arrival of 50 religiously and ethnically diverse male judges from different parts of Iraq. Arriving, none made eye contact with Barbara Dillon Hillas, the female member of our International Advisory Board who was serving as the Institute's interim executive director and was in charge of the programme. The *pro bono* faculty for the two-week training course on 'Judging in a Democratic Society' were a former chief justice of the Supreme Court of the State of Washington, an exiled Iraqi lawyer from Sweden, an Austrian Supreme Court justice, a trial court judge from Los Angeles, and an expert in federal court administration from Utah.

In Iraq, the departure of the judges was delayed because their safety could not be guaranteed. One judge scheduled to attend was assassinated. When the group did arrive, security concerns were high. Some had been victims of the Hussein regime; others had relatives who had been tortured or murdered; some had survived assassination attempts; and the bodyguards protecting one of the judges had been killed. These courageous and sophisticated judges faced daunting challenges, among them varied legal traditions (including the Code of Hammurabi, as well as French, Egyptian, and *Sharia* law), heavy caseloads, crippled infrastructure, hours-long lapses in electricity, and having to write decisions in longhand.

While in Prague, this group of judges bonded, bridged cultural and language divisions, and embraced Barbara Hillas, the woman in charge of the programme. Deputy US Secretary of State, Richard Armitage, met with them and discussed their being the first wave of the effort to bring the rule of law to Iraq. The Czech Foreign Minister shared the Czech Republic's experiences of transitioning from an autocratic regime. The judges departed after an emotional farewell speech by Washington State Supreme Court Justice Robert Utter, one of CEELI's most effective and committed volunteers. They returned to Iraq where going to the office every day was viewed as an act of bravery. After returning home, two of the judges trained at the CEELI Institute were killed.

The second and third groups of Iraqi judges followed. The second group included three of Iraq's 15 female judges, one of whom, as an unmarried woman, had been banned from being a judge under Sadam Hussein. Topics discussed included the UN International Covenant on Civil and Political Rights, DNA testing of evidence, media freedom, and ethics. Michael Diedring, who became the CEELI Institute's next executive director and served from August 2004 to 2008, observed that no other country group of participants had taken the course as seriously as the judges from Iraq.

1.4 More programmes, more floors

With support from major donors, the Institute continued and expanded its post-graduate course offerings. A grant from the World Bank enabled a programme on judicial sector reform for Georgia, Armenia, Serbia, Kyrgyz Republic, Moldova and Kazakhstan. For participants from countries seeking admission to the European Union, the Institute offered a course in EU Law and Practice. Another on International Human Rights was held for lawyers from Serbia and Montenegro. By the end of 2004, the Institute had trained 395 lawyers and judges from 26 different countries.

In 2005, restoration of the second floor was completed. Dramatic features included the large handsome meeting room (once the massive bedroom of Moritz Grobe), the grand staircase from the main lobby, and the ornate ceiling above the staircase, restored with the exception of the centre octagonal tile on which the communist occupants had painted a gold hammer and sickle. For historical reasons and a touch of irony, that tile remains unchanged.

To dedicate the second floor, as had become our wont, we cut another ribbon at the top of the staircase at our 2005 annual meeting. Joining that meeting and its discussions was Justice Anthony Kennedy of the US Supreme Court. Justice Kennedy participated in the ribbon-cutting, along with other distinguished guests at that meeting, including the chief justice of Iraq; Beverly McLachlin, chief justice of the Supreme Court of Canada; Vojtech Cepl of the Czech Constitutional Court; Institute board member Eliska Wagnerova, chief justice of the Supreme Court of the Czech Republic; and Justice Karim Pharaon of the Supreme Court of Jordan. The ribbon-cutting honours were performed by Czech Institute board member, Jirina Novakova, and Institute chair, Homer Moyer. Other participants in the annual meeting included Lado Chanturia, former chairman of the Supreme Court of Georgia, Justice Murad of the Supreme Court of Afghanistan, and Justice Viktor Kryvenko a Supreme Court justice and head of the Council of Judges of Ukraine, who gave a stirring address praising fundamental principles of the rule of law.

At that same meeting, the CEELI Institute board of directors dedicated the main foyer of the Institute, naming it the 'Homer Moyer Entry Hall'. This kind and generous act of the Institute's boards prompted some of Homer's friends to claim that but for them the plaque might have read the 'Moyer Foyer' or, worse yet, the 'Lawyer Moyer Foyer'.

Through 2005 and 2006, Institute programmes continued to expand. Training of Iraqi judges continued. By Spring of 2005, the number of Institute programmes had tripled since early 2003. It opened an Anti-Corruption Legal Advocacy Centre in Baku, Azerbaijan, held Street Law summer camps and classes in Armenia and Turkmenistan, and released its updated Judicial Reform Index.

In 2006, the Institute inaugurated 'Investigating and Prosecuting Official Corruption', which has become one of the Institute's regularly over-subscribed signature courses addressing what has emerged as one of the most pervasive threats to establishing and maintaining the rule of law. In 2006, the restored public park in which the CEELI Institute is situated was reopened after substantial improvements, supported in part by a contribution by the Institute that was a condition of its lease.

By that time, the CEELI Institute established itself as an independent institution. Launched by the ABA and forever a part of its legacy, the CEELI Institute and the ABA agreed in 2004 that the Institute's law reform and rule of law programmes, now operating in numerous countries, could be more effective if the Institute were a free-standing Czech institution based in Central Europe and not an international extension of an association of American lawyers. The Institute is a proud beneficiary of the ABA's willingness to take bold steps to advance the rule of law and proud to continue to work in parallel, as well as jointly, with the ABA and ROLI in seeking to advance the rule of law in the world.

Throughout the creation and growth of CEELI and, later, of the CEELI Institute, the foresight and support of a succession of ABA presidents has been an important asset, supporting the creation of both CEELI and the CEELI Institute. In addition to years of Sandy D'Alemberte's continuing encouragement, several other ABA presidents have also provided valuable guidance and encouragement.

2. A rejuvenated home – at last

On 8 June 2007, Czech President Vaclav Havel, US Supreme Court Justice Sandra Day O'Connor, and Institute founder and chair Homer Moyer cut one final ribbon, dedicating the fully renovated Villa Grebovka as the home of the CEELI Institute. Inside, we also named and dedicated the Maurice R Greenberg/Starr Foundation Main Hall and the Mary and David Boies Reading Room. Those in attendance included former ABA presidents Sandy D'Alemberte, Martha Barnett and Karen Mathis; Mark Ellis, executive director of the IBA and former CEELI executive director, former ABA executive director Bob Stein, IBA president Fernando Pombo and future IBA president Martin Solc, Prague 2 Mayor Michal Basch, Salzburg Seminar president Stephen Salyer, US Court of Appeals Judges Robert Henry and Thomas Griffith, as well as many other friends, supporters and CEELI Institute board members, friends and volunteers.

Leading up to this milestone event, there had been an intense effort to complete renovations of the villa's 34 guest suites, the villa's upper two floors and the residential Landhaus, all professionally handled by SKANSKA's talented artisans, architect Michal Hron, and project manager Hedvika Hronova. Soon to follow was the addition of a first-floor fitness facility, which was added thanks to the generosity of Essam Al Tamimi – a member of our International Advisory Board – of Al Tamimi & Company in Dubai. As the 2007 festivities and board meeting ended, the CEELI Institute found itself with a handsome, historic and highly functional headquarters that has served us well, along with some last-minute debt required to meet the renovation deadline of the lease, and some unpaid obligations to our friends at SKANSKA. These financial obligations preoccupied us for the next eight-and-a-half years, as the Institute both flourished and hung on by its fingernails.

3. The Institute: growing into its second decade

The Institute's tenth anniversary, in 2010, seemed far removed from the early days of conducting training in borrowed classrooms and inspecting a 40,000 square foot 19th-century structure considered by many to be a dilapidated white elephant. But with a knowing nod of support from Sandy D'Alemberte, a legendary institution builder, the encouragement and generosity of many, and the incentivising scepticism of a few, we pushed ahead, with a stream of volunteers to follow, helping to create and build the CEELI Institute. Their efforts paved the way for many programmes and initiatives to support the rule of law around the world in the years to follow.

Encouragers of the CEELI Institute included US Ambassadors to the Czech Republic. The first encounter came when Mark Ellis and I sat down with US Ambassador Shirley Temple Black to outline our idea for a postgraduate rule of law institute, while trying not to betray our delight at brainstorming with someone who was both an effective ambassador and a Hollywood icon. Others followed, all offering encouragement and bipartisan enthusiasm: John Shattuck, a former Assistant Secretary of State and later president of the Central European University; Craig Stapleton, who retains interests in the Czech Republic, was a booster and is still a friend of the Institute; Bill Cabaniss immediately saw the potential of the Institute and provided extraordinary official support and a strong personal commitment to our mission; Richard Graber and Norm Eisen were both supporters as the Institute came of age with a renovated home in Villa Grebovka; Andrew Schapiro, another lawyer-ambassador; and Steve King, a friend who was ambassador for our 20th anniversary.

Continuing the public interest, *pro bono* traditions of CEELI, the CEELI Institute established a tradition of enlisting expert faculties from America, Europe and other regions willing to participate on a *pro bono* basis, a practice that contributes significantly to the Institute's unusual cost-effectiveness. By 2009, CEELI Institute volunteers had numbered 250, with more than 130 governmental, corporate, foundation and individual financial supporters. Leading up to its 10th anniversary, the CEELI Institute had begun a Judicial Integrity Roundtable for senior judges in the region, training on human rights and judicial independence for Iraqi lawyers and judges, and increasingly popular training on combating official corruption, a pervasive threat to the rule of law.

In 2010, our tenth anniversary, the Institute hosted its second Integrity Roundtable, led by US Court of Appeals Judges John Walker (Second Circuit) and Clifford Wallace (Ninth Circuit), with presentations by both Justice Sandra Day O'Connor and former chief justice of the Washington State Supreme Court, Robert Utter. The Institute's annual summer meeting featured a retrospective of rule of law highlights of CEELI and the CEELI Institute, a discussion of war crimes as fundamental failures of the rule of law, official corruption as a growing threat to the rule of law, and future challenges, including human trafficking, terrorism, ethnic conflict and gender discrimination. Justice Sandra Day O'Connor, recalling the important role that American lawyers and judges played since the dissolution of the Soviet Union, said that the establishment of 26 separate, functioning nation states was a "breath-taking accomplishment".

The CEELI Institute board expressed its great appreciation for the generosity of David and Mary Boies and of J Larry Nichols, the chairman of Devon Energy. Their support was timely as well as generous and without it the continued operation of the CEELI Institute would have been at risk. Valuable support of the CEELI Institute also came from, among others, IBA presidents Fernando Pombo, Fernando Pelaez-Pier, David Rivkin, Martin Solc and IBA executive director Mark Ellis. Funding by the Eligible Fund of the IBA enabled renovation of one of the two wings of guest suites at the Institute, as well as additional programming.

4. CEELI Institute hallmarks

Beginning its second decade, the Institute has continued practices and traditions that have become hallmarks of the CEELI Institute.

4.1 Expert, *pro bono* faculties

One has been its ability to attract expert, international faculty members who are willing to participate on a *pro bono* basis. A tradition dating back to the beginning days of CEELI, this practice taps into the extraordinary willingness of members of our profession to contribute their time and energy to promote the rule of law and the benefits that it provides. Today, approximately 150 legal experts and leaders volunteer to teach at the CEELI Institute each year.

4.2 Interactive, participatory training

A second secret of the Institute's success has been its development of interactive, participatory training programmes in lieu of just lectures, the still dominant method of instruction in many parts of the world. Institute programmes require participants to engage, face both legal and real-life challenges, and learn by doing much of the work themselves. This approach has generated much positive feedback as participants have, sometimes hesitantly, engaged in learning by working collectively with colleagues under the guidance of international experts.

4.3 Second generation issues

Third, of necessity, the CEELI Institute has increasingly dealt with 'second-generation issues' – issues that were not at the top of reformers lists in the early 1990s, but which have emerged as critically important in promoting the rule of law. High on this list is the phenomenon of official corruption, which can corrosively undermine the rule of law. Similarly, innovations and more refined issues have appeared in Institute programmes focused on maintaining independent, fair-minded, competent judiciaries and lawyer training programmes that increasingly address both aspects of professionalism and substantive expertise that are necessary to an independent, effective legal profession.

Quinn O'Keefe, the Institute's energetic executive director early in our second decade, led both growth in the Institute's programmes and its further expansion into areas beyond Central and Eastern Europe. With programmes in Asia, the Middle East and North Africa, the Institute's footprint grew dramatically, a trend that Quinn's successor, Chris Lehmann, continued, beginning in 2014, as recounted below.

These developments, along with the 2016 refined articulation of the Institute's vision and mission, continue to guide the growth and expansion of the CEELI Institute. As its programmes and geographical reach have expanded, the Institute's financial strength has also grown, bringing the promise of a sustainable and permanent institution dedicated to advancing the rule of law in the world. A few of the highlights of the CEELI Institute's second decade define its growth path to 2020.

5.   Institute milestones

The growth of the CEELI Institute has been marked by a series of milestones – prominent programmes that have become part of the Institute's core curriculum: geographical expansion into the Middle East, Africa and south Asia; innovative, groundbreaking new initiatives; productive partnerships and collaborations; and programmes the Institute initiated that have become ongoing, semi-independent traditions. All have been undertaken with a continuing commitment to excellence and fidelity to the Institute's rule of law mission.

5.1   Independent courts and professional judges

The two judicial training programmes with which the CEELI Institute began building its curriculum for judges – 'Judging in a Democratic Society' and 'Justice in a Market Economy' – remain a core part of the Institute's curriculum and continue to draw participants from a wide range of countries. On these two building blocks, the Institute's programmes and activities in support of independent courts – an essential cornerstone of the rule of law – have proliferated.

5.2   Conference of chief justices

In 2010, following the CEELI Institute's annual meeting, the Institute hosted a Judicial Integrity Roundtable led by Justice O'Connor, US Court of Appeals Judges John Walker of the Second Circuit and Clifford Wallace of the Ninth Circuit, and former chief justice of the Supreme Court of the State of Washington, Robert Utter. At that roundtable, the participants, who were chief justices, presidents, and other high officers of Supreme Courts in the region, voted to return to the CEELI Institute the following summer to begin an annual conference of chief justices.

Accordingly, in July 2011, the chief justices of the Supreme Courts of 16 countries, including Justice John Roberts, of the US Supreme Court, launched the first conference of chief justices of Central and Eastern Europe. Justice Roberts, who spoke on 'Equal Justice Under Law', participated in that inaugural session, which was otherwise led by Judge John Walker, Judge Wallace, and former US District Court Judge and Harvard Law School professor, Nancy Gertner. US Ambassador to the Czech Republic Norm Eisen and CEELI Institute chair Homer Moyer also spoke at the conference, which was coordinated by Institute executive director, Joel Martin.

The participating chief justices voted to make the conference of chief justices an annual affair at which they could discuss among themselves issues of common interest. They agreed that on a rotating basis, one chief justice would host each annual conference and that, to encourage candour and confidentiality, there would be no press, no quotes for attribution, and outside participants only by invitation. The CEELI Institute would co-sponsor and support these conferences, with Judge John Walker agreeing to advise and assist each host chief justice in turn, which he continues to do.

In 2015, at the conference held in Brijuni, Croatia, the 16 assembled chief justices signed 'The Brijuni Statement of Principles of the Independence of the Judiciary'. Developed by the chief justices over the course of three years, the Brijuni Principles reaffirm fundamental principles of judicial independence and integrity, recognising that true independence, both institutional and individual, is indispensable to the successful functioning of the judiciary under the rule of law. Now signed by judges of the 19 countries that participate in the chief justices' annual conferences, the Brijuni Statement of Principles stands alongside the Bangalore Principles of Judicial Conduct and other international instruments embracing an independent judiciary as fundamental to the rule of law.

5.3   The Judicial Exchange Network

Beginning in 2012, with funding from the US State Department's Bureau of International Narcotics and Law Enforcement Affairs, the CEELI Institute launched the Central and Eastern European Judicial Exchange Network. The first gathering of this Network brought together 32 lower court judges and court administrators from 15 different countries across the region. Drawing, in part, on the conference of chief justices, the Institute designed a series of exchanges and instruction on best practices and began the process of building a 'sustainable peer support network' focusing on judicial integrity and court efficiency.

On returning home, one participating judge presented a proposal to develop bench books in criminal law and civil law, and a book for court executives. Another published a summary of his take-aways from the roundtable to share with his colleagues and proposed a separate office of court management. Another began work creating a special room for interviewing children who are witnesses or victims in proceedings. Two years later, in 2014, the number of participating judges nearly doubled to 63 from 19 countries. They held a strategic planning session, agreed to form a Network Advisory Board, and adopted a Network mission statement.

In 2015, Network judges, with coordinating assistance from the CEELI Institute, conceived, developed and published the *Manual on Independence, Impartiality and Integrity of Justice: A Thematic Compilation of International Standards, Policies and Best Practices*. Based on a systematic review of 130 documents setting forth relevant international standards, the Manual reflects impressive commitments of time, research and energy by the Network judges themselves. The result is an easy-to-use reference tool available to judges worldwide, especially societies in which judiciaries are struggling to assert and establish full independence.

In its first eight years, the Judicial Exchange Network brought together over 150 young, reform-minded judges – 'some of the best and brightest' – who continue to meet one or more times a year to discuss judicial independence, judicial ethics, comparative disciplinary procedures, dealing with the media, lustration, and mechanisms for earning public trust.

5.4   Tunisian judges

Following the Arab Spring, the CEELI Institute in 2011, together with the International Legal Assistance Consortium (ILAC) and the IBA, began an extraordinary multi-year project to train nearly 1,000 Tunisian judges on judging in a democracy and judicial accountability. Funded by the Swedish International Development Cooperation Agency, this project entailed twice-monthly trainings on judicial independence and building the public's confidence in the judiciary. Half of the trainings were conducted by the CEELI Institute, half by the IBA. Joel Martin, former CEELI liaison and former Institute executive director, masterfully managed this project.

All of the training sessions, which were built on the Institute's 'Judging in a Democratic Society' course, were conducted in Tunis. In March 2012, the Institute conducted the first of the 11 training sessions it was to hold that first year. The judges who led the training sessions came from the United States, Sweden, the Czech Republic and a host of other Central and East European countries. Inviting feedback at the end of each session, participants noted that the interactive, participatory course, which included a focus on practical problems, was unlike any other they had ever taken. Their evaluations were overwhelmingly positive. The following year the Institute was asked also to work with Tunisia's new Anti-Corruption Agency.

Beginning in 2017, after the Institute and the IBA had together trained nearly 1,800 Tunisian judges, the Institute developed, in coordination with Tunisian judges and other stakeholders, a follow-up curriculum. With Tunisians having lived for many years under an authoritarian government, the follow-up curriculum focused on efforts to promote and build public trust in the judiciary. This project was overseen and managed by Joel Martin, who had become the Institute's Senior Advisor for Judicial Affairs, Joel's third CEELI title.

5.5 Expanded judicial offerings, partnerships, workshops, exchanges

In the CEELI Institute's second decade, the number and variety of judicial programmes continued to grow both substantively and geographically. As trainings on judicial independence and court administration continued – including, for example, trainings in Burma on 'Judging in a Democratic Society' – the interests and needs of courts and judges led to new Institute initiatives.

In 2011, judges from Ukraine and Moldova came to the Institute for training in intellectual property – copyright, trademark and patent law. The years that followed also brought a variety of workshops for judges on bench book innovations (held with the National Office for the Judiciary of the Hungarian Academy of Justice), public pressures and corruption, caseload management, evaluating the performance of judges, judicial ethics, CLE for judges, new technologies in the administration of justice, EU law, the role of NGOs in monitoring court proceedings and judicial functions, dealing with the media, and helpful and unhelpful uses of social media by judges.

With the continuing involvement of Judge Jack Tunheim, chief judge of the US District Court in Minnesota, and others, the Institute initiated programmes on good practices in handling complex litigation involving terrorism or issues of national security. Undertaken jointly with the International Institute for Justice and the Rule of Law in Malta, these courses focus in part on the Global Counterterrorism Forum's 'The Hague Memorandum Good Practices for the Judiciary in Adjudicating Terrorism Offenses'. Participants for these programmes were drawn from the Balkans, the Middle East, and North Africa, and a similar programme for Bangladeshi judges conducted with the National Centre for State Courts also included work on a specialised bench book for terrorism cases. In 2017, with a focus on good practices in cases involving terrorism or national security crimes, the Institute, the National Judicial Academy of India, and the US Federal Judicial Center began a multi-year programme promoting exchanges between Indian and US judges.

These various programs have reached not only judges in Central and Eastern Europe and Central Asia, but also judges in Iraq, Jordan, Lebanon, Tunisia, Pakistan, India, Burma and Syrian judges in exile in Turkey.

5.6   The role of US judges

American judges from all levels of courts in the United States have played critical roles in both CEELI and the CEELI Institute. They have involved themselves in judicial training, judicial exchange programmes, and innovative, specialised initiatives, as well as governance of CEELI and the CEELI Institute. Some have participated in literally dozens of programmes and events, commonly travelling long distances. They have shared their experiences and insights with judges in countries around the world and have furthered the goal of establishing independent, impartial, efficient, incorruptible courts and judiciaries. Most took on projects as active judges, while managing ongoing responsibilities and active dockets; others joined in or continued after retiring from the bench. We, and particularly the judicial colleagues with whom they collaborated, are grateful for their efforts on behalf of the rule of law.

5.7   Postgraduate training for lawyers

Another core part of the CEELI Institute's curriculum, postgraduate training for lawyers, continues to grow. In addition to the large number of anti-corruption prosecutors and investigators, the Institute offers skills training, substantive courses and support for human rights and defence lawyers through a variety of programmes.

The Institute has provided advocacy skills training for young lawyers throughout the region and beyond. Through one- and two-week programmes, young professionals receive training from experienced lawyers from various countries, including interactive training developed for use in clinical training programmes, such as international programmes run by the National Institute for Trial Advocacy (NITA). Participants in these trainings have included young lawyers from Burma, Iran and other countries beyond Central and Eastern Europe.

Other programmes have been tailored to the needs of criminal defence lawyers seeking to maintain the rule of law, particularly in countries in which the independence of the legal profession or of the defence bar is under stress. Beginning with the question of access to counsel, these programmes include litigation strategies for representing clients and for challenging repressive laws. Among the available tools is the use of international law and international conventions as a check on national laws and practice. One three-part training course developed in cooperation with the Centre de la Protection Internationale in Strasbourg focuses on representing clients before the European Court of Human Rights in cases involving violations of rights guaranteed by the European Convention on Human Rights. The jurisdiction of the European Court of Human Rights extends to appeals from final judgments in the 47 member states of the Council of Europe.

The Institute's programmes in Burma, in cooperation with the Burma Center

Prague, have for four years included trainings for lawyers engaged in *pro bono* legal defence efforts. These trainings, which include practical skills components, have been conducted in 13 different cities in Burma. These programmes have also included roundtables with lawyers and members of the Burmese Parliament who are seeking reform of repressive laws and to increase recourse to the underutilised Constitutional Court, established by the Burmese Constitution drafted in 2008 by the country's previous military regime.

For human rights lawyers working under difficult conditions in countries with a hostile or authoritarian environment, the Institute provides short-term residential fellowships at the Institute. These fellowships provide an opportunity for lawyers to re-group, connect with colleagues, and participate in or audit Institute programmes. Fellows are sometimes placed in longer-term internships in other organisations throughout Europe. This programme of providing short-term sabbaticals has been in place since 2015. The Institute also conducts workshops for and other civil society organisations which are seeking to ensure transparent government processes, obtain access to information, and enhance government accountability.

The Institute works with a variety of other organisations in hosting events and programmes devoted to enhancing the rule of law, human rights and democracy. Included in this variety of activities have been collaborations with ABA ROLI, including a 2017 Working Discussion on the Rule of Law, Governance, and Human Rights Assistance in Europe & Eurasia held in Washington DC. Each summer's annual meeting of the Institute's governing board in Prague includes an examination of successes, challenges, issues and trends in the rule of law, and the effectiveness of Institute programmes.

5.8 Young lawyers from Palestine and Israel

Beginning in 2014, the CEELI Institute and the IBA, with funding from the IBA, began to shape a programme bringing together young Israeli and Palestinian lawyers to meet one another, to utilise some novel communication tools to promote dialogue, and to create discussions on Israel-Palestine issues critical to the Middle East and of concern throughout the world. The young lawyers – including a third category of young Palestinian lawyers who lived and worked in Israel and were thus Israeli citizens – arrived in Prague for our first meeting not knowing one another and wondering, we later learned, whether the experiment would last a few hours, or less, before the shouting started.

Unexpected was that we would try communication techniques sometimes used in couples counselling (known to Imago therapists as an 'intentional dialogue') during which participants attempt to mirror or replicate comments made by others rather than comment on or challenge statements made. To guide this undertaking were an Israeli Imago therapist and a Palestinian Imago therapist skilled in this technique. Following a couple of practice rounds –

through which it became clear that listening was the essential skill and that regardless of what anyone said, no one was going to challenge or attack them – participants were asked to comment on what about the Israeli-Palestinian relationship most bothered them. The second commenter, a Palestinian, described delays and hassles he experienced when having to pass checkpoints when travelling to visit his father in Jerusalem. His story caused the Israeli lawyer seated next to him to cry. Apologising for her response, she explained that although she did not frequently cry, the story had deeply touched her.

During the six three-day meetings of this group that followed over the next two to three years, participants learned about one another, realised many things they had in common, and heard perspectives and narratives they had never before been exposed to. Friendships were formed; officials, diplomats, and negotiators joined some of the sessions; and, as relationships strengthened, mixed groups discussed intractable issues that have polarised and plagued the region. The meetings did not produce agreement on hard questions or dissolve differences. They stunningly showed, however, the potential of addressing and bridging bitter, historical enmities that were culturally deeply embedded and assumed to be irreparable.

The courageous young lawyers who agreed to participate in this project were inhibited primarily by fears of the potential repercussions and reprisals they might suffer from fellow countrymen if it became public that they had agreed to participate in a project such as this. Some who were interviewed as candidates for the project declined, believing the risks were too great; one withdrew for fear that it would foreclose her hope of ever becoming a judge; and one law professor whom we consulted for recommendations advised that several universities had agreed not to cooperate with any project that was designed to achieve normalisation of relations between Palestine and Israel.

Fear of the consequences of becoming publicly associated with the project affected both Israeli and Palestinian lawyers. After two years, however, at a meeting of the IBA in Washington, six participants agreed to discuss their experiences in the project at a programme at which press was not allowed and at which they were introduced by first names only. Their open, often poignant discussion with members of the project's steering committee – which included a prominent Israeli lawyer and a prominent Arab lawyer who had become long-time friends through the IBA – prompted an exuberant, standing ovation by the audience of several hundred.

Facing practical and political limits to publicising the remarkable achievements of this mixed dozen of young lawyers, this project nonetheless offered a glimpse of achieving the impossible. Perhaps this low-visibility project will continue in the future to inspire its participants and, perhaps, their friends and colleagues.

5.9   Anti-corruption

The emergence of official corruption as a holdover of privilege from authoritarian regimes and a pervasive threat to building the rule of law prompted the CEELI Institute to include anti-corruption training as part of its core curriculum. An area of active legal practice and of intense corporate concern for little more than a generation, anti-corruption/foreign bribery laws have increased exponentially, based on a flurry of international conventions adopted since 1995 to which more than 100 countries are now signatories. In former communist or autocratic countries, anti-corruption is an even less familiar discipline.

The CEELI Institute's signature training course is 'Investigating and Prosecuting Official Corruption', a highly interactive training programme built around a hypothetical case study which participants are asked to analyse and evaluate in breakout groups based on facts and information made available to them over the course of a week. Because foreign bribery laws have been aggressively enforced by the United States and some other countries since the 1990s, it has been possible to enlist faculties of private practitioners, former prosecutors and forensic accountants with extensive real-world experience. They deserve credit for the success of this popular programme.

Since first offered in 2011, this programme has become a twice-a-year, typically over-subscribed programme. Participants, in groups of 30 to 40, from countries throughout the region (and as distant as Bhutan) have come to the Institute for this programme, which has, in turn, led to the additional anti-corruption training programmes noted below. As needed, simultaneous translation is provided throughout the course. One visiting UN official kindly reported to us that the Institute's anti-corruption training programmes "are considered to be the best in Europe".

The feedback from those who have participated in the course has also been positive and gratifying: "more than excellent, just outstanding" (2012); "this was really the best quality course I have ever attended" (2014); "the training is one of the finest things to happen in the fight against corruption globally" (2015); "this is the best training I have ever participated in" (2015); "one of the best experiences of my professional life" (2016); "absolutely outstanding course" (2017).

In the Institute's second year of training judges in Tunisia, Samir Anabi, the head of the new Tunisian Anti-Corruption Agency who had attended the Institute's anti-corruption training course the year before, asked the CEELI Institute to provide training and assistance to his new agency. In 2017, the Institute launched an initiative to provide guidance and training to anti-corruption activists across the region, including lawyers, civil activists, journalists and representatives of civil society organisations.

In 2018, the Institute offered its first course for practitioners, in-house counsel and others under the standards of the US Foreign Corrupt Practices Act, the UK Anti-Bribery Law, and the UN Convention Against Corruption (UNCAC). The same year, the CEELI Institute partnered with the International Foundation Electoral Systems (IFES) on a programme to strengthen anti-corruption standards in the Balkans, focusing on implementing the recommendations of GRECO (the Council of Europe's Group of States Against Corruption) in Bulgaria, Romania and Montenegro.

In 2019, the Institute responded to requests for advanced anti-corruption training, the Institute debuted an intensive follow-up course ('Anti-Corruption 2.0'), focusing on complex procurement fraud, forensic accounting, use of meta data and data analytics, money laundering, and multi-jurisdictional investigations. Most participants had attended the basic course, 'Investigating and Prosecuting Official Corruption'. And in 2020, the Institute scheduled, but had to postpone because of the coronavirus, a new multi-disciplinary anti-corruption training course. The concept of this new course is to focus on a single country and to include in the training not only prosecutors and investigators, but also parliamentarians, judges, a representative of the office of the President, journalists, and NGOs. Not only does such a disciplinary mix provide a variety of perspectives on official corruption, but it can provide a critical mass that can be more effective in dealing with political inertia or indifference to official corruption and the costs it extracts.

6. The Institute's coming third decade

The next decade will see the Institute's footprint and impact grow. Entering its third decade, the Institute engaged more than 12,000 participants from nearly 50 different countries in central Europe, central and south Asia, the Middle East, and Africa. Although the global pandemic has imposed constraints on operations, it has also been a catalyst to innovate and develop new techniques, which will greatly expand the capabilities and sophistication of the Institute's training programmes.

As it continues, the Institute will be guided by both a vision and a clearly articulated mission statement. The CEELI Institute's vision is simple and worthy, if ambitious: 'Globalisation of the rule of law'.

Its mission 'to advance the rule of law in the world' was refined in 2016 to note the benefits that can accompany the rule of law and the broad consequences that make it such a powerful engine for humanity:

To advance the rule of law in the world in order to: protect fundamental rights and individual liberties; promote transparent, incorruptible, accountable governments; lay the foundation for economic opportunity and growth; and encourage peaceful resolution of disputes.

Chapter 6. Rule of law initiatives: tackling the problem of knowledge – 30 years of rule of law learning[1]

Elizabeth A Andersen
World Justice Project

1. Introduction

The modern era of rule of law development was launched with the fall of the Berlin Wall, and at the forefront of this effort was the American Bar Association (ABA), through its Central and Eastern European Law Initiative (later redubbed the Central European and Eurasian Law Initiative, also known as ABA CEELI, and eventually the global Rule of Law Initiative, ABA ROLI). In the early 1990s, as ABA volunteers were deployed throughout Eastern Europe, there was a fair amount of trial and error and learning on the fly, often to very good effect, but not shaped by the rigorous assessment, programme design, monitoring and evaluation that characterise development efforts today. Nonetheless, from its earliest days, learning about the rule of law and what works in promoting it has been a focus of the ABA's efforts. Through that learning, the ABA has made important contributions to the advancement of the rule of law development field as it has evolved over the past 30 years.

In 2003, the Carnegie Endowment's Tom Carothers penned "Promoting the Rule of Law Abroad: The Problem of Knowledge", arguing that the "field of rule-of-law assistance is operating from a disturbingly thin base of knowledge – with respect to the core rationale of the work, how change in the rule of law occurs, and the real effects of the changes that are produced."[2] This was about the time that I joined CEELI as its executive director, and I took this critique as a personal challenge. As I looked into the matter, I found that while Carothers' critique of

---

1   This chapter was originally published in *Building the Rule of Law: Firsthand Accounts from a 30-year Global Campaign*, edited by James R Silkenat and Gerold W Libby (© 2021 American Bar Association. All rights reserved. Reproduced with kind permission). It was greatly enriched by interviews with and feedback from a number of colleagues who worked with and for the ABA rule of law programmes over the years, including Scott Carlson, Angela Conway, Lisa Dickieson, Mark Dietrich, Mary Greer, Michael Maya, Andrew Solomon, Salome Tsereteli-Stephens and Nancy Ward. I am grateful to them and to WJP colleagues Bill Neukom, Alejandro Ponce and Ted Piccone, who provided feedback on an earlier draft.
2   Tom Carothers, "Promoting the Rule of Law Abroad: The Problem of Knowledge", p13 (Carnegie Endowment for International Peace Working Paper, January 2003) https://carnegieendowment.org/2003/01/28/promoting-rule-of-law-abroad-problem-of-knowledge-pub-1169.

the field had some merit, ABA CEELI was already taking important steps to solve this problem with its assessment methodologies, research office and thought leadership initiatives.

In 2007, with the launch of the World Justice Project (WJP), the ABA brought additional scholarly rigour to the field, developing a universally resonant definition for the rule of law and a methodology for measuring it that has become the gold standard. More recently, ABA ROLI and the CEELI Institute have continued to expand research and learning on rule of law topics, contributing a number of important studies, tools and on-ground assessments to the field, and regularly convening colleagues to share best practices and improve programming.

This chapter surveys the leadership role that the ABA and its rule of law initiatives have played over the years in improving understanding of the rule of law, why it matters and the mechanisms through which development assistance can strengthen it. The chapter highlights key contributions that the ABA has made to tackling the problem of knowledge in the rule of law field, the challenges that these efforts confront, and opportunities to continue to lead in the next 30 years.

2.   Defining the problem of knowledge

The ABA's rule of law efforts were launched in the heady optimistic days of the early 1990s, as the Berlin Wall and Soviet bloc autocracies crumbled and a swift transition to democracy and free-market economies throughout the region seemed inexorable. With a little technical guidance about the constitutional arrangements, institutions and laws that were important to the rule of law in the West, many thought that justice sector leaders in emerging democracies would be able quickly to replicate the rule of law foundation required to support successful political and economic transitions.

As many ABA CEELI liaisons deployed to Eastern Europe and the former Soviet Union in the 1990s soon learned, rule of law transition proved much more challenging and halting than initially anticipated. Reform efforts often ran up against entrenched interests or inadequate resources and competing priorities. Deep-seated public distrust of institutions was a significant problem in many transitioning countries, yet rule of law assistance programmes rarely included public opinion polling common today, so reform efforts often overlooked this important dimension. In some countries, political instability and armed conflict made progress impossible. Even where there were successes, sustaining them proved difficult. In the best cases, rule of law progress seemed to be on a two-steps-forward, one-step-backward trajectory. By the late 1990s, it was clear that rule of law development would be a long-term project. When the 9/11 attacks drove home that gaps in the rule of law helped create conditions for violent extremism and terrorism, it became a more urgent, global project.

As rule of law development programmes expanded and matured from a transitional effort into a permanent field of development practice – akin to public health and food security – rule of law programmes and their objectives, methodologies and effectiveness came under increased scrutiny. A US Government Accountability Office 2001 report on nearly a decade of US rule of law assistance in the former Soviet Union had the startling title, "U.S. Rule of Law Assistance Has Had Limited Impact".[3] The report lamented that none of the US agencies responsible for rule of law assistance programming had "effective monitoring and evaluation systems in place to assess fully the longer-term results and sustainability of their efforts and reorient their projects based on a thorough understanding of the lessons learned".[4] In his essay, "The Problem of Knowledge", and a subsequent edited volume,[5] Tom Carothers took the critique further, arguing that those of us working to advance the rule of law had neither a clear definition of the concept nor evidence that it supports democracy and economic development, let alone much understanding of what works in promoting it. As such, he questioned whether "the rule of law field" was a "field" at all.

These were trenchant critiques of rule of law development efforts, but they were not news to those at the ABA with boots on the ground, living these challenges in their daily work helping progressive deans and professors to open law school clinics in Russia, supporting the development of an independent judiciary in Albania, or introducing adversarial criminal processes in Armenia and Bosnia. Indeed, drawing on a long ABA tradition of support for research and standard-setting in support of the rule of law in the United States, ABA CEELI styled itself as a learning organisation from the beginning. Because of the ABA's size and influence and the leadership roles that its liaisons and staff have gone on to play in other organisations, the story of learning through the ABA's rule of law initiatives over the past 30 years is a significant part of the larger story of the development of the rule of law field worldwide.

3.   Thirty years of rule of law learning

In many ways, learning was baked into the DNA of the ABA's rule of law initiatives from the beginning. A founding and abiding principle of ABA CEELI and the projects that followed was that assistance must be responsive to the needs of local partners. The ABA did not purport to have all the answers nor to

---

3   Government Accountability Office, "U.S. Rule of Law Assistance Has Had Limited Impact", preface, April 2001 www.gao.gov/assets/240/231403.pdf.

4   *Ibid*, p4. A USAID study commissioned in 2002 concluded more optimistically (if defensively) that "major transformations have taken place in rule of law and justice practices worldwide and that US foreign assistance programs, implemented through USAID and its partners, have made a substantial contribution to those transformations". USAID, "Achievements in Building and Maintaining the Rule of Law: MSI's Studies in LAC, E&E, AFR, and ANE", November 2002.

5   Thomas Carothers, ed, *Promoting the Rule of Law Abroad: In Search of Knowledge* (2006).

insist that there was a single path to the rule of law. Rather, the ABA CEELI approach was to make available to national and local actors information, models and expertise from which they could draw lessons for reform efforts tailored to their needs. This approach was reflected even in the title given to CEELI's first *pro bono* field representatives – 'liaisons' – whose role was not to impose a predetermined solution but to connect partners to expertise and resources relevant to their needs and interests, empowering them to find their own solutions.

In the early 1990s, CEELI liaisons arrived without a clearly defined work plan, open to input, ready to learn and to play this connecting role for in-country partners. This approach was initially supported by flexible funding, much of it from USAID, which allowed for false starts and adjustments to on-ground realities and opportunities. Ironically, the professionalisation of the rule of law development field over the years, while bringing needed rigour and discipline to the provision of technical assistance, may also have cramped this important on-ground real-time learning and adaptive programming. Although they did not have today's acronyms and methodologies for 'political economy analysis' and 'thinking and working politically',[6] the most effective liaisons were indeed approaching their work in that vein and became quick studies of the local legal context.

"Most of us had been lawyers practising in the US without significant comparative law experience and so were not familiar with some important institutions like constitutional courts," recalls early liaison Mark Dietrich. "We had to educate ourselves about the civil law systems, with the overlay of Soviet or socialist law. This all meant that the base of our knowledge was really quite low, but it also drove us to learn more about the history and roots of the common law and US legal traditions, which in itself was educational and interesting, and made us better, more informed lawyers and advocates for change in the countries we were working in."[7] This learning posture was critical to CEELI's early successes and, as detailed below, it has deepened and been institutionalised over the years, through knowledge management initiatives, the development of assessment methodologies, data collection and analysis, and monitoring and evaluation. As we reflect on that evolution, it is instructive to recall the early spirit of collective discovery and to consider ways in which it can continue to infuse current rule of law development efforts.

3.1   Early initiatives in rule of law knowledge management

The earliest institutional manifestation of ABA CEELI's learning agenda was its

---

6   See eg, USAID, Center for Excellence in Democracy, Rights and Governance, "Thinking and Working Politically through Applied Political Economy Analysis: A Guide for Practitioners" (2018), www.usaid.gov/sites/default/files/documents/1866/PEA2018.pdf.
7   Author's email exchange with Mark Dietrich, 9 August 2020.

midyear and annual meetings – the gatherings of CEELI liaisons and board members to share experiences and lessons learned. Generally convened in a country in which CEELI had a long-standing presence, the meetings had a bit of a reunion feel, yet serious learning and problem solving occurred as liaisons presented their work to the board and underwent cross-examination by the likes of Sandra Day O'Connor, Ab Mikva, Max Kampelman and Pat Wald, all of whom sat on the board and were actively engaged in the work.

Some of the most important learning was led by CEELI host country staff gathered at these meetings. CEELI was fortunate to hire many of the brightest young reform-minded lawyers in each country in which it operated. Their understanding of the local context and the political and practical constraints and opportunities it presented contributed enormously to many early CEELI successes. The midyear and annual meetings afforded these staff attorneys an opportunity to share insights and approaches with colleagues in other countries with similar laws, institutions, traditions and challenges. "The key to successful programming in each country, and a critical legacy of ABA's work, was the local staff," recalls Lisa Dickieson, another early liaison, country director, and eventually director of the ABA Asia Rule of Law Council (later the Asia Division of ABA ROLI). "We were creating a cadre of individuals able to take the work forward, which was critical to the longer-term sustainability of the work. And through the midyear and annual meetings we also were creating a network of like-minded and trained reformers."[8]

These meetings continue, if less regularly, to this day. Although contemporary technology facilitates ongoing exchange, there is nothing like the impromptu and generative learning that programme directors working in different parts of the world can undertake when they unexpectedly discover they are grappling with similar substantive or operational challenges. These gatherings became even more important as CEELI grew beyond Europe and Eurasia and eventually morphed into ROLI, with colleagues working across the globe. Indeed, a major rationale for merging the ABA's regional rule of law entities into ROLI was that it would facilitate the sharing of expertise, resources and learning among the regional programs. I remember well the first global annual meeting in 2005, gathering staff of what were still separate regional ABA rule of law entities in Istanbul. It was incredibly exciting to see colleagues from across the globe connecting the dots and sharing effective strategies for achieving programme goals. Colleagues working to support clinical legal education in China or the transition to accusatorial criminal justice systems in Latin America had much to learn from a decade of similar efforts in Eastern Europe and the former Soviet Union.

Just as CEELI and ROLI annual meetings were effective learning

---

8   Interview with Lisa Dickieson, 5 August 2020.

opportunities for ABA staff and volunteers, some of the most valuable ABA rule of law programs over the years have fostered this kind of learning among programme partners in countries in which we worked. In the early days, CEELI-supported clinical legal education faculties throughout the former Soviet Union came together to support and learn from one another. Another effort convened women's rights activists across Eurasia to share strategies for combating domestic violence and human trafficking. Later, the ROLI-sponsored Arab Women's Legal Network provided a forum for women in the Middle East region to support and learn from one another, and the Balkans Regional Rule of Law Network provided a similar space for the criminal defence bar in that region. In the same vein, the CEELI Institute has cultivated judicial networks as critical learning communities in Central and Eastern Europe. The conference of chief justices of Central and Eastern Europe, first convened by the Institute, is now a self-sustaining forum for learning and mutual support among judicial leaders, a number of whom have in recent years withstood significant threats to their independence. The Institute also supports a parallel network of up-and-coming young judges, which gathers regularly to share best practices on issues of judicial independence, integrity, accountability and court management. The group recently published the *Manual on Independence, Impartiality and Integrity of Justice: A Thematic Compilation of International Standards, Policies, and Best Practices*, collecting key guidance from 160 international standards.

Michael Maya, who as a liaison in Uzbekistan and later CEELI and ROLI deputy director was involved in many such convenings, argues that such regional networks and convenings were among the most valuable programmatic approaches pursued by the ABA initiatives. "It was so powerful when we could bring together legal professionals from different countries grappling with the same challenges, and enable them to learn from each other," he recalls. "The sharing of best practices caught on like wildfire, with many attendees maintaining contact after our gatherings, and replicating and supporting each other's efforts in different countries."[9] Colleagues from the former Soviet Union had the added advantage of all speaking the same language and being able to trade materials in Russian. Lisa Dickieson also recalls this singular ABA contribution: "The ABA contributed incredibly to building up relationships and trust, which supported exchanges of information. It was hugely important."[10] To a great extent, this spirit has also animated the World Justice Forum, convened by the WJP, first as a project of the ABA in Vienna in 2008, and since then biennially bringing together rule of law innovators from around the world for a week of collective learning and problem-solving.

---

9   Interview with Michael Maya, executive director, North America, International Bar Association, 23 July 2020.
10   Interview with Lisa Dickieson, 5 August 2020.

Another early hub of learning at CEELI was its Research Office, established at the Washington DC headquarters in the mid-1990s to provide comparative and international legal research support to liaisons, helping them connect partners to relevant information, standards and models. From the outset, a core principle of the ABA's rule of law work was that it would not seek to export an American model; liaisons would draw on comparative and international best practices in providing technical assistance. Nonetheless, most of the liaisons were US-trained lawyers, so the system they knew best was an American model. The research office was established to fill this knowledge gap.

The first director of the research office was Angela Conway, who later went on to launch and direct ABA ROLI's programmes in the Middle East and North Africa. Angela had started with CEELI in 1993, when, as an associate in a law firm, she pitched in as a *pro bono* volunteer in the Washington DC, CEELI office. She became enthralled with an early *pro bono* assignment to compile comparative models and standards as a resource for those drafting the Russian constitution. So, when CEELI's first executive director, Mark Ellis, invited Angela to direct a new research office full-time, she jumped at the opportunity, and today she is nearing her own 30th anniversary of rule of law development work.[11] The research office – comprising just one other staff attorney in addition to Angela and as many as six interns at a time – compiled collections of model laws and best practice guides on a wide range of topics. In this way, the research office began to address Carothers' definitional question – what is the essence of the rule of law? – by assembling a menu of options comprising best practices in obtaining recognised normative elements of the rule of law, such as independent and accountable bar associations and a fair and effective criminal process.

The late 1990s also saw the development of another valuable learning initiative in the form of practice groups among CEELI liaisons and staff working on common problems. The groups were organised by areas of CEELI programme focus – initially judicial reform, legal profession reform, and legal education reform, with criminal law reform, anti-corruption and gender issues following later – often referred to as focal or thematic cones. (Group leaders were, in a nod to Saturday Night Live humour, dubbed 'coneheads'.) Networked across the organisation, these groups facilitated the sharing of lessons learned, information resources, curricula, and the names of experienced and effective trainers among colleagues working in different CEELI countries and eventually in all of ROLI's regional programmes. Long before Dropbox and Google, by the early 2000s, the ABA had built a custom web-based document-sharing platform to help staff exchange resources and learning across its programmes. Through listservs and periodic calls, the coneheads provided important substantive

11   Interview with Angela Conway, director, ABA ROLI MENA Division, 29 July 2020.

connective tissue facilitating learning between mid-year and annual meetings. Michael Maya, who led the gender issues group, remembers a tight-knit cohort, regularly sharing articles, resources and names of experts, and gathering at annual meetings, where both US and host country staff discussed best practices, setbacks and trends in the region, such as early legislative efforts to combat domestic violence and human trafficking.

While ABA CEELI was in these various ways a learning organisation from its earliest days, throughout its first decade, the emphasis was principally on responding to in-country partners' requests for assistance, not building and perfecting the rule of law field of development practice. Indeed, some within the organisation even opposed developing the focal cones, arguing that to do so would be too prescriptive and contrary to ABA CEELI's principle of providing technical assistance only in response to in-country partners' requests. Nonetheless, by the end of the 1990s, it became clear that promoting and sustaining the rule of law would be a long-term project, and as questions mounted about the impact of a decade of ABA CEELI assistance, USAID engaged Richard Blue of Management Systems International to conduct an external evaluation of ABA CEELI's work. Blue's assessment was positive, concluding that CEELI had supported lasting change throughout the region. The report specifically credited CEELI with contributing to stronger and more independent judiciaries, independent professional legal associations and "highly praised" and sustainable continuing legal education programmes.[12] It singled out for praise efforts to strategically advance the rule of law through related policy objectives, such as environmental protection and women's rights, and it hailed in particular regional programming that networked likeminded reformers across national boundaries. The evaluation was validating of ABA CEELI's approach, but it also marked a turning point, as the need to justify ongoing donor investments drove increased emphasis on quantifying and documenting programme impact and brought more rigorous development practices to the ABA and the rule of law field more generally.

3.2   Assessment methodologies

In the early 2000s, ABA CEELI's learning efforts took a quantum leap with the development of the first of its tools for systematic assessment, the Judicial Reform Index (JRI). The initiative to develop a standard assessment methodology emerged in response to both internal learning and external pressures. "We realised that if we were going to promote an independent judiciary, we had to have an idea of what that is," recalls Lisa Dickieson, of early

---

12   Richard Blue, Silvy Chernev, Robyn Goodkind and Siegfried Wiessner, "Evaluation of the Rule of Law Program in Central and Eastern Europe and the Newly Independent States: The American Bar Association/Central and East European Law Initiative (ABA/CEELI) – Final Report", 28 January 1999, pii.

efforts to ground CEELI's judicial reform efforts in international standards. At the same time, USAID was increasingly insisting on defined work plans that were based on assessments and evaluated against measurable indicators. USAID funded development of the JRI tool as part of a cooperative agreement with the RIGHTS consortium led by Freedom House, the National Democratic Institute, and the ABA, which included as a programme goal development of technical leadership tools for the rule of law field.

The work on the JRI tool had begun in the late 1990s, with an initiative led by Lisa Dickieson, Mark Dietrich and a panel of expert advisers to draft a Judicial Independence Index (JII). Mark and Lisa piloted the methodology with an assessment in Macedonia in late 1999, after which Scott Carlson picked up the mantle to develop the tool.

Then CEELI director for Central and Eastern Europe, Scott had spent 1994–95 as a CEELI liaison in Albania, and there he witnessed first-hand the ebbs and flows of judicial reform. During his liaison year, Scott had worked closely with the chief justice of the Albanian Supreme Court to support initiatives reinforcing the court's independence, such as establishing a judges' association and publishing court decisions. At first, he was gratified by the pace of progress, but the change proved too fast for some, and by the end of his liaison year, a backlash stalled the reforms and sent the chief justice into asylum in the United States. Although the seeds sown by Scott and the chief justice that year would eventually take root and be reflected in constitutional reform adopted four years later, it was becoming clear in Albania, as elsewhere in the region, that rule of law progress would not be linear. "I began to think of rule of law as a pendulum, swinging back and forth but progressing over time," Scott recalls.[13]

After several more years overseas, Scott had returned to CEELI headquarters, "obsessed with what it is that motivates judicial reform". He trained that obsession on the development of the tool, but with the scars of his efforts in Albania still fresh, Scott urged a more expansive and perhaps less politically charged take on the topic than that contemplated in the draft Judicial Independence Index. He thought the tool should look not just at factors of independence but also at other dimensions affecting judicial performance, such as judicial education, resources, representativeness, accountability and transparency. The resultant JRI methodology focused on 30 factors in total, tied to international standards and best practices codified by the United Nations, Council of Europe, and International Bar Association.

This methodology also benefited from lessons learned during the 1999 JII pilot assessment in Macedonia. The original JII methodology had focused on interviewing judges, but in the course of their pilot assessment, Lisa Dickieson and Mark Dietrich quickly determined that other data sources would be

---

13   Interview with Scott Carlson, Director of Programs, ABA ROLI, 29 June 2020.

required to obtain an accurate assessment of the state of the judiciary. Drawing on their experience, the JRI methodology was developed further to entail a qualitative *de jure* and *de facto* evaluation of a country's judiciary against international standards through in-depth interviews with at least 35 key informants in the judiciary, legal profession and academy, as well as documentary analysis of the country's legal framework governing the judiciary. CEELI decided to forego scoring or ranking of countries to avoid alienating or distracting key constituents needed to drive a judicial reform agenda, opting instead for directional assessments ('positive', 'negative' or 'neutral') and qualitative descriptions of conditions under each factor. This decision was in tension with preferences voiced by USAID representatives, who were eager for quantifiable measures, but the ABA CEELI board thought it inappropriate for the ABA to score and rank foreign judiciaries.

The JRI quickly became a mainstay of CEELI judicial programming in Europe and Eurasia, with assessments completed in 20 countries since 2001 and in several countries multiple times. The original idea was to conduct the JRI regularly in each country to track progress over time. "We were trying to tackle the problem of knowledge systematically with qualitative data," Scott explains. Unfortunately, the assessments were viewed by some donors as too costly, and donor interest proved inconstant. While the JRI was not conducted sufficiently consistently to support analysis of rule of law progress over time, it did facilitate effective diagnosis of rule of law gaps and reform needs, and it developed into an important early tool of programme design.

Building on this successful assessment model, the ABA (CEELI and eventually ROLI) developed similar methodologies to systematically assess other justice sector institutions through its Prosecutorial Reform Index, Legal Education Reform Index, and Legal Profession Reform Index. Next came a series of tools for evaluation of laws and practices against substantive standards such as women's rights, anti-trafficking norms and best practices, international human rights and access to justice. Each was developed based on international standards and comparative best practices and vetted with a panel of external experts in the respective topics.

Over the next two decades, ABA ROLI developed 11 rule of law assessment tools that became a critical reference point for ROLI, US government donor agencies, and other implementing organisations – clarifying the essence of the rule of law, identifying standards against which laws, institutions and practice could be measured, and serving as a diagnostic to focus reform efforts and assistance.

As experience drove home the importance of local ownership to effective, sustainable reform, the tools were used to empower local actors to develop their own assessments. In particular, the Convention on the Elimination of Discrimination Against Women (CEDAW) Assessment Tool (later renamed the 'Status of Women Assessment Tool') proved a useful methodology in the hands

ABA assessment tools and methodologies
- Judicial Reform Index
- Legal Education Reform Index
- Legal Profession Reform Index
- Prosecutorial Reform Index
- Detention Procedure Assessment Tool
- International Covenant on Civil and Political Rights Legal Implementation Index
- Status of Women Assessment Tool
- Human Trafficking Assessment Tool
- Global Supply Chain Trafficking Risk Assessment Methodology
- HIV/AIDS Legal Assessment Tool
- Access to Justice Assessment Tool

of local women's rights activists, guiding their preparation of shadow reports and advocacy before the UN CEDAW Committee about their government's respect for women's rights. CEELI increasingly focused efforts on training in-country partners to carry out the assessments rather than sending its own international expert assessors. One of the latest tools to be developed, the Access to Justice Assessment Tool, was designed from the beginning as an assessment methodology to be implemented by national and local stakeholders interested in evaluating their own justice system and designing reform initiatives to address justice gaps.

Another ABA contribution in the field of rule of law assessments came in the form of the International Legal Assistance Consortium (ILAC). The brainchild of then-CEELI executive director Mark Ellis and CEELI's first liaison Bill Meyer, among others, ILAC was conceived in the late 1990s at a series of meetings convened with support from the Stanley Foundation to address the particularly vexing problem of knowledge in post-conflict settings. From the Balkans to the Great Lakes Region of Africa, the 1990s had witnessed peace-building operations plagued by haphazard and poorly coordinated efforts to rebuild justice systems. Through a nimble and collaborative model, drawing on expertise from a variety of legal assistance organisations, ILAC aimed to deploy assessment teams quickly, evaluate conditions and generate recommendations for coordinated post-conflict reconstruction of the justice sector. Eventually organised as a Swedish non-governmental organisation, today ILAC has more than 80 institutional and individual members, including ABA ROLI, the CEELI Institute and the WJP, which together undertake assessments and work to build knowledge about peace-building in some of the world's most challenging rule of law contexts.

3.3 Defining and measuring the rule of law

A watershed in the ABA's contributions to solving the problem of knowledge came in 2007, with the launch of the WJP, first as a presidential initiative of then-ABA president Bill Neukom, and later as an independent non-governmental organisation. The WJP seized the challenge of defining the rule of law, developing a universally resonant definition vetted with scholars from throughout the world.[14]

Figure 1. Four universal principles of the rule of law

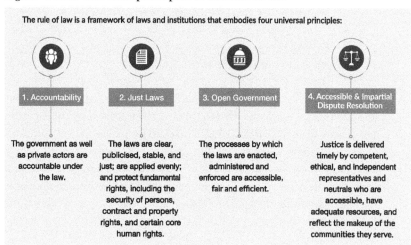

Source: From the WJP Rule of Law Index® 2019, p9. Copyright 2019 by The World Justice Project. Reprinted with permission.

In addition, the WJP developed a methodology for systematically measuring the rule of law across jurisdictions. That methodology – the WJP Rule of Law Index – brought quantitative tools to bear on the issues previously addressed with the JRI and other ABA assessment tools. The WJP Index draws on surveys of households and expert practitioners in each country to assign scores for eight factors and 44 sub-factors of the rule of law. First piloted in a handful of countries, the methodology was refined over time, and the country coverage was expanded to reach 139 countries and territories by 2021. Over the past

---

14   The WJP definition dovetails with that articulated by Secretary General Kofi Annan in a 2004 report, and subsequently embraced by the General Assembly and other UN bodies. See, Report of the Secretary General, "The Rule of Law and Transitional Justice in Conflict and Post-Conflict Societies", S/2004/616 (2004), www.un.org/ruleoflaw/files/2004%20report.pdf. ("[The rule of law] refers to a principle of governance in which all persons, institutions and entities, public and private, including the State itself, are accountable to laws that are publicly promulgated, equally enforced and independently adjudicated, and which are consistent with international human rights norms and standards. It requires, as well, measures to ensure adherence to the principles of supremacy of law, equality before the law, accountability to the law, fairness in the application of the law, separation of powers, participation in decision-making, legal certainty, avoidance of arbitrariness and procedural and legal transparency.")

Figure 2. Conceptual framework of the WJP Rule of Law Index

The conceptual framework of the WJP Rule of Law Index comprises eight factors further disaggregated into 44 sub-factors. These factors and sub-factors are presented below and described in detail in the section that follows.

Constraints on Government Powers
- 1.1 Government powers are effectively limited by the legislature
- 1.2 Government powers are effectively limited by the judiciary
- 1.3 Government powers are effectively limited by independent auditing and review
- 1.4 Government officials are sanctioned for misconduct
- 1.5 Government powers are subject to non-governmental checks
- 1.6 Transition of power is subject to the law

Absence of Corruption
- 2.1 Government officials in the executive branch do not use public office for private gain
- 2.2 Government officials in the judicial branch do not use public office for private gain
- 2.3 Government officials in the police and the military do not use public office for private gain
- 2.4 Government officials in the legislative branch do not use public office for private gain

Open Government
- 3.1 Publicised laws and government data
- 3.2 Right to information
- 3.3 Civic participation
- 3.4 Complaint mechanisms

Fundamental Rights
- 4.1 Equal treatment and absence of discrimination
- 4.2 The right to life and security of the person is effectively guaranteed
- 4.3 Due process of the law and rights of the accused
- 4.4 Freedom of opinion and expression is effectively guaranteed
- 4.5 Freedom of belief and religion is effectively guaranteed
- 4.6 Freedom from arbitrary interference with privacy is effectively guaranteed
- 4.7 Freedom of assembly and association is effectively guaranteed
- 4.8 Fundamental labour rights are effectively guaranteed

Order & Security
- 5.1 Crime is effectively controlled
- 5.2 Civil conflict is effectively limited
- 5.3 People do not resort to violence to redress personal grievances

Regulatory Enforcement
- 6.1 Government regulations are effectively enforced
- 6.2 Government regulations are applied and enforced without improper influence
- 6.3 Administrative proceedings are conducted without unreasonable delay
- 6.4 Due process is respected in administrative proceedings
- 6.5 The government does not expropriate without lawful process and adequate compensation

Civil Justice
- 7.1 People can access and afford civil justice
- 7.2 Civil justice is free of discrimination
- 7.3 Civil justice is free of corruption
- 7.4 Civil justice is free of improper government influence
- 7.5 Civil justice is not subject to unreasonable delay
- 7.6 Civil justice is effectively enforced
- 7.7 Alternative dispute resolution mechanisms are accessible, impartial, and effective

Criminal Justice
- 8.1 Criminal investigation system is effective
- 8.2 Criminal adjudication system is timely and effective
- 8.3 Correctional system is effective in reducing criminal behaviour
- 8.4 Criminal justice system is impartial
- 8.5 Criminal justice system is free of corruption
- 8.6 Criminal justice system is free of improper government influence
- 8.7 Due process of the law and rights of the accused

Source: From the WJP Rule of Law Index® 2019, p10. Copyright 2019 by The World Justice Project. Reprinted with permission.

decade, the WJP Rule of Law Index has become the leading source of original data on the rule of law, widely relied upon by governments and intergovernmental organisations, scholars, the media and private sector to evaluate governance.

Drawing on nearly two decades of modern rule of law development efforts and a peer review process that tapped expertise across the globe, the Index took a position on a number of conceptual questions about the definition and essential elements of the rule of law. On the question posed by Carothers and others – whether the rule of law simply comprises certain institutional arrangements or also requires certain normative outcomes – the Index looks at both, conceptualising the rule of law "in terms of specific outcomes that are informative of the extent to which rule of law principles are observed in practice and that policy makers might want to influence".[15] The eight outcomes (or factors) that the Index measures reflect both constraints on government powers (eg, anti-corruption and fundamental rights norms) and obligations governments owe their citizens (eg, order and security and effective regulatory, civil and criminal justice). In an important innovation, the Index defines and measures the rule of law comprehensively, looking at a variety of factors equally rather than prioritising a single dimension as other rule of law indicators do. As such, it captures effectively the multi-faceted nature of the rule of law and supports the targeting of reform efforts to areas of greatest need, based on what in-country survey respondents identify as the main gaps in their own experience with the rule of law. Finally, by focusing on outcomes and employing surveys to construct Index scores and rankings, the Index elevates people's experience of governance as an important measure of the rule of law. This approach reflects learning in the field that the rule of law entails both an institutional supply side (eg, laws, judiciaries, bar associations, etc) and also a societal demand side (eg, citizen understanding of their rights, their experience of the law and government institutions, and their ability to access justice).

In addition to making these contributions to conceptualisation of the rule of law, the WJP has also strengthened the evidence base for the asserted relationship between rule of law and economic, social and political development. In collaboration with the American Bar Foundation, the WJP supported the 2009 publication of *Global Perspectives on the Rule of Law*, a collection of essays edited by James Heckman, Robert Nelson and Lee Cabatingan. Featuring contributions from leading scholars from a range of disciplines, the volume grappled with the complexity of the rule of law and its relationship to economic and democratic development, illustrated through both contemporary and historical case studies. There is a clear correlation between the rule of law as measured by the Index and a number of standard measures of development. More work remains to be done to understand these correlations, the rule of law factors at work and causal relationships reflected in them, but the Index provides an invaluable foundation for this future learning.

---

15   Juan C Botero and Alejandro Ponce, "Measuring the Rule of Law", World Justice Project Working Paper Series 001, p8 (November 2010), https://papers.ssrn.com/sol3/papers.cfm?abstract_id=1966257.

3.4　Monitoring and evaluation

An important area of more recent evolution in ABA ROLI's learning agenda has been the development of its capacity to monitor and evaluate programme impacts. Although the ABA reported programme results from its earliest days, these reports did not take advantage of modern social science evaluation methodologies. In the early 2000s, it was not just Tom Carothers and rule of law development practitioners who were grappling with the problem of knowledge; the development field as a whole was becoming increasingly preoccupied with monitoring and evaluation (M&E) as a critical tool to ensure and document programme effectiveness.[16] Over the past two decades, this emphasis has only grown – reflected in, for example, the US Foreign Aid and Transparency and Accountability Act of 2016 and its implementing regulations, which significantly expand evaluation requirements on US-funded development efforts.

In 2012, an external strategic assessment of ROLI's work flagged M&E as an area of needed investment, and in 2013, Salome Tsereteli-Stephens was hired as the first ABA ROLI M&E manager. Salome had benefited from CEELI's work in her native post-Soviet Georgia, where the law school library, well-stocked with CEELI-provided materials, enriched her legal education. "It doesn't seem like much, but having been on the other side, as a law student during the CEELI years, I can tell you, having a modern library makes a difference," she recalls.[17] Salome is committed to bringing modern M&E tools to bear on the rule of law field, to contribute a rigorous evidence base to evaluation of the interventions she has seen make a difference in her country.

A critical challenge for M&E and related efforts to identify what works in the rule of law development field is the length of time it takes for rule of law change to occur. Most programme interventions last 18 months to three years, and funders seek M&E analyses that track the interventions, looking for impact upon programme completion, not five or 10 or even 20 years later when it may emerge. As Salome summarises the challenge: "If we are only looking at three-year indicators, we are going to miss impact."

Today, as director of ROLI's office of monitoring, evaluation, and learning, Salome is leading efforts to fill the learning gap about programme effectiveness. Taking advantage of ROLI's long-standing presence and engagement on core rule of law challenges in a number of countries, Salome has been able to use cutting-edge methodologies to evaluate these programmes over time. She has documented, for example, how ROLI's nearly two decades of support for the legal profession in Armenia has strengthened Armenian citizens' access to

---

16   See eg, United Nations Development Program, Evaluation Office, "Handbook on Monitoring and Evaluating for Results", 2002, http://web.undp.org/evaluation/documents/handbook/me-handbook.pdf.
17   Interview with Salome Tsereteli-Stephens, director, Monitoring, Evaluation, and Learning, ABA Rule of Law Initiative, 26 June 2020.

redress before the European Court of Human Rights.[18] Salome is encouraged that donors have increased support for long-term *ex post* evaluation of rule of law interventions and sees valuable learning emerging from those efforts. "Nobody thinks cookie-cutter approaches will work," she notes, "but we can identify certain elements that help. For example, if you are going to support constitutional reform, it's important to emphasize public participation. We have learned this over the years, academics have captured it." Acknowledging the complexity of rule of law development, Salome nonetheless believes that rigorous M&E can lead to better outcomes, and she is determined to mine the ABA's three decades of experience across the globe for insights into what works. "We have to try," she urges.

4. Challenges and opportunities for rule of law learning

As outlined above, the ABA's rule of law initiatives and their progeny have contributed significantly to the development of a greater understanding of the rule of law, its dimensions and role in society, and effective strategies for cultivating it. This is not to say that the problem of knowledge has been solved, however. Much work remains to be done to understand this dimension of good governance better and in particular to identify and document strategies that work in developing it. This learning agenda has over the years faced (and continues to face) some significant impediments, some of them practical, others conceptual. Future progress requires coming to terms with these challenges.

Notwithstanding considerable commitment to learning at the ABA and among others working in the rule of law field, solving the problem of knowledge has over the years presented considerable practical difficulties. First among these is the dearth of funding for such learning. With some notable exceptions, such as USAID's 1999 evaluation of ABA CEELI's programmes and its support for the development of the ABA's JRI and other assessment methodologies, historically donors have not devoted adequate resources to the kinds of research required to draw meaningful findings about what works to build the rule of law. Most projects implemented by ABA ROLI over the past 30 years did not include funding for rigorous and comprehensive baseline assessments so important for effective programme design and evaluation. ABA ROLI colleagues interviewed for this chapter could identify no more than a handful of projects in which a donor funded such a study at the outset of a programme. When they did, the results were significant. For example, following an in-depth six-month comprehensive diagnostic study of corruption in Morocco carried out in 2012–13, ABA ROLI was able to implement a much more nuanced, targeted and effective programme that focused on particular localities

---

18   Gergana Danailova-Trainor, James Filpi, Norman Greene and Salome Tsereteli-Stephens, "Beyond Good Intentions: New Legislation on Foreign Aid Effectiveness" 53 Int'l L 1, 6 (2020).

and employed public education and criminal justice strategies designed in collaboration with local authorities identified through the study as committed partners.[19] Such research at the inception phase of development projects may be more common in large-scale institution reform efforts typically implemented by for-profit contractors, but they are a rare luxury in smaller grant-funded technical assistance, educational and capacity-building efforts implemented by non-profit organisations such as the ABA.

When donors do fund assessments and evaluations, the focus is often too narrow, on a particular three-year project funded by a single donor agency, rather than the totality of interventions over the decade or two that it may take for the consequences – positive and negative – to play out. A 2002 USAID study of its rule of law assistance in 34 countries recognised the importance of taking the long view and captured some valuable lessons learned, yet most evaluations that USAID and other donors supported continued to look for short-term project-based results.[20]

There are welcome signs that donors increasingly recognise the importance of learning over the longer term. A recently published USAID Rule of Law Practitioner's Guide highlights effective approaches identified over several decades of programming.[21] USAID is also currently developing an updated Rule of Law Achievements Guide, reviewing its programmes in each region over the past 10–15 years to identify lessons learned and inform new rule of law policy and practice.[22] Another recent positive step was an *ex post* study commissioned by the US State Department's Office of Democracy, Human Rights, and Labor (DRL) to evaluate its programmes implemented under 62 grants over five years.[23] This unusual exercise made valuable findings about the strengths and weaknesses of different programme approaches. While steps in the right direction, these studies look at interventions by just the sponsoring agency, one among many US agencies funding rule of law development. Even more valuable would be long-term *ex post* studies that evaluate all US rule of law programming, or indeed that of all international development agencies, in a given country over time.

The focus of these US government agencies on evaluating just their own work highlights another practical challenge to rule of law learning: the siloed and competitive nature of the field that stymies the sharing of lessons learned

---

19   Interview with Angela Conway, director, MENA Division, ABA Rule of Law Initiative, 29 July 2020; interview with Mary Greer, senior criminal law adviser, ABA Rule of Law Initiative, 22 July 2020.

20   USAID, "Achievements in Building and Maintaining the Rule of Law: MSI's Studies in LAC, E&E, AFR, and ANE", November 2002, https://gsdrc.org/document-library/achievements-in-building-and-maintaining-the-rule-of-law-msis-studies-in-lac-ee-afr-and-ane/ ("The objective of the study underlying this Occasional Paper was to take a step back, and look at the higher level, cumulative impacts that can only be measured over a longer time horizon, in as unbiased a manner as possible.")

21   USAID, "Rule of Law Practitioner's Guide", p11 (July 2020), www.usaid.gov/sites/default/files/documents/USAID-Rule-of-Law-Practitioners-Guide-July-2020.pdf.

22   Interview with Andrew Solomon, senior rule of law adviser, USAID, 26 June 2020.

23   US Department of State, Office of Democracy, Human Rights, and Labor, "Ex Post Evaluation of DRL Rule of Law (ROL) Programs: Final Report", 18 November 2019.

across donors and among implementing agencies. Even among US agencies that support rule of law development, coordination and information-sharing is notoriously weak.[24] I have personally had the experience of having senior USAID mission personnel ask me if ABA ROLI might be in a position to undertake programming that we were already implementing in the country with funding from the US State Department Bureau of International Narcotics and Law Enforcement Affairs. Lamentably, these USAID mission colleagues had no idea what programming their State Department colleagues housed across town at the embassy were supporting, let alone what they were learning from it. USAID's annual conference for its democracy, rights and governance (DRG) officers and implementing partners is rarely attended by colleagues from other US government agencies working on these issues. Coordination of programming and learning among different bilateral, multilateral and foundation donors is even weaker than it is among US government agencies.

The problem is not just with the donors. Implementing organisations competing for funding are proprietary about their learning and also loath to share. ABA ROLI has not been immune to this impulse, though it has tried to set a different tone for the rule of law community, convening an annual conference on contemporary rule of law issues and inviting speakers from across the community to share learning and highlight best practices emerging in the field.

Again, a number of recent developments promise better coordination and improved learning across the field. Multiple reports by the Government Accounting Office have highlighted the problem and inspired donor agency commitments to do better. The enactment of the US Foreign Aid and Transparency and Accountability Act of 2016 is driving better practices, and Congressional oversight is keeping the pressure on donors and implementers alike. USAID is investing in developing a 'rule of law evidence gap map' to highlight publicly available learning across agencies and partners. It has developed a robust DRG learning agenda and during the pandemic it has rekindled a previously moribund DRG implementing partner community of practice for bi-weekly Zoom calls to pursue the agenda.

Perhaps most promising for rule of law learning is the work that ABA ROLI and the Rule of Law Collaborative at the University of South Carolina are leading through the State Department-funded Justice Sector Training, Research, and Coordination Plus Program (JUSTRAC+). The programme represents a significant investment of resources with the goal of enhancing coordination, learning and knowledge sharing among US government agencies and implementing partners and with foreign government and international

---

24   Government Accounting Office, "Rule of Law Assistance: Agency Efforts Are Guided by Various Strategies, and Overseas Missions Should Ensure that Programming is Fully Coordinated", June 2020, www.gao.gov/assets/gao-20-393.pdf.

organisations. This programme has already produced two practice notes on important aspects of strengthening the rule of law – court efficiency and the nexus of anti-corruption and transnational crime.

In a similar vein, the WJP has launched its Rule of Law Solutions initiative to identify, document and profile effective approaches to stimulating rule of law progress. A new post-doctoral fellow – funded with support from the American Council of Learned Societies, the Mellon Foundation, and the Dutch-funded Knowledge Platform on Security and the Rule of Law – is working to document promising solutions in challenging contexts, such as access to justice in the Sahel and corruption in southeast Asia. These learnings will be compiled in a series of blogs and podcasts and a guidebook of good practices that will be shared widely with the international rule of law community. The WJP's World Justice Challenge competition provides another vehicle for identifying and sharing innovative projects and best practices on specific rule of law challenges from across the globe. The 2021 competition features a knowledge platform for continuous education around such issues as access to justice and accountable governance in the context of emergencies such as the COVID-19 pandemic.

Beyond the practical issues, there is a conceptual challenge to rule of law learning. To some extent, the problem of knowledge is unsolvable. The complexity and context-specific nature of the way the rule of law works means that it defies ultimate knowing. We cannot expect to be able to identify a defined blueprint for effective, accountable and just governance that will produce predictable economic, political and social outcomes. The best that we can do – as the WJP has done with its definition and Index – is to identify principles and outcomes at a sufficient level of abstraction or generality that they can be observed in a consistent and comparable way across jurisdictions. How those outcomes are realised in a particular context will vary and depend on many factors, but through research and rigorous programme evaluation, we can identify those factors and develop a menu of options and proven effective strategies for pursuing them. These in turn can be shared with colleagues to inform their work to build and sustain the rule of law. This is, it is important to note, work that is never done.

In this way, the solution to the problem of knowledge is not knowledge *per se* but a process – an informed process, strengthened by a learning community. It is a process that inspires and supports collective discovery, learning and problem-solving, as we have seen develop so effectively in the CEELI- and ROLI-supported network meetings and World Justice Forum convenings over the years. It is a process that the ABA has in many important ways sustained in the United States for over 140 years. This experience has meant that the ABA has been well-placed to stimulate learning processes around the world these past 30 years. Along the way, it has helped to build a global rule of law movement of committed stakeholders learning together.

Chapter 7. Official corruption: a threat to the rule of law

Kathryn Cameron Atkinson
Homer E Moyer, Jr
Miller & Chevalier

In the 1990s, following the fall of the Berlin Wall and the dissolution of the Soviet Union, the phrase, 'rule of law', became widely popularised. It was used by both reformers in the approximately two dozen countries transitioning from Soviet domination to independence and by the many advisers and supporters who offered technical legal assistance. These newly independent countries knew firsthand the absence of the rule of law in countries dominated by the Soviet Union, and there was broad public support for establishing new, law-based societies. The 'absence of the rule of law' became a common reference in pronouncements of newly formed governments, in reports of governments offering assistance, and in accounts and commentary in the popular press.

As former Soviet Bloc satellite countries and former Soviet republics gained independence, they began to address the daunting question of how to design new governments and build the rule of law. For many countries, drafting a new constitution was a first step. Throughout the region, elections were held, new leadership assumed power, and new officials were appointed. In some countries, lustration laws limited the ability of former officials to hold public positions.

As reform processes continued, countries in transition identified numerous new laws that were needed. They included laws in areas that had not been the subject of previous legislation and areas not typically found in communist legal structures. Implementing new laws and structures also required new and modified institutions. Priorities included both political legislation and economic legislation.

With these urgent, competing needs, official corruption was rarely among the first priorities of transitional countries. Despite privilege and corruption on the part of public officials and ruling elites being by no means new, a focus on cross-border corruption by individuals and companies seeking business opportunities was not widespread. Although the United States attracted international attention when it enacted the US Foreign Corrupt Practices Act in 1977 (FCPA), few countries quickly followed suit.[1] Bribery of government officials was commonplace in many countries, and in previously communist

---

1   See section 2.1 below.

countries, the old guard of those who had been in power were sometimes able to retain a privileged status.

In the mid-1990s, however, cross-border corruption began to receive more attention. The president of the World Bank gave a widely reported, landmark speech on the "Cancer of Corruption";[2] the anti-corruption organisation, Transparency International (TI), was founded;[3] and the United States brought a highly publicised enforcement action against a US aerospace corporation that resulted in both a large fine and prison sentences for executives. The confluence of the collapse of Soviet domination, the rise of civil society in Asia and Latin America, and the reopening of West Africa to foreign oil majors all contributed to a sharp rise in awareness that international and multinational anti-corruption measures were needed to facilitate economic and social progress.[4]

As enforcement and publicity grew, so too did public awareness of cross-border official corruption and its diverse, harmful consequences. And in the latter half of the 1990s the first international anti-corruption conventions were concluded and entered into force.

Various organisations also began to examine the issue in greater depth and quantify its effects. In a 1998 speech, the International Monetary Fund's managing director, Michael Camdessus, suggested that global money laundering transactions could account for "2 to 5 percent of global GDP".[5] Analyses by the World Bank and other organisations identified multiple costs and consequences. The World Bank Institute dramatically highlighted the macro-economic costs, estimating a decade ago that a total of approximately $1 trillion is paid in bribes each year to corrupt public officials.[6] By accepting bribes, corrupt officials cause their governments to pay more for goods and services than they otherwise would. Doing so imposes additional costs on their citizens – the equivalent of an additional tax – and, by taking bribes, corrupt officials effectively steal from their own countries and citizens. Large corrupt payments made to secure major, highly profitable government projects or procurements were termed 'grand corruption', and the acts of officials who solicited, or accepted, such illicit payments were deemed to constitute the 'demand side' of official corruption.

With greater scrutiny also came the realisation that official corruption can often facilitate serious international crimes. Human traffickers, drug smugglers and black-market arms traders typically need to cross national borders and must

---

2   See section 2.4 below.

3   See section 2.3 below.

4   James G Tillen and Leah Moushey, "Global Overview", in James G Tillen and Leah Moushey, (eds), *Getting the Deal Through – Anti-Corruption Regulation* (2021), p3.

5   Frank Vogel, "The Supply Side of Global Bribery", *International Monetary Fund: Finance and Development*, No 2 (Vol 35, June 1998), www.imf.org/external/pubs/ft/fandd/1998/06/vogl.htm.

6   Juanita Olaya, "Looking Under Every Stone: Transparency International and the Fight Against Corruption" in *The Global Competitiveness Report 2006–2007* (2006), p123, The World Economic Forum, www3.weforum.org/docs/WEF_GlobalCompetitivenessReport_2006-07.pdf.

often bribe customs officials to do so. Such facilitation often requires only so-called 'petty' corruption, that is, the payment of relatively small bribes or 'grease payments' to customs officials, immigration officials or other non-senior government employees. When minor or seemingly benign 'facilitating payments' are made to enable major international crimes – not just to obtain local telephone service – the related crimes can obviously be far more serious than the bribes themselves. The failure of governments to deal with low-level bribery that enables major crimes has also been cited as a source of public distrust of governments' ability to deal with major transnational crime.[7]

The World Economic Forum approximated in 2018 that corruption cost was at least $2.6 trillion globally, which is the equivalent to 5% of the global GDP.[8] Additionally, survey-based indexes published by TI – in particular, the Corruption Perceptions Index – have highlighted countries that are unattractive markets for trade and investment because of their perceived levels of corruption. Moreover, research showed that a combination of a weak rule of law and perceived corruption is closely related to stunted economic development, obstacles to an escape from poverty, and human rights abuses.[9]

Increasingly, the toll that official corruption takes has led to public intolerance and demands for change. In every country involved in the so-called Arab Spring, for example, official corruption was cited in the calls for change as a governmental abuse.[10]

1.   Facets of cross-border official corruption

The advent of anti-corruption laws and conventions, publicity from a crescendo of enforcement, analyses of the economic consequences of official corruption, and greater public awareness have unsurprisingly led to a range of responses in seeking to combat official corruption and its consequences, including erosion of the rule of law. These responses have often distinguished between official corruption's so-called 'supply side' and 'demand side', imperfect terms that broadly differentiate between payers and recipients of bribes. In addition, 'intermediaries' – individuals or entities through which bribes are sometimes transferred – have necessarily become an important category in both prevention

---

7   Homer Moyer, José Carlos Ugaz Sánchez-Moreno, Paul A Volcker and Stephen S Zimmerman, "The challenge of corruption to the rule of law", in Robert A Stein and Richard Goldstone (eds), *The Rule of Law in the 21st Century* (2015), p46.

8   Meetings Coverage and Press Releases, Security Council, "Global Cost of Corruption at Least 5 Per Cent of World Gross Domestic Product, Secretary-General Tells Security Council, Citing World Economic Forum Data", UN Press Release SC/13493 (10 September 2018), www.un.org/press/en/2018/sc13493.doc.htm#:~:text=The%20World%20Economic%20Forum%20estimates,trillion%20in%20bribes%20every%20year.

9   Volcker, footnote 7 above at p47 (citing Stephanie F Dyson, "The Clash Between Corruption and Codes of Conduct: The Corporate Role in Forging a Human Rights Standard", 17 Conn J Int'l L 335, 343 (2002), citing Igor Abramov, Speech to the Second Annual Meeting of the OECD Anti-Corruption Network for Transitional Economies, "Anti-Corruption: Fostering a Rule of Law Environment Through Integrity in Public-Private Relations" (3 November 1999)).

10   See "Slovenian coalition loses majority as Civil Lists quit", BBC News Europe (23 January 2013), www.bbc.com/news/world-europe-21166763.

and compliance. The three categories are distinct, and combating each presents different issues.[11]

1.1 The 'supply side'

Those who pay, or supply, bribes to government officials are typically those seeking some benefit or advantage from a government employee or official who can, if corrupt, provide it. In transnational business, the payor is commonly a company wanting to advance its own commercial interests by obtaining improper benefits or advantages. This can occur in a wide variety of contexts, including seeking to enter or qualifying to do business in a particular market, obtaining permits, avoiding regulatory requirements, securing contracts, corrupting a formal procurement process, disqualifying competitors, influencing a regulator or judge, or corruptly gaining any other business advantage. Payments can be made directly by company officials or employees or indirectly through any other complicit third party or intermediary.

To date, enforcement has predominantly focused on supply side violations – individuals and entities that pay, offer to pay, or assist in paying bribes. While enforcement in the early years of the FCPA focused on corporations, enforcement against individuals has sharply increased.[12] In countries where there is no corporate criminal liability, the absence of criminal sanctions has sometimes increased enforcement attention on individuals.

The tension with supply side enforcement is that countries are called on to enforce their anti-corruption laws against companies created or operating in their own countries, companies that the government may otherwise be seeking to support or help prosper. This, however, is common to all government regulation of commercial activity and, in the case of laws prohibiting cross-border bribery, is undercut by the fact that the broad extraterritorial reach allows the prosecution of both domestic and foreign companies. US jurisdiction, for example, extends to any company that has securities traded on US exchanges, and of the largest fines imposed under the FCPA, a majority have been against non-US companies that were nonetheless subject to US jurisdiction.

It should also be noted that the prohibitions of both the FCPA and the historic Organisation for Economic Co-operation and Development (OECD) convention, among the earliest prohibitions against cross-border bribery, contain supply side prohibitions only – reaching only the payments side of official corruption. Laws prohibiting US officials from accepting bribes are

---

11   Homer Moyer, José Carlos Ugaz Sánchez-Moreno, Paul A Volcker and Stephen S Zimmerman, "The challenge of corruption to the rule of law", in Robert A Stein and Richard Goldstone, (eds), *The Rule of Law in the 21st Century* (2015), p54.

12   See eg, Press Release, US Dept of Justice, "Six Defendants Indicted in Alleged Conspiracy to Bribe Governmental Officials in India to Mine Titanium Minerals" (2 April 2014), www.justice.gov/opa/pr/six-defendants-indicted-alleged-conspiracy-bribe-government-officials-india-mine-titanium.

covered by separate US statutes. Subsequent international conventions, including the widely applicable United Nations Convention against Corruption (UNCAC), however, prohibit both supply side and demand side corruption.

One consequence of the early enforcement focus on the supply side been the emergence of an entire industry focused on corporate anti-corruption compliance programmes and initiatives, as discussed below.

1.2 The 'demand side'

The demand side of official corruption, referring to government officials or employees who seek or accept bribes, is also an imprecise term in that bribes can be offered and accepted without an official ever demanding or requesting a bribe. (The alternative characterisations of 'active' and 'passive' bribery, referring respectively to paying and receiving bribes, may be even less apt, as the demand side is not always passive; indeed, in some instances the official is the active, initiating party.)

An obvious incentive for unscrupulous public officials to accept bribes is self-enrichment and, in the case of substantial bribes, to accumulate wealth. Revelations have for years disclosed situations in which senior government officials or heads of state have engaged in egregious corruption. The countries in which that happens are typically ranked poorly in TI's Corruption Perception Index, lessening their attractiveness to businesses and investors.

Enforcement of anti-corruption laws against officials who receive bribes has proved to be more difficult than supply side enforcement, presumably in part because a country is enforcing its own laws against its own officials, who may be colleagues or political allies of those in power. If a country's head of state is himself or herself corrupt, the awkwardness and resistance may be even greater and, as numerous examples have shown, may result in no enforcement at all. One consequence is that there have been many highly publicised, well-documented enforcement actions against corporations that paid bribes to foreign officials, but which have prompted no enforcement actions against the offending officials.

In some highly corrupt countries, a sense of impunity can develop, causing corrupt officials to believe they face little risk of prosecution. If corruption runs rampant, the belief that they are immune from accountability can extend to prosecutors, law enforcement officials, judges and other officials. This obviously increases not only the risk that corruption is tolerated, but also that officials may even extort both foreign companies and their own country's companies and citizens for bribes.[13]

---

13   Homer Moyer, José Carlos Ugaz Sánchez-Moreno, Paul A Volcker and Stephen S Zimmerman, "The challenge of corruption to the rule of law", in Robert A Stein and Richard Goldstone, (eds), *The Rule of Law in the 21st Century* (2015), pp49–50, para 3.

There have also been, of course, numerous examples of backlash against corrupt senior officials and corrupt heads of state – both domestic prosecutions and actions forcing corrupt officials to resign from office. These efforts have sometimes been facilitated by financial disclosure laws and laws prohibiting unexplained 'unjust enrichment' by foreign officials. Another counterforce to impunity can be national efforts to recover funds illicitly paid to corrupt officials in order to restore them to their national treasury. These efforts, often difficult, routinely involve tracing illicitly obtained funds through anti-money laundering laws and other techniques.

1.3   Intermediaries

As official corruption came under increasing scrutiny, bribery schemes became more complex and creative. Bribe payers and recipients sought ways to transfer money, inducements or other economic benefits surreptitiously from one individual or entity to another through other methods than a direct payment. A common ruse to disguise or keep illicit payments secret was to make payments indirectly, through one or more third parties, or intermediaries. Using go-betweens was (and still is) seen as a way to disguise illicit payments, prevent their discovery, make tracing funds more difficult and to give participants the ability to deny when asked if they paid or received a bribe.

Theoretically, any individuals or entities can act as intermediaries – sales agents, local representatives, consultants, sub-contractors, employees of affiliates, privately held companies, partnerships, etc – even individuals who are themselves 'foreign officials'. Likewise, as a second layer of obfuscation, funds being paid to an official can be transferred through multiple banks or other financial institutions to make the money trail more difficult to follow, and funds can be paid not to the official personally but to a family member, a front company controlled by the official, or another related participant.

Although the FCPA and international conventions anticipated these ruses, few of the early enforcement cases involved intermediaries. In recent years, however, that pattern has reversed itself. Today, most enforcement actions involve indirect payments made through intermediate third parties.

2.   Four responses to official corruption

With the advent of international anti-corruption conventions, a wave of implementing national laws prohibiting payment of bribes to foreign government officials, and growing public awareness of the effects of official corruption, there developed a wide variety of efforts to combat cross-border bribery. Some addressed the supply side of bribe payers. Others, such as rigorous ethical standards, financial disclosure laws and greater transparency in public proceedings, focused on the demand side. Many addressed both.

Four prominent responses were among the first, beginning with the global legal structure created by international conventions and implementing national laws and regulations. Likewise, the proliferation and growth of corporate compliance programmes have had a transformative impact on the corporate private sector. Reactions from non-governmental organisations (NGOs) and civil society and initiatives of international financial institutions have paralleled and reinforced the criminalisation of cross-border official corruption. To be sure, there have been many more, including investigative reporting by the media, stronger reporting and disclosure requirements for public companies, tightened accounting rules, private litigation, asset recovery programmes, and strengthened anti-money laundering laws. The four discussed below added significant momentum to the early efforts to combat cross-border official corruption.

2.1   Enforcement of anti-corruption laws and conventions

In the 1970s, investigations into the Watergate political scandal and illicit corporate campaign financings activity led to the discovery that more than 400 US corporations had paid more than $300 million in questionable payments to various foreign government officials, often made from off-book accounts not reflected in companies' public accounting records. Those revelations were a catalyst that eventually led to today's network of laws outlawing bribes to foreign government officials. In 1977, the US Congress enacted the FCPA, which prohibits US companies and individuals from bribing foreign officials in exchange for business and requires companies that issue certain securities on US securities exchanges, regardless of domicile, to implement systems of internal controls and to maintain accurate and complete books and records to protect against misuse of corporate assets.[14] The FCPA provided for criminal and civil penalties and was amended in 1998 to conform to the OECD Anti-Bribery Convention.[15]

Between 1996 and 1999, various combinations of countries concluded agreements on four international anti-corruption conventions. These international conventions and the laws enacted to implement them have created a new international legal framework. There are now 187 states that are parties to the United Nations Convention against Corruption (adopted in 2005), and all parties are obliged to implement the convention through national legislation of their own. The resulting international legal structure has moved us from the days of a single unilateral law against bribing foreign government officials to an overlapping web of international agreements and implementing national legislation that establish principles and prohibitions against official corruption.

---

14   US Dept of Justice & Sec Exch Commn, FCPA: *A Resource Guide to the US Foreign Corrupt Practices Act* (July 2020, 2d edn), www.justice.gov/criminal-fraud/file/1292051/download.
15   *Ibid.*

The parallel rise in enforcement became evident first in the United States. As US officials began to take advantage of the broad jurisdiction and the inherently extraterritorial reach of the statute's prohibitions, enforcement of the FCPA quickly extended beyond US companies and US borders. With multilateral agreements, the number of national anti-corruption laws dramatically expanded. Although consistent enforcement is not universal, the web of anti-corruption laws is now truly global.

In 2020, the US Department of Justice (DOJ) and the US Securities and Exchange Commission (SEC) had resolved 22 FCPA enforcement actions by early December.[16] In those matters alone, the DOJ and SEC recovered more than $2.9 billion in penalties.[17] This averages to $224.1 million per enforcement action, more than twice the average for each year in the previous 10 years (which averaged to $79.2 million).[18]

In the quickly changing anti-corruption enforcement landscape, details of anti-corruption investigations and dispositions have become available in a variety of publicly available sources:

- public dispositions of anti-corruption enforcement actions;
- media reports of official and internal investigations;
- disclosures in corporate filings with securities regulatory agencies and stock exchanges;
- private litigation between companies and former employees;
- monitoring reviews and reports by international organisations;
- voluntary corporate disclosures to enforcement authorities;
- occasional confessions or exposés of implicated individuals;
- public statements by enforcement officials;
- statistics compiled by NGOs and international organisations; and
- findings of anti-corruption commissions, World Bank reports and academic studies.[19]

As legal regimes go, anti-corruption law is still maturing, well behind the precedents and practices of such older legal specialities as competition law, tax treaties, and trade and investment laws. Nonetheless, upward trends continue in overall anti-corruption enforcement, in prosecutions of individuals and corporations, and in the penalties imposed on both.

2.2 Corporate compliance programmes
Changes in enforcement have led to a proliferation of anti-corruption programmes inside corporations doing business internationally. These

---

16   Tillen and Moushey, footnote 4 above, at pp7–8.
17   *Ibid.*
18   *Ibid.*
19   *Ibid* at pp5–6.

programmes, in turn, have required company vendors and suppliers and their employees to agree to abide by certain standards of conduct and adhere to certain internal controls processes. Suppliers, sales agents, distributors and other third parties are sometimes required to comply with or implement the substantive equivalent of a company's anti-corruption and internal controls programme.

According to the OECD's *Good Practice Guidance on Internal Controls: Ethics and Compliance* (18 February 2010), certain factors are highly effective in preventing corrupt and unethical behaviour:

- a strong commitment from senior management;
- a clearly articulated anti-bribery policy;
- accountability and oversight;
- specific measures applicable to subsidiaries that are directed at the areas of highest risk;
- internal controls;
- documented training;
- appropriate disciplinary procedures; and
- modes for providing guidance and reporting violations.[20]

In addition, the International Organization for Standardization (ISO) published a paper on the "new standard on antibribery management positions", ISO 370001, in September 2016. Although the extent to which international agencies and authorities will defer to this new standard is not clear,[21] ISO certification may be useful for multinational corporations in establishing anti-corruption accreditation when undergoing due diligence projects.[22]

The impact on the private sector and, in particular, the impact on companies doing business internationally, has been far-reaching. Trends of the last 25 years suggest that corporate compliance programmes may continue to become more elaborate and innovative. Although many specific elements of corporate compliance programmes are not explicitly required by statute, large multinational companies in particular have found that effectively preventing their own participation in corruption requires significant investment in and monitoring of the controls and compliance measures they implement.[23]

Looking ahead, new dynamics shaping both public and corporate attitudes foreshadow continued emphasis on anti-corruption law. The international legal structure that has emerged is now being reinforced by a growing public and corporate awareness of the costs of official corruption. Not only do bribes to

---

20   *Ibid*, at p8.
21   *Ibid*.
22   *Ibid*.
23   For a more in-depth discussion of the evolution of corporate anti-corruption compliance programmes, see Kathryn Cameron Atkinson and Andrew T Wise, "Effective Anti-Corruption Compliance Programs", 67 Rocky Mtn Min L Inst 19-1 (2021).

officials constitute a hidden tax, but they also deprive a country's taxpayers of the efficiencies and savings that marketplace competition creates.

More aggressive enforcement will lead to prosecutions of more companies and individuals. The resulting fines, penalties, debarments and, in the case of individuals, imprisonment, will negate the hoped-for benefits or illicit payments and will propel the continuing development and refinement of corporate compliance programmes. Heightened international awareness also suggests that anti-corruption work will continue to be at the forefront of the private sector milieu in the coming years, perhaps expanding a growing belief that a clean business is a better, more sustainable business.

2.3 Transparency International and other anti-corruption NGOs

A milestone occurred in Germany in 1993 with the founding of TI, an NGO devoted to fighting corruption.[24] The creation of TI inspired the formation of other NGOs and the broader engagement of civil society in addressing the costs of official corruption.[25]

TI's Corruption Perceptions Index, which ranks countries in terms of their perceived levels of official corruption, and the Bribe Payers Index, which measures how likely corporations from the world's largest economies are to pay overseas bribes, provide visibility and raise public awareness of the prevalence of official corruption.[26] Citing widespread corruption as an important reason for underdevelopment and erosion of confidence in governance, TI's indices have highlighted the risks of trade and investment in countries seen to be highly corrupt.[27] Through its indices and other initiatives, TI became recognised as an effective voice in the global fight against corruption.[28] However, adverse publicity alone has not been sufficient, as TI's corruption indices continue to confirm.[29]

Since the early 1990s, non-governmental entities combating official corruption have proliferated. TI now has a network of local chapters in countries around the globe. The rule of law training programmes of the CEELI Institute in Prague prioritise judicial integrity, and its interactive anti-corruption training programmes for prosecutors and investigators are routinely over-subscribed.[30] The American Bar Association's Rule of Law Initiative (ROLI) includes a variety of anti-corruption initiatives. The World Justice Project, which annually publishes its closely-watched WJP Rule of Law Index, includes as its second rule of law factor "the absence of corruption".[31]

---

24   Tillen and Moushey, footnote 4 above, at p3.
25   Ugaz Sánchez-Moreno, footnote 13 above, at p50, para 6.
26   *Ibid.*
27   *Ibid.*
28   www.transparency.org/en/what-we-do.
29   Ugaz Sánchez-Moreno, footnote 13 above, at p50.
30   CEELI Institute, *Combatting Corruption*, https://ceeliinstitute.org/combatting-corruption/.
31   World Justice Project, *Rule of Law Index*, https://worldjusticeproject.org/rule-of-law-index/factors/2020/ Absence%2520of%2520Corruption.

Other organisations, such as TRACE, the Basel Institute on Governance, Global Witness, Alexei Navalny's Anti-Corruption Foundation in Russia, Integrity Initiatives International, and many others have joined the swelling number of anti-corruption and good government organisations seeking to combat official corruption. These organisations, which support enforcement of anti-corruption laws and conventions, complement the work of multilateral organisations supporting international conventions, such as the OECD's Anti-Bribery Group and Anti-Corruption Network and the United Nations' Global Programme against Corruption.

Such non-governmental organisations and civil society initiatives provide another bridge between the necessary enforcement of anti-corruption conventions and national laws, and public attitudes, which are themselves an important element of the effort to eliminate official corruption.

2.4   The World Bank

Three years after the formation of TI, the World Bank joined the battle to stem official corruption.[32] Since the 1996 speech by James Wolfensohn, then president of the World Bank, on dealing with the "cancer of corruption", the World Bank has initiated over 600 global programmes to combat corruption.[33] The World Bank implemented multiple reforms in July 2004 and August 2006 that established a two-step process for sanctions review.[34] The first tier was review by a chief suspension and debarment officer, and the second tier involved review from the World Bank's Group Sanctions Board if sanctions were challenged.[35] Although the goal of these reforms was to support unconventional solutions for eradicating poverty, distrust of government and public services serve as additional barriers to a strong rule of law.[36]

The World Bank broadened its position in bringing high integrity ethics to its projects through oversight and by anticipating the risks of corruption. One of these approaches includes the foundation of the INT, the World Bank's Integrity Vice-Presidency, which, although limited in jurisdiction, looks to "expand its impact from anecdotal prosecutions to more systematic deterrence and sustainable change".[37] In this regard, the World Bank Group signed an agreement with four other international banks in 2010 to encourage global anti-corruption initiative formations through recognition of their respective debarment verdicts.[38] The World Bank created the International Corruption Hunters Alliance (ICHA) in October 2010.[39] The ICHA's mission is to bring

---

32   Ugaz Sánchez-Moreno, footnote 13 above, at p50.
33   *Ibid.*
34   *Ibid.*
35   *Ibid.*
36   Zimmerman, footnote 11 above, at p51.
37   Zimmerman, footnote 11 above, at p53.
38   Zimmerman, footnote 11 above, at pp52–53.
39   Ugaz Sánchez-Moreno, footnote 13 above, at p50.

together international anticorruption authorities to investigate cross-border anticorruption and fraud cases.[40] Lastly, by growing its range of partnerships with authorities and development organisations, the World Bank has bolstered the potential and widened the net of many countries' capacity to fight corruption.[41]

Other International Financial Institutions have also fostered anti-corruption initiatives. The European Bank for Reconstruction and Development (EBRD), for example, publishes a yearly Integrity and Anti-Corruption report.[42] The EBRD also maintains a list of parties who are ineligible to become Bank Counterparties due to fraud and corruption.[43] This list serves to discourage entities from engaging in corrupt activity so that they can participate in EBRD initiatives. The African Development Bank Group (ADBG) also publishes anti-corruption reports. In 2018, the ADBG initiated the Office of Integrity and Anti-Corruption's (PIAC) Annual Report.[44] The ADBG also performs Due Diligence Reviews and Project Integrity Reviews.[45] Finally, in January 2018, Asian Development Bank (ADB) published an article titled, "Realizing the Potential of Public–Private Partnerships to Advance Asia's Infrastructure Development", which included a commentary on the challenges of securing investor confidence in the region while facing corruption.[46] The bank intends to mitigate investment risks by creating distinct legal and economic entities to promote transparency, avoid corruption, and help secure investor confidence.[47]

Although the World Bank has created a successful internal structure to manage its own rule of law system, it recognises that there is a growing need to support rule of law initiatives in its member countries.[48] The World Bank's corruption initiatives continue to grow in influence and status, but still face challenges from countries where corruption is, or has been, prominent.[49]

3.   Conclusions

The far-reaching repercussions of official corruption are today broadly understood. Reformers recognised early that official corruption was a form of theft from the public treasury and thus imposed unnecessary costs and an

---

40   *Ibid.*
41   *Ibid.*
42   European Bank for Reconstruction and Compliance, "Integrity and Compliance", www.ebrd.com/integrity-and-compliance.html.
43   *Ibid.*
44   African Development Bank Group, PIAC Integrity and Prevention Division's Annual Reports 2018 and 2019 (24 August 2020), p1, www.afdb.org/en/documents/piac-annual-reports-2018-and-2019.
45   *Ibid.*
46   Asian Development Bank "Realizing the Potential of Public–Private Partnerships to Advance Asia's Infrastructure Development" (January 2019), www.adb.org/publications/potential-ppp-asia-infrastructure; Asian Development Bank, "Boosting Public Private Partnerships for Development", https://data.adb.org/story/boosting-public-private-partnerships-development.
47   *Ibid.*
48   Zimmerman, footnote 11 above, at p53.
49   Ugaz Sánchez-Moreno, footnote 13 above, at p50.

unseen tax on citizens. Official corruption can also deprive governments and societies of the free-market forces that reward quality and price, thereby distorting procurement of public goods and services. The financial costs of grand corruption can obviously be high, as World Bank studies and numerous cases illustrate.

Corruption, even so-called 'petty' corruption, can facilitate international crimes such as trafficking in drugs, arms, or human beings, and violations of laws designed to protect the environment. As awareness of the need for environmental protection continues to grow, the implications of significant official corruption in countries that host the world's greatest natural resource reserves critical to the health of the biosphere loom large. Illegal 'facilitating payments' can erode trust in law enforcement agencies, customs and immigration agencies, and public services ranging from telephone services to visa or driver's licence offices.

Corruption can taint governmental agencies, whether they are dispensing benefits or regulating business activities. Even public educational institutions are not immune, as has occasionally been demonstrated by bribes paid to admit unqualified applicants or improve grades, thereby discrediting both academic degrees and academic achievement. Most destructive of all, perhaps, is corruption in a country's judiciary, the branch of government that can be a society's place of last resort for addressing lawlessness or injustice.

By definition, official corruption can undermine the rule of law. If official corruption is unchecked, it can become pervasive, cutting across all functions of government. It can then broadly undermine public confidence in the integrity and fairness of government. Public apathy, cynicism or acceptance of public corruption can, in turn, cripple a country's ability to embrace and sustain the rule of law.

By disregarding principles inherent to the rule of law – accountable public officials who are themselves bound by legal norms and duties, independent courts with honest judges, equal treatment of all before the law, limited and responsive government, freedom of expression and a free press, and protection of fundamental human rights and freedoms – official corruption can corrosively reduce public confidence in government and government functions and erode a country's commitment to the rule of law. It is this greater threat that must be counted among the potential risks of unchecked official corruption.

The tools for protecting against official corruption's corrosive effects are the lessons learned over recent decades in preventing corruption in government, detecting corruption in its many manifestations, and sanctioning those who participate in it. As discussed above, this requires addressing and attacking corruption's various elements: so-called supply side participants who authorise and pay bribes or provide other illicit benefits to public officials; demand side participants who solicit, extort or accept bribes or other inducements to influence the execution of their official responsibilities; intermediaries and the sometimes imaginative mechanisms they use to channel improper payments and benefits to corrupt officials; and the secrecy on which all participants rely.

Failing to address official corruption can perpetuate and worsen the economic, social and political costs that corruption imposes. It can fuel and help sustain authoritarian governments that are dismissive of human and individual rights and that maintain power through repressive means. For democracies and other countries attempting to embrace and implement the rule of law, persistent official corruption risks compromising or nullifying the many social, political and economic benefits that the rule of law can enable.

The authors wish to express their appreciation for the excellent and timely assistance of two of their colleagues, Nicole Gokcebay and Julia Herring, in the preparation of this chapter.

Chapter 8. The rule of law through the lens of international criminal law

Mark S Ellis
International Bar Association

"Fiat justitia, et pereat mundus" [Let there be justice, though the world perishes].[1]

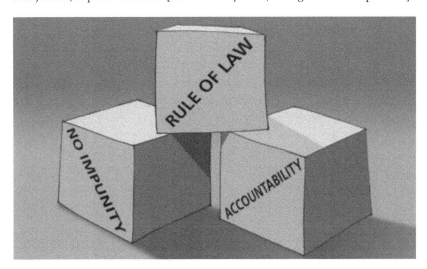

1. Introduction

The rule of law is a concept with numerous definitions and approaches. Scholars and legal entities have proffered a range of lenses for understanding and operationalising what has come to be a fundamental measure. Examples include: AV Dicey,[2] Lon Fuller,[3] Joseph Raz,[4] Lord Tom Bingham,[5] the

1   The sentence was the motto of Ferdinand I, Holy Roman Emperor, and probably originated in Johannes Manlius's, *Loci Communes* (1563). Immanuel Kant famously paraphrased the line in his 1795 work *Perpetual Peace* (*Zum ewigen Frieden: Ein philosophischer Entwurf*) to summarise the counter-utilitarian nature of his moral philosophy: "Let justice reign even if all the rascals in the world should perish from it."
2   Albert Venn Dicey, *An Introduction to the Study of the Law of the Constitution* (1885) (referring to the rule of law); AV Dicey, *New World Encyclopedia*, 2 April 2008, www.newworldencyclopedia.org/entry/A._V._Dicey.
3   José Maria Maravall and Adam Przeworski (eds), *Democracy and the Rule of Law* (CUP, 2003) p68.
4   Joseph Raz, Columbia Law School, www.law.columbia.edu/faculty/joseph-raz.
5   Philippe Sands, "Lord Bingham of Cornhill Obituary", *The Guardian* (London, 11 September 2010), www.theguardian.com/law/2010/sep/11/lord-bingham-of-cornhill-obituary.

International Bar Association (IBA),[6] the UN Secretary-General,[7] John Rawls,[8] US Supreme Court Justice Anthony Kennedy,[9] the US military,[10] The World Bank[11] and the World Justice Project Rule of Law Index.[12]

Likewise, the rule of law has a myriad of meanings across cultures and legal traditions. For example, the Anglo-Saxon rule of law and its German equivalent (*Rechtsstaatlichkeit*) show significant differences in terms of their relationship with the nation state. The constitutions of Afghanistan and Sudan grant extensive law-making powers to the executive with little interaction by parliament. In the Islamic Republic of Iran, the idea of the rule of law (*hākemiyat-e qānun*) is in constant conflict with the rule of *Sharia* (*hākemiyat-e shari'at*), barring legislation that departs from the official Shiite school of Islamic law.[13]

This variation across states suggests a degree of elasticity in what the rule of law means, which creates quite a quandary. One of the most compelling aspects of the rule of law principle is that it has the support and endorsement of a diverse group of global entities. Still, it has been said that "there are almost as many conceptions of the rule of law as there are people defending it".[14] An equivocal and malleable definition of the rule of law means its implementation can be challenging.

Yes, the rule of law is characterised by a nomocracy premised on the superiority, predictability and enforcement of law. However, governments can hide behind a body of law – clear, publicised, and upheld by judges – while ignoring fundamental human rights. Unjust governments flout basic legal principles and commit egregious human rights violations, despite the existence of robust legal institutions, statutes and procedures. This practice is, of course, antithetical to the rule of law, where legal and institutional instruments exist, in part, to protect citizens against the power of the state.

Tyranny against citizens has no place in a state founded on the rule of law. As Madison wrote in the *Federalist Papers*: "You must first enable the government to control the governed; and in the next place oblige it to control

---

6   International Bar Association, Commentary, *Rule of Law Building Blocks*, www.ibanet.org/rule-of-law-videos-en.

7   UN Secretary-General, *The Rule of Law and Transitional Justice in Conflict and Post-Conflict Societies*, para 6, UN Doc S/2004/616 (23 August 2004).

8   John Rawls, *A Theory of Justice* (52 rev ed, Harvard, 1999).

9   Robert Stein, *Rule of Law: What Does It Mean?*, 18 Minn J Int'l L 293 (2009), https://scholarship.law.umn.edu/faculty_articles/424.

10   US Dept of the Army, *Field Manual 3-07: Stability Operations* 1-9 ¶ 1-40 (2008). This definition was also adopted by the Multinational Corps-Iraq Commander as early as 2006. See Appendix 2 to Annex G to MNC-I Operation Order 06-03.

11   The World Bank, *Initiatives in Legal and Judicial Reform* (2002), p3.

12   Mark David Agrast, Juan Carlos Botero and Alejandro Ponce, *Measuring Adherence to the Rule of Law around the World*, (Rule of Law Index 2.0, 7 November 2009), http://worldjusticeproject.org/rule-of-law-index/index-2009/Executive-Summary.

13   Yannic Körtgen, "Rule of Law and Conflict – The different roles of law and justice in conflict and fragility" (2019) 11 *GIZ Law Journal* 18.

14   Olufemi Taiwo, "The Rule of Law: The New Leviathan" (1999) 12 Can J L & Jurisprudence 151, 154.

itself."[15] Thus, the rule of law must transcend the structure of the state to ensure justice is upheld. Yet, for centuries this simply did not occur.

The Treaty of Westphalia, which in 1648 ended the Thirty Years' War in Europe, set forth a standardised legal principle that territorial sovereignty was sacrosanct. It assured non-interference by any state over the internal, sovereign actions of another state. This principle remained a pillar of international law, until the 20th century when the unimaginable atrocities of the Holocaust revealed important ethical limits of sovereignty.

The nefarious crimes committed by Nazi Germany were largely conducted under a government that adhered to formulated statutes enforced and publicised in official gazettes. It was 'rule *by* law', law in a narrow, undemanding design. The legal construct was never sufficient to deter the arbitrary and capricious acts by a government intent on committing atrocity crimes. Nor did it represent 'rule *of* law', incorporating norms of justice and substantive legal protections.

World War II was, thereafter, the catalyst for a transformation of international criminal law and, consequently, the rule of law, once seen as the exclusive domain of states.[16] Protecting the sovereignty of the state became secondary to protecting the human rights afforded to individuals. States should be held accountable for violating the rights of the individual including their own citizens.

What emerged from the horror of the Holocaust, and the debate thereafter, was a titanic shift towards a new legal doctrine – one which would change the international legal order forever.[17] It reimagined the rule of law to include accountability and punishment for government authorities who flagrantly violated the sanctity of individual rights. Too often, states allow international crimes to go unpunished.[18] But the rule of law signifies a covenant among nations to uphold universal standards of justice. The international community recognised this in one of the most important post-War international proclamations in history: the 1948 Universal Declaration of Human Rights. Stated clearly in the preamble is the view that "human rights should be protected by the *rule of law*" [emphasis added].[19] Fundamental to these standards, and consistent with the rule of law, is the notion that justice comes first and foremost through accountability.[20]

---

15 James Madison, *The Federalist No. 51: The Structure of the Government must Furnish the Proper Checks and Balances Between the Different Departments* (first published 1788).
16 See Mark S Ellis, "Combating Impunity and Enforcing Accountability as a Way to Promote Peace and Stability – The Role of International War Crimes Tribunals" (2006) 2 *Journal of National Security Law & Policy* 1.
17 Mark Ellis, Yves Doutriaux and Timothy Ryback, *Justice and Diplomacy*, Cambridge University Press (2018), p3.
18 Mark S Ellis, "Combating Impunity and Enforcing Accountability as a Way to Promote Peace and Stability – The Role of International War Crimes Tribunals" (2006) 2 JNSL&P.
19 Universal Declaration of Human Rights, General Assembly Resolution 217 A (III), A/RES/3/217A (10 December 1948), Preamble.
20 Mark S Ellis, "International Justice and the Rule of Law: Strengthening the ICC through Domestic Prosecutions" (2009) 1 *Hague Journal on the Rule of Law* 79–86.

This idea bridges the Nuremberg and Tokyo tribunals of the 1940s to today's Agenda 2030 and the Sustainable Development Goals (SDGs) – the world's ambitious "blueprint to achieve a better and more sustainable future for all".[21] Within this framework, SDG 16.3 aims to promote the rule of law at the national and international levels and ensure equal access to justice for all. At the outset, then, the rule of law is seen as a precondition and catalyst not only to establish and maintain peace and justice, but to all other areas of human development.

This aspirational goal can also be quantified. The World Justice Project (WJP) Rule of Law Index is one of the most authoritative measurements of the rule of law.[22] Accountability, one of the index indicators, is one of four 'universal principles' of the rule of law.[23] It requires that states sanction those officials who engage in illegal acts. There is no impunity – only accountability consistent with the maxim that no one is above the law.

States have also unambiguously supported the nexus between the rule of law and accountability. During UN General Assembly meetings, a significant number of states have identified 'accountability' and the 'fight against impunity' as key elements of the rule of law. For instance, Switzerland found that "the fight against impunity was fundamental for the implementation of the rule law" and emphasised the importance of the International Criminal Court's (ICC) role in this fight.[24] Denmark, speaking on behalf of the Nordic countries, echoed this same sentiment stating that "fighting impunity and ensuring accountability for the most serious crimes of concern to the international community is a pillar of the rule of law".[25]

In short, promoting and strengthening the rule of law is commensurate with, and requires commitment to, ending impunity and enhancing accountability at both national and international levels.

2. Ending impunity in support of the rule of law

There were earlier efforts to establish a solid principle against impunity for international crimes. After the armistice that ended World War I, the Allies agreed to bring the defeated German Emperor Kaiser Wilhelm II to trial. This was a radical and tantalising shift in the annals of international justice. The very idea

---

21   United Nations, "Sustainable Development Goals", www.un.org/sustainabledevelopment/sustainable-development-goals/.

22   The World Justice Project Rule of Law Index is created by surveying over 130,000 households and over 4,000 legal practitioners worldwide, to measure the experience and perception of the rule of law in every country. World Justice Project, https://worldjusticeproject.org/about-us/overview/what-rule-law.

23   WJP Rule of Law Index 2020, p11, https://worldjusticeproject.org/sites/default/files/documents/WJP-ROLI-2020-Online_0.pdf.

24   UN General Assembly Official Records, 72nd Sess, 5th mtg at p13, UN Doc A/C.6/72/SR.5 (13 November 2017).

25   UN General Assembly Official Records, 71st Sess, 5th mtg at p5, UN Doc A/C.6/71/SR.5 (31 October 2016).

of holding a leader responsible for atrocity crimes was unprecedented.[26] Article 227 of the Treaty of Versailles stated that Kaiser Wilhelm would submit to, and be tried by, an international court for the supreme crime against international morality and the sanctity of treaties.[27] It was the first time states created an international criminal tribunal. Sadly, the trial never took place. Much to the consternation of his victims, the Kaiser was never brought to justice.

There was also a debate in 1937 at the League of Nations, which focused on the creation of the Convention for the Creation of an International Criminal Court.[28] However, this court did not come into being either.

There was yet another attempt towards ending impunity during the early years of World War II. The United Nations War Crimes Commission (UNWCC) was established on 20 October 1943 by 17 Allied nations,[29] charged with investigating crimes committed during the war.[30] Each Allied government[31] established a national office for the purpose of preparing charges against alleged war criminals.

The UNWCC recognised that, in general, the appropriate jurisdiction for the prosecution and trial of such crimes would be national courts.[32] However, the UNWCC also discussed the idea of an international court to try war criminals.[33]

---

26   See Mark Ellis, *The Kaiser's Trial: How a Case that Never Happened Helped Create the International Criminal Justice System*, Los Angeles Review of Books (8 April 2019).

27   *Ibid.*

28   League of Nations, "Convention for the Prevention and Punishment of Terrorism and the Convention for the Creation of an International Criminal Court" (16 November 1937) 10 *League of Nations Official Journal* C.546.M.383.1937.V; UN General Assembly, *Historical Survey of the Question of International Criminal Jurisdiction – Memorandum submitted by the Secretary-General*, A/CN.4/7/Rev.1, 1949, http://untreaty.un.org/ilc/documentation/english/a_cn4_7_rev1.pdf.

29   The state parties to the UNWCC: Australia, Belgium, Canada (according to Hard Copy Documents (HC) p2.28; Canada was not represented on the Commission), China, Czechoslovakia, France, Greece, India, Luxembourg, the Netherlands, New Zealand, Norway, Poland, the United Kingdom, the United States, Yugoslavia and South Africa (however South Africa only took part in the creation of the UNWCC, but did not hold national trials and according to HC p2.28; South Africa was not represented on the Commission). Denmark later joined the UNWCC in July 1945; The HC page numbers refer to the handwritten page numbers on the hard copy documents retained by the author. This set of documents included 1. Minutes of the first UNWCC meetings; 2. Commission and Committee Meetings and Documents; and 3. National Offices Conference Meetings and Documents. All hard copy documents and other UNWCC documents can be found at www.legal-tools.org/en/go-to-database/ltfolder/ 0_28455/#results.

30   *Annex V – Establishment of closer cooperation between the UNWCC and the National Offices*, 2 June 1945, NOC 5 (HC p3.77). The Moscow Declaration was signed during the Moscow Conference in October 1943 by China, the Soviet Union, the United Kingdom and the United States. Under the Declaration, "those German officers and men and members of the Nazi party who have been responsible for or have taken a consenting part in the above atrocities, massacres and executions will be sent back to the countries in which their abominable deeds were done in order that they may be judged and punished according to the laws of these liberated countries and of free governments which will be erected therein". Thus, those who committed crimes "will know they will be brought back to the scene of their crimes and judged on the spot by the peoples whom they have outraged". See http://avalon.law.yale.edu/wwii/moscow.asp.

31   'Each Government' refers to each government that was party to the UNWCC; Australia, Belgium, China, Czechoslovakia, France, Greece, India, Luxembourg, the Netherlands, New Zealand, Norway, Poland, South Africa, United Kingdom, United States and Yugoslavia.

32   Draft Convention for the Establishment of a United Nations War Crimes Court, 3 September 1944, C 50(1) (HC p2.33).

33   One important issue that was raised was the fact that the Allied courts were unable to try Germans who committed crimes in Germany, Members of the Commission argued that the creation of an inter-Allied court would offer a solution: "[t]he campaign of racial extermination of the Jews has special features which do not generally fall within the scope of the National Offices, as for instance the case of German Jews murdered in Germany"; See Annex VI – Chairman's Introductory Speech, 31 May 1944, NOC 6, (HC p3.86).

An initial draft convention (Draft Convention for the Creation of an International Criminal Court) was adopted by the London International Assembly in February 1944.[34] But in the end, the idea of an international criminal court underwhelmed, and like its previous iterations, failed to materialise.

While attempts to establish an international criminal court did not succeed in the first half of the 20th century, the underlying aspiration to end impunity for atrocity crimes did, in fact, take hold. By the end of War World II, the international community had set in motion a lasting and irrevocable effort to enshrine an anti-impunity stance in international law – a concept that remains at the core of the rule of law today in the eloquent form of the Nuremberg Principles. The principles make clear that: "[t]he fact that a person who committed an act which constitutes a crime under international law acted as Head of State or responsible Government officials does not relieve him from responsibility under international law".[35] Coupled with impunity was a commitment to accountability: "[a]ny person who commits an act which constitutes a crime under international law is responsible therefore and liable to punishment".[36]

The Nuremberg Principles also established a set of crimes punishable under international law. They included 'crime against peace', 'war crimes' and 'crimes against humanity'.

A series of conventions followed: the Genocide Convention,[37] the Geneva Conventions,[38] the Convention against Torture,[39] and the prohibition (although not a convention)[40] of crimes against humanity. These conventions and prohibitions aimed to identify and prevent crimes that shocked the conscious of humanity; they are today binding customary international law and mark a legal prohibition on granting impunity for atrocity crimes.

Several of the conventions also impose inviolable obligations on states to

---

34   UNWCC, Draft Convention for the Creation of an International Criminal Court, submitted to the London International Assembly, II/2, 14 February 1944.

35   *Ibid*, Principle II.

36   United Nations, "Principles of International Law Recognized in the Charter of the Nürnberg Tribunal and in the Judgment of the Tribunal" (UN 1950) p28, https://legal.un.org/ilc/texts/instruments/english/draft_articles/7_1_1950.pdf.

37   Convention on the Prevention and Punishment of the Crime of Genocide, Paris (adopted 9 December 1948, entered into force 12 January 1951), 78 UNTS 277, Article 1.

38   Convention (No I) for the Amelioration of the Condition of the Wounded and Sick in Armed Forces in the Field, Geneva (adopted 12 August 1949, entered into force 21 October 1950), 75 UNTS 31; Convention (No II) for the Amelioration of the Condition of Wounded, Sick and Shipwrecked Members of the Armed Forces at Sea, Geneva (adopted 12 August 1949, entered into force 21 October 1950), 75 UNTS 85; Convention (No III) Relative to the Treatment of Prisoners of War, Geneva (adopted 12 August 1949, entered into force 21 October 1950), 75 UNTS 135; Convention (No IV) Relative to the Protection of Civilian Persons in Time of War, Geneva (adopted 12 August 1949, entered into force 21 October 1950), 75 UNTS 287.

39   Convention Against Torture and Other Cruel, Inhuman or Degrading Treatment or Punishment, New York, 10 December 1984, in force 26 June 1987, 1465 UNTS 85.

40   There is currently a draft Convention on the Prohibition and Punishment of Crimes Against Humanity presently before the 6th Committee of the UN General Assembly.

extradite or prosecute a person found in their territory who is suspected of certain international crimes. For the 'core crimes' of torture and grave breaches of the Geneva Conventions, there is a treaty-based obligation *aut dedere aut judicare* [either extradite or prosecute]. The conventions require states to undertake prosecutions at the national level or transfer the case to a country that will prosecute. The prohibition of both crimes has become a norm of *jus cogens*. The crime of genocide, and crimes against humanity, are often seen in the same light.

The 1949 Geneva Conventions direct states parties to enact domestic legislation to punish persons committing grave breaches of the Conventions.[41] The Genocide Convention also requires states parties to enact punitive measures against those who commit genocide.[42] Many states accept that other atrocity crimes are covered under customary international law and, thus, imposes similar obligations and norms.

3.   Accountability mechanisms in support of the rule of law

World War II ushered in a number of accountability mechanisms to ensure there would be no impunity for gross violations of human rights and mass atrocities. The military tribunals in Nuremberg and Tokyo[43] represented the initial accountability mechanisms for crimes committed by Nazi Germany and Japan, respectively.

The horrors witnessed in Cambodia, the former Yugoslavia and Rwanda accelerated efforts to create additional accountability mechanisms to combat impunity for atrocity crimes.

The creations of domestic and international accountability mechanisms engendered an 'indispensable requirement' to strengthen the rule of law.[44] The proceedings came in the form of the UN Security Council's Resolutions 827 and 955, which established the International Criminal Tribunal for the former Yugoslavia (ICTY)[45] and the International Criminal Tribunal for Rwanda (ICTR).[46] The UN, in cooperation with the government of Cambodia, established the Extraordinary Chambers in the Courts of Cambodia (ECCC),[47] and also created a special crimes unit to prosecute cases before Special Panels for Serious Crimes in East Timor.[48]

---

41   See Geneva Conventions, footnote 38 above.
42   See Genocide Convention, footnote 37 above.
43   Harvard Law School Library, Nuremberg Trials Project: A Digital Document Collection, https://nuremberg.law.harvard.edu; United Nations, "International Military Tribunal for the Far East" (UN 1959), www.un.org/en/genocideprevention/documents/atrocity-crimes/Doc.3_1946%20Tokyo%20 Charter.pdf.
44   See Barrie Sander, "The Human Rights Agenda and the Struggle Against Impunity", *Lawfare Blog* (6 February 2017), www.lawfareblog.com/human-rights-agenda-and-struggle-against-impunity.
45   SC Res 827, Int'l Crim Trib for the Former Yugoslavia (25 May 1993).
46   SC Res 955, Int'l Crim Trib for Rwanda (8 November 1994).
47   GA Res 57/228, Extraordinary Chambers in the Courts of Cambodia (18 December 2002).
48   SC Res 1272, Special Panels for Serious Crimes in East Timor (25 October 1999).

Other accountability mechanisms followed, including the Kosovo Specialist Chamber (KSC),[49] the Special Court for Sierra Leone (SCSL),[50] the Supreme Iraqi Criminal Tribunal,[51] the Special Tribunal for Lebanon (STL),[52] the Office of the War Crimes Prosecutor in Serbia,[53] the War Crimes Chamber of the Court of Bosnia-Herzegovina,[54] and the International Crimes Tribunal of Bangladesh.[55]

Together, the accountability tribunals and mechanisms represented a sea change in how the world would address atrocity crimes. They have influenced and shaped global and domestic legal policies, evolving protections of fundamental human rights and commitments to state responsibility and accountability.

The tribunals have also created a lexicon in international criminal law based on the names of notorious perpetrators brought to justice: Charles Taylor, Thomas Lubanga, Slobodan Milošević, Radovan Karadžić, Ratko Mladić, Nuon Chea, Bosco Ntaganda and Germain Katanga, to name just a few.

Indeed, the ICTY is an example of an international tribunal that integrated the role of accountability into the rule of law concept. In the *Erdemović* case, the Tribunal saw its role, in part:

> *[t]o contribute to the settlement of the wider issues of accountability, reconciliation and establishing the truth behind the evils perpetrated in the former Yugoslavia. Discovering the truth is a cornerstone of the* rule of law *and a fundamental step on the way to reconciliation* [emphasis added].[56]

The most dramatic shift in accountability came about with the creation of the ICC.[57] The ICC, which came into existence on 1 July 2002, is the first permanent court ever to be established to investigate and try individuals for the most serious violations of international criminal law, including war crimes, crimes against humanity and genocide. The overarching aim that motivated the establishment of the ICC was "to put an end to impunity for the perpetrators of [the most serious] crimes and, thus, to contribute to the prevention of such crimes".[58] In the arc of justice, starting after WWI, the ICC is the pinnacle.

David Miliband, former UK Secretary of State for Foreign and

---

49   The Kosovo Specialist Chamber, 2015 (L No 05/L-053) (Kos).
50   SC Res 1315, Special Court for Sierra Leone (14 August 2000).
51   Coalition Provisional Authority No 48: Delegation of Authority Regarding an Iraqi Tribunal, CPA/ORD/48 (9 December 2003) (IST Statute).
52   SC Res 1664, Special Tribunal for Lebanon (29 March 2006).
53   Act on Public Prosecution Services (*Official Gazette of the Republic of Serbia*), Nos 116/2008, 104/2009, 101/2010, and 78/2011 (1 July 2003).
54   Office of the High Representative, *War Crimes Chamber Project: Project Implementation Plan Registry Progress Report* (20 October 2004), www.ohr.int/ohr-dept/rule-of-law-pillar/pdf/wcc-project-plan-201004-eng.pdf.
55   International Crimes (Tribunals) Act 1973, Act No XIX (Bangladesh) (amended in 2008).
56   United Nations International Residual Mechanism for Criminal Tribunals, "Drazen Erdemovic Sentenced to 5 Years of Imprisonment" (UN 1998), www.icty.org/sid/7686.
57   In 1947, the UN General Assembly requested the International Law Commission (ILC) (then referred to as the Codification of International Law) to begin to codify the principles of international law that emerged from the Nuremberg Tribunal. The first draft statute for establishing an international criminal court was completed in 1950. Finally, in 1994, the International Law Commission produced a comprehensive draft statute for an international court which was submitted to the UN General Assembly. Four years later, on 19 July 1998, the Rome Statute of the International Criminal Court was adopted.
58   Rome Statute of the International Criminal Court pmb, 17 July 1998, 2187 UNTS 90.

Commonwealth Affairs, sees this development as "the fight against impunity – the capacity of actors to commit crimes without facing justice – and for accountability [that] provides at once more practical and inclusive than previous efforts to bring values to foreign policy".[59] I would add that this adherence to accountability also brings indispensable value and relevance to the rule of law. Without accountability, the rule of law is fictional.

The same principle holds for the victims of atrocity crimes. Without recourse, they will "languish in a post-conflict environment that lacks the very cornerstone of the rule of law – the notion of accountability".[60]

4. The principle of complementarity and the rule of law

The connection between accountability and the rule of law at the domestic level is most discernible in the legal document governing the work of the ICC – the Rome Statute.[61] Enshrined in the Rome Statute is the principle of *complementarity*.[62] Complementarity refers to the principle that the ICC may gain jurisdiction only when domestic legal systems are 'unwilling' or genuinely 'unable' to carry out an investigation or prosecution of an accused, that is, there is a breakdown in the national system of justice or a state simply fails to act. This is an important element.

The ICC actually exists to support states in bolstering the rule of law. The principle of complementarity emphasises the devolution of authority to national judicial systems in accordance with the standard of the rule of law. The tenet aims to encourage and facilitate genuine national proceedings. It strengthens domestic law and national capacity building. By examining the 'genuineness' of national investigations and proceedings, the ICC upholds the rule of law internationally with the view to end impunity.

The concept of complementarity encourages states to retain control over prosecuting nationals responsible for atrocity crimes. Additionally, the potential benefits of complementarity also came into play when states create domestic legislation that adequately covers the jurisdiction *ratione materiae* of the ICC Statute. The Rome Statute specifically requires states parties (ie, states that ratify the statute) to "ensure that there are procedures available under their national law for all of the forms of cooperation". Thus, states parties must update their domestic legislation to achieve complementarity with the ICC.[63] This includes fighting against impunity.

---

59   David Miliband, *Foreign Affairs*, "The Age of Impunity and how to Fight It", 13 May 2021.
60   Mark Ellis, "Bringing Justice to an Embattled Region – Creating and Implementing the Rules of the Road for Bosnia-Herzegovina", 17 *Berkeley J of Int'l L* 1, 24–25 (1999).
61   Statute of the International Criminal Court, UN Diplomatic Conference of Plenipotentiaries on the Establishment of an International Criminal Court, UN Doc A/Conf 183/9 (1998) (hereinafter ICC Statute).
62   The principle of complementarity as enshrined in Article 1 of the Rome Statute.
63   For instance, the crime of murder found in national law is not the same as a crime against humanity – since it lacks the requirement of intent – or other acts that constitute a crime against humanity.

Customary international law bestows heads of state and diplomatic officials with immunity from prosecution by foreign states.[64] However, under Article 27 of the Rome Statute, these officials are not immune from prosecution for crimes committed within the jurisdiction of the ICC. Therefore, states parties must ensure that their national legislation does not allow for the innovation of any immunities for ICC crimes.

To date, 123 states have agreed to become states parties to the Court and, most importantly, to adopt implementing legislation ensuring that jurisdiction for punishing these crimes also exists at the national level. Thus, the ICC is shaping the domestic laws of nearly two-thirds of the world obliging states to commit to the rule of law by ensuring individuals are brought to justice for violating international criminal law.

Of course, implementation is lacking in many parts of the world and outcomes are far from perfect.[65] However, the Rome Statute will continue to influence domestic jurisdictions as states incorporate punishment for war crimes, genocide, and crimes against humanity into their national legislation.

Ukraine, which is a signatory to the Rome Statute, is a good recent example. In May 2021, the Ukrainian Parliament adopted amendments to the criminal code regarding international humanitarian and international criminal law.[66] The new law specifically provides a domestic mechanism to prosecute war crimes committed in the occupied territory of Crimea.[67]

Prior to the law's passage, Ukraine's domestic criminal law was insufficient to hold perpetrators of atrocity crimes to account.[68] Previously, crimes committed in the context of armed conflict in the Ukraine were classified under separate articles of the Ukraine's criminal code and were subject to statutes of limitation.[69] The 2021 law brings Ukraine's legislation up to the standards of current international law and the Rome Statute.[70]

Changes like the one in Ukraine fundamentally reinforce the rule of law principle of accountability and, by extension, the rule of law itself. The legislative amendments do not solely focus on substantive law; states will introduce new or improved criminal procedural law too.

For instance, promoting international criminal law also ensures that judges

---

64   See Vienna Convention on Diplomatic Relations, Article 31(i).

65   Of the 123 state parties to the ICC Statute, 40% have yet to enact national implementing legislation. See Daley J Birkett, "Twenty Years of the Rome Statute of the International Criminal Court: Appraising the State of National Implementing Legislation in Asia" (2019) 18(2) *Chinese Journal of International Law* 353–392.

66   Gaurav Gupte, "Ukraine parliament adopts law allowing accountability for war crimes committed in Crimea", *Jurist*, 23 May 2021, www.jurist.org/news/2021/05/ukraine-parliament-adopts-law-allowing-accountability-for-war-crimes-committed-in-crimea/.

67   *Ibid.*

68   "Ukraine: Closer to Accountability for International Crimes", Parliamentarians for Global Action, 10 February 2021, www.pgaction.org/news/ukraine-closer-accountability-for-international-crimes.html.

69   "Ukraine: International Crimes Bill Adopted", Human Rights Watch, 21 May 2021, www.hrw.org/news/2021/05/21/ukraine-international-crimes-bill-adopted.

70   *Ibid.*

undertaking accountability assessments must be qualified and able to uphold principles of independence and impartiality consistent with international standards of fairness and human rights guarantees.

Another example of international criminal law directly supporting the rule of law at the national level is in the area of victim and witness support and protection. Accountability for atrocity crimes is not possible without ensuring this support. This is particularly true at the national level where crimes are often committed in small, close-knit ethnic communities.[71]

My own experience in Serbia is illustrative of the issue. Serbia's decision to undertake domestic war crimes trials was a formidable task. The trials took place in Belgrade and non-Serbs simply did not trust the Serbian courts, nor were they open to travelling to Belgrade. However, Nataša Kandić of the Humanitarian Law Center undertook a major campaign in cooperation with the Court's newly created Victim and Witness Unit, which ultimately made possible the testimony of victims and witnesses in the judicial process.

In further support of the rule of law at the national level, states will likely extend their own criminal law penalising a series of offences set forth in the Rome Statute. These could include offences like giving false testimony, presenting false or forged evidence, and attempting to influence witnesses. Countering these and other offences are fundamental to an effective independent judicial system and also form part of an effort to ensure that states' domestic judicial systems incorporate and adhere to principles of due process recognised by international law.

The principle of complementarity requires all domestic criminal proceedings to meet the highest standards of international law. In essence, state procedures must protect judicial independence, impartiality and equality – all fundamental to the rule of law.

5.   Universal jurisdiction and the responsibility to protect

International criminal law has also emboldened the rule of law through the ancillary doctrines of universal jurisdiction and the responsibility to protect.

While these doctrines remain different in nature (ie, one legal and the other political), they share a common theoretical underpinning and goal to end mass atrocities. The similarities mean the two doctrines are often amalgamated into tandem mechanisms to jointly address gross human rights abuses – two sides of the same coin.

5.1   Responsibility to protect

Responsibility to protect – known as R2P – is a global political commitment and

---

71   For a general discussion, see Mark S Ellis, *Sovereignty and Justice: Balancing the Principle of Complementarity between International and Domestic War Crimes Tribunals* (Cambridge Scholars, 2014), p265.

an international norm in formation. It seeks to ensure that the international community decisively halts the mass atrocity crimes of genocide, war crimes, ethnic cleansing, and crimes against humanity. R2P was unanimously adopted in 2005 at the UN World Summit which stressed the need for "universal adherence to and implementation of the rule of law at both the national and international levels".[72]

More recently, on 18 May 2021, the UN General Assembly adopted Resolution A/75/277 on "the responsibility to protect and the prevention of genocide, war crimes, ethnic cleansing and crimes against humanity". In adopting this resolution, the General Assembly agreed to include R2P on the annual agenda and requested an annual report on the topic from the Secretary General.[73]

A year earlier, on 17 July 2020, the Human Rights Council adopted Resolution 44/14 on the "Fifteenth anniversary of the responsibility to protect populations from genocide, war crimes, ethnic cleansing and crimes against humanity, as enshrined in the 2005 World Summit Outcome". In adopting this Resolution, the Human Rights Council decided to convene an intersessional panel discussion on R2P with participation from states, relevant UN bodies and agencies, treaty bodies, civil society, etc.[74]

R2P rests on three pillars: state responsibility; international assistance; and timely and decisive action by the international community.[75]

This last pillar is the most dramatic: when domestic jurisdictions fail to ensure citizens are protected from state abuse, the international community is able to intervene, including via the use of force as a measure of last resort.

The R2P concept emerged in response to the failure of the international community to respond adequately to mass atrocities committed in Rwanda and the former Yugoslavia during the 1990s. The International Commission on Intervention and State Sovereignty developed R2P during 2001. It is premised on the notion that "domestic atrocity anywhere could have systematic impact everywhere".[76]

When reviewing R2P, it becomes apparent that there is a close link to the complementary principle of the ICC. As aforementioned, the ICC focuses its mandate and jurisdiction over states that are unwilling or unable to prosecute those responsible for atrocity crimes in their jurisdiction. The R2P principle is essentially founded on this same idea of complementarity. The primary

---

72   2005 World Summit Outcome, 24 October 2005, A/RES/60/1, para 134.
73   *UN General Assembly Adopts New Resolution on the Responsibility to Protect*, Global Centre for the Responsibility to Protect, 18 May 2021, www.globalr2p.org/publications/un-general-assembly-adopts-new-resolution-on-the-responsibility-to-protect/.
74   Human Rights Council Resolution A/HRC/RES/44/14 (17 July 2020).
75   See Arif Saba and Shahram Akbarzadeh, "The ICC and R2P: Complementary or Contradictory?" (2020) 28(1), *International Peacekeeping*.
76   See William W Burke-White, "Adaption of the Responsibility to Protect", in Jared Genser and Irwin Cotler, *The Responsibility to Protect* (OUP, 2012), p18.

responsibility to protect lies with the state itself,[77] where R2P interacts with the rule of law at the domestic level. This is an important point because when the rule of law is threatened or attacked at the domestic level, it exacerbates the failure of a state to protect its citizens and, consequently, these same vulnerable citizens fall victim to atrocity crimes.

R2P is a broad encompassing obligation. Ensuring adherence to the rule of law domestically is crucial in preventing atrocity crimes from occurring. States must ensure that their institutions remain independent, credible and impartial.[78] In this way, the rule of law and R2P go hand in hand. If states continue to promote, strengthen and adhere to the rule of law at home, the international community succeeds in upholding compliance with international law. If the application of the rule of law is cemented at the domestic level, then it is less likely that a situation will arise where the international community must react under the second and third pillars of R2P. The end result is to prevent human suffering before it occurs.[79]

However, the relationship between the rule of law and R2P does not come without risks and challenges, and it is rife with controversy. For example, it has been argued that "the attempt to hold accountable the Libyan regime for atrocity crimes eventually resulted in legitimizing military intervention and regime change under the R2P mandate".[80]

Within the R2P toolbox, the ICC can be an instrument of deterrence. Former UN Secretary-General Ban-Ki Moon has argued that the early threat of prosecution could deter perpetrators and ultimately prevent atrocity crimes. In this regard, he sees the ICC as an "essential tool for implementing the responsibility to protect [principle]".[81]

Regional courts have also expressed support. The Grand Chamber of the European Court of Human Rights (ECHR) ruled that member states have a responsibility to ensure that their citizens are protected against the arbitrary actions of governments in violations of the European Convention on Human Rights (eg, Article 3 which prohibits torture and inhumane or degrading treatment).[82]

---

77 See Gareth Evans and Mohamed Sahnoun, "The Responsibility to Protect" (2002) 81 *Foreign Affairs* 99–110.
78 Jeremy Sarkin, "The Role of the United Nations, the African Union and Africa's Sub-Regional Organizations in Dealing with Africa's Human Rights Problems: Connecting Humanitarian Intervention and the Responsibility to Protect" (2009) 53 J of Afr L.
79 Stephen Marks and Nicholas Cooper, "The Responsibility to Protect: Watershed or Old Wine in a New Bottle?" (2010) 2 Jindal Global L Rev 97.
80 See Arif Saba and Shahram Akbarzadeh, "The ICC and R2P: Complementary or Contradictory?" (2019) 28 *International Peacekeeping*.
81 "Report of the Secretary-General on Implementing the Responsibility to Protect" (2009) United Nations, para 23; Ban, Ki-moon, "Responsibility to Protect: Timely and Decisive Response" (2012) United Nations, para 29.
82 See *El-Masri v The former Yugoslav Republic of Macedonia* 39630/09 (2009) and *Osman v United Kingdom* 23452/94 (1998).

5.2   Universal jurisdiction

Universal jurisdiction holds, at its core, the principle that every country has a responsibility, and obligation, to bring to justice perpetrators of the most heinous international crimes regardless of the nationality of the perpetrators or their victims. The principle abandons the more traditional approaches of adjudicative jurisdiction which require a nexus between the prosecuting state and the crime. Universal jurisdiction is interlaced with the precept that some international norms are obligations bound to the entire world – *erga omnes* – and binding on all states – *jus cogens*.

In its most literal interpretation, this is universal jurisdiction in its 'absolute' form. The principle does not require an assessment of relevant 'personal jurisdiction'; any state can pursue any individual for the crimes. The crimes most commonly viewed as subject to universal jurisdiction include slavery, piracy, crimes against humanity, selected war crimes, torture and genocide.[83] The crimes are rightfully seen as an affront "against the law of nations" and as an "offence against the universal law of society".[84]

Two of the most famous examples of the application of absolute universal jurisdiction are the trials of Adolf Eichmann and Augusto Pinochet.

Adolf Eichmann was the high-ranking Nazi *Schutzstaffel* (SS) bureaucrat who played an indispensable role in the implementation of the Holocaust. After a 16-year manhunt, Israeli intelligence forces captured and smuggled him out of Argentina to face trial in Israel.

In its judgment, the Israeli Court ruled that its jurisdiction was based on the universal nature of the crimes:

> *The abhorrent crimes defined under this Law are not crimes under Israeli law alone. These crimes, which struck at the whole of mankind and shocked the conscience of nations, are grave offences against the law of nations itself* (delicta juris gentium). *Therefore, so far from international law negating or limiting the jurisdiction of countries with respect to such crimes, international law is, in the absence of an international court, in need of the judicial and legislative organs of every country to give effect to its criminal interdictions and to bring the criminals to trial. The jurisdictions to try crimes under international law is universal.*[85]

The case of former Chilean President General Augusto Pinochet is another landmark case for universal jurisdiction. Pinochet led a *coup d'état* which overthrew the government of Chile in 1973. He subsequently led the military junta that committed an extensive number of atrocity crimes in the country. As a private citizen, Pinochet visited London, England and was apprehended based

---

83   See Stephen Macedo, *Princeton Principles on Universal Jurisdiction* (Program in Law and Public Affairs, 2001), https://lapa.princeton.edu/hosteddocs/unive_jur.pdf.
84   See *United States v Smith*, 18 US 153 (1820).
85   Holocaust Education and Archive Research Team, "The Trial of Adolf Eichmann", Holocaust Research Project (2007), http://holocaustresearchproject.org/trials/eichmanntrial.html.

on an international arrest warrant issued by Spain. After a series of complex legal proceedings, the UK House of Lords ruled that it had jurisdiction and denied immunity for Pinochet based on universal jurisdiction as required under the Convention against Torture.[86]

The decision was not without controversy[87] but the Pinochet case remains significant as the first time a national court rejected functional immunity for a head of state for having committed atrocity crimes.

Of course, the principle of universal jurisdiction is not without its critics. Henry Kissinger, former US Secretary of State, has argued that universal jurisdiction is a breach of each state's sovereignty, claiming that "widespread agreement that human rights violations and crimes against humanity must be prosecuted has hindered active consideration of the proper role of international courts. Universal jurisdiction risks creating universal tyranny – that of judges".[88]

According to Kissinger, since any number of states could set up universal jurisdictional tribunals, the process could quickly degenerate into politically driven show trials attempting to place a quasi-judicial stamp on a state's enemies or opponents.[89]

A number of states agree with this view, which has resulted in selected states attempting to circumvent the 'absolute' form of universal jurisdiction and move towards a 'conditional' structure. Conditional universal jurisdiction requires some degree of nexus between the crime and the state asserting jurisdiction. For example, the nexus could be the requirement for the victim or accused to be a citizen of the prosecuting state or requiring the state, through a federal prosecutor, to approve the initiation of the prosecution.

However, the trend to embrace the concept of universal jurisdiction continues on the upturn.

According to a 2012 Amnesty International report, more than 160 countries have enacted legislation supporting universal jurisdiction over one or more atrocity crimes[90] (though there remains controversy over this figure).[91]

Universal jurisdiction also plays an important role in advancing the rule of law at the national level. Just as the ICC's principle of complementarity counsels states to create strong substantive and procedural legal processes through implementing legislation, universal jurisdiction requires nation states

---

86   *R v Bow Street Metropolitan Stipendiary Magistrate, ex parte Pinochet Ugarte* [1998] UKHL 41, [2000] 1 AC 61.
87   A number of politicians from the Czech Republic, Poland and the Assembly of the Council of Europe vehemently opposed the extradition of Pinochet. They saw him as a hero who brought "stability to Chile". See "In their own words" (1999) 6(3) *Transactions* 14.
88   Henry A Kissinger, "The Pitfalls of Universal Jurisdiction" (2001) 80(4) JSTOR 86, www.jstor.org/stable/20050228?origin=crossref.
89   *Ibid*.
90   See "Universal Jurisdiction", International Justice Resource Center, http://ijrcenter.org/cases-before-national-courts/domestic-exercise-of-universal-jurisdiction/.
91   The article "Just Security" by Ryan Goodman explores the idea that perhaps the figure provided by Amnesty International has been somewhat 'inflated'. See International Criminal Court: Rome Statute of the International Criminal Court, www.icc-cpi.int/resource-library/documents/rs-eng.pdf.

to do the same – that is, to strengthen their capacity to uphold the rule of law through accountability.

A recent example of the power of universal jurisdiction occurred in Finland. In February 2021, the trial of Gibril Massaquoi, a Sierra Leone national accused of committing war crimes during Liberia's second civil war, began in Finland's Tampere District Court.[92] Massaquoi had been a resident of Finland for 10 years and was granted a residence permit due to his cooperation with the SCSL in the early 2000s.[93] He is thought to have been a high-ranking official of an insurgent group called the Revolutionary United Front.[94] He was detained by police in March of 2020 after an inquiry conducted by the National Bureau of Investigation.[95] The Bureau requested that Massaquoi be placed in custody due to suspicions of murder, war crimes and crimes against humanity committed during the war.[96]

Under Finland's universal jurisdiction laws and customary international agreements, Finland has an obligation to investigate and prosecute perpetrators of war crimes when necessary.[97]

In a rare decision, the Finnish court temporarily moved to Liberia and Sierra Leone in order to hear live testimony from victims and witnesses of Massaquoi's alleged war crimes.[98]

In another recent example, the German Federal Court of Justice (BGH) ruled in 2021 that war crimes committed abroad can be tried in the German courts.[99]

The BGH decided that criminal prosecution of the accused in Germany under the application of international law does not conflict with the procedural obstacle of state official immunity.[100] The BGH ruled that the court could rule on acts "committed by a defendant in the exercise of foreign sovereign activity" when the defendant is indicted on charges that constitute war crimes.[101]

This decision continues German recognition of universal jurisdiction for war crimes in German courts, while also eliminating immunity for foreign officials in such cases.[102]

Another example is Ukraine. Because of Russia's occupation of the Crimea

---

92   Sahana Devarajan, "Sierra Leone national accused of war crimes appears in Finland court", *Jurist*, 3 February 2021, www.jurist.org/news/2021/02/sierra-leone-national-accused-of-war-crimes-appears-in-finland-court/.
93   Thierry Cruvellier, "The Massaquoi Trial: Double or Quits Before a Finnish Court", *Justice Info* (March 2021), www.justiceinfo.net/en/74574-massaquoi-trial-double-or-quits-before-finnish-court.html.
94   Sahana Devarajan, "Sierra Leone national accused of war crimes appears in Finland court", *Jurist*, 3 February 2021, www.jurist.org/news/2021/02/sierra-leone-national-accused-of-war-crimes-appears-in-finland-court/.
95   *Ibid.*
96   *Ibid.*
97   *Ibid.*
98   *Ibid.*
99   Judgment of 28 January 2021 – 3 StR 564/19, www.bundesgerichtshof.de/SharedDocs/Pressemitteilungen/DE/2021/2021019.html?nn=10690868.
100   *Ibid.*
101   *Ibid.*
102   *Ibid.*

since 2014, Ukraine recently adopted universal jurisdiction in Ukraine for crimes of aggression, genocide, crimes against humanity and war crimes.[103]

6. Conclusion

The remarkable shift in international law towards ending impunity through accountability is incontrovertible. The conventions emerging after World War II to prescribe crimes repugnant to humanity, as well as the accountability mechanisms that followed, established a firm foundation to ensure that those responsible for atrocity crimes would be brought to justice. This anti-impunity, pro-accountability foundation was reinforced by the adoption of both the responsibility to protect and universal jurisdiction principles.

International criminal law, including the statutes and the jurisdiction exercised by a long string of ever-evolving international criminal tribunals, brought forward the global rule of law agenda, and is one of the most significant tools to move the world closer to achieving its ambitious goal of justice for all.

Of course, it remains a central challenge to achieve consistent adherence by nation states. International justice is sadly not equitable. Too often powerful states escape accountability; the powerless cannot.

For example, during his last days in office, US President Donald Trump issued full pardons to four former military Blackwater contractors, who were earlier convicted of killing civilians during the Iraq wars.[104] A year earlier, Trump pardoned three military soldiers for murdering civilians in the Iraq and Afghan wars.[105]

Unsurprisingly, the pardons resulted in strong condemnation from human rights groups and Iraq. They argued that Trump's actions "violate US obligations under international law and more broadly undermine humanitarian law and human rights at a global level".[106]

President Donald Trump was not the only recent US president to embrace impunity. President Barack Obama failed to uphold accountability for those US officials accused of committing acts of torture during the so-called 'war on terror' after 9/11. President Obama stated that the country needed to "look forward as opposed to looking backwards".[107] The Obama administration made active efforts to assert impunity for Bush administration officials accused of

---

103   Gaurav Gupte, "Ukraine parliament adopts law allowing accountability for war crimes committed in Crimea", *Jurist*, 2021, www.jurist.org/news/2021/05/ukraine-parliament-adopts-law-allowing-accountability-for-war-crimes-committed-in-crimea/.

104   "Trump Grants Clemency to Former Blackwater Contractors Convicted of War Crimes in Iraq and Associates Prosecuted Following the Mueller Investigations" (2021) 115(2) *The American Journal of International Law* 329.

105   *Ibid.*

106   "US pardons Blackwater guards: an 'affront to justice' – UN Experts", UN News, 30 December 2020 https://news.un.org/en/story/2020/12/1081152. As quoted *ibid*, at 333.

107   Adam Sewer, "Obama's Legacy of Impunity for Torture", *The Atlantic*, 14 March 2018, www.theatlantic.com/politics/archive/2018/03/obamas-legacy-of-impunity-for-torture/555578/.

torture. Civil lawsuits by former detainees were blocked by the Administration based on the state secrets doctrine.[108] A US Department of Justice inquiry into alleged torture ended in no charges.[109] President Obama announced that he would provide absolute immunity for any official involved in torture that aligned with approved techniques by the Bush administration.[110] In the end, the Obama administration blocked all avenues – civil, criminal and professional – for any form of accountability for those US citizens who violated international criminal law.[111] Unfortunately, this idea of American exceptionalism when enforcing human rights is all too pervasive in US politics.

Other world leaders embrace a similar view of accountability. Recently, Russian President Vladimir Putin signed a new law that grants lifetime immunity to former Russian presidents, including from criminal charges, detention, arrest, search and interrogation.[112] They are to be immune in their person, as well as their personal effects, correspondence, residence and offices.[113]

It's important to note that the actual number of individuals held accountable for atrocity crimes is depressingly low. The 20th century shall be remembered as a time when more than 200 million civilians were killed in war, internal conflict, and as a consequence of repressive state regimes.[114] Yet, fewer than 900 persons have been held accountable for their crimes by international, regional or state courts.[115]

The 'impunity trend' sadly continues. The number of civilians killed in conflict between 2016 and 2020, was two-and-a-half times higher than in the previous five-year period.[116]

There also remains a legalistic split on the issue of impunity. In the Belgian Arrest Warrant case,[117] the International Court of Justice (ICJ) ruled on a dispute between Belgium and the DRC. The Belgian authorities had issued an arrest warrant for the DRC's minister of foreign affairs for having made various speeches inciting racial hatred. The ICJ found that, other than before

---

108   *Ibid*.
109   *Ibid*.
110   Glenn Greenwald, "Obama's justice department grants final immunity to Bush's CIA torturers, *The Guardian*, 31 August 2012, www.theguardian.com/commentisfree/2012/aug/31/obama-justice-department-immunity-bush-cia-torturer.
111   For instance, Gina Haspel, who oversaw a black-site where at least one detainee was tortured, was chosen to lead the CIA during the Trump administration (see Sewer, footnote 107 above).
112   M Tyler Gillett, "Putin signs laws expanding immunity and office-holding eligibility of former Russian presidents", *Jurist*, 24 December 2020, www.jurist.org/news/2020/12/putin-signs-laws-expanding-immunity-and-office-holding-eligibility-of-former-russian-presidents/.
113   *Ibid*.
114   See Mark Ellis, *Sovereignty and Justice – Balancing the Principle of Complementarity between International and Domestic War Crimes Tribunals* (Cambridge Scholars Publishing, 2014); see also M Cherif Bassiouni, "Assessing Conflict Outcomes: Accountability and Impunity" in M Cherif Bassiouni (ed), *The Pursuit of International Criminal Justice: A World Study on Conflicts, Victimization, and Post-Conflict Justice*, 2 Vols (Oxford: Intersentia, 2010), Vol 1.
115   *Ibid*.
116   See David Miliband, *Foreign Affairs*, "The Age of Impunity and how to Fight It", 13 May 2021.
117   Case concerning the Arrest Warrant of 11 April 2000 (*Democratic Republic of the Congo v Belgium*), Judgment, ICJ Reports 2002, at 3.

international criminal tribunals, foreign ministers would enjoy immunity in foreign national courts. Moreover, the Court found that under customary international law there was no "exception to the rule according immunity from criminal jurisdiction and inviolability to incumbent Ministers for Foreign Affairs, [even when] they are suspected of having committed war crimes or crimes against humanity".[118]

However, the international community continues to gravitate towards the goal of supporting the rule of law through international criminal law. Some have dismissed the possibility of the emergence or existence of this type of 'international rule of law'[119] at times even calling it a 'myth'.[120] However, I am not a student of this proposition. As proffered in this chapter, there are two elements common to the rule of law in every legal system and which have their genesis in international law: accountability and the fight against impunity.

In terms of atrocity crimes, customary international law is now clear – immunity for senior state officials does not exist for international criminal tribunals. At the national level, rulings are increasingly guided by the Charter of the Nuremberg Tribunal which declared that impunity for acts of government officials is inapplicable to acts which are condemned by international criminal law.[121] In short, states today continue to advance the position that *jus cogens* violations of international criminal law do not warrant immunity protection.[122]

With a fierce abhorrence to impunity and an unyielding demand for accountability, international criminal law provides a bedrock for the rule of law on both the international and national levels. Accountability for atrocity crimes is a core component of the rule of law that continues to reverberate throughout the international community.

---

118   *Ibid*, at para 58.
119   See Martti Koskenniemi, "The Politics of International Law" (1990) 1 EJIL 4; Jacob K Cogan, "Noncompliance and the International Rule of Law" (2006) 31 Yale J Int'l L 189.
120   Jacob K Cogan, "Noncompliance and the International Rule of Law" (2006) 31 Yale J Int'l L 189 at 206.
121   Formulation of the Nuremberg Tribunal Principles, ILCY B Vol 2, 103 (1950).
122   For example, see *A v Ministère Public de la Confédération, B and C* (2012) (Fed Cr Ct Switz, 25 July 2012).

Chapter 9. Rule of law and sex discrimination: women and the American judiciary

Mariah A Lindsay
University of Wisconsin-Madison
Allison M Whelan
University of Pennsylvania

1.   Introduction

Sex discrimination, sex inequality, and reproductive justice are pivotal battlegrounds in the 21st century, much like race and the 'color line' were during the 20th century (and continue to be today).[1] Scholars, activists, and lawmakers frequently perceive the 'rule of law'[2] as essential to eliminating discrimination and promoting various forms of egalitarianism, including sex equality. Hard legal rules are viewed as fundamental to "effectively addressing and eliminating social inequalities, because legal rules are thought to be transparently written and enacted, equally enforced, and independently adjudicated".[3] This chapter focuses on that third component – adjudication – by examining the role of women judges in protecting reproductive rights and promoting reproductive justice.[4] Scholars acknowledge an important role for women judges in enforcing the rule of law and ensuring access to justice for women.[5] Our question, therefore, is whether meaningful representation of women in the judiciary furthers the values of reproductive justice.[6]

---

1   See WEB Du Bois, *The Souls of Black Folks* (first published 1903, WW Norton & Co, 1999), pp5, 35 (describing Jim Crow laws and racial intolerance as defining and consuming democracy in the United States and yet hurting it as a nation); Michele Goodwin and Allison M Whelan, "Reproduction and the Rule of Law in Latin America" (2015) 85 *Fordham L Rev* 2577, 2578.

2   Despite the wide use of the term, there is no concrete agreement as to its definition. As defined in the 2004 Report of the Secretary General of the United Nations, the rule of law:

   refers to a principle of governance in which all persons, institutions and entities, public and private, including the State itself, are accountable to laws that are publicly promulgated, equally enforced and independently adjudicated, and which are consistent with international human rights norms and standards. It requires, as well, measures to ensure adherence to the principles of supremacy of law, equality before the law, accountability to the law, fairness in the application of the law, separation of powers, participation in decision-making, legal certainty, avoidance of arbitrariness and procedural legal transparency.

   UN Secretary General, *The Rule of Law and Transitional Justice in Conflict and Post-Conflict Societies: Report of the Secretary-General*, UN Doc S/2004/616 at 6 (23 August 2004).

3   Goodwin and Whelan (footnote 1 above), 2578.

4   The authors acknowledge that women are not the only people capable of becoming pregnant (eg, transgender and non-binary people) and in need of access to full reproductive health, rights, and justice. We also recognise that not all women have uteruses. While we use the word 'women' due to the nature of research we rely on (which often specifically identifies cisgender women) and because the chapter focuses on women, we do so with the intent of being inclusive of all women and people with uteruses.

The theory of critical mass is important when thinking about women's representation in the federal judiciary and elsewhere. The theory of critical mass refers to a minimum or sufficient percentage of individuals who share ideology or affinity, collectively believe in an ideal, or contribute to an action such that they are able to exert influence, inspire interest in their platforms, produce desired outcomes, and avoid tokenism.[7] Without a critical mass of women, sociological and normative illegitimacy can be produced, including within courts. Indeed, "[a] body that lacks a critical mass of women can produce and reify tokenism, and it can create barriers to meaningful participation and persuasion".[8] But when an organisation or entity achieves critical mass, there is a "potential to enhance governance and achieve substantive equality goals".[9] As explained by one of the foundational works on critical mass theory, "[g]roups fortunate enough to have a critical mass can enjoy the collective good", such as rights and privileges, but "less fortunate groups cannot".[10] Thus, for purposes of our research, if women judges exhibit distinctive behaviours in cases involving reproductive rights, then achieving a critical mass of women judges could have important implications for reproductive health, rights, and justice.

This chapter emerges at a time when women have made, and continue to make, tremendous strides towards equality. Nevertheless, there is still much work to be done, and stagnation and regression remain ever-present threats to women's full inclusion in the distribution of social, political, and economic power. Troublingly, the World Economic Forum's 2021 Global Gender Gap Report estimated that it would take an average of 135.6 years for women and

---

5   See, eg, Sandra Day O'Connor and Kim K Azzarelli, "Sustainable Development, Rule of Law, and the Impact of Women Judges" (2011) 44 *Cornell Intl LJ* 1; Vanessa Ruiz, "The Role of Women Judges and a Gender Perspective in Ensuring Judicial Independence and Integrity", UN Office on Drugs and Crimes, www.unodc.org/dohadeclaration/en/news/2019/01/the-role-of-women-judges-and-a-gender-perspective-in-ensuring-judicial-independence-and-integrity.html ("Achieving equality for women judges, in terms of representation at all levels of the judiciary and on policy-making judicial councils, should be our goal – not only because it is right for women, but also because it is right for the achievement of a more just rule of law. Women judges are strengthening the judiciary and helping to gain the public's trust."); Americas Quarterly, "Women in Robes", 24 July 2012, www.americasquarterly. org/women-in-robes/ ("[E]qual representation for women in the judiciary strengthens the rule of law and should be a goal across the Americas").

6   The concept of 'reproductive justice' has been defined as having "three primary principles: (1) the right *not* to have a child; (2) the right to *have* a child; and (3) the right to *parent* children in safe and healthy environments. In addition, reproductive justice demands sexual autonomy and gender freedom for every human being", Loretta J Ross and Rickie Solinger, *Reproductive Justice: An Introduction* (University of California Press, 2017), p9.

7   See Rosabeth Moss Kanter, *Men and Women of the Corporation* (Basic Books, 1977), pp206–221; Rosabeth Moss Kanter, "Some Effects of Proportions on Group Life: Skewed Sex Ratios and Responses to Token Women" (1977) 82 American J of Sociology 965, 966, 969–977; Drude Dahlerup, "From a Small to a Large Minority: Women in Scandinavian Politics" (1988) 11 *Scandinavian Political Studies* 275, 280; see also Pamela Oliver and others, "A Theory of the Critical Mass. I. Interdependence, Group Heterogeneity, and the Production of Collective Action" (1985) 91 American J of Sociology 522, 524 (calling attention to collective action depending on a critical mass). See generally Mancur Olson, *The Logic of Collective Action: Public Goods and the Theory of Groups* (Harvard University Press, 1965).

8   Michele Goodwin and Mariah Lindsay, "American Courts and the Sex Blind Spot: Legitimacy and Representation" (2019) 87 *Fordham L Rev* 2337, 2361.

9   *Ibid*, 2361.

10   Oliver and others (footnote 7 above), 542.

men to reach parity across key factors related to power and economic security worldwide due to the COVID-19 pandemic, instead of the 99.5 years found in the 2020 report – an extra 36 years.[11]

This chapter focuses on just one facet of sex inequality – women's representation on the US federal courts of appeals, which serves as a proxy for the larger problem of women's inequality. Sex inequality permeates myriad issues that constitute a violation of the rule of law, and sex inequality bears itself out far beyond the judiciary, in many industries and areas of life. This chapter highlights a few of those sectors to illustrate the continuing pervasiveness of sex inequality and how inequality in one area frequently intersects with and exacerbates inequality in others. Equality in one area cannot be truly attained and maintained without equality in others. This chapter highlights the areas below given their relation to the legal field, but they are by no means exhaustive.[12]

1.1   Law

The exclusion of women and their planned and unplanned, premature departures in the legal field are ongoing problems. In 2018, women surpassed the number of men enrolled in US law schools, yet they comprised barely one-third of practising attorneys.[13] United States law firms now hire and promote greater numbers of women and people of colour, but diversity decreases dramatically the higher one ascends the leadership ladder. In 2019, women made up 52.2% of law firm summer associates, 47.25% of associates, 40.35% of counsel, 30.61% of non-equity partners, 22.31% of equity partners, 24.68% of all partners (equity and non-equity), and 36.88% of all attorneys.[14] Women of colour fared worse, making up 19.89% of summer associates, 15.23% of associates, 7.35% of counsel, 5.30% of non-equity partners, 3.31% of equity partners, 3.88% of all partners (equity and non-equity), and 9.44% of all attorneys.[15]

---

11   The report looked at four indicators: 'economic participation and opportunity', 'educational attainment', 'health and survival' and 'political empowerment', World Economic Forum, *Global Gender Gap Report 2021*, March 2021, p15, www3.weforum.org/docs/WEF_GGGR_2021.pdf; World Economic Forum, "Pandemic Pushes Back Gender Parity by a Generation, Report Finds", 31 March 2021, www.weforum.org/press/2021/03/pandemic-pushes-back-gender-parity-by-a-generation-report-finds/.

12   Inequality experienced by women is far too pervasive to address comprehensively in this chapter, but similar trends appear across many industries, such as the fields of business and science, technology, engineering, and mathematics (STEM). For example, as of 21 May 2021, women accounted for only 41 of the 500 Fortune 500 chief executive officers (CEOs). Emma Hinchliffe, "The Number of Female CEOs in the Fortune 500 Hits an All-Time Record", *Fortune*, 21 May 2020, https://fortune.com/2020/05/18/women-ceos-fortune-500-2020/; see also Catalyst, "Historical List of Women CEOs of the Fortune Lists: 1972–2020", May 2020, www.catalyst.org/wp-content/uploads/2019/06/Catalyst_Women_Fortune_CEOs_1972-2020_Historical_List_5.28.2020.pdf. And in engineering, one report found that women make up only 15.7% of engineers, American Association of University Women, "The STEM Gap: Women and Girls in Science, Technology, Engineering, and Math", www.aauw.org/resources/research/the-stem-gap/; see also Goodwin and Lindsay (footnote 8 above), 2350 and n 86 (discussing and citing examples of inequality in the medical field).

13   Kristina Davis, "Why are Women Leaving the Law Profession?", *San Diego Union-Tribune*, 5 February 2018, www.sandiegouniontribune.com/news/courts/sd-me-women-law-20180205-story.html.

14   *2020 Vault/MCCA Law Firm Diversity Survey Report* (2020), p7, www.mcca.com/wp-content/uploads/2021/02/2020-Vault_MCCA-Law-Firm-Diversity-Survey-Report-FINAL.pdf.

15   *Ibid* p7.

And in the courtroom, research indicates that women are less likely to take on a leading attorney role.[16]

This chapter focuses on federal appellate judges and whether women's unequal representation in the federal appellate judiciary impacts reproductive health, rights, and justice. State court judges, however, also play a critical role in the protection of rights and furtherance of justice.[17] State judges are not representative of the US population, as women and people of colour are starkly underrepresented.[18] Specifically, recent data show that women make up approximately 51% of the US population, but they account for only 30% of state court judges.[19] People of colour make up almost 40% of the US population, and yet they make up less than 20% of state judges.[20] This disparity suggests that these gaps have their basis, at least in part, in historical and modern discrimination and exclusion.

1.2   Government

Women remain underrepresented in all levels of government in the United States. The first women elected to a state legislature (Utah) were Clara Cressingham, Carrie C Holly, and Frances Klock in 1894. Martha Hughes Cannon, also of Utah, was the first woman elected to a state senate in 1896. A woman was not elected to the US Congress until 1916, when Jeannette Rankin, from Montana, was elected to the House of Representatives. And finally, in 1948, Margaret Chase Smith, from Maine, became the first woman elected to the US Senate.[21]

Since those firsts, progress remains slow. As of mid-2021, only 58 women have served in the US Senate.[22] There were only 24 women senators serving as of mid-2021, which accounted for slightly less than a quarter of the Senate (24%), and only three senators (3%) were women of colour.[23] As of 15 January 2021, women made up roughly 27% of the House of Representatives, with

---

16   See Stephanie A Scharf and Roberta D Liebenberg, *First Chairs at Trial: More Women Need Seats at the Table* (American Bar Foundation and the Commission on Women in the Profession, 2015), p8, www.americanbar.org/content/dam/aba/administrative/women/first_chairs_final.pdf (finding, based on a random sample of cases filed in 2013 in the US District Court for the Northern District of Illinois, that men were two times more likely to appear as lead counsel or trial attorneys in civil cases and four times more likely to appear as trial counsel in criminal cases).

17   See, eg, David E Allen and Diane E Wall, "The Behavior of Women State Supreme Court Justices: Are They Tokens or Outsiders?" (1987) 12 *The Justice System Journal* 232 (finding that women state Supreme Court justices were more 'prowoman' on cases involving women's issues).

18   Tracy E Georgy and Albert H Yoon, *The Gavel Gap: Who Sits in Judgment on State Courts?* (American Constitution Society, 2018), pp2, 12, www.acslaw.org/wp-content/uploads/2018/02/gavel-gap-report.pdf.

19   American Constitution Society, "The Racial and Gender Breakdown of State Court Judges", www.acslaw.org/wp-content/uploads/2018/02/infographic-2.jpg.

20   Georgy and Yoon (footnote 18 above), p3.

21   Center for American Women and Politics, "Facts: Milestones for Women in American Politics" https://cawp.rutgers.edu/facts/milestones-for-women.

22   US Senate, "Women Senators", www.senate.gov/senators/ListofWomenSenators.htm.

23   *Ibid*; Center for American Women and Politics, "Women of Color in Elective Office 2021", https://cawp.rutgers.edu/women-color-elective-office-2021; see also Center for American Women and Politics, "Women Serving in the 117th Congress 2021–22", https://cawp.rutgers.edu/list-women-currently-serving-congress.

women of colour making up approximately 10.6% of the House.[24] At the state level, the number of women serving in state legislatures has more than quintupled since 1971, but as of October 2021, women still held only 28.3% of state senate seats and 32.0% of state house or assembly seats, with women of colour only holding 8.2% of state legislative seats.[25]

As to executive offices, the United States has not elected a woman president, and only as of January 2021 has the United States had a woman vice president. Vice President Kamala Harris also represents the first Black person and the first Asian American Pacific Islander (AAPI) to hold the office. At the state level, there have only been 47 women governors since the first woman governor was elected in 1925.[26] As of October 2021, only 20% of states have women governors.[27]

1.3   Academia

Academia, despite its progressive pretenses, is not immune to the historic and modern exclusion of women. This is true along the typical markers of success, such as tenure, institution, position, and salary. In 2018, women in the United States held nearly half of tenure-track positions, but held only 39.3% of tenured positions. In contrast, women held 57% of all 'instructor' positions, which are among the lowest ranking positions in academia. Following the pattern seen elsewhere, women of colour fared worse: Asian women held 5.3% of tenure-track positions and 3.5% of tenured positions, Black women held 3.8% of tenure-track positions and 2.3% of tenured positions, and Latinas held 3.1% of tenure-track positions and 2.6% of tenured positions.[28] At doctoral institutions in 2019–2020, women made up only 28.8% of those at the highest rank (professor), but held the majority of the lowest rank positions of instructor and lecturer (56.4% and 55.2%, respectively).[29] At the leadership level, women comprised 30% of college presidents in 2016,[30] and only 5% of college presidents were women of colour.[31]

24   Pew Research Center, "Women Make Up More than a Quarter of U.S. Congress' Membership", 14 January 2021, www.pewresearch.org/fact-tank/2021/01/15/a-record-number-of-women-are-serving-in-the-117th-congress/ft_21-01-06_womenincongress_1a/; "Women of Color in Elective Office 2021" (footnote 23 above).
25   Center for American Women and Politics, "Women in State Legislatures 2021", https://cawp.rutgers.edu/women-state-legislature-2021.
26   This number was determined by adding the number (as of 4 October 2021) of women governors listed on the National Governors Association's (NGA) website (10) to the number of former women governors (37) listed on the NGA's website using the "Find a Former Governor" database and searching by gender. See National Governors Association, "Governors", www.nga.org/governors/; National Governors Association, "Find a Former Governor", www.nga.org/former-governors/search/?govq_name=&govq_state=&govq_keyword=&govq_party_affiliation=&govq_birth_state=&govq_school=&govq_awards=&govq_military_service=&govq_status=&govq_profession=&govq_gender=Female&govq_race=&govq_natl_office_served=&govq_terms=.
27   "Governors" (footnote 26 above).
28   Catalyst, "Women in Academia: Quick Take", 21 January 2020, www.catalyst.org/research/women-in-academia/.
29   Glen T Colby, *The Annual Report on the Economic Status of the Profession, 2019–20* (American Association of University Professors, May 2020), p21, www.aaup.org/sites/default/files/2019-20_ARES.pdf.
30   American Council on Education, "Women Presidents" (2017), www.aceacps.org/women-presidents/.
31   American Council on Education, "Minority Presidents" (2017), www.aceacps.org/minority-presidents/.

Troublingly, the inequalities discussed above barely scratch the surface of the inequalities experienced by women. Contributing to this inequality is a history of sex bias located in the US Supreme Court's jurisprudence, which perpetuates harmful sex stereotypes relating to women's rights and autonomy.[32] Given this, "one measure of judicial legitimacy is sex representation[,] and not simply how judges cast their votes".[33] The composition of the judiciary matters not only for political persuasion but also for sex equality and competency. And when important matters such as the reproductive health and safety of women are at stake, who sits on the courts, in the legislature, and in executive offices "is more than a lofty academic concern ... The active presence of women in the body politic is a question of women's basic personhood, which implicates quality of health, life, and even death".[34]

This chapter builds on prior work by Michele Goodwin and Mariah Lindsay, described further in section 2, which argued that the legacy of explicit sex bias and discrimination with relation to political rights and social status begins with the government.[35] Based on two years of empirical research that examined each federal appeals court's record on abortion and each judge's vote on a particular case, they sought to determine whether women – regardless of whether they were appointed by a Democratic or Republican president – are more likely than their male counterparts to affirm reproductive rights. The short answer is 'yes'. The chapter then takes up where Goodwin and Lindsay left off, analysing whether President Donald Trump's judicial appointees – who are described as "ideologically driven" and "ultra-conservative"[36] – follow this pattern and, if not, how and why that matters for the rule of law and equality. Even though we found that President Trump's women judges appear to be 'outliers', disrupting the pattern discovered by Goodwin and Lindsay, we ultimately believe this further evidences the need for a critical mass of women on the courts and elsewhere in society. The chapter concludes by acknowledging the precarious nature of progress, while also noting reasons for optimism based on the Biden Administration's commitment to diversity and early actions to diversify the government.

---

32   For a more detailed discussion, see Goodwin and Lindsay (footnote 8 above), 2337.
33   *Ibid*, 2361.
34   *Ibid*, 2362. For example, data suggests that women are 14 times more likely to die carrying a pregnancy to term than terminating the pregnancy. This fact was noted by Justice Breyer in *Whole Woman's Health v Hellerstedt*, 136 S Ct 2292, 2315 (2016). See also Elizabeth G Raymond and David A Grimes, "The Comparative Safety of Legal Induced Abortion and Childbirth in the United States" (2012) 119 *Obstetrics and Gynecology* 215, at 215–219.
35   Goodwin and Lindsay (footnote 8 above).
36   See, eg, *Courts, Confirmations, & Consequences* (Lambda Legal, January 2021), pp1, 3, www.lambdalegal.org/sites/default/files/judicial_report_2020.pdf; National Organization for Women, "Do the Math: Trump Has Added More Right-Wing Judges to the Courts than Any Other President", 2 June 2020, https://now.org/media-center/press-release/do-the-math-trump-has-added-more-right-wing-judges-to-the-courts-than-any-other-president/; Mario Recio, "Trump Makes Mark on Texas Judiciary", *Statesman*, updated 16 February 2020, www.statesman.com/news/20200214/trump-makes-mark-on-texas-judiciary.

2.   The starting point: the research of Goodwin and Lindsay

Goodwin and Lindsay's study examined decisions in 302 abortion-related cases across US federal courts of appeals and assessed each judge's vote on each case to inform whether women judges are more likely than male judges to affirm reproductive rights. Their research "tells an important story about the composition of the federal appellate judiciary and the slow climb for women, including women of color, within the elite branches of the courts".[37] It also reflects the historical marginalisation of women within the law more generally. For example, women did not join the courts of appeals until well after they were established in 1891, when Florence Allen was appointed to the Sixth Circuit in 1934.[38] Another woman did not serve on a US court of appeals until 1968, when Shirley Ann Mount Hufstedler was appointed to the Ninth Circuit.[39]

Updated data show that as of 14 March 2021, 796 judges have served on the US courts of appeals, and only 99 – approximately 12% – of those judges have been women.[40] As of March 2021, there were 286 sitting judges in the federal circuit courts and only 76 were women. These updated data reaffirm what Goodwin and Lindsay found: "the historic legacy of women's exclusion and the recent trickling of inclusion".[41] That is, of the 99 women to ever sit on the courts of appeals, 76 were currently serving in March 2021. And despite recent progress, women still only represented approximately 27% of the judges serving on the bench in March 2021. And in two circuits, the First and Eighth, as few as two women had ever served as a judge. As noted by Goodwin and Lindsay, "[t]oday, this cannot be explained away by a lack of women law graduates or women's diminished intellectual capacity in relation to their male colleagues".[42]

This chapter focuses primarily on sex. Even so, it is critical to mention that the lack of diversity on the federal bench is not limited to sex, and includes other demographic factors such as race, class, religion, geography, and education. And when these demographics intersect – as they do for women of colour, for example – levels of inequality magnify. The majority of women judges serving at both state and federal levels are white, and white women are more likely than women of colour to be nominated to the federal judiciary. For example, even though women of colour were still significantly less likely to be

---

37   Goodwin and Lindsay (footnote 8 above), 2346.
38   The courts of appeals were established in the following years:
       First–Ninth: 1891.
       Federal: 1893.
       Tenth: 1929.
       District of Columbia: 1948.
       Eleventh: 1980.
       Ibid, 2351.
39   *Ibid*, 2351–2352.
40   Unless otherwise noted, all calculations and data are based on data provided by the Federal Judicial Center. See Federal Judicial Center, "Biographical Directory of Article III Federal Judges, 1789–Present", www.fjc.gov/history/judges/search/advanced-search.
41   Goodwin and Lindsay (footnote 8 above), 2352.
42   *Ibid*, 2368.

appointed under President Barack Obama, the effort he made to appoint women of colour to the federal bench has been praised as "historic" and "unprecedented", which "likely reflects the near absence of consideration of women of color for federal judgeships during prior administrations".[43]

Even with President Obama's historic appointments, the integration of women of colour to the federal appellate judiciary is slow and incomplete. To make this more concrete: as of March 2021, no women of colour have ever served as appellate judges on the Third, Fifth, Eighth, or Tenth Circuits. These circuits include Arkansas, Louisiana, Mississippi, New Mexico and Texas, among other states. Common among those states "are historically dense populations of people of color, as well as histories of racial subordination buttressed by institutional impediments of slavery and entrenched Jim Crow practices".[44]

With that background and understanding, Goodwin and Lindsay began with the question: "Do women judges, appointed by conservative presidents, review and judge reproductive rights cases outside the party line?"[45] In short, Goodwin and Lindsay found that they do, but "the answer, like the question, is not so simple".[46] They framed their questions "on Republican axes specifically because the Republican Party platform explicitly targets the dismantling of women's reproductive civil liberties and rights in several ways, including denying abortion access, limiting contraception, and abolishing or reshaping sex education".[47] This platform stands in contrast to the views of the majority of women in the United States.[48] Goodwin and Lindsay thus asked, "[m]ight women on the bench share the perspectives of the majority of American women?"[49]

Goodwin and Lindsay's research found that women judges more frequently write or join pro-choice majority, concurring, and dissenting opinions. Of the 302 abortion cases reviewed, only 160 (53%) had at least one woman sitting on the three-judge panel or *en banc* with the entire court. Of those 160 cases, 88 were pro-choice, 44 were anti-abortion, and 28 had 'mixed' holdings.[50] For purposes of this chapter, mixed holdings are those that could be categorised as simultaneously pro-choice and anti-abortion, including those where the

---

43   *Ibid*, 2354. For a more detailed discussion of the broader problem of homogeneity, see *ibid*, 2347–2348, 2353–2356, 2362–2368.

44   *Ibid*.

45   *Ibid*, 2368.

46   *Ibid*.

47   *Ibid*.

48   *Ibid*. For example, one survey found that 70% of women do not want *Roe v Wade* overturned and 60% of women say that abortion should be legal in all or most cases. Pew Research Center, "U.S. Public Continues to Favor Legal Abortion, Oppose Overturning Roe v Wade", 29 August 2019, www.pewresearch.org/politics/2019/08/29/u-s-public-continues-to-favor-legal-abortion-oppose-overturning-roe-v-wade/; see also NPR/PBS NewsHour/Marist Poll, "National Tables May 31st Through June 4th, 2019", June 2019, http://maristpoll.marist.edu/wp-content/uploads/2019/06/NPR_PBS-NewsHour_Marist-Poll_USA-NOS-and-Tables-on-Abortion_1906051428_FINAL.pdf#page=3 (reporting that 60% of women identified as 'pro-choice').

49   Goodwin and Lindsay (footnote 8 above), 2368.

50   *Ibid*, 2369.

outcome was arguably pro-choice, but where the rhetoric and language used by the court suggest it reached its decision only because it was 'required' to do so by precedent.[51]

Goodwin and Lindsay's study suggests that "[w]omen, no matter the party of the appointing president, are more committed to the autonomy, liberty, and reproductive rights of women than their male counterparts".[52] They found that "[i]n every circuit apart from the Fifth Circuit, in cases regarding abortion for which one or more women were sitting on the three-judge panel, [women] judges were more likely to join or write an opinion upholding reproductive rights".[53] Their research revealed that in the majority of abortion-related cases, women leaned towards pro-choice opinions. Thus, they predicted that broader representation of women in the judiciary could lead to greater protections for reproductive health, rights, and justice. They noted, however, that this is likely to occur only by achieving a critical mass of women in the judiciary and avoiding tokenism.[54]

3.   The outliers: President Trump's judicial appointments

This chapter builds on the research of Goodwin and Lindsay by analysing whether President Trump's judicial appointees follow the pattern they found. During his four-year term, President Trump appointed 229 judges to the federal courts, including three Supreme Court justices. As of mid-2021, more than a quarter of currently active federal judges were Trump appointees, which he achieved in just four years as president.[55] Of the 229 appointments, 174 (76%) were men (of which 85% were white) and only 55 (24%) were women.[56] Importantly, only 11 women of colour were appointed (comprising only 4.8% of all appointments), including two Black women, three Latinas, five AAPI women, one Native American woman, and one Chaldean woman.

---

51   For example, in *Price v City of Chicago*, 915 F 3d 1107 (7th Cir 2019), the majority upheld Chicago's abortion clinic buffer zone law, but the panel's opinion indicates that it did so only because the law was identical to a Colorado law upheld by the Supreme Court in *Hill v Colorado*, 530 US 703 (2000), and thus they were bound by precedent. The opinion stated that "*Hill* is incompatible with current First Amendment Doctrine" and that "[a]bortion clinic buffer-zone laws 'impose serious burdens' on core speech rights", *Price*, 1109, 1117 (quoting *McCullen v Coakley*, 573 US 464, 487 (2014)) (emphasis added). Much of the opinion was spent explaining why the court believed the Supreme Court's decision in *Hill* was wrong and ended by informing the plaintiffs that they "must seek relief in the High Court", *ibid*, 1119. See also *Planned Parenthood of Greater Texas Family Planning and Preventative Health Services, Inc v Smith*, 913 F 3d 551, 569 (5th Cir 2019) (Jones J, concurring in judgment) (concurring because of precedent, but writing separately to request rehearing *en banc* to reconsider the precedent case), *vacated Planned Parenthood of Greater Texas Family Planning and Preventative Health Services, Inc v Kauffman*, 981 F 3d 347 (5th Cir 2020) (*en banc*).
52   Goodwin and Lindsay (footnote 8 above), 2373.
53   *Ibid.*
54   *Ibid.*
55   John Gramlich, "How Trump Compares With Other Recent Presidents in Appointing Federal Judges", Pew Research Center, 13 January 2021, www.pewresearch.org/fact-tank/2021/01/13/how-trump-compares-with-other-recent-presidents-in-appointing-federal-judges/.
56   Unless otherwise noted, calculations and data are based on data provided by the Federal Judicial Center. See "Biographical Directory of Article III Federal Judges, 1789–present" (footnote 40 above).

For the courts of appeals specifically, President Trump appointed 54 judges in total, which includes Amy Coney Barrett, who was later appointed to the Supreme Court. Of those 54, 43 (80%) were men and 11 (20%) were women (again including Amy Coney Barrett). Forty-six (85%) were white and eight (15%) were people of colour. Importantly, President Trump did not appoint a single Black or Native American judge to the courts of appeals. Of the 54 judges, only two (4%) were women of colour: one AAPI woman and one Latina.

Shockingly, despite these low numbers, President Trump was slightly *more* likely than other recent Republican presidents to appoint women judges. Women accounted for approximately one-quarter of President Trump's federal judicial appointees (24%). This is slightly higher than the share of women judges appointed by Republican Presidents George W Bush (22%) and George HW Bush (19%), but below the proportion appointed by Democratic Presidents Obama (42%) and William Clinton (28%). However, President Trump appointed a smaller share of non-white federal judges than other recent presidents, including the prior Republican president, President George W Bush.[57]

President Trump's circuit court judges were very young, the youngest of any president since at least the beginning of the 20th century. According to *The Washington Post*,[58] which used data compiled by the Federal Judicial Center, President Trump's appellate judges were, on average, 47 years old when nominated, five years younger than President Obama's judicial nominees. Of the 54 judges appointed by President Trump to the federal courts of appeals, six were in their 30s, 20 were under the age of 45, and only six were older than 55. By comparison, President Obama nominated 55 appellate judges during his two terms, with none in their 30s, only six under 45, and 21 over 55.

President Trump's judicial appointments were also heavily influenced by the Federalist Society, a conservative legal group with increasing influence over the nomination and appointment of federal judges. Indeed, President Trump himself said during his presidential campaign that his judges would be "great", "conservative", and "picked by the Federalist Society".[59] He kept this campaign promise – an article from June 2020 states that all but eight of President Trump's 53 appointees are tied to the Federalist Society, a group described as "basically a breeding ground for lawyers who hate reproductive freedoms".[60]

To supplement Goodwin and Lindsay's research and to gain an understanding of the impact of President Trump's appointees on the federal appellate courts, women judges, and abortion jurisprudence, we conducted a similar review of each circuit court's record on abortion-related cases. We

---

57   Gramlich (footnote 55 above).
58   Micah Schwartzman and David Fontana, "Trump Picked the Youngest Judges to Sit on the Federal Bench. Your Move, Biden", *The Washington Post*, 16 February 2021.
59   Ian Millhiser, "Trump Says He Will Delegate Judicial Selection to the Conservative Federalist Society", *ThinkProgress*, 15 June 2016, https://archive.thinkprogress.org/trump-says-he-will-delegate-judicial-selection-to-the-conservative-federalist-society-26f622b10c49/.

focused on the circuits to which President Trump appointed judges and reviewed abortion-related cases decided between 1 January 2018 and 14 March 2021 and available on Westlaw at the time of our research, which took place during the end of March and beginning of April 2021.[61]

In total, we found 74 cases implicating the right to abortion. Of those 74 cases, 55 (74.3%) had at least one woman sitting on the three-judge panel or *en banc* with the entire court. This is a higher percentage than that found by Goodwin and Lindsay (52.5%), but it is important to note that a man was present in 100% of the 74 cases, and men were frequently in the majority. That is, while there were 19 all-men panels, there were no all-women panels. This reflects the history of the American judiciary and the importance of critical mass, as women can only make a difference when present and represented in similar numbers to men. As aptly stated by Justice Ruth Bader Ginsburg: "When I'm sometimes asked 'When will there be enough [women on the Supreme Court]?' and I say 'When there are nine,' people are shocked. But there'd been nine men, and nobody's ever raised a question about that."[62]

Women appointed by President Trump only served on panels in 10 of the cases reviewed. On the Fourth Circuit, Judge Allison Jones Rushing joined two anti-abortion opinions (including a dissent in an *en banc* case) and one pro-choice opinion.[63] On the Sixth Circuit, Judge Joan L Larsen wrote one anti-abortion majority opinion and joined one anti-abortion majority *en banc* opinion.[64] On the Seventh Circuit, then-Judge Amy Coney Barrett joined three anti-abortion opinions (two *en banc* dissents and one *en banc* majority) and one mixed opinion.[65] Interestingly, Judge Amy Joan St Eve wrote or joined only pro-

---

60 Lisa Needham, "Trump's 200th Judge Will Mean Decades of Fighting for Our Rights", *Rewire News Group*, 24 June 2020, https://rewirenewsgroup.com/article/2020/06/24/trumps-200th-judge/. Needham's article was written before Justice Barrett was elevated to the US Supreme Court and before Judge Kirsch replaced Justice Barrett on the Seventh Circuit. Judge Kirsch was also a member of the Federalist Society. Thus, 46 of President Trump's 54 total circuit court appointees are tied to the Federalist Society. See "US Senate Commission on the Judiciary, Questionnaire for Judicial Nominees: Thomas Lee Kirsch II", www.judiciary.senate.gov/imo/media/doc/Thomas%20Lee%20Kirsch%20II%20Senate%20Questionnair e%20(PUBLIC).pdf.

61 President Trump did not appoint any judges to the First Circuit or the Federal Circuit, and he did not appoint any women judges to the Second, Third, Fifth or Eighth Circuit. We found abortion cases by searching each circuit's cases on Westlaw from 1 January 2018 through 14 March 2021 using the term 'abortion'. The First Circuit and Federal Circuit, to which President Trump did not appoint any judges (men or women), did not decide any abortion cases during this period.

62 Jay Croft, "10 Quotes that Help Define the 'Notorious RBG' Legacy of Ruth Bader Ginsburg", CNN, 20 September 2020, www.cnn.com/2020/09/19/politics/best-ruth-bader-ginsburg-quotes-trnd/index.html.

63 *Mayor and City Council of Baltimore v Azar*, 778 F App 212 (4th Cir 2019) (anti-abortion); *Mayor and City Council of Baltimore v Azar*, 799 F App 193 (4th Cir 2020) (pro-choice); *Mayor of Baltimore v Azar*, 973 F 3d 258, 297 (4th Cir 2020) (Richardson J, dissenting) (anti-abortion).

64 *Planned Parenthood of Greater Ohio v Hodges*, 917 F 3d 908 (6th Cir 2019); *EMW Women's Surgical Center, PSC v Friedlander*, 978 F 3d 418 (6th Cir 2020).

65 *Planned Parenthood of Indiana and Kentucky, Inc v Commissioner of Indiana State Department of Health*, 727 F App 208 (7th Cir), *vacated*, 917 F 3d 532 (7th Cir 2018) (anti-abortion); *Planned Parenthood of Indiana and Kentucky, Inc v Commissioner of Indiana State Department of Health*, 917 F 3d 532 (7th Cir 2018) (Easterbrook J, dissenting) (anti-abortion); *Planned Parenthood of Indiana and Kentucky, Inc v Box*, 949 F 3d 997, 999 (7th Cir 2019) (mem) (Kanne J, dissenting) (anti-abortion); *Price v City of Chicago*, 915 F 3d 1107, 1109 (7th Cir 2019), *cert denied sub nom Price v City of Chicago, Illinois*, 141 S Ct 185 (2020) (mixed).

choice opinions (four in total), even in cases where Judge Barrett and others dissented.[66] Of the 55 cases with at least one woman sitting on the panel (Trump appointees and/or non-Trump appointees), 25 (45%) were pro-choice, 21 (38%) were anti-abortion, and 9 (16%) had mixed holdings.

Despite the small sample size, the pattern seen thus far suggests that President Trump's women appointees are not, in general, following the pattern found by Goodwin and Lindsay. That is, they do not appear more likely than their male counterparts to affirm reproductive rights. As discussed next, President Trump's judicial outliers expose the precarious nature of progress and reaffirm the importance of women achieving a critical mass not only in the judiciary, but in all areas of law and society.

4.   Why this matters: reproductive rights and the precarious nature of progress

Women's presence within the legal profession, and specifically the judiciary, matters because men too often fail to uphold the rights of women, particularly when women are vulnerable to abuse by state authorities.[67] And despite the rights affirmed by *Roe v Wade*[68] and *Planned Parenthood of Southeastern Pennsylvania v Casey*,[69] which provide merely a baseline for realising full reproductive autonomy for all women, many state legislatures continue to

---

66   These cases, however, were decided largely for procedural reasons and did not address the merits of any abortion law and therefore do not provide much insight as to how Judge St Eve might decide a case involving substantive issues of abortion law. See *Planned Parenthood of Indiana and Kentucky, Inc v Commissioner of Indiana State Department of Health*, 727 F App 208 (7th Cir), *vacated*, 917 F 3d 532 (7th Cir 2018) (voting to deny rehearing *en banc*); *Planned Parenthood of Indiana and Kentucky, Inc v Commissioner of Indiana State Department of Health*, 917 F 3d 532 (7th Cir 2018) (reinstating part of the panel's opinion that had been vacated on *en banc* review after a judge was found ineligible to vote on the *en banc* petition, which resulted in a lack of majority vote to hear the case *en banc* in the first instance); *Planned Parenthood of Indiana and Kentucky, Inc v Box*, 949 F 3d 997, 998 (7th Cir 2019) (denying appellants' petition for rehearing and rehearing *en banc*); *Planned Parenthood of Wisconsin, Inc v Kaul*, 942 F 3d 793 (7th Cir 2019) (mem) (denying state legislature's motion to intervene).

67   The 1927 decision in *Buck v Bell*, in which the US Supreme Court upheld a Virginia law permitting the compulsory sterilisation of individuals deemed socially, morally, or mentally 'unfit', illuminates this concern. For a more detailed discussion of this decision and other court cases that have affected women's rights and presence in the judiciary and other professions, see Goodwin and Lindsay (footnote 8 above), 2348–2352; see also *Buck v Bell* 274 US 200 (1927).

68   410 US 113 (1973) (holding that inherent in the Due Process Clause of the 14th Amendment is a fundamental right to privacy – balanced against the government's interest in protecting women's health and the 'potentiality of human life' – that protects a woman's right to choose whether to have an abortion).

69   505 US 883 (1992) (reaffirming *Roe* in a 5-4 decision and imposing a new 'undue burden' standard to assess abortion restrictions).

70   See Ruth Dawson and others, "An Even-More-Conservative U.S. Supreme Court Could Be Devastating for Sexual and Reproductive Health and Rights", Guttmacher Institute, updated 28 October 2020, www.guttmacher.org/article/2020/09/even-more-conservative-us-supreme-court-could-be-devastating-sexual-and-reproductive ("Justice Kavanaugh's confirmation in 2018 led antiabortion state policymakers to abandon all pretense with a new wave of abortion bans intended to cut off access and tee up cases for the Supreme Court to consider"); Elizabeth Nash and Lauren Cross, "2021 is on Track to Become the Most Devastating Antiabortion State Legislative Session in Decades", Guttmacher Institute, updated 14 June 2021, www.guttmacher.org/article/2021/04/2021-track-become-most-devastating-antiabortion-state-legislative-session-decades ("[S]tate policymakers are testing the limits of what the new U.S. Supreme Court majority might allow and laying the groundwork for a day when federal constitutional protections for abortion are weakened or eliminated entirely").

infringe on reproductive rights and are increasingly emboldened to do so as the judiciary becomes more conservative.[70] In fact, by mid-2021, the year was on track to be "the most damaging antiabortion state legislative session ever".[71]

On 9 March 2021, for example, Arkansas Governor Asa Hutchinson signed into law Senate Bill 6, a near-total ban on abortion. Under this law, abortion is allowed only when necessary to save the life of the mother during a medical emergency or to save the life or health of the fetus. It does not provide any exceptions for rape or incest. US District Court Judge Kristine G Baker blocked the Arkansas law temporarily, calling it "categorically unconstitutional".[72] The preliminary injunction remains in effect until further order from the court. In Texas, a state law went into effect on 1 September 2021, which bans abortions after a fetal heartbeat is detected.[73] This can be as early as six weeks' gestation – before many women know they are pregnant. Like the Arkansas law, there are no exceptions for rape or incest. Unlike most state restrictions on abortion, which are enforced by government officials, the Texas law "effectively deputiz[es] ordinary citizens" – Texas residents and non-residents – to sue clinics and others who violate the law.[74] The law awards them at least $10,000 per violation if they are successful. The law went into effect after the US Supreme Court, in a 5-4 ruling, declined to intervene to halt its enforcement. As of this writing, litigation is ongoing.[75]

There is no doubt that one purpose of these laws is to compel the Supreme Court to reconsider *Roe* and subsequent decisions that establish the right to an abortion. Indeed, the Arkansas bill itself states that "[i]t is time for the United States Supreme Court to redress and correct the grave injustice and the crime against humanity which is being perpetuated by its decisions in *Roe v Wade*, *Doe v Bolton*, and *Planned Parenthood v Casey*".[76]

State legislatures are achieving their goal. On 17 May 2021, the Supreme Court agreed to hear a case "concerning a Mississippi law that seeks to ban most abortions after 15 weeks of pregnancy", which is well before viability and, as a result, much earlier than what *Roe* and its progeny allow.[77] In addition to these extreme, near-total abortion bans, state legislatures also propose or pass

---

71   From 1 January 2021 through 7 June 2021, 561 abortion restrictions, including 165 abortion bans, were introduced across 47 states. Eighty-three of those restrictions had been enacted across 16 states, including 10 bans. These numbers are unprecedented. "To put those figures in context, by the same date in 2011 – the year previously regarded as the most hostile to abortion rights since *Roe* was decided – 70 restrictions had been enacted, including seven bans." See Nash and Cross (footnote 70 above).

72   *Little Rock Family Planning Services, et al v Jegley et al*, No 4:23-CV-00453-KGB, 2021 WL 3073848 (ED Ark 20 July 2021).

73   SB 8, 87th Legislature (Texas 2021).

74   Sabrina Tavernise, "Citizens, Not the State, Will Enforce New Abortion Law in Texas", *The New York Times*, updated 2 October 2021, www.nytimes.com/2021/07/09/us/abortion-law-regulations-texas.html.

75   Maggie Astor, "How the Supreme Court Quietly Undercut *Roe v. Wade*", *The New York Times*, 2 September 2021, www.nytimes.com/2021/09/02/us/politics/roe-v-wade-supreme-court.html.

76   SB 6, 93rd General Assembly, Regular Session (Arkansas 2021) (emphasis in original).

77   Adam Liptak, "Supreme Court to Hear Abortion Case Challenging Roe v. Wade", *The New York Times*, 17 May 2021, www.nytimes.com/2021/05/17/us/politics/supreme-court-to-hear-abortion-case-challenging-roe-v-wade.html.

legislation that seeks to chip away at abortion rights, rather than set up a case that would overturn *Roe* whole cloth.[78] Thus, if the Supreme Court is unwilling to go so far as to overturn *Roe*, abortion rights may be more likely to "die a death by a thousand cuts" through restrictive state laws under *Casey* rather than outright bans.[79]

The judiciary plays a key role in determining whether reproductive rights will be dismantled or affirmed and protected. Given that these state laws have constitutional implications, they will be litigated in federal courts. The role of federal appellate courts is particularly important because they are frequently the last stop before the Supreme Court, and most federal litigation ends there, meaning that their decisions are binding on lower courts within the particular circuit.[80] For these reasons, contemporary threats to dismantle reproductive rights and forging that platform through courts add urgency to evaluating the legitimacy of the judiciary. In the realm of reproductive health, these can be matters of life or death. Indeed, some of the states that are most hostile to abortion and other reproductive rights are those with the highest rates of maternal mortality.[81]

This chapter neither denies nor discounts the progress made in women's representation on the courts of appeals since their founding. However, women have not achieved a critical mass and, as of mid-2021, still make up only 26.6% of all sitting judges on the courts of appeals. As discussed in section 3, President Trump's appointees to the courts of appeals were 20.4% women, whereas Obama's appointees were 43.6% women. And President Trump did not appoint any women to four of the 11 courts of appeals to which he appointed at least one judge. Given Goodwin and Lindsay's prior research finding that men are less likely to affirm reproductive rights, this matters.

Even though President Trump appointed only 11 women judges to the

---

78   For example, a bill was passed and approved by the Governor of Oklahoma that allows only physicians to provide abortions. HB 1904, Regular Session (Oklahoma 2021). In February 2021, the Kentucky legislature overrode Governor Andy Beshear's veto of HB 2, which gives the state's attorney general greater authority to regulate, sue, and penalise abortion clinics for violations of state law or regulation. HB 2, Regular Session (Kentucky 2021). And a bill has been introduced in Arizona that expands the rights of health care facilities and providers to refuse to provide abortion services. SB 1362, First Regular Session (Arizona 2021). These are but a few examples, as 561 abortion restrictions were introduced in state legislatures between 1 January 2021 and 7 June 2021. See Nash and Cross (footnote 70 above).

79   Serena Mayeri, "How Abortion Rights Will Die a Death by 1,000 Cuts", *The New York Times*, 30 August 2018, www.nytimes.com/2018/08/30/opinion/brett-kavanaugh-abortion-rights-roe-casey.html; Justin Franz, "States Aim to Chip Away at Abortion Rights with Supreme Court in Mind", KHN, 2 March 2021, https://khn.org/news/article/anti-abortion-legislation-conservative-states-gnaw-at-roe-wade-destination -supreme-court/.

80   See US Courts, "Appellate Courts and Cases – Journalist's Guide", www.uscourts.gov/statistics-reports/appellate-courts-and-cases-journalists-guide. The courts of appeals hear more than 50,000 cases per year, with 10% or fewer being appealed to the US Supreme Court. Of those appealed, the US Supreme Court generally hears fewer than 100 cases per year. *Ibid.*

81   Arkansas, for example, had a maternal mortality rate of 45.9 per 100,000 live births in 2018. Of the 25 states reporting maternal mortality rates for 2018, Arkansas had the highest (45.9), followed by Kentucky (40.8), Alabama (36.4), Oklahoma (30.1) and Georgia (27.7). US Department of Health and Human Services, Center for Disease Control and Prevention, National Center for Health Statistics, "Maternal Mortality by State, 2018", www.cdc.gov/nchs/maternal-mortality/MMR-2018-State-Data-508.pdf.

courts of appeals, we acknowledge that this small number did not negatively impact the overall percentage of women judges on the appellate courts. On the date of President Trump's inauguration, 26.2% of sitting judges on the courts of appeals were women. At the end of his presidency, women made up 26.6% of all sitting judges on the courts of appeals. Thus, while President Trump did not reverse progress, he did little to achieve the goal of improving women's representation in the judiciary. Any period of stagnation, particularly one in which the women who are appointed to the courts are outliers with respect to their decisions on reproductive rights, is detrimental and puts women's reproductive rights and health at risk.

Furthermore, President Trump left a highly conservative mark on the entire federal judiciary, which will last for years to come. He appointed three Supreme Court justices and roughly as many appellate judges in just four years as President Obama appointed in eight (54 versus 55, respectively). As of mid-2021, more than a quarter of active federal judges were Trump appointees.[82]

Under Article III, section 1 of the Constitution, Article III judges "hold their offices during good behavior", which in practice means that many judges have long careers on the bench. As discussed above in section 3, President Trump's appointees were the youngest of any president since at least the beginning of 20th century. *The Washington Post* explains the import of this:

> *We can do some rough calculations to put the age advantage for Republican-appointed judges in perspective. Recall that Obama and Trump nominated almost the same number of appellate judges (55 and 54, respectively). Assume these judges all serve to the same retirement age, which is usually about 68 years old for appellate judges. Based on their ages at nomination – and assuming that other factors such as early death don't affect one group more than the other –* Trump's judges will serve on the bench for 270 more years than Obama's judges. *Take it a step further: Assuming that federal appellate judges decide, on average (and conservatively), at least several hundred cases per year,* Trump's judges will decide tens of thousands more cases than their Obama-appointed counterparts. *To put it bluntly: The age of judges matters.*[83]

Furthermore, the women appointed by President Trump show a troubling outlier trend. With respect to their decisions on reproductive health, rights, and justice, President Trump's conservative mark is playing out in ways not seen with women judges appointed by other Republican presidents.

Indeed, even if he had appointed more women, our research shows that thus far, the women appointed by President Trump appear to be outliers, in that they do not seem to follow the general pattern seen in Goodwin and Lindsay's prior research: that women judges are more likely to affirm reproductive rights,

---

82   Gramlich (footnote 55 above).
83   Schwartzman and Fontana (footnote 58 above) (emphasis added).

regardless of the appointing president's political party. We recognise that our conclusions are limited based on the small number of cases reviewed. Nevertheless, there will be significant ramifications for reproductive rights if the pattern we found continues, as women judges appointed by President Trump join forces with their male colleagues to issue decisions that curtail reproductive rights, setting the stage for one or more Supreme Court cases that could have broad, long-lasting consequences for women. And given their youth, President Trump's appointees will have decades to leave their mark.

We do not, however, think these findings discount the conclusions of Goodwin and Lindsay or suggest that achieving a critical mass of women judges is not important. Rather, we conclude that the comparatively extreme ideologies of President Trump's judicial appointees make them outliers, just as the Fifth Circuit was found to be an outlier in the prior research.[84] Indeed, President Trump's appointees appear more ideologically driven and are described as ultra-conservative.[85] For example, an analysis conducted by *The New York Times* of more than 10,000 published decisions and dissents (from all federal courts, not just the courts of appeals) through December 2019 found that "[w]hen ruling on cases, [President Trump's appointees] have been notably more likely than other Republican appointees to disagree with peers selected by Democratic presidents, and more likely to agree with those Republican appointees, suggesting they are more consistently conservative".[86] Another analysis found that President Trump's appointees were, on average, 20% more conservative than the appointees of President George W Bush.[87] Indeed, President Trump selected his appointees "for their rock-solid conservative credentials, including at least seven that had previous jobs with Mr. Trump's campaign or his administration".[88] Ultimately, all but eight of President Trump's

---

84   See Goodwin and Lindsay (footnote 8 above), 2381–2383 (finding that "women on the Fifth Circuit appointed by Republican presidents tend to vote closer to the ideological party line of the nominating president").

85   See, eg, *Courts, Confirmations, & Consequences* (footnote 36 above), pp1, 3; National Organization for Women (footnote 36 above); Recio (footnote 36 above) ("These are ultra-conservative jurists with records that erode critical rights and liberties" (quoting Daniel Goldberg, legal director of the Alliance for Justice)).

86   Rebecca R Ruiz and others, "A Conservative Agenda Unleashed on the Federal Courts", *The New York Times*, updated 16 March 2020, www.nytimes.com/2020/03/14/us/trump-appeals-court-judges.html.

87   Jon Green, "The Ideology of Trump's Judges", Demand Justice, January 2019, https://demandjustice.org/reports/ideology-of-trump-judges/.

88   Ruiz and others (footnote 86 above).

89   *Ibid*.

90   Susan B Anthony List, "About Susan B. Anthony List", www.sba-list.org/about-susan-b-anthony-list; see also, eg, Susan B Anthony List, "Pro-Life Victory: Judge Joan Larsen Confirmed", 1 November 2017, www.sba-list.org/newgsroom/press-releases/pro-life-victory-judge-joan-larsen-confirmed (celebrating the confirmation of Judge Larsen to the Sixth Circuit); Susan B Anthony List, "SBA List Praised President Trump's Expanded Supreme Court List", 17 November 2017, www.sba-list.org/newsroom/press-releases/sba-list-praises-president-trumps-expanded-supreme-court-list (praising Judges Amy Barrett and Britt Grant); Susan B Anthony List, "SBA List Celebrates Kyle Duncan's Confirmation to the Fifth Circuit", 24 April 2018, www.sba-list.org/newsroom/press-releases/sba-list-celebrates-kyle-duncan-confirmation-fifth-circuit; Susan B Anthony List, "SBA List Praises President Trump's Judicial Nominees", 12 September 2019, www.sba-list.org/newsroom/press-releases/sba-list-praises-president-trump-judicial-nominees (praising the nomination of Judge Barbara Lagoa for the Eleventh Circuit).

appointees were connected to the Federalist Society, nearly twice as many those of President George W Bush.[89] President Trump's judicial nominations and confirmations were also endorsed and celebrated by anti-abortion groups such as the Susan B Anthony List, an organisation with a mission "to end abortion by electing national leaders and advocating for laws that save lives, with a special calling to promote pro-life women leaders".[90]

The presence of a President Trump appointee on a panel also makes non-unanimous decisions more likely. Generally, there is a culture of consensus in most circuits, and the analysis performed by *The New York Times* found that appellate judges of both parties agreed with one another the majority of the time. But when there was not agreement, President Trump's appointees stood out. On panels with judges appointed by presidents of the same party, dissent occurred 7% of the time and that rate increased to 12% on panels with a mix of judges appointed by presidents of both parties. But when a President Trump appointee wrote an opinion for a panel with a single Democratic appointee, or served as the only Republican appointee, the dissent rate rose to 17%. This means that the likelihood of dissent was nearly 1.5 times higher if a President Trump appointee was on the panel.[91]

Because we conclude that President Trump's women appointees are outliers, achieving a critical mass of women judges who are not outliers (that is, who would follow the general pattern found by Goodwin and Lindsay) could help counteract the tendency of President Trump's appointees to uphold anti-abortion laws. Our updated research also shows, however, that a critical mass of women on the judiciary alone is not enough and that a period of outliers, whatever the cause, could have long-term, widespread detrimental consequences for reproductive health, rights, and justice. Women's representation and equality matter in all areas of life – be it political, economic, academic, social, or otherwise. Equality in one does not guarantee equality in another, nor does it guarantee that women's civil liberties will be protected, as our research shows.

With respect to reproductive rights and the role of the judiciary in protecting those rights, one could hypothesise that if women reach a critical mass in state legislatures and can exert meaningful influence, the role of the federal judiciary in protecting those rights might take on less importance. This might occur, for example, if states with a critical mass of women legislators are less likely to introduce and pass laws hostile to reproductive rights in the first place, such that no federal case would transpire. Future research could explore whether women legislators, regardless of their political party, are more likely to vote against anti-abortion laws and/or introduce or vote for pro-choice laws. Such research could also explore whether, once they achieve a critical mass, women legislators are better able to "exert influence, inspire interest in their

---

91   Ruiz and others (footnote 86 above).

platforms [such as reproductive health, rights, and justice], [and] produce desired outcomes".[92]

Further, it must be remembered that equality and diversity at the top, be it in the legislature, judiciary, academia, or otherwise, require equality and representation at the bottom, that is, in the pipeline. However, sheer numbers in the pipeline are not enough, and must coincide with more aggressive policies to end discrimination so that the women in the pipeline have an equal chance to move up.[93] The problem, however, is that achieving equality at and advancement from the bottom to the top generally require sufficient numbers at the top to champion the policies that will help those rise from the bottom. Thus, there must be a critical mass of women at the top to influence policies that will help women progress through the pipeline.

Moreover, women's ability to make a real impact is limited until they reach a critical mass. In our research, for example, of the 55 cases in which women were on the panel, women did not have an equal or meaningful presence in 34 cases (meaning there was only one woman on a three-judge panel or women represented less than 50% of the judges on an *en banc* panel). In other words, in 61.8% of the cases where women were on the panel, women alone were not present in sufficient numbers to alter the outcome of the case.

Dr Julie C Suk takes up the issue of equal representation by appealing to Pauli Murray's written testimony in support of the Equal Rights Amendment (ERA) before the Senate Judiciary Committee in 1970. That testimony suggested that "what the opponents of the Amendment most fear is not equal rights but equal power and responsibility".[94] Murray argued that the disproportionate power of men created a dangerous imbalance in society that would lead to an abuse of power and prevent progress on key issues of justice, including pollution, poverty, racism and war. She also identified the importance of the unique perspective and experience brought by women, which undoubtedly includes their perspective on reproductive health, rights, and justice. In line with critical mass theory, Murray suggested that the

---

92 Goodwin and Lindsay (footnote 8 above) 2361 n 148.
93 In academia, for example, merely increasing the pool of qualified women has not led to a commensurate number of women rising to the top levels of academia. Women still end up in lower paid jobs and less 'prestigious' positions and continue to earn less than men in comparable positions. See data discussed in section 2; see also Goodwin and Lindsay (footnote 8 above), 2368 ("Empirically, women continue to encounter barriers to nomination and confirmation to the federal bench (and other senior positions within the legal profession). And women experience fewer nominations to the federal bench by raw number and percentage. Today, this cannot be explained away by a lack of women law graduates or women's diminished intellectual capacity in relation to their male colleagues"). Data "clearly show that fewer women work in academia than would be expected, given the relatively comparable numbers of male and female graduate students currently entering the market", Kristen Renwick Moore and William F Chiu, "Gender Equality in the Academy: The Pipeline Problem" (2010) 43 *PS: Political Science and Politics* 303, 306. The same could be said about law firm partners, given the relatively equal representation of men and women law school students and law firm associates. See Davis (footnote 13 above) and accompanying text; Enjuris, "Law School Rankings by Female Enrollment" 2020, www.enjuris.com/students/law-school-women-enrollment-2020.html (reporting that in 2020, 54.09% of law students identified as women, 45.70% identified men, and 0.20% identified as other).
94 Julie C Suk, "A Dangerous Imbalance: Pauli Murray's Equal Rights Amendment and the Path to Equal Power" (2021) 107 *Virginia L Rev Online* 3, 14.

dangerous imbalance would persist until Congress was "composed of at least one-third women".[95] Fifty years after Murray's remarks, Congress has more women than ever before, but women still "only constitute twenty-five percent of Congress, still short of the one-third Murray proposed as an antidote to the 'dangerous imbalance' that impaired solutions to 'pollution, poverty, racism and war'".[96] As of mid-2021, women have yet to break the threshold of holding one-third of the seats in Congress, meaning there are not enough women to block a constitutional amendment, or the confirmation of a judicial nominee for that matter.[97]

As a final point, this is not just about equal representation, but also equal participation. If women's voices are not raised and heard, their presence will mean little. Our research does not focus on women's ability to participate on an equal basis, which is an important component of critical mass theory: the ability to exert influence and avoid tokenism. This should be explored in future work. One should consider, for example, whether President Trump's women appointees might feel implicit or explicit pressure to write or join opinions that align with what is expected of them. In the context of abortion, these expectations would lead them to affirm anti-abortion laws and strike down pro-choice laws. Future work could explore whether the length of time a judge has been on the bench influences a judge's decisions. That is, as they gain seniority and confidence in their positions, do they find their own voice, making them more likely to take positions that are contrary to expectations, such as writing a pro-choice dissent against an anti-abortion majority opinion? In the legislative context, one could explore whether women legislators are more or less likely to propose or vote for legislation on particular topics, such as reproductive rights. Such research could illuminate an underlying premise of this chapter – that representation and equality, everywhere and in every way, matter.

5.   Conclusion

The potential dismantling of reproductive rights that President Trump put in motion through his judicial appointments and other actions[98] is extremely

---

95   *Ibid*, 15.
96   *Ibid*.
97   See text accompanying footnotes 22–24 above; National Archives, "Constitutional Amendment Process", www.archives.gov/federal-register/constitution. ("The Constitution provides that an amendment may be proposed either by the Congress with a two-thirds majority vote in both the House of Representatives and the Senate or by a constitutional convention called for by two-thirds of the State legislatures"); Georgetown Law Library, "Nomination & Confirmation Process", https://guides.ll. georgetown.edu/c.php?g=365722&p=2471070 ("A simple majority of the Senators present and voting is required for the judicial nominee to be confirmed").
98   For example, one of President Trump's first acts in office was to reinstate and expand the 'global gag rule' (also known as the Mexico City Policy), which eliminates federal funding for non-governmental organisations abroad if they provide abortion counselling or referrals for abortion. He also issued a 'gag rule' that prohibits Title X providers from telling patients how to access legal and safe abortions. And in 2018 he became the first sitting president to directly address the annual March for Life anti-abortion rally. For a discussion of additional actions taken by President Trump that restricted access to abortion and reproductive health care more generally, see Planned Parenthood, "Donald Trump: President of the United States", www.plannedparenthoodaction.org/tracking-trump/player/donald-trump.

troubling. This chapter emerges at a time when "[j]udges ... have become the most consequential policymakers in the nation",[99] while at the same time they remain the branch of government least answerable to the people. Even though judicial independence and relative isolation are important for a governmental body that is supposed to adhere to fixed rules in an unbiased manner, they are far less so when the judiciary strays from its central and intended role. The legitimacy of the Supreme Court and lower federal courts are in question, as is their ability to protect civil liberties and civil rights, including the interests of women in matters of health and reproduction.

The many Supreme Court decisions, rooted in stereotypes, which banned women from serving on juries, denied them equal rights to contract for longer workdays like men, or restricted their range of employment exemplify this inequality. "The sex blind spot is a deep and abiding problem; it will persist in American politics and within courts until more women attain these offices."[100] And this cannot occur just in the judiciary – equal representation and participation everywhere matter.

Notwithstanding the stagnation and setbacks caused by the Trump Administration's actions and the outlier judges appointed by President Trump, there is reason to be optimistic that this was temporary. And despite President Trump's outlier women judges, we agree with the ultimate conclusion of Goodwin and Lindsay "that with more women on the bench, the interests of all women will advance".[101]

President Joseph Biden is taking steps to counter President Trump's impact on the federal courts. Through both words and actions, the Biden Administration showed an early commitment to diversity in the government, including the judiciary. The Biden Administration is the first to have a woman Vice President and, not only that, Vice President Harris is also a woman of colour. Additionally, President Biden's cabinet nominations included a record number of women, women of colour, and members of other underrepresented groups. Among others, President Biden nominated, and the Senate subsequently confirmed, the first Native American Cabinet leader (Deb Haaland, Secretary of the Interior); the first openly gay man to run a Cabinet department (Peter Buttigieg, Transportation Secretary); and the first openly

---

99   Ian Millhiser, "What Trump has Done to the Courts, Explained", Vox, 29 September 2020, www.vox.com/policy-and-politics/2019/12/9/20962980/trump-supreme-court-federal-judges.
100   Goodwin and Lindsay (footnote 8 above), 2384.
101   Ibid.
102   Brian Naylor, "Pete Buttigieg Confirmed as Transportation Secretary", NPR, 2 February 2021, www.npr.org/sections/president-biden-takes-office/2021/02/02/963217201/pete-buttigieg-confirmed-as-transportation-secretary; Nathan Rott, "Deb Haaland Confirmed as 1st Native American Interior Secretary", NPR, 15 March 2021, www.npr.org/2021/03/15/977558590/deb-haaland-confirmed-as-first-native-american-interior-secretary; Laurel Wamsley, "Rachel Levine Makes History as 1st Openly Trans Federal Official Confirmed by Senate", NPR, 24 March 2021, www.npr.org/2021/03/24/980788146/senate-confirms-rachel-levine-a-transgender-woman-as-assistant-health-secretary.

transgender federal official (Rachel Levine, Assistant Secretary for Health in the Department of Health and Human Services).[102]

President Biden's nominations for the federal judiciary follow this same pattern of intentional and thoughtful inclusion. His first 11 judicial nominations for the federal district courts and courts of appeals were highly diverse and included nine women, including seven women of colour. The two remaining nominees were also diverse and included a Black man and an AAPI man.[103] President Biden also pledged to nominate a Black woman to the Supreme Court if a vacancy occurs during his presidency.[104]

Taken together with Goodwin and Lindsay's work, our research offers a compelling case that representation in the judiciary and elsewhere matters. In government, this means that a critical mass of women is important in all three branches of federal and state governments. Our updated research shows that while women judges, on the whole, are more likely to affirm reproductive rights regardless of the appointing president, the pattern seen with President Trump's women appointees makes clear that one branch of government cannot be relied upon to protect women's interests. As the number of women in government grows, we cannot become complacent. Progress is precarious and as the impact of the Trump Administration shows, can easily stagnate or be reversed. Women have an important role to play in enforcing the rule of law and ensuring access to justice for women, and we must build institutions that allow for and encourage women to take on these roles in significant numbers. Justice, fairness, and the rule of the law depend on it.

---

103   See Ann E Marimow and Matt Viser, "Biden's First Slate of Judicial Nominees Aims to Quickly Boost Diversity in Federal Courts", *The Washington Post*, 30 March 2021; White House, "President Biden Announces Intent to Nominate 11 Judicial Candidates", 30 March 2021, www.whitehouse.gov/briefing-room/statements-releases/2021/03/30/president-biden-announces-intent-to-nominate-11-judicial-candidates/.

104   See John Fritze, "Biden Wants to Put a Black Woman on the Supreme Court, Putting Spotlight on Lack of Diversity in Lower Courts", USA Today, 17 February 2021, www.usatoday.com/story/news/politics/2021/02/17/supreme-court-advocates-ask-joe-biden-name-black-women-judges/6722856002/.

Chapter 10. Judicial independence in Islam

Essam Al Tamimi
Al Tamimi & Company

1. Introduction: the origins of Islam and Islamic law

The independence of the judiciary is an essential principle of the rule of law. The judiciary in Islam is supreme, impartial and of fundamental importance.

Islam is one of the three monotheistic religions. The Prophet Mohamed peace be upon him (pbuh), the chosen recipient and messenger of the word of God (Allah SWT) through divine revelations. Divine revelations are considered the direct words of Allah (SWT) and this is central to the birth of Islam.

In terms of dates, Islam dates from shortly before the Islamic (*hijri*) calendar. The *hijri* calendar commenced in AD622 and is named in connection with the *hijra* or migration of the Prophet Mohamed (pbuh) and his followers from Mecca to Medina, both cities currently in Saudi Arabia. The move from Mecca to Medina marked the first year of the Islamic calendar and we are currently at year 1442.

In Medina, Prophet Mohamed (pbuh) continued to receive divine revelations. On the strength of those revelations a community was built (arguably the beginning of the first Islamic state). As a result of the example provided by this community of faith in Medina, the subsequent structures of successive Islamic states was foreshadowed. The hallmark of these successor states is the application of the Divine Code of Law (*Sharia*), settled in substantially the form we recognise today under the reign of the Caliph Uthman.

Sources of law under *Sharia* are divided into revealed and non-revealed:

- The revealed comprises the Quran and *Sunna* or *Hadith* (referring to Prophet Mohamed's (pbuh) deeds and accepted citations by learned authorities on matters where the Prophet Mohamed (pbuh) had expressed approval or disapproval); and

- The non-revealed, or *Ijtihad*, consists of *Ijma* (the consensus of the community of scholars), *Qiyas* (reasoned analogy by Islamic jurists deducing what the aforementioned three sources (*Sunna*, *Hadith* and *Ijtihad*) would have said in response to a similar question) and *Istihsan* (seeking the most equitable solution according to Islamic jurists).

Added to the non-revealed sources of *Sharia* are also *Istislah* (seeking the best solution for the general interest according to Islamic jurists or, where this is not possible, by reference to what may be in the wider public interest) and *Taqlid* (precedents).

The main sources are mentioned in the following Quranic verses:

O ye who believe! Obey Allah, and obey the messenger, and those charged with authority among you. If ye differ in anything among yourselves, refer it to Allah and His Messenger if you do believe in Allah and the Last Day: that is best, and most suitable for final determination.[1]

The religion of Islam, transmitted by Prophet Mohamed (pbuh) in perfection of the prophets that came before him, was an expressly *human* model for people to follow. All prophets and scriptures were sent by God for the establishment of justice on Earth, as the Quran says:

We sent aforetime our apostles with Clear Signs and sent down with them the Book and the Balance (of Right and Wrong) that men may stand forth in justice.[2]

Islam is, therefore, not seen just as an abstract religion but as a practical way of life and, as a necessary corollary, as a system of justice.

The following provisions of the Quran explain the basis of justice which the Prophet Mohamed (pbuh) and any Muslim is subject to:

And if you judge, judge between them with justice.[3]

O you who have believed, be persistently standing firm in justice, witnesses for Allah, even if it be against yourselves or parents and relatives. Whether one is rich or poor, Allah is more worthy of both. So follow not [personal] inclination, lest you not be just. And if you distort [your testimony] or refuse [to give it], then indeed Allah is ever, with what you do, acquainted.[4]

O you who have believed, be persistently standing firm for Allah, witnesses in justice, and do not let the hatred of a people prevent you from being just. Be just; that is nearer to righteousness. And fear Allah; indeed, Allah is acquainted with what you do.[5]

Accordingly, impartiality and justice was and remains a very important characteristic of any Islamic judiciary as indicated in the *Quran* and implemented by the Prophet Mohamed (pbuh). After the death of Prophet Mohamed (pbuh) in 632CE, the subsequent leaders (or caliphs) headed the judiciary in the nascent Islamic state. Rightly guided caliphs followed the same practice as Prophet Mohamed (pbuh). As the Islamic states expanded beyond the Arabian Peninsula, governors in different states were then appointed to represent the caliph. These governors were appointed as judges, or they themselves appointed judges, to deal with the community's affairs.

---

1   Holy Quran, Sura 4, Aya 59.
2   Holy Quran, Sura 57, Aya 25.
3   Holy Quran, Sura 5, Aya 42.
4   Holy Quran, Sura 4, Aya 135.
5   Holy Quran, Sura 5, Aya 8.

Some may view the combination of the judicial and ruling power as contrary to the principle of the independence of the judiciary. However, the three branches of executive, legislature and judiciary operated independently and separately from each other under the supervision of the head of the state. At the time when Prophet Mohamed (pbuh) established the judiciary, there was no need for a specialised judiciary and Prophet Mohamed (pbuh) delegated some of his judicial powers to his companions who were not part of the executive. In Islam, a system of justice to protect the rights of the weak in society was seen as fundamental and the independence of this judicial system was respected, honoured and kept within the highest authority of the community. Prophet Mohamed (pbuh) did provide guidance during his lifetime. In an early *Hadith* it is reported that:

> *Mu'adh [(a judge appointed by Prophet Mohamed (pbuh) in Yemen)] said, "I will judge according to what is in the Book of Allah." The Prophet said: What if it is not in the Book of Allah?*
>
> *Mu'adh said, "Then with the tradition (Sunnah) of the messenger of Allah." Prophet Mohamed (pbuh) said: What if it is not in the tradition of the messenger of Allah? Mu'adh said, "Then I will strive to form an opinion (Ijtihad)." Prophet Mohamed (pbuh) said*
>
> *All praise is due to Allah who has made suitable the messenger of the Messenger of Allah.*

The system was in the hands of Prophet Mohamed (pbuh) during his lifetime and, thereafter, in the hands of the rightly guided caliphs Abu Bakr, Umar and Uthman. Only those who were most honourable and trustworthy were appointed as governors and given the judicial power to implement and interpret the *Sharia* principles derived from the Quran and *Sunna* in the event of any ambiguity or doubt (for the benefit of the defendant). Caliphs Abu Bakr and Umar were the first to separate the judiciary from the executive and entrusted the *Qadhis* (judges) with power to decide suits of a purely civil nature. The judges used to have great powers and respect even when it comes to state matters. A famous historical incident provides an example of the independency of judges. At the time of Ruler (Caliph) Omar Ibn Abdul Aziz, the Islamic army took over the land of Samarkand district. The people of Samarkand objected to Omar that the army had entered their city in violation of the Islamic rules. Omar appointed a judge and the judge ruled against the Islamic army and ordered the army to vacate the city.

2. The four major schools of Islamic thought and doctrine

Before *Sharia* principles and their application are elaborated on, it is important to first discuss the establishment of the four major schools of Islamic thought and doctrine that were founded (in the sequence which follows) after the death of Prophet Mohamed (pbuh), namely those under jurists Hanafi, Maliki, Al

Shafi'i and Hanbali. These scholars are preeminent among those who first construed the meaning of *Sharia* derived from the Quran and *Sunna*, helping Muslims in their prayers, daily life and transactional dealings and assisting judges in applying the principles of *Sharia* to ensure justice and equity.

Equity is considered a strong and fundamental principle of *Sharia*. The dispensation of adl (impartial justice) is the common concern of all Muslims and the *Ummah* (community) is collectively responsible for its administration. It is therefore *faradh kifayah* – an act where performance is required from the whole community and not from each individual.[6]

During Prophet Mohamed's (pbuh) time, Muslims not only followed Islamic principles derived from the *Quran* and *Hadith* but also adopted a practical *modus operandi* for the community. This was promulgated verbally by Prophet Mohamed (pbuh) and has become known in its written form as the Constitution of Medina. According to the Maliki school, this unwritten and customary set of principles constituted a formal agreement between Prophet Mohamed (pbuh) and all of the significant tribes and families of Medina, which included Muslims, Jews, Christians and pagans.

The Constitution of Medina was built upon the concept of one community of diverse tribes living under the sovereignty of one God.[7] It instituted peaceful methods of dispute resolution among diverse groups living as one people but without their assimilation into one religion, language or culture.[8] In particular, the Constitution was drawn up to bring an end to inter-tribal fighting and established, among other things, a judicial system for resolving disputes relating to warfare, tax and civil matters.

Although the Constitution of Medina was originally an unwritten and customary set of principles to underpin the establishment of an Islamic community, over time the concepts it contains further evolved under the guiding principles of *Sharia*. These principles were applied by the four juristic schools mentioned above, based on their interpretations of *Sharia*, in order to clarify any ambiguity that may cause controversy among believers. The doctrines and schools are still followed today to interpret different principles of *Sharia* and religious practice.

3.   The principles of Islamic law

The Islamic legal principles that apply to the judicial system can be found in both the Quran and the *Sunna*. The seven key principles are as follows:

- "No punishment is given on dubious proof." *Hadith* (narrated by Aishah) that the Messenger of Allah (pbuh) said: "Avert the legal penalties from

---

6   Ubaidullah ibn Masud Sadr al Shariah, Ubaidullah ibn Masud, 2 Al Taudhih.
7   L Ali Khan, "Commentary on the Constitution of Medina", in Hisham M Ramadan (ed), *Understanding Islamic Law: From Classical to Contemporary* (2006).
8   Hisham M Ramadan (ed), *Understanding Islamic Law: From Classical to Contemporary* (2006).

the Muslims as much as possible; if he has a way out then leave him to his way, for if the Imam makes a mistake in forgiving it would be better than making a mistake in punishment."[9]

- "No one can bear the burdens of another."[10]
- "People before you were ruined because if a noble man committed theft, he would go unpunished and if a poor man committed theft he would be punished."[11] (In other words, a criminal's social status or family influence should not obstruct the administration of justice.)
- "O you who have believed, be persistent in standing firm for Allah, witnesses in justice, and do not let the hatred of people prevent you from being just. Be just; that is nearer to righteousness, and fear Allah; indeed, Allah is acquainted with what you do."[12]
- "Indeed, Allah commands you to render trusts to whom they are due and when you judge between people to judge with justice. Excellent is that which Allah instructs you. Indeed, Allah is ever hearing and seeing."[13]
- "Act justly. Indeed, Allah loves those who act justly."[14]
- "And say, 'Do [as you will], for Allah will see your deeds, and [so, will] His Messenger and the believers'. And you will be returned to the Knower of the unseen and the witnessed, and He will inform you of what you used to do."[15]

The above are the fundamental principles for judicial process in Islam. However, the Quran and *Sunna* contain not only the judicial process but also the substantive law in dealing with civil, commercial and criminal matters. These assist judges in the implementation of justice and application of these principles to different cases that are heard before a judge. A very good synopsis of how the application of *Sharia* law works in practice, given this wealth of source material, is provided by the learned French authority, Georges Affaki:

> *Shari'a's casuistic approach mandates that the relevant rule be extracted from the general principles of the Koran and the Sunna. This process, called Ijtihad, allows competent scholars to use analogical or deductive reasoning such as Qiyas, Istihsan and Istislah to identify the solution to a given problem. The rules thus extracted will have a heightened normative nature were they to benefit in addition from Ijma', the Shari'a scholars' consensus.*[16]

---

9   At-Tirmidhi (1424).
10 Holy Quran, Sura 35, Aya 18.
11 *Hadith* – narrated by Urwa bin Az Zubair (Bukhari 4304).
12 Holy Quran, Al Maida, Sura 5, Aya 8.
13 Holy Quran, Al Nisa, Sura 4, Aya 58.
14 Holy Quran, Al Hujurat, Sura, Aya 8.
15 Holy Quran, Al Toba, Sura 9, Aya 105.
16 Commission on Islamic Finance, Proposal, Group on Governing Law and Dispute Resolution in Islamic Finance, 21 September 2009.

As the Islamic community grew into a series of states, certain issues became more complex. Thus, new principles were adopted through the four schools of jurisprudence. The creation of new rules and regulations dealt with fresh issues that arose both in day-to-day life and in the administration and governance of the Islamic states.

The most comprehensive and famous law that incorporated and codified some of the *Sharia* principles and introduced modern legal principles to deal with a number of civil and commercial issues was the *Majalla*. This was published by the Ottomans to help with the administration of the Ottoman Empire. It specifically provided the judges with procedures to deal with cases and a substantive body of law with which to adjudicate matters.

On the periphery of Europe, the independence of the judiciary from the executive system is also seen as a vital principle of the rule of law. The concept can, arguably, be seen in the Magna Carta (1215), although that document is controversial. The context in which the document was produced is often neglected. Claims are made for its foundational import (particularly in the United States) which are questionable. Four aspects which are frequently cited are of particular note:

- It was the first document to challenge the authority of the English king, and it served to protect his people from feudal abuse. It established the rule of law, meaning that the law itself should be the absolute ruler and not the monarch.

  The document could equally be interpreted as a kind an oligarch's charter – governing the conduct of the head oligarch towards his *capo regime* with no application to the wider English population who were, at the time, still subject to Norman colonial rule.

- It set out the principle of *habeas corpus*, or right to due process and a trial by jury: "No free man shall be seized or imprisoned, or stripped of his rights or possessions, or outlawed or exiled ... except by the lawful judgment of his equals or by the law of the land."

  The key terms here are 'free man' and 'equals', each of which were categories which in 1215 only could apply to the colonial Norman aristocracy. The Magna Carta was of no avail to the Jewish population of England who in 1218 were obliged to wear an identifying badge (under the Edict of the Badge), and who were expelled outright in 1290 under the Edict of Expulsion. For most normal English people of this era the semi-mythical outlaw character of Robin Hood – a kind freelance distributor of justice would have had more resonance.

- Not only did it grant all free men the right to due process, but it also set out the principle of proportionality such that the punishment for a crime must be proportionate to the crime itself.

  Hardly. See above.

- The liberties guaranteed in the Magna Carta were not limited to a privileged elite; they were the rights of all the free subjects of the monarch.

  Flat out wrong – again note the word 'free'. It should be noted that England was only part of what was a multi-polar feudal empire at the time. French was the *lingua franca* of the court until much later. French was the mother tongue of every English king from William the Conqueror (1066–1087) until Henry IV (1399–1413). Henry IV was the first to take the oath in English, and his son, Henry V (1413–1422), was the first to write in English. That the Magna Carta has come to achieve such prominence in terms of an English foundational national myth perhaps shows an understandable desire to stake a claim for some kind of moral *bona fides* in the historical record. What we tend to lose sight of is that, during this period, the English were themselves the colonised.

Nonetheless, and despite its somewhat anachronistic and sentimental treatment, the Magna Carta was and remains an important document. It did curtail the absolute power of the monarch and set a precedent for so doing. Looking towards mainland Europe during the same epoch, the Statute of Kalisz (1264) is perhaps a better analogue to the Constitution of Medina. A law adopted by the King of Poland to cater for an influx of migrants escaping persecution in the west, the law provides a concrete basis for their presence in the state recognising differences and, because of those differences, enshrining certain key rights in the interests of societal harmony. The Statute was ratified by subsequent Polish Kings in 1334, 1453 and 1539. Like the Magna Carta, the Statute has various anachronistic claims made about it regarding human rights.

The principles claimed by its modern supporters for the Magna Carta have always been present within Islamic societies and were commonly used by judges and the caliphs in their governing of the Islamic state.

It is well established from history that as societies and civilisations evolved and grew, they naturally learned from each other and adopted the principles and styles of other civilisations. The Islamic state was no different. The integrity, independence and process of the judicial system in Islam was founded on a solid foundation from the date of the establishment of the Islamic states. The importance of a judicial system and the independence of judges, along with the principle of justice itself, have all been recognised as key principles for the success and the sustainability of Islam.

The religion of Islam is based on justice, fairness and equality. Adjudication in a fair and independent way remains extremely important. The Quran stresses that it is the fundamental duty of the messengers of Allah to protect the rights of all the people and to establish a society in which the rights of all people are guaranteed on the basis of equity and justice.

4.   The rule of law in Islam

The establishment of the judiciary in Islam highlights the importance that Islam has attached to justice and to its smooth and impartial administration. This is demonstrated by the cases at the time Islam was founded. These cases evidence how Islam truly comprehended and applied the principles of impartiality and accessibility more than 1,400 years ago.

One *Hadith* that clearly illustrates the principle of independence and impartiality is when Prophet Mohamed (pbuh) was head of the Islamic state in Medina. He was petitioned to intercede for a noble lady who had committed theft. In response, the Prophet Mohamed (pbuh) said:

> *The nations before (us) were destroyed because if a noble person committed theft, they used to leave him, but if a weak person amongst them committed theft, they used to inflict the legal punishment on him. By Allah, if Fatima, the daughter of Muhamed, committed theft, Muhamed would cut off her hand!*[17]

This *Hadith* illustrates that even if the Prophet Mohamed's (pbuh) daughter had committed a crime, notwithstanding his position as the head of Islamic state, he would have implemented the same criminal punishment upon his daughter without favour.

After the death of the Prophet Mohamed (pbuh), the first caliph (successor) was Abu Bakr Al Siddiq who ruled the Islamic states which were mainly in the Arabian Peninsula, Iraq and part of Iran. Before his death, Abu Bakr named Umar as his successor. This was a decision that was accepted by the large community because of Umar's record of early and enormous service to Islam. Umar Ibn Al-Khattab became caliph in 634CE. He was known for his pious and just nature, which earned him the epithet *Al-Farooq* (the one who distinguishes between right and wrong).

Umar appointed a judge in Al Kufa, a city in Iraq – Judge Abu Moosa Al-Ash'ari. Umar also appointed Omar Ali Ibn Abi Taleb as judge in the capital ensuring a separation of judicial authority. Umar wrote a letter to the Abu Moosa advising him on how to rule as a judge for the people in Iraq, doubtless drawing on the earlier *Hadith* regarding the Prophet Mohamed's (pbuh) interaction with Ibn Jabal regarding the proper enforcement of judgments. The letter states the following:

> *Pronouncing judgment is an established and unequivocal ordinance and followed practice. You must try to understand the case which comes before you because the pronouncement of a judgment which cannot be put into effect is of no use. Treat people equally in the way you attend to them and hold court so that a nobleman may not expect you to be partial to him and a weak man may not despair of your justice. The onus of proof is on [the] plaintiff and the oath on the one who denies [the charge]. Conciliation is permissible between Muslims, except a conciliation*

---

17   Holy Quran, Sura 5, Aya 41.

which makes licit forbidden or forbids what is licit. Set a term for a person who advances a plea, taking into consideration a potential right and giving him a deadline to produce a proof. If he produces a proof, he will receive his due; if not, it is permissible to issue a judgment against him – doing so will remove any doubts, will clear any ambiguities and will leave no excuse behind. Let not a judgment which you judged yesterday, but over which you re-consulted yourself and were guided to your rectitude, prevent you from retracting to justice/right, for nothing can invalidate justice and retraction to justice/right is better than long persistence in a thing which is invalid. The Muslims are persons whose testimony is admissible (they are udool) except for a person who has received a whipping for [an offence against morality] involving a fixed penalty, or from whom false testimony has been experienced, or one who is suspect on account of client relationship [to a litigant] or lineage. Allah is well aware of your hearts and averts [punishment] from you on account of evidence and oaths. Pay attention to comprehending a matter that has no Qur'anic indication or practice of the Prophet applicable to it and become acquainted with similarities and analogies and then after that, compare matters. Then have recourse to that which is the most preferable to Allah and most in conformity of them to justice/right as you see it. Have a care to avoid impatience, vexation and annoyance with people and denying the rights of the litigants when they are on the right side. If you do so, Allah will confer reward and give you a good name. For whoever has a sincere intention to establish the truth, even against his own interests, Allah will suffice him and protect him from the people. And whosoever decks himself out for the world with something other than what Allah knows of him, Allah will bring shame upon him for Allah accepts worship only if performed with good intention. So keep in mind Allah's rewards both in this life and in the hereafter.[18]

This letter clearly sets out the basic principles of Islam and *Sharia*, the fundamental principles upon which justice is based, and the judicial independence and integrity that most modern-day societies try to achieve. This letter was not written by a professor or a scholar in a law school. It was written by a Bedouin, a warrior in the Arabian Peninsula, born in the city of Mecca, a dear companion of Prophet Mohamed (pbuh), who worked with him for the establishment of the Islamic states. During his caliphate, Umar Ibn Al-Khattab was known to be very just and fair in addition to being very strong and tough in his approach to some matters. He learnt to apply the principles of Islam derived from the Quran and *Sunna*. He summarised some of those principles in the above-mentioned letter, and the letter encapsulates principles matched by those behind present-day international law – the independence and integrity of the judiciary.

There is a lot of emphasis in the letter on the principle of equality before the

---

law, the presumption of innocence, a fair hearing in public, the need for the judge to be independent and impartial, and respect for the rights of the parties. The letter established the need for a transparent procedure during the hearing and a ruling to be made by applying the law. It also emphasised the need not only to guarantee justice and independence but also to be seen as just and independent. The final decision had to be made free from pressure or inducement. This letter also provides a reminder to the judge to remember that God is fully aware of his actions (and therefore of the need to be just and to apply equitable rights in *Sharia*).

This letter was written nearly 1,400 years ago – its relevance today is as fresh as it was when first authored. The principles contained within it enable any judge to reach a sound ruling and to follow a proper procedure for trial, and it also provides the basis for an independent judiciary.

5.   Practical application of *Sharia*

It should be noted that the Islamic judicial system does not limit the judicial process to Islamic principles of *Sharia*, which today are criticised by modern scholars who have no real knowledge or understanding of the application of those principles or the *Sharia* process.

To illustrate the application of the principles found in *Sharia* even among the caliphs, a dispute before Caliph Umar in Medina involving Ali Bin Abi Talib can be recounted. (Ali was one of the most influential and respected persons in Islam and was the first cousin of Prophet Mohamed (pbuh). He was also the fourth caliph of Islam.)

At the time when Umar Ibn Al-Khattab, the second caliph, was the caliph and the judge, Ali Bin Abi Talib lost one of his shields – he believed it was stolen. At a time when he was working in the market, he realised that his shield was on offer to be sold by a Jewish merchant. He argued with the merchant that it was his shield and it was stolen, while the merchant argued that he purchased it legitimately and the shield was his. Following a long argument, they both agreed to go to Judge Umar Ibn Al-Khattab to argue the case before him. Ali Bin Abi Talib and the merchant walked to the courtroom, which was presided over by Judge Umar Ibn Al-Khattab. As they entered the court, naturally Umar Ibn Al-Khattab received both parties and greeted Ali Bin Abi Talib – who was known to him as a prominent person of the community – with warm greetings and asked him to sit down by calling him father of Hassan and welcoming him. The merchant objected to the style in which his opponent was received by the court. Judge Umar Ibn Al-Khattab acknowledged his mistake and decided to dismiss the case because there was misconduct by him in the process by favouring one of the parties at the court hearing as against the other. The case was dismissed and the Jewish merchant was allowed to keep the shield. Ali Bin Abi Talib agreed to the judgment as well as acknowledging the misconduct at the hearing.

This story is well documented in Islam's judicial history, among other similar cases of justice and trials before the court in Islam. These cases not only demonstrate the importance of the independence and impartiality of the judge but also the need for a lack of prejudice against other religions before the judiciary. It is therefore an example of a strong judicial process. It is also established – as we have learned recently in modern society – that justice must not only be done but must also be seen to be done. People – rich or poor, from high society or otherwise – must be treated equally before the court; all are equal before the law.

Islam does not permit any discrimination on the basis of race, colour, religious affiliation, or social or economic status. The code that Judge Umar Ibn Al-Khattab followed in deciding the case against Ali Bin Abi Talib is this basic Islamic rule of *Sharia* – the only principles that Judge Umar Bin Al-Khattab had to follow in determining cases before the court. Notwithstanding Ali's status in the community and relationship to the Prophet Mohamed (pbuh), the dispute was still referred to the judicial authority to determine under the law. No one is above the law and the law is available and accessible to all. The judicial system is the only process to determine disputes among people in commerce and in their conduct.

6.   The rule of law in modern-day Islam

There is a question that is often asked nowadays: if all these principles of Islamic law were to be fully applied within society and the judicial system, why is it that the judicial systems in certain Middle Eastern and African states in the 19th and 20th century did not progress to the level and standard that could be seen during the time of the Prophet Mohamed (pbuh) and the caliphs?

It is a true and realistic assessment that the Middle East and North Africa did not progress but rather lost their direction, until recent years where there have been some efforts to develop and modernise their judicial systems. This is attributed to three very important and crucial factors which have affected Islamic states and their institutions (but not their judicial systems). They are as follows:

- Following the internal fights between factions within Islam, the Ottoman Empire was a Turkish-dominated empire. In the main, soldiers within the Islamic states took control of most of the Arab states. In other words, most of the Arab states in the Arabian Peninsula, the Levant and, to some extent, North Africa were ruled by the Ottoman Empire. That empire spread east and west and ruled the region for more than 400 years. However, during the last 100 years of their rule, which started shortly before World War I, the Ottoman Empire suffered from serious internal problems as well as weak government. As a consequence, corruption emerged within the political as well as the judicial systems.

This was accompanied by a weaker understanding and poor knowledge of *Sharia* within those states, which ultimately infected the judicial institutions in the Middle East and contributed to a decline in the relevant Middle Eastern countries, especially with respect to law, knowledge, science, innovation, education and religion.

- As a result of the division of the Ottoman Empire provided in the Sykes–Picot Agreement (where the countries involved were under the 'protection' of the British and the French), colonialism in the Middle Eastern states occurred and contributed to the decline of the Middle East. During this time, very little investment was made in infrastructure, education, healthcare or anything that would benefit the Middle Eastern states. If anything, those states were either in the process of being used for the benefit of the occupying states or were starting resistance movements that in some cases lasted decades. Not only was there no investment in infrastructure but also none in the judicial system or the judiciary. There were isolated improvements in major economic hubs such as Baghdad, Beirut and Cairo where they had good legal systems, but those were not sufficient and were limited to those capital cities. By and large, Middle Eastern countries (like England in 1215 at the time of Magna Carta) were still under the control of the colonial nations and suffered the consequent effects.

- The independence movement which took place in the 1930s until the 1960s in most Middle Eastern countries depleted all the countries' resources. This had nothing to do with Islam. The struggle not only destroyed the infrastructure in a lot of countries but also destroyed any efforts to invest in any of their institutions or infrastructures, including the legal and judicial systems. Worst of all, these movements brought about dictatorships and oligarchies and inexperienced regimes that had no knowledge of working with and maintaining legal organs, let alone an independent judicial system.

It was only recently, particularly during the late 1970s and the 1980s, that some of the countries in the Middle East started to invest in and work towards building a good judicial system. With the establishment of modern constitutions, proper legal systems, transparency, independence and the growth of the media, proper judicial systems and processes were once again starting to be introduced into Middle Eastern and North African countries.

The principles of the rule of law always existed, and the evidential records of that are available; the assistance of UN models and norms was not needed. However, the implementation of *Sharia* was flawed and led to a dark period in the history of the Middle East that has lasted more than 200 years. The correct principles are nevertheless now being reiterated and referenced in modern laws and modern constitutions today. Table 1 shows how the 20th and 21st centuries saw the birth of several such constitutions. Notable exceptions would be the Kingdom of Saudi Arabia and the State of Israel each of which, although having a basic law and a number of key derivative laws, do not have a formal constitution. Moreover, in the case of the Kingdom, the Basic Law provides that the Quran is the constitution.

Table 1: Formal written constitutions in modern-day Middle Eastern nations

Country	Year of first constitution	Year of current constitution	Number of constitutions to date
Bahrain	1973	2002	2
Iran	1906	1979	2
Iraq	1925	2005	7
Jordan	1952	1952	2
Kuwait	1962	1962	1
Lebanon	1926	1926	1
Palestine		2003	4
Qatar	1972	2004	2
Saudi Arabia	1992	1992	1
Turkey	1921	1982	4
United Arab Emirates	1971	1971	1

A serious effort has been made by most Middle Eastern countries to modernise their judicial systems, which paradoxically means going back to the true practice that was in force more than a thousand years ago. As Mark David Welton states:

The Islamic world, too, has a devotion to the Rule of Law that has prevailed through much of its history and while severely impaired in the nineteenth and twentieth centuries by Western colonization and its aftermath, has resurfaced, as a deserved virtue, fully compatible with Islamic law and tradition.[19]

Ultimately, the judiciaries of the Middle Eastern states have a strong legacy to look to in the basic principles of Islam, in which the judiciary's independence and the rule of law are supreme and guaranteed.

As mentioned above, the Islamic culture has a huge repository of practices and principles that serve as references and bases upon which new practices should be built. However, due to the development in the human life, the need is necessary to consider and develop new practices based on the Islamic culture and its foundations of justice, equality and independence that were referred to above.

---

19   Mark David Welton, "Islam, the West and the Rule of Law", 19 *Pace Int'l Law Review* 169 (2007), available at http://digitalcommons.pace.edu/pilr/vol19/iss2/2.

Chapter 11. Rule of law programmes: a primer

Michael Maya
International Bar Association

Since the publication of the first edition of this book, several trends have stood out as threats to the rule of law. None, however, is more ominous than China's transformation from a country singularly focused on elevating the economic well-being of its own citizens, to one that, seemingly overnight, signalled its intention to vigorously promote its model of governance to other countries. China's marketing is backed up by more than talk, with its generously funded Belt and Road Initiative a central feature of China's global charm offensive.

To state the obvious, the 'China model' is decidedly unfriendly to the rule of law, and of course democracy as well.[1] It is, after all, the world's premier surveillance state, the likes of which even George Orwell might have dismissed as an impossibility.[2] It also is profoundly corrupt, as most Chinese who have had run-ins with the local communist party bureaucracy can attest to. Sadly, it is an increasingly brutal and paranoid country, something virtually any journalist, democracy activist, human rights lawyer or Uyghur or ethnic Kazakh in Xinjiang Province also can attest to.[3]

---

1   It also is unfriendly to global public health. China's failure to adhere to the rule of law did not give rise to the COVID-19 pandemic, but its absence surely was the chief, and arguably most consequential, accelerant. Had China had an independent media free to report on the first suspected cases of COVID-19, and had it not suppressed and 'disappeared' whistle-blowers, there is little doubt it could have altered COVID-19's trajectory, and dramatically so. In fact, a University of Southampton study estimated China could have reduced the pandemic's spread by a staggering 95% had it heeded the calls of whistle-blowers and instituted anti-pandemic measures just three weeks earlier, or by 86% had interventions commenced two weeks earlier. Such is the nature of pandemics, where every day counts. See www.southampton.ac.uk/news/2020/03/covid-19-china.page. Ironically, the American Bar Association's Central European and Eurasian Law Initiative spearheaded in 2005 a Rule of Law Symposium at which one of the sessions was presciently titled "Pandemics and the Rule of Law". It would be a harbinger of events to come, with panelists agreeing that countries not bound by the rule of law – especially repressive regimes – represented an existential threat to the world. Why? Among other things, such countries generally lacked a free press capable of sounding the alarm about an incipient pandemic. Fifteen years later, China and COVID-19 would follow the doomsday scenario foretold at the 2005 Symposium all too faithfully, with disastrous consequences for the world.
2   In 2021, Freedom House once again rated China as "not free", one of 54 countries so designated. In fact, China was among the 12 *least* free countries in the world, earning its inclusion in Freedom House's "Worst of the Worst" category, alongside North Korea, Turkmenistan, Eritrea, Syria, etc.
3   Both the Biden and Trump Administrations have labelled ongoing abuses in Xinjiang Province a genocide; so, too, have several think tanks and human rights NGOs. Whether China's conduct in Xinjiang rises to the level of genocide is unsettled, but it is a virtual certainty that it has violated most of the crimes of humanity enumerated in the Rome Statute, the International Criminal Court's guiding standard. Further, its relentless repression in Hong Kong has been chilling. On 17 June 2021, police escorted *Apple Daily* editors and executives out of their building in handcuffs, the final nail in the coffin

The likelihood of a hot war between China and the United States is unlikely, but still frighteningly possible given China's designs on Taiwan, a US ally that China claims as its own. Thus, a likely best-case scenario is that we will be consigned to yet another multi-decade Cold War, certain to be as disruptive and perilous as the previous one, which pitted the West against a vanquished, and dangerously humiliated Russia, a country that, for decades, seemingly kept the Soviet Union together with glue, duct tape and the KGB.[4]

In a perfect world, where facts not only matter, but win the day, oddsmakers would have China losing the new Cold War, and losing it decisively. One need only look at Hong Kong and Taiwan to conclude the China model is a poor substitute for the rule of law and democracy. Whether one looks to the United Nations Human Development Index, the World Happiness Index or most other indices that shed light on the overall well-being of a country, the China model cannot even compete with Hong Kong and Taiwan, which, but for their embrace of the rule of law and democratic norms, are largely mirror images of China. That is, in many key respects – ethnically, culturally, linguistically – they are strikingly similar. Yet, they have wildly outperformed Mainland China, and if left alone, they would continue to do so, owing in large measure to their adherence to the rule of law.

The China model seems to be succeeding at providing only one of the three things most people covet in life once their basic needs are taken care of: (1) growing prosperity – yes; (2) justice and fairness – no; and (3) to be left alone – no. It is no accident that Hong Kong, now firmly in Beijing's clutches, is declining in all three categories after a remarkable, multi-decade run, most of it under the aegis of the United Kingdom, a rule of law stalwart that gave us the Magna Carta. All of this is to say that promoting the rule of law, and promoting it vigorously, has never been more important. Why? Because China is more formidable and arguably a far greater menace to the rule of law and democracy than the Soviet Union, the latter a congenital economic laggard. China's 'ideology' combined with its vast resources are far more compelling to onlookers than was Soviet ideology coupled with its crippled economy and persistent scarcity. What, other than China, is a deeply worrying menace to the global rule of law? Sadly, it is the decline of the rule of law in the United States.[5]

---

for Hong Kong's vaunted, once raucously free press. The final edition of the *Apple Daily* was on 24 June 2021, with Hong Kongers vying to get their hands on a copy of its very final, million-strong print run. The *Apple Daily* posted its final digital version the previous day.

4   Technically, the former Soviet Union comprised 15 countries. The three Baltic countries – Estonia, Latvia and Lithuania – were dragooned into the Soviet Union in 1940, and until the Union's collapse in 1991, were the most openly defiant of Moscow's hegemony. By 2004, all three Baltic countries had joined the European Union, and today are classified by the World Bank as high-income countries. According to the IMF, in 2021, Estonia's GDP per capita was $26,470. Russia, sandwiched between the Maldives and Malaysia, had a GDP per capita of $11,654.

5   Freedom House observed in its 2021 *Freedom in the World* report that: "Over the past 10 years, the U.S.'s aggregate score has declined by 11 points, placing it among the 25 countries that have suffered the largest declines in this period." Nearly a third of the United States' decline came in 2020 alone.

That, together with the shattering of democratic norms, particularly in the last five years, undermine US soft power, arguably the most compelling power of all, especially when it comes to winning hearts and minds in the developing world. Foundations, NGOs and other institutions that once looked abroad as the most sensible place to invest their rule of law dollars might be wise to look for ways to direct some of their largesse at a weakened US, perhaps beginning by funding civic and rule of law education for American youth.[6]

1.   Introduction

Rule of law promotion efforts were first undertaken nearly 60 years ago by a small group of lawyers and professors, with funding from a handful of government donors and foundations. Together, the sum total of individuals involved in these early efforts might have had a difficult time filling a high-school assembly hall. In the past 30 years, however, there has been an explosion of rule of law promotion efforts. Today, it is a *bona fide* industry.[7] The World Bank, the European Commission, the United Nations, the US Department of State, the US Agency for International Development (USAID) and numerous other national aid agencies and private foundations are all actively involved in promoting the rule of law in both low- and lower middle-income countries around the world. Individuals who were, or are now, involved in rule of law promotion efforts number well into the thousands. Most are lawyers, but many are not.

The discussion of rule of law promotion efforts in this publication is divided into two chapters. This chapter provides a brief primer on past rule of law promotion efforts, tracking the arc of the rule of law promotion movement over the last 60 years. Further, it identifies donors and implementers active in the rule of law field today, the substantive areas in which they work most intensively (eg, judicial reform) and the modes of assistance they employ most frequently. Both this and the next chapter were written with the following audiences in mind:

---

6   One of the gold standards for civic education was established by the creators of School House Rock's cartoon, "How a Bill Becomes Law". This once ubiquitous 'infomercial' was aimed at schoolchildren watching Saturday morning cartoons. It is the reason countless American adults know how legislation is passed in the US Congress. Lessons also may be drawn from Hong Kong, once famous for its culture of corruption. Hong Kong provides one of the most dramatic and successful efforts to promote a culture of lawfulness and reduce corruption in the modern era. In the wake of student-led protests against corruption in 1973, Hong Kong, then under British rule, responded by creating an Independent Commission Against Corruption (ICAC) that instituted a three-pronged approach to combating corruption: (1) law enforcement, (2) prevention and (3) community education. The oft-studied Hong Kong model is impressive on many levels, most notably its creative use of the media, such as the airing of television and radio dramas based on actual corruption cases, coupled with public education initiatives that enlisted television, radio and print to disseminate information about ICAC's work. Notably, Japan's post-World War II schoolchildren were exposed to American-sponsored civic education courses and textbooks, explaining at least in small part how Japan managed to transform itself into the democratic, rule of law-abiding country it is today.
7   Over 700 entities are listed in the International Bar Association's *Rule of Law Directory*. See www.roldirectory.org/Default.aspx.

- seasoned rule of law professionals who implement field-based programmes in developing countries;
- individuals who manage field-based rule of law programmes from their organisation's 'home office' (ie, ABA Rule of Law Initiative or Chemonics, both headquartered in Washington DC);
- donor agency and foundation personnel who oversee rule of law programmes, either in the field or in their organisation's headquarters;
- host country recipients of rule of law assistance (eg, judges, lawyers, justice ministers);
- individuals who are new to the rule of law promotion field; and
- commentators and academics who write and/or teach about the rule of law and promotion efforts.

The next chapter identifies a handful of potential trends that may affect how rule of law assistance providers carry out their work in the future, and areas in which more assistance may be needed.[8]

Together, these chapters will address the challenges faced by donors, implementers and host country beneficiaries with what is arguably the most vexing conundrum in international development: how to help control corruption and build a rule of law culture in countries where recalcitrant elites as well as entrenched and often rapacious bureaucrats resist change. It is not difficult to identify the habits and practices that together form a millstone around a country's neck (ie, nepotism, patronage networks), preventing the rule of law from taking hold and frustrating development generally. However, replacing old habits and practices with new ones that approach international standards or best practices, or simply constitute a modest advance, is maddeningly difficult. It can take several generations – and it usually does.

To be sure, donors and implementers also cling to bad habits and practices that undermine well intentioned efforts to advance the rule of law in the developing world. As a consequence of these practices, resources are squandered, and not just financial resources. Another resource is the finite hopefulness of a cynical public, which often responds with a collective rolling of the eyes when their government announces another hollow anti-corruption initiative, often at the urging of a donor country or international organisation whose funding or other spoils are being sought by those in power. Despite these challenges and shortcomings, rule of law promotion efforts have proved to be an essential tool for bringing countries into the world's rule of law community and, in so doing, improving the lives of citizens around the world.

---

8   Some of the best suggestions found in Chapter 12 of this book were offered by seasoned implementers, donors and academicians interviewed for this chapter, most of them with 25–35 years of experience in the rule of law field.

2.   Overview of rule of law promotion efforts

Before delving into the many dimensions of rule of law promotion efforts, and technical assistance in particular, it might be helpful to first describe how rule of law promotion fits within the larger field of international development. That field is large and growing, especially now that China has entered the field with great vigour and resources. Development assistance increased from roughly $60 billion in 2000 to at least $161 billion in 2020.[9] Some of the most generously funded areas of assistance include: agriculture (eg, food security), transportation, economic development, education, environment/climate change, health, humanitarian relief and, lastly, democracy and governance.

Technical assistance in the rule of law sphere is one of the myriad types of assistance that donors provide, mostly to lower- and lower-middle-income countries with a weak rule of law, such as DR Congo and the Philippines, respectively. This assistance comes mainly from: Australia, Japan, and wealthy Western countries; a handful of international institutions such as the United Nations and the World Bank; and private foundations, primarily based in the United States and Western Europe. Like every form of international development, there are many reasons why various governmental and private institutions engage in rule of law promotion efforts. Some donors, especially foundations, are driven by sheer altruism. Just as often, donors, namely governmental donors, are motivated by self-interest or the interests of commercial enterprises that lobby for rule of law assistance in countries in which they have *existing* investments, or in promising countries in which they would like to make *prospective* investments. Governmental donors also regularly seek to promote the rule of law in their so-called backyard – such as the EU assisting poorer countries in Eastern Europe or the United States providing assistance to Central American countries – in a bid to thwart illegal immigration, drug trafficking issues or other ills.

Rule of law promotion generally falls under the rubric of democracy and governance (D&G) or some variation on that phrase. In addition to rule of law promotion, key thematic areas falling under the D&G rubric include: elections

---

9   See www.oecd.org/dac/financing-sustainable-development/development-finance-standards/official-development-assistance.htm. The true figure assuredly is much greater than $161 billion, as this does not include, for example, generous assistance provided by China, especially in Africa and Asia. This figure *does* include the contributions of all the OECD Development Assistance Committee (DAC) members (eg, United Kingdom, Japan, United States, Germany, New Zealand, Australia), as well as non-DAC members (Estonia, Hungary, Israel, Latvia, Russia, Turkey and the United Arab Emirates). While $161 billion is a sizeable sum, it is not much more than the GDP of Algeria. In 2018, China created a new aid agency called the China International Development Cooperation Agency (CIDCA). CIDCA does not seem eager to engage in rule of law promotion efforts; however, commendably, it does appear eager to link its Belt and Road Initiative with the UN's 2030 Agenda for Sustainable Development (aka Agenda 2030), which includes Sustainable Development Goal 16 that focuses on "Peace, Justice and Strong Institutions". See Kristen A Cordell, *Chinese Development Assistance: A New Approach or More of the Same?* (Carnegie Endowment for International Peace, March 2021). See also White Paper defining China's approach to foreign assistance published in January 2021 by the China International Development Cooperation Agency, http://epaper.chinadaily.com.cn/a/202101/11/WS5ffb7d83a31099a23435323b.html.

and political processes, civil society, labour rights, media freedom (including internet freedom), governance, anti-corruption and human rights. Some donors lump rule of law, anti-corruption and governance together, at times simply calling it 'governance'. Typically, assistance in the D&G arena is not the most generously funded form of assistance provided by government donors or foundations, although no individual or institution appears to have successfully determined with any precision the amount spent annually on promoting the rule of law.[10]

While donor-funded technical legal assistance efforts are the focus of this chapter, it goes without saying that there are countless other means by which the rule of law can be promoted, such as: the establishment of law-related accession criteria that countries must meet to join highly prized 'clubs' such as the European Union, NATO and the World Trade Organization; the use of diplomacy, including the strategic use of carrots and sticks; the establishment of war crimes tribunals or transitional justice initiatives in the wake of armed conflict; reporting by the media and human rights organisations on breakdowns in the rule of law; and the publication of indices that encourage countries to improve their performance in law-related areas.[11]

2.1   Areas of assistance

Assisting host country partners with legislative drafting and writing or reforming constitutions is the best-known form of rule of law assistance, but it represents a small fraction of the actual assistance provided today. Some of the primary areas in which donors and implementers devote their efforts are listed below:

- *judicial reform:* training judges on, for example, newly passed laws and fair trial standards; helping to establish or increase the capacity of judicial training centres; strengthening judicial associations; assisting in drafting judicial codes of ethics;
- *legal profession reform/prosecutorial reform:* continuing legal education programmes that focus on skills development, especially in response to the passage of new laws or to facilitate transitions to hybrid adversarial/

---

10   The lower end of estimates of worldwide expenditure on rule of law promotion is probably $3 billion a year, with the US government, the World Bank, European Commission and United Nations topping the list of most generous donors. There are no reliable figures on the amount foundations and other private sources devote to rule of law promotion efforts, but the largest appears to be the Open Society Foundations, which in 2020 devoted nearly $400 million of its roughly $1.2 billion annual budget in four areas: (1) justice reform and the rule of law, (2) human rights movements and institutions, (3) economic equity and justice, and (4) equality and anti-discrimination. Of that amount, $107 million was spent on programmes within the United States, perhaps in response to perceived incursions on fundamental rights and the rule of law by the Trump Administration.

11   A few examples include the World Justice Project's Rule of Law Index, the State Department's *Trafficking in Persons* report, Transparency International's Corruption Perceptions Index, various Freedom House reports, and the World Bank/International Finance Corporation's *Doing Business* report, which measures the quality of business regulations, their enforcement and the overall ease with which business entities are able to operate in 190 countries.

inquisitorial systems; bar association development; assisting in drafting codes of ethics;

- *court reform:* building and refurbishing courts; installing advanced case management equipment and procedures; trial monitoring and reporting; training non-legal court personnel to provide more user-friendly court services, and to communicate more effectively with the public; helping to re-orient the courts to become more 'people-centred';
- *access to justice:* increasing the public's access to legal counselling and recourse, including, increasingly, through paralegal programmes in both rural and urban areas; supporting 'travelling lawyers' programmes and implementing mobile courts that provide legal services and bring justice to people in remote areas; training non-lawyers and non-paralegals (ie, nurses) who regularly come in contact with underserved populations to provide basic legal assistance;
- *human rights:* working with non-governmental organisations (NGOs) and, to a lesser degree, governments, to address abuses and discrimination directed at minority and disadvantaged populations, especially, in recent years, the LGBTI community;
- *transitional justice:* helping local communities or entire countries to redress legacies of human rights abuses through judicial and non-judicial means, usually a short period after a conflict has subsided; integrating child soldiers into society;
- *police reform:* training on human rights and specialised crimes, especially human trafficking;
- *traditional/informal/customary justice:* working to link informal justice systems with state institutions, and training local arbiters of justice and community members (ie, 'elders') on how to avoid violations of basic human rights standards and/or discriminatory outcomes, especially with respect to women and girls;
- *anti-corruption/public integrity:* helping to draft comprehensive anti-corruption legislation, assisting anti-corruption commissions to operate more effectively, and devising means to empower the public to join the fight against corruption, including through public education; training law enforcement on asset tracing and other investigative skills needed to combat money laundering;
- *women's rights:* enhancing access to justice for women, and combating violence against women, particularly domestic violence but also rape and workplace violence;
- *legislative strengthening:* working with parliaments to improve bill drafting capacity and various legislative processes;
- *legal education:* curriculum reform, teaching interactive training techniques, and opening law school clinics that often serve indigent clients;

- *criminal law:* working to rewrite and implement criminal and criminal procedure codes; working to reduce unlawful pre-trial detentions and to a lesser degree abuses in connection with juvenile justice; introducing bail reform; working on prison reform that includes building or refurbishing prisons; helping to transition to an accusatorial (as opposed to inquisitorial) type of criminal law system;
- *commercial law:* helping to revise commercial law frameworks (including tax laws) and establishing processes to render the business environment more friendly to both domestic and foreign investors (note: commercial law reform is sometimes characterised as economic development as opposed to rule of law development, meaning that, for some donors, it may not fall under the rubric of democracy and governance programmes);
- *alternative dispute resolution (ADR)/mediation:* helping to establish ADR or mediation centres, and helping courts to establish court-ordered arbitration/mediation in order to reduce case backlogs;
- *civic education/promoting a culture of lawfulness:* conducting educational activities directed at the public, and especially youth, on topics such as conflict mitigation and human rights through in-person trainings (eg, 'street law'), community theatre, and radio and television programmes; disseminating 'know your rights' brochures and materials on topics such as voters' rights in the run-up to a major election.

Together, the myriad programmes that fall under these and other thematic areas are designed to address what one commentator has called the "four objects of rule of law reform":

1. *The Laws: Get the Rules Right*
2. *Institutions: Ensure Proper Training, Equipment, and Funding*
3. *The Power Structure: Create Formal and Informal Checks and Balances on Power*
4. *Social Norms: Enhance Public and Professional Cultures that Support the Rule of Law.*[12]

2.2 Methods of providing technical legal assistance

The means by which rule of law implementers ply their trade has evolved. In the early years, assistance tended to be supplied episodically. Experts typically would fly in for short periods to provide targeted assistance and training, and then return to their home countries, often for extended periods. In an era when international calls were prohibitively expensive and before the advent of email,

---

12   Rachel Kleinfeld, *Advancing the Rule of Law Abroad: Next Generation Reform* (Carnegie Endowment for International Peace, 2012), pp79–108.

Zoom, Skype or even FedEx and fax machines, this type of assistance was trying at best.

Later, many donors and implementers came to agree that the optimal method for providing assistance was by deploying long-term expatriate experts who resided in the host country for extended periods, spoke the local language and had a profound understanding of the culture, politics and power centres in the country, not to mention a deep understanding of the public's aspirations and its appetite for (or tolerance of) reform.

Today, rule of law experts with years of field experience under their belt increasingly are available for such deployments. That was not the case 30 years ago, when the demand for seasoned rule of law implementers outstripped the supply by a wide margin. After the fall of the Berlin Wall in 1989 and the Soviet Union's collapse in 1991, how many rule of law implementers spoke fluent Kyrgyz, Russian, Georgian, Czech, Estonian or Bulgarian? How many of them could boast a profound understanding of those countries' cultures? More recently, too few rule of law implementers spoke Arabic or Pashtu or understood the complex cultures and politics of Iraq or Afghanistan before setting off for either or those two countries, the site of the most generously funded rule of law reform efforts to date. Whether it was rule of law assistance or some other type of assistance, vast amounts of development resources were squandered in both Afghanistan and Iraq, in part because so few people understood either country well, or were willing to face the realities of what was transpiring in each.[13]

Over the last decade in particular, there has been a greater effort to identify host country professionals to manage foreign-funded rule of law programmes. These coveted 'chief of party' positions once were the sole province of foreign experts. No longer. In fact, today, it is not uncommon for donor agencies such as USAID to mandate that top positions are filled by host country professionals.

Every rule of law assistance professional recognises the value of investing in local talent, but some experts interviewed for this chapter wondered whether this shift to host country chiefs of party was happening too quickly, citing the added influence a seasoned foreign chief of party might have with, say, a minister of justice or other senior government official. Another consideration is that, in some countries with ethnic and/or sectarian divisions, having a host country chief of party affiliated with one or another ethnicity or religion might undermine their effectiveness. There is no meaningful data on whether foreign chiefs of party are more effective than locally hired professionals. This author has seen spectacular successes and failures using both approaches. On balance,

---

13   See Craig Whitlock, *The Afghanistan Papers: A Secret History of the War – At War with the Truth*, 9 December 2019. ("A confidential trove of government documents obtained by *The Washington Post* reveal[ed] that senior U.S. officials failed to tell the truth about the war in Afghanistan throughout the 18-year campaign, making rosy pronouncements they knew to be false and hiding unmistakable evidence the war had become unwinnable.")

however, the increasing reliance on host country professionals to shape and implement rule of law development programmes is surely the correct approach. That said, there will always be a place for expatriate professionals to provide an outsider's vantage point and to provide expertise that simply does not exist in the host country.

One variation on the foreign expert model discussed above is to place experts inside a host institution, such as a ministry of justice, law school or courthouse, for extended periods (ie, a year or more). At times, it can be difficult to fully grasp how an institution operates unless one is actually working within it. Embedding someone for a meaningful duration can solve that problem. 'Embeds' are underused. In part, this may be due to distrust on the part of host country governments, who may not want outside experts, especially foreign experts, to see the underbelly of their institutions.[14] But implementers also do not propose this as an option with local partners as often as they should.

Other forms of rule of law assistance abound, including the provision of fellowships and scholarships to host country reformers to study abroad.[15] It usually is quite easy to identify rising stars who could be enriched immeasurably by living and studying in a country with a robust rule of law. This could be, for example, a year-long Master's programme (LLM) or a term-long course of study.[16] Another valuable form of assistance entails bringing together legal professionals from neighbouring countries to exchange best practices.[17] Participants in such exchanges are quick to report that learning from their peers from nearby countries is uniquely valuable, especially if some of those peers are from countries that are developmentally one or two steps ahead of their own (eg, a legal professional from a country that has just emerged from conflict learning from a peer whose country's conflict ended 10 years earlier).[18] Study tours to countries that are not significantly ahead on the development spectrum also reduce the risk that an individual will return from an overseas study tour dispirited; having seen how a well-funded German or US courthouse operates, they may conclude their own courts have no real prospect of operating at or

---

14   In Penelope Nicholson and Sally Low, "Local Accounts of Rule of Law Aid: Implication for Donors", 5 *Hague Journal of the Rule of Law* 1 (2013), available at http://papers.ssrn.com/sol3/papers.cfm?abstract_id=2453379, the authors noted that the contributions of a Japanese expert posted within a Vietnamese court were especially prized. Assistance providers have placed 'embeds' in many other countries (Rwanda, Burundi and Bahrain), seemingly to good effect. The track record of embeds merits further investigation.
15   Implementers find host country counterparts who have spent, say, a year or more studying at an overseas university or high school to be among the most forward-thinking counterparts with whom to work.
16   Loyola University Chicago's School of Law offers an LLM programme in Rule of Law in its Rome, Italy, campus. www.luc.edu/law/academics/centersinstitutesandprograms/ruleoflawfordevelopmentprogram/.
17   These gatherings also provide a critical opportunity for beleaguered judges, lawyers, women's rights activists, etc, to commiserate about the challenges they face, particularly individuals from highly repressive countries who feel constrained or unsafe discussing these issues in their own country. Institutions such as the CEELI Institute in Prague excel at conducting such trainings.
18   When peers from a region share a common language and culture (eg, Middle East and North Africa or Latin America), these gatherings can be especially effective.

near that level in their lifetime. Unfortunately, because of funding constraints and the time and effort needed to plan these exchanges, they occur all too rarely.

One of the most common modes of technical assistance are all-day or multi-day training or workshops/conferences. Regrettably, trainings and conferences are routinely conducted without a clear and measurable end-goal in mind. Too often, they have limited impact, in part because they use presenters who lack a mastery of adult learning principles and interactive training techniques.[19] Arguably, the most effective mode of assistance is one-on-one mentoring and coaching. Because that is often not a viable option, practice-based training in small groups with close supervision and real-time feedback is a good alternative. For example, jury trial training in Russia in the 1990s was typically conducted in small groups. Presentations and oral arguments by Russian lawyers were videotaped and shortly thereafter each participant was provided with detailed feedback on the content of their presentations, voice modulation, body language and so on. This type of practice-based training is far from cutting edge. It has been around for decades, and yet it is used too infrequently, even today.

Finally, we are only beginning to understand the full potential of distance learning, including self-paced, asynchronous learning, that relies on prepared, online resources as opposed to real-time, teacher-led interactions. The COVID-19 pandemic accelerated interest in this mechanism for transmitting know-how, especially to legal professionals who are in hard-to-reach areas that historically have been bypassed on account of funding constraints. The opportunities in this area are enormous, and of course with the advent of Zoom and similar platforms, it is also possible to conduct real-time, teacher-led trainings to far more people than was ever thought possible, and at a fraction of the cost of in-person training.[20]

2.3 'Top down' versus 'bottom up' reform efforts (supply side versus demand side)

One of the most basic ways to categorise rule of law reform efforts (and D&G efforts generally) is to refer to them as either 'top down' or 'bottom up' – or, put differently, supply side versus demand side.

Examples of top-down reform efforts include court reform, judicial reform,

---

19 It goes without saying that trainers who lack fluency in the local language should be used sparingly. Further, a rigorous training-of-trainers component should be a key component of workshop-intensive programmes and deserves an appropriate allocation of resources. A smaller number of expertly led workshops yields more impact than a larger number with sub-par trainers.
20 Naturally, speedy internet is essential for real-time, teacher-led interactions, raising the question of whether legal communities in poorer countries will be able to avail themselves in the near term of the enormous opportunities that internet-based learning offer. As a side note, donors and implementers must also concede that, while the cost savings of remote training are enormous, there also may be a material drop in its efficacy *vis-à-vis* live training. In due course, reliable data likely will confirm that most people do not learn or retain as much from online training.

prosecutorial reform, anti-corruption initiatives, police reform and other reforms that directly affect the functioning of governmental organs that make up the legal system. Top-down (or supply side) reform efforts require buy-in from government officials, often at the highest levels – that is, the president, prime minister, or monarch, for example. Without proper buy-in or political will, top-down reforms have very little chance of succeeding.

Top-down projects often are conceived by individuals who lack a full appreciation of just how hard it is to institute these reforms, even where there is buy-in at the highest levels. Every rule of law implementer has encountered mid-level bureaucrats, judges, prosecutors and police chiefs who possess a preternatural ability to undermine reforms, often by stalling long enough for a reform-minded president to lose a re-election bid or for a reformist justice minister to be sacked for one reason or another. By playing the game deftly, courts, prosecutor's offices and police stations have found themselves awash with shiny equipment purchased by donors, all by feigning support for reform efforts but without altering their practices in any meaningful way. This game has been played so often on so many hapless donors and implementers that the only appropriate response is: 'fool me once, shame on you; fool me twice, shame on me'. As one American with first-hand experience overseeing costly, sometimes ill-conceived rule of law programmes in Afghanistan lamented: "The Afghans had our number."

In contrast, bottom-up or demand-side efforts focus on civil society and the public, and on a limited number of private institutions such as private law schools. They include efforts such as building the capacity of human rights NGOs, helping to open student-run law school clinics that provide *pro bono* assistance to the poor, working with NGOs and law students to educate the public about their rights, working with women's rights groups to advocate for the passage of legislation that enhances women's rights, providing training to environmental NGOs on international conventions, and strengthening lawyers' and judges' associations in order to promote their independence. It took decades for many commentators to begin speaking out forcefully about the futility of many top-down reform efforts, especially those attempted in repressive countries that evince no political will to implement reforms. Fortunately, donors are focusing increasingly on bottom-up efforts – a welcome development.[21]

---

21   As one very seasoned implementer noted: "Ideally you have demand and supply in a symbiotic relationship, where demand side pressure results in supply side reforms that bolster the legitimacy of the democratic state." A detailed study commissioned by the State Department's Bureau of Democracy, Human Rights and Labor supports this assertion.

3. Key members of the rule of law assistance community

3.1 Donors

Since the 1960s, rule of law promotion has been dominated by donors and implementers from highly developed countries (ie, Australia, United Kingdom, Norway, Sweden, Canada, Japan and United States). For a while, there was much interest in engaging lesser developed countries, such as Brazil, Poland, Hungary and South Africa, to undertake largely self-funded, regional rule of law promotion efforts. However, these and other countries experienced rule of law/democratic recessions during the period from 2010 to the present. At least in the near term, they are no longer seen as having a meaningful role to play in promoting the rule of law outside their borders.[22]

While obtaining budgetary figures for rule of law programmes is exceedingly difficult, what follows is a list of some of the larger donors in the rule of law field, both governmental and non-governmental.

(a) Governments

- United States: USAID, Department of State, Department of Justice, Department of Commerce, Millennium Challenge Corporation;[23]
- European Union: European Commission;
- United Kingdom: Foreign and Commonwealth Development Office (formerly known as DFID, or the Department for International Development, before merging with the Foreign and Commonwealth Office);
- Belgium: Enabel (Belgian Development Agency);
- Canada: Canadian International Development Agency;
- Finland: Ministry for Foreign Affairs of Finland;
- Netherlands: Ministry of Foreign Affairs, Dutch Development Cooperation;
- Norway: Ministry of Foreign Affairs, Norwegian Agency for Development Cooperation;
- Sweden: Swedish International Development Agency;
- Denmark: Danish International Development Agency;
- Switzerland: Swiss Agency for Development and Cooperation;
- Germany: Deutsche Gesellschaft für Internationale Zusammenarbeit;
- Japan: Japan International Cooperation Agency; and
- Australia: Australian Agency for International Development.

---

22   Even rule of law promotion stalwarts such as the US lost some of their lustre during this same period, especially during the period from 2016–2020, when, as noted earlier in this chapter, the US saw its scores on various rule of law and democracy indices drop significantly.

23   The Millennium Challenge Corporation (MCC) was created by the US Congress in 2004. It is an independent US foreign aid agency that provides large grants – 'compacts' in MCC parlance – to a small number of eligible developing countries. To date, the MCC has entered into 37 compacts with 29 countries, worth more than $13 billion.

(b)   *International organisations*

- Association of Southeast Asian Nations;
- Council of Europe;
- Organization of American States;
- Organization for Security and Cooperation in Europe;
- United Nations:[24] United Nations Development Programme, Department of Peacekeeping Operations, United Nations High Commissioner for Refugees, United Nations Office on Drugs and Crime; and
- World Bank Group.

(c)   *Private foundations*

- Germany: German Foundation for International Cooperation, Konrad Adenauer Foundation;
- Switzerland: Aga Khan Foundation;
- United Kingdom: Sigrid Rausing Trust, Atlantic Philanthropies, Oak Foundation, Westminster Foundation for Democracy; and
- United States: National Endowment for Democracy, Ford, MacArthur, Open Society Foundations, Gates Foundation.[25]

3.2   Assistance instruments used by donors

The instruments that a donor uses to fund rule of law programmes can affect how a programme is implemented and by whom, as explained below. The three instruments used by USAID represent an example of the funding tools at a donor's disposal: (1) grants, (2) cooperative agreements and (3) contracts. These instruments are listed in the order of the relative autonomy they accord to implementers. Grants provide implementers with the greatest level of autonomy and conversely provide donors with the least amount of control. USAID primarily uses cooperative agreements and contracts when conducting D&G programmes, including rule of law programmes. That said, the largest and most ambitious rule of law programmes, especially top-down programmes that include large procurements involving computers and other hardware, are typically implemented through contracts.

---

24   In 2002, only eight UN entities provided rule of law assistance, with that number growing to 40 by 2008. By 2014, the United Nations was providing rule of law assistance in more than 150 countries; in 70 of those countries at least three UN entities were reactively providing such assistance. See David Marshall, *The International Rule of Law Movement: A Crisis of Legitimacy and the Way Forward* (Harvard University Press, 2014), pxiv.

25   In 2006–2007, the author and Bill Neukom – former American Bar Association President and World Justice Project (WJP) founder – secured from the Gates Foundation $1.75 million in seed funding to the ABA, which at the time was working hand in hand with the then nascent WJP to develop the first iterations of the WJP's Rule of Law Index. Much credit is owed to the Gates Foundation for investing in a project the success of which was far from assured. Above all, credit is owed to Bill Neukom for showing all-too-rare vision and commitment to the rule of law. At least in the United States, only George Soros, through his Open Society Foundations, comes to mind as another philanthropic thought leader with a long-term commitment to promoting the rule of law.

Under US regulations, contracts provide USAID with a high degree of control over the project, including significant discretion in approving or rejecting personnel that implementers propose to carry out a project. Contracts also allow implementers to derive an agreed-upon profit. Notably, for philosophical and occasionally practical reasons, some implementers refuse to operate under a contract. They argue that contracts unduly impinge on their autonomy or render them too closely tied to the US government for their own comfort. For that very reason, some implementers refuse to take any government funds, irrespective of the funding instrument used. Other implementers, usually for philosophical reasons, are willing to accept funds from some parts of the government (eg, USAID), but not others (eg, US Department of Defense). The vast majority of funding instruments from governmental and non-governmental sources, such as private foundations, are for relatively short periods of one to three years. This is regrettably short. Most rule of law programmes operate for well under $1 million a year, but ambitious projects that involve, say, the overhaul of court management systems, can easily exceed $7 million a year and may operate for three or more years. Virtually no donors provide more than five years of funding for a given rule of law project, although the donor may conduct a competitive bidding process to carry out a follow-on project with similar goals that may last another, say, three to five years.

3.3   Implementers

Because the US government was the first government donor to provide significant funding for rule of law programmes, it is not surprising that many of the most established providers are US organisations. These organisations generally fall into one of two camps: non-profit organisations on the one hand, and for-profit consulting companies on the other.

(a)   Non-profit organisations

Some of the leading non-profit implementers around the world include:
- American Bar Association Rule of Law Initiative;
- Asia Foundation;
- Central and Eastern European Law Initiative (CEELI) Institute;
- Danish Institute for Human Rights;
- East-West Management Institute;
- Freedom House;
- German Foundation for International Legal Cooperation;
- Hague Institute for the Internationalisation of Law;
- International Bar Association Human Rights Institute;
- International Center for Not-for-Profit Law;
- International Commission of Jurists;
- International Legal Assistance Consortium;

- International Senior Lawyers Project;
- Lawyers without Borders;
- National Center for State Courts;
- Open Society Justice Initiative;
- Partners for Democratic Change;
- Street Law, Inc;
- The Carter Center;
- The World Justice Project, and;
- US Institute for Peace.

(b) *Private consulting companies*

Some of the leading private contractors include:

- Adam Smith International;
- Cardno;
- Checchi;
- Chemonics;
- Democracy International;
- Development Associates International;
- Palladium;
- Management Systems International Sofreco; and
- Tetra Tech.

Notably, over the last decade, donors have increasingly provided grants directly to host country actors, namely civil society organisations. In the past, rule of law implementers almost always served as a 'middle-man' for such grants – that is, they provided sub-grants to these local organisations and could monitor closely how these funds were spent. Further, these implementers typically enjoyed significant latitude in deciding which local organisations would receive the sub-grants in the first instance. While some have raised concerns about the capacity of local actors, especially smaller civil society organisations, to handle even moderately sized grants, there is little doubt that, over time, they will develop said capacity.[26]

3.4 Host country recipients

The primary recipients of technical legal assistance can be divided into two categories: governmental and non-governmental.

---

26 Anyone who has worked in the field of international development for any length of time will be able to recount instances of misspent funds, or worse still, funds that have disappeared courtesy of personnel working in the implementers' own overseas office, or personnel at the offices of a sub-grantee. However unfortunate, it is inevitable that some donor funds will be misused or stolen. Ultimately, the onus is on donors and implementers (aka sub-grantors) to keep malfeasance to an absolute minimum by, for example, intense vetting of recipients and by providing training on best practices with respect to financial oversight, good governance, etc.

(a) *Governmental*

Governmental recipients include:

- ministries of justice;
- courts (including high courts, such as supreme or constitutional courts, but also lower courts, including trial courts in rural areas);
- the judiciary;
- court personnel (usually non-lawyers);
- publicly funded law schools;
- parliaments/legislatures;
- prosecutor offices;
- police and investigators;
- anti-corruption commissions;
- truth and reconciliation commissions;
- national human rights institutions (NHRIs);
- judicial training centres;
- judicial commissions or similar entities that oversee all or a portion of a country's judicial functions, including budgetary functions in some countries; and
- prisons and detention centres.

(b) *Non-governmental*

Non-governmental recipients include:

- human rights NGOs;
- women's rights NGOs;
- bar associations and law societies;
- judicial associations;
- private law schools;
- private mediation and arbitration centres;
- paralegal programmes;
- informal justice actors;
- domestic violence centres (including safe houses);
- land rights NGOs;
- climate justice NGOs;
- environmental NGOs;
- legislative advocacy actors;
- think tanks;
- labour unions;
- civic education NGOs;
- prison reform NGOs; and
- juvenile justice reform NGOs.

4. Brief history of rule of law promotion

The Law and Development movement, which began in the 1960s and fizzled out without much fanfare by the late 1970s, constituted the first sustained effort to promote the rule of law in modern times. It was led mostly by American lawyers and academics, funded primarily by USAID. Early adherents of the movement sought to promote development in Latin America, and to a lesser degree in Africa and Asia, by encouraging host countries to adopt American-style legal institutions and laws, including through exchange programmes and the transmission of legal know-how by experts who travelled to various countries in these regions. In part, the Law and Development movement was designed to thwart the spread of communism during the Brezhnev era of the Cold War.

By the mid-1970s several leaders of the Law and Development movement began levelling withering attacks on a movement they had earlier embraced, claiming there was no proof that meaningful results were being achieved. Critics questioned the very utility of sharing know-how about the American legal system in countries that were radically different politically, culturally and otherwise. Although many scholars at the time came to agree with the view that the Law and Development movement was a failure, more recent analyses have suggested that there were some salutary benefits; further, while critics today would naturally decry the ham-handed effort to transplant American-style legal processes without adequate regard for local conditions, several commentators have noted that significant results could not possibly have been achieved in that time frame, given what is now known about the pace of rule of law reforms in most countries. As numerous commentators have noted, a situation that has taken several centuries to develop is not easily altered in 10 or 25 years; in fact, it can easily take two or more generations.

In the 1980s, donors and implementers, chastened by the perceived failures of the discredited Law and Development movement, ushered in a second phase of the rule of law movement. This time, the focus was on the 'administration of justice' in countries where political will for legal reform was in evidence.[27] Latin America continued to receive the lion's share of attention and resources, with Asia a distant second and Africa receiving little attention at all, with the exception of South Africa.[28] Once again, USAID served as the lead governmental

---

27 Martin Schonteich, *A Mandate to Promote the Rule of Law, Promoting the Rule of Law, A Practitioner's Guide to Key Issues and Development* (American Bar Association, 2013), p32; see also James Goldston, *New Rules for the Rule of Law, The International Rule of Law Movement: A Crisis of Legitimacy and the Way Forward* (Harvard University Press, 2014).

28 South Africa is a special case, one in which a multitude of actors and donors, most of them American, helped build the capacity of the South African legal community to play a significant role in dismantling the apartheid regime. After travelling to the US to study public interest legal centres, South African lawyer Felicia Kentridge helped establish the Legal Resources Centre (LRC) in Johannesburg in 1979. The LRC was modelled after the NAACP Legal Defence and Educational Fund in the US, seeking to use the law to pursue justice and protect human rights in South Africa. It also served as a practical training

donor, with foundations also providing significant funding. Rule of law promoters of the 1980s focused on passing key legislation, namely criminal codes, and on reforming the judicial sector, including through judicial training and court modernisation projects. Efforts also were made to increase the competency of prosecutors, public defenders and investigators, and to increase the capacity to combat transnational crime, particularly in Latin America.[29] After roughly a decade, critics once again claimed there was little evidence that these efforts were having an impact. Before long, seismic shifts in the world order – starting with the fall of the Berlin Wall in 1989 – would render rule of law efforts beyond the perimeter of Eastern Europe and the former Soviet Union almost an afterthought.

Prior to 1990 few people would have referred to rule of law promotion as a recognised discipline or 'industry'. Nor were there many practitioners who would have described themselves as rule of law professionals or rule of law assistance providers prior to the 1990s. That changed with the fall of the Berlin Wall in 1989 and the collapse of the Soviet Union in 1991. A discipline, a profession and an industry were effectively born in the early 1990s. The relatively nascent rule of law movement appeared to have found its moment.

It was widely understood there was unlikely to be a similar moment again: triumphalism, euphoria and hopefulness abounded in equal measure – at least in the West. Here was a situation ready-made for rule of law and democracy promoters. After all, donors all seemed to agree there was no mass poverty, disease or widespread illiteracy to eradicate, with the possible exception of small pockets of rural Central Asia. Instead, the two main deficits that most agreed needed attention was the lack of a free-market mindset and accompanying institutions on the one hand, and the lack of the rule of law and democratic institutions (ie, free press, state apparatus to conduct free elections) on the

---

ground for black lawyers and law students. With the help of White House Counsel Lloyd Cutler, Professor Emeritus Louis Loss of Harvard and US Solicitor General Erwin Griswold, the LRC received funding from the Rockefeller Foundation, Ford Foundation and the Carnegie Corporation. The latter's President, Allan Pifer, hired David Hood to revitalise the Corporation's South Africa projects, with a focus on challenging the legitimacy of apartheid in the courts. Such funding would begin in 1973 with the watershed, Ford-funded conference on 'Legal Aid in South Africa' and continue well beyond the formal end of apartheid. Founding member Arthur Chaskalson, who would go on to serve as President of the Constitutional Court of South Africa, later noted that the Ford and Rockefeller foundations, among others, provided him and his colleagues with access to the finest constitutional scholars in the US. A similar role was undertaken by the National Institute of Trial Advocacy, a US not-for-profit organisation that trained young black advocates. Further, Georgetown University's Law Center, funded in part by the United States Information Agency, placed young black lawyers in leading commercial law firms in Washington DC and New York, allowing them to gain invaluable legal training. A parallel effort by the Aspen Institute trained South African jurists on advocating for greater human rights protections. Other examples of American technical legal assistance include the provision by American constitutional lawyers of assistance in drafting the Inkatha Freedom Party's Bill of Rights and the KwaZulu Bill of Rights. Even the first black law clerk in South African history, hired by Judge Richard Goldstone, was an African-American Yale Law student named Vernon Grigg. In short, the degree to which US legal assistance helped to advance South Africa's rule of law, and to dismantle apartheid, may never be fully understood, but there is little doubt it was highly consequential.

29   Comparatively few resources were directed at improving the handling of non-criminal cases or bolstering the capacity of civil society organisations to advocate for advances in the rule of law.

other. Suddenly there was a proliferation of NGOs and for-profit contractors eager to deploy experts to Warsaw, Bratislava, Sofia, Bucharest and, later, to Moscow, Kiev, Tbilisi and Tashkent. There was great urgency to the work of the rapidly expanding rule of law community, as both donors and implementers were eager to seize the moment. Seasoned development experts opined that it might take roughly five to seven years of intensive assistance from the West to get the Eastern bloc countries on track, after which they would find their own way. It was hoped that the European Union or privately funded efforts would mop up whatever messes might still remain.[30]

Although there has always been a certain amount of pessimism among some commentators and academics about the effectiveness of rule of law promotion efforts, those critics overlook myriad small and significant successes. What was achieved in Eastern Europe in the 1990s and the ensuing decade is the most significant of these successes. What transpired there was nothing short of remarkable, with former bastions of communism and state control, such as Poland, transforming themselves with staggering speed. However, it became apparent almost overnight that Eastern Europe and the former Soviet Union would likely remain on very different development trajectories, not only with respect to rule of law development, but in almost every other respect as well.

It is no accident that Poland and other Eastern European countries advanced at an entirely different pace compared with the former Soviet republics. First and foremost, their level of development (legal and otherwise) prior to their domination by the Soviet Union was in many cases significantly greater. Also, many countries in Eastern Europe had enjoyed a vibrant civil society prior to falling under Soviet domination. Thus, civil society was reignited with relative ease in many Eastern European countries, at least compared with the former Soviet republics. There, civil society was anaemic even before being brought under Soviet control – some as early as the 1920s (eg, Azerbaijan in 1922, and Uzbekistan in 1924).

A further divergence between Eastern Europe and the former Soviet Union was the deplorable leadership in virtually all the former Soviet republics. When the Soviet Union collapsed in late 1991, the authoritarian heads of the communist parties of several Soviet republics engineered takeovers, becoming presidents of their newly formed countries, virtually overnight. Through repression, the murder of opposition leaders, control of the media, or sham elections, many held on to these positions for 15 years or longer after their countries gained independence from the Soviet Union.[31] In contrast, free and fair elections were held throughout Eastern Europe within a decade of the collapse of the Berlin Wall.

---

30   From the outset, Western Europeans were far less sanguine about the speed with which Eastern bloc countries would find their way. Perhaps their experience rebuilding their ravaged continent after two world wars rendered them less optimistic about the likely pace of reforms.

Another significant difference between the two regions was the European Union's willingness to accept certain Eastern European countries as EU members so long as they could meet certain criteria. These criteria included rigorous rule of law-oriented requirements, not least of which was the integration of 80,000 pages of EU law (*acquis communautaire*). The frenzied race to satisfy the European Union's accession requirements was a boon to Eastern European reformers and the mostly expatriate rule of law advisers working alongside them.[32] Technical legal assistance proved especially critical to a country's accession prospects. Why? Because of the many EU accession requirements, rule of law requirements were often the most difficult for aspirant countries to satisfy. As a result, the amount of energy and resources devoted to helping aspirant (and non-aspirant) countries reform their legal systems from 1990 to 2010 was staggering, especially when compared with the comparatively limited rule of law promotion efforts of previous decades.

Interestingly, commentators writing about rule of law promotion efforts rarely credit technical legal assistance providers for helping to advance the rule of law in Eastern Europe from 1990 to 2010. Even though assistance providers were at times naïve or prone to missteps, especially in the early 1990s, their efforts on balance were successful and profoundly consequential. Host country beneficiaries are usually quick to describe their sustained interaction with Western rule of law professionals during these years of state building not only as helpful, but decisively so. Beneficiaries from Eastern bloc countries had to learn a new language of sorts and new concepts. Just as law students around the world typically attend classes full time for three to five years to learn a new language and master the confounding aspects of, say, tax law, the leaders and technocrats who brought their countries into compliance with the European Union's rule of law criteria also had to learn a new lexicon. In fact, they had to learn an altogether new approach to governing, including managing a market economy for the first time in decades, revamping their elections systems and adopting a bevy of new laws and creating altogether new legal institutions. It was as if one had to learn how to ride a bicycle for the first time, with the added challenge of learning how to juggle while still pedalling. It is not reasonable to

---

31   For example, until his death in 2016, Islam Karimov was Uzbekistan's only president, ruling that country with an iron fist and earning a reputation as one of the most egregious human rights violators in the world. Joining Karimov in the pantheon of grave human rights violators was Saparmurat Niyazov (aka Turkmenbashi), who ruled Turkmenistan until his death in 2006. He and Karimov, both endowed with feral instincts, shared a fondness for repression and a quick-triggered willingness to use lethal force to silence restive citizens.

32   While EU accession provided an indisputably powerful incentive, justice sector actors in Eastern Europe demonstrated a strong desire to reform their legal systems before EU accession was presented as an option. The political will to institute legal reforms was linked in part to regional rivalries, with many leaders motivated by the uncomfortable prospect of a 'lesser' neighbour outpacing them on the reform front. Donors and implementers learned to make sure key players stayed apprised of the progress being made by neighbouring countries. Unfortunately, this well-known, mostly positive phenomenon has a fraternal twin: declines in the rule of law in one country also increase the likelihood of declines in neighbouring countries. That is, a regressing country can precipitate a race to the bottom in the region.

assume they could have done all of this by reading textbooks alone – ie, without the intensive, often years-long partnerships they forged with foreign technical assistance providers posted in their countries.

In contrast with Eastern Europe, rule of law providers found the former Soviet Union to be a far more challenging environment. The devastating effects of decades of Soviet repression, propaganda and paranoia were apparent from the outset. Countries run by the old guard, especially in Central Asia, continued to rely on repressive tactics to keep the population in check, often enlisting a rubber-stamping legislature to pass laws that evinced some measure of political will for reform. In some former Soviet republics, the courts became more politicised and less independent, with judges sometimes more cowed than they were even in Soviet times. Some countries, such as Georgia and Kyrgyzstan, and to a lesser degree Moldova, emerged as mavericks; they showed great promise, in part because civil society was permitted to flourish (by post-Soviet standards) under the leadership of their comparatively moderate presidents. Even Russia enjoyed a fairly robust civil society and was making fitful progress on the rule of law prior to Vladimir Putin's assumption of the presidency on 31 December 1999.[33] Putin's influence on rule of law assistance efforts would begin to be felt shortly after assuming power (eg, increased harassment of technical assistance providers by the FSB, the successor to the Soviet KGB). After watching the 'Coloured Revolutions' in Georgia (2003), Ukraine (2004) and Kyrgyzstan (2005), a nervous Putin had seen enough. Putin's efforts to undermine democratic movements in Russia's 'backyard' suddenly took on great urgency. He began to romance neighbouring autocrats, bringing them more closely into Russia's orbit, and insisting that they distance themselves from the United States and the West. Before the West could blink, Putin's deft statecraft had brought to a halt much of the positive momentum generated in the 1990s and the early 2000s, instead ushering in an era of backsliding that lingers to this day.[34]

---

33 Examples of progress made under Yeltsin and the first years of Putin's presidency included: landmark criminal law reforms, including the reintroduction of jury trials for the first time since tsarist times and a dramatic revision of its criminal procedure code; the professionalisation of Russia's commercial courts and arbitration centres; significant progress in combating domestic violence and human trafficking; the successful introduction of clinical legal education and interactive teaching methods in law schools throughout Russia; a growing respect for the right of free association and assembly, and a surprisingly free media, especially compared with the tightly controlled media in many former Soviet Republics.

34 Notably, from 2005 to 2013, Freedom House's Judicial Framework and Independence ratings for Georgia and Moldova remained static, while they declined in every other former Soviet republic. Russia tied Azerbaijan and Uzbekistan for the second most precipitous ratings drop during this eight-year period. Ukraine, under the leadership of Russian-backed President Viktor Yanukovych, saw the biggest slide of all. See Freedom House, *Nations in Transit* (2014). Today, two of the 10 most repressive countries in the world – Turkmenistan and Tajikistan – are former Soviet Republics, an ignominious distinction they share with China, North Korea, Equatorial Guinea and South Sudan, among others. (See Freedom House, *Freedom in the World Report 2021*.) Despite the significant challenges of promoting the rule of law in the former Soviet Union, technical assistance providers helped host country reformers achieve significant gains, and in fact continue to do so. These achievements include: increasing access to justice in criminal and civil courts; reforming law schools and successfully introducing legal clinics and interactive training methodologies in law schools throughout the former Soviet Union; the successful lustration of Georgia's

The next distinct phase of rule of law assistance is inextricably linked to the Afghanistan and Iraq wars and US efforts to remake the Middle East in the wake of the September 11 attacks. This had implications for assistance efforts in Eastern Europe and the former Soviet Union, with the United States significantly reducing rule of law budgets throughout the region, with just a few exceptions, such as the Central Asian republics.[35] This partial retreat from the region by the United States rested on the assumption that the European Union would fill the void created by the US government's new-found focus elsewhere. Roughly at this same time, private foundations also began to shift their funding elsewhere, especially to Asia and Africa, where poverty and governance challenges were more extreme.

As US ambitions to promote the rule of law increased in the Middle East and North Africa, so too did D&G budgets.[36] One of the signature programmes commenced under President George W Bush's administration was the State Department's Middle East Partnership Initiative (MEPI), which, in its early years, supported rule of law promotion efforts throughout the Middle East and North Africa. Despite US government rhetoric about the importance of promoting the rule of law in the Middle East, rule of law interventions have been surprisingly episodic, with a few exceptions such as the more sustained assistance provided to Egypt and Jordan. Even after an Arab Spring that saw rulers forced from power in Tunisia, Egypt, Libya and Yemen, US-funded rule of law programmes have tended to be of relatively short duration and modestly funded – although, again, there have been exceptions.[37] One seasoned implementer expressed particular disappointment that rule of law programmes

---

judiciary; assisting the environmental law movement in places such as Ukraine; promoting women's rights; combating domestic violence and human trafficking; helping to launch civic education and 'know-your-rights' initiatives for youth and adults; expanding the cadre of human rights defenders throughout the region; and training advocacy organisations to challenge unlawful governmental practices, including by bringing cases to the European Court of Human Rights.

35   In part because of their proximity to Afghanistan, funding for rule of law assistance programmes in Central Asia increased after 9/11, at least for a short while. In 2005, once-warm relations between Uzbekistan and the US deteriorated abruptly in the wake of a massacre in Andijan, a city in Uzbekistan's restive Ferghana Valley. There, Uzbekistani forces killed roughly 500 unarmed civilians. Vibrant rule of law programmes came to a halt shortly thereafter, as numerous USAID-funded NGOs working on D&G programmes were forced out of the country by the Uzbekistani government, mostly in response to US criticism of President Karimov's actions in Andijan. Not until Karimov's death in 2016 did relations between Uzbekistan and the United States warm again, with US government support for rule of law programming resuming after a protracted hiatus.

36   Funding levels for rule of law programmes in Iraq and Afghanistan were extremely high – in fact, unprecedentedly high. Because both environments were highly insecure, a significant percentage of rule of law budgets were devoted to implementers' security needs, reducing the funds available to conduct actual programming.

37   Egypt's judiciary and courts, for example, have received significant assistance, although few would characterise Egypt as a rule of law success story. Some of the most important successes in the Middle East and North Africa region have been in the area of criminal justice reform. For example, Bahrain has established a programme on alternatives to detention, providing courts with discretion to impose sentences ranging from probation to community service. Similarly, Tunisia has adopted a programme of alternatives to incarceration, and is working to establish probation offices throughout the country. Donors and implementers have also devoted considerable resources to addressing acute needs in the areas of gender-based violence and combating trafficking in persons. The impact of such interventions appears promising.

in Tunisia and Libya – important, transitioning countries – have been comparatively underfunded, and that Syria, a country with acute needs, has been largely ignored.

During the Obama era (2008–2016), donors began devoting greater resources to promoting the rule of law in two regions in particular: Asia and sub-Saharan Africa. With the announcement of President Obama's 'pivot' to Asia in 2011, rule of law programming in the region rose, including, for a time, in China. But the increase was quite modest, with commitments of funding and personnel not commensurate with the rhetoric about Asia's importance to the United States and the West.

To their credit, most donors and implementers active in China were appropriately cautious, resisting the temptation to conduct programming certain to raise China's ire (such as aggressive human rights programmes). One area where Western assistance providers met with success in China was in bolstering the anti-domestic violence (DV) movement, culminating in the 2016 passage of a domestic anti-DV law. Notably, today there is virtually no foreign-funded rule of law activity in China.

As was the case in China, rule of law implementers also had to exercise caution in countries such as Vietnam, where the government restricted the space in which D&G assistance providers could operate. Cambodia, on the other hand, initially was more receptive to externally funded rule of law programmes but became less receptive over time; many in the Western rule of law community attributed the contraction of space in which civil society and rule of law promoters could operate to China's rise as a benefactor. After all, China was often willing to provide generous assistance to countries such as Cambodia with few strings attached, and none of the perceived sanctimony.[38] Several countries in Asia, such as the Philippines, Indonesia, Sri Lanka and even Laos, have been more receptive than others to collaboration with rule of law assistance providers.[39]

Turning to sub-Saharan Africa, the scale of rule of law assistance there has been quite modest, especially when compared with assistance efforts in Iraq and Afghanistan, or even past efforts in Eastern Europe and the former Soviet Union. In part, this is because donors have focused their efforts on addressing the high concentrations of poverty and related challenges such as health and education deficits. But in the last two decades, donors increasingly have begun

---

38   For example, China remained silent at the same time that Western aid providers and embassies criticised the Cambodian government for illegal land grabs that deprived scores of villagers of their land and livelihood without just compensation.

39   The Philippines has a history of strong judicial leadership, which has embraced technology and innovation more enthusiastically than many other developing countries in the Asia Pacific region. The roll-out of an innovative small claims court system in the Philippines, for example, has reduced court backlogs and increased access to justice for many individuals and businesses that once avoided the court system altogether.

to emphasise the 'soft' forms of development assistance, such as D&G programmes. Some of the countries that have received the most technical legal assistance in recent years include Liberia, Sierra Leone, Tanzania, Central African Republic and the Democratic Republic of the Congo. With Africa of intense interest on account of its economic potential and vast resources, it is almost certain that donor agencies, development banks and foundations will maintain a strong interest in rule of law promotion efforts in Africa. Arguably, the most important development is that Western donors, and the United States in particular, are increasingly vying with China for influence in Africa, and to a much lesser degree, with Russia. Thus, all forms of assistance to Africa will almost certainly remain robust in the coming years, including assistance in the D&G arena generally, and the rule of law specifically.

Finally, and coming full circle, it is very likely we will see a resurgence in rule of law promotion efforts in Latin America, home to some of the earliest such efforts during the Law and Development era in the 1960s. In reality, the US government has been providing generous rule of law funding to Mexico, Columbia, etc, for years. Assistance to both countries will surely continue, but in the coming years it is likely that the United States will redouble its assistance to the 'Northern Triangle' (Guatemala, Honduras and El Salvador) in particular. This is a case of US domestic politics helping to shape US assistance efforts abroad. Instability, repression and criminal activity in the Northern Triangle are driving many to migrate illegally into the United States, resulting in an uproar among the US electorate and fuelling in part President Trump's rise to power in 2016. Already, the Biden administration is mobilising resources in an effort to improve the lives of ordinary people in those countries, in the hopes of reversing the steady flow of US-bound migrants. USAID and State/INL will almost surely provide generous funding for rule of law, anti-crime, and anti-corruption programmes in that region in the coming years, and perhaps in subsequent administrations as well.

The author would like to acknowledge IBA legal interns Danilo Angulo Molina and Scott Reid, and IBA program coordinator Ashna Basnet, for their significant assistance in updating Chapters 11 and 12 of this book. He also wishes to acknowledge former legal interns Ashley Houlihan and Chayada Polpun, former legal fellow Sandra Ovcinikova, and former program associate Jason Davis for their assistance with the first edition of these chapters. Finally, I would like to thank the many individuals from the rule of law assistance community who agreed to be interviewed for these chapters. They are a remarkable cadre of committed professionals, at once idealistic, but also wide-eyed and savvy. They have seen it all.

Chapter 12. Rule of law promotion efforts moving forward

Michael Maya
International Bar Association

1.   Introduction

This chapter aims to provide further context for assessing the contributions of past rule of law promotion efforts. It also aims to temper expectations about what the rule of law promotion community can be expected to achieve in the near and medium term in light of the grey clouds hovering over a growing list of countries around the globe, especially over the last 15 years.

The penalties for being a rule of law laggard have significantly diminished in the last 15 years, owing in large part to China's rise and the succour Russia provides to virtually any country willing to be a burr in the West's saddle. Irrespective of whether one ascribes malign intent to one or both countries, the reality is that the largely unipolar world the United States and the West enjoyed from, say, 1990–2005, no longer exists. This has rendered it far more difficult for the West to create an enabling environment for host country reformers and rule of law implementers. This is borne out by recent Freedom in the World reports, discussed below.

This chapter also offers observations and suggestions about how donors, implementers and recipients of assistance might make better use of finite resources, and urges adherence to time-tested best practices. It closes by identifying a handful of potential trends that may affect the arc of the rule of law movement in the coming decades.

2.   Building on successes, learning from past missteps

Commentators have long called for a 'reform of the reformers', namely rule of law donors and implementers.[1] This is a challenge that always should be accepted. It may lead to greater humility, introspection and intellectual honesty

---

1   Valuable works on this subject include: Rachel Kleinfeld, *Advancing the Rule of Law Abroad: Next Generation Reform* (Carnegie Endowment for International Peace, 2012); David Marshall, *The International Rule of Law Movement: A Crisis of Legitimacy and the Way Forward* (Harvard University Press, 2014); Linn Hammergren, *Balanced Justice and Donor Programs: Lessons from Three Regions of the World* (Open Society Institute, 2009); Pip Nicholson and Sally Low, "Local Accounts of Rule of Law Aid: Implications for Donors", 5 *Hague Journal on the Rule of Law* (2013) 1–43; Thomas Carothers, *Promoting the Rule of Law Abroad* (Carnegie Endowment for International Peace, 2006).

than have been on display by all parties in the rule of law field. More importantly, it may give rise to greater innovation in the rule of law field, which to date has seen insufficient risk taking, especially by donors.

At the same time, commentators have consistently been glass-half-empty observers of rule of law assistance efforts. By and large, they have not given credit where it is due, despite numerous examples of successes, large and small. It is possible that commentators have fallen into the trap of 'watching the needle' – that is, scrutinising rule of law indices to determine whether the rule of law has increased in a given country, and using that information to infer whether individual rule of law programmes have had any impact in a given country. This is a mistake. One must take a far more nuanced and careful look at changes on the ground to determine whether progress is being made, and whether outside assistance can rightly share the credit for these advances.

A 2013 article authored by Pip Nicholson and Sally Low about rule of law assistance in Vietnam helps make this point. They write:

> In conclusion, the contemporary Vietnamese court system is beset by lack of resources (including challenges in attracting judges), allegations of corruption, and an under-educated workforce needing additional training in what the law is and to apply it. These criticisms need to be tempered by acknowledging the extraordinary developments witnessed in the courts over the last twenty years. Lawyers are today experimenting with litigating in courts … Judges are developing a nascent legal discourse. Further, some lawyers agitate for more nuanced interpretations of the law, relying at least in part on legal argument rather than on their relationships … to secure judgments. And there is great activity reforming substantive laws …[2]

If one looks at the World Bank's rule of law score for Vietnam in 2013, it is slightly worse than it was in 1996. One conclusion, of course, is that there had been no progress whatsoever in advancing the rule of law in Vietnam and that any external efforts to promote it have been a fool's errand. Yet, anyone who knows Vietnam or countries like it knows that progress was in fact being made during this period, even though a well-regarded index suggested otherwise. Is it possible that the indices at our disposal are not sensitive enough to measure the progress that has in fact occurred, or that there is a lag before progress can be registered by certain indices? The "extraordinary developments" that Nicholson and Low observed suggest that Vietnam had in fact made significant headway, thanks to its own efforts and those of outside assistance providers. Notably, during the six-year period after the above referenced article was written (2013–2019), Vietnam's rule of law score improved dramatically, both in absolute terms, but also compared to other countries around the world. Vietnam's rule of

---

2   Pip Nicholson and Sally Low, "Local Accounts of Rule of Law Aid: Implications for Donors", 5 *Hague Journal on the Rule of Law* (2013) 1–43, at 4–6; footnotes omitted. This article also contains thoughtful critiques of certain donor and implementer practices, and provides valuable lessons for both groups of actors.

law score in 2013 placed it in the 39th percentile in the world, but by 2019 it had jumped to the 53rd percentile. Perhaps Nicholson and Low were prescient. More likely they were accurately describing genuine progress they observed, progress that somehow had eluded indices such as the World Bank's.

A lack of realistic expectations has plagued the field of law promotion since the 1960s. When taking note of slower than hoped for progress in the rule of law field, it is important to factor in global trends that either promote or thwart progress. Especially since 2006, host country reformers and assistance providers active in the field of democracy and governance have faced more headwinds than tailwinds. As alluded to above, two countries – China and Russia – stand out as active instigators or enthusiastic supporters of anti-democratic and anti-rule of law movements around the globe The findings of Freedom House's dispiriting *Freedom in the World 2021* report[3] regrettably can be summarised in their six-word summary: "The long democratic recession is deepening." Here are a few other observations:

- 2020 saw the 15th consecutive year of decline in global freedom.
- "[C]ountries experiencing deterioration outnumbered those with improvements by the largest margin recorded since the negative trend began in 2006."
- "The ongoing decline has given rise to claims of democracy's inherent inferiority. Proponents of this idea include official Chinese and Russian commentators seeking to strengthen their international influence while escaping accountability for abuses, as well as anti-democratic actors within democratic states who see an opportunity to consolidate power. They are both cheering the breakdown of democracy and exacerbating it, pitting themselves against the brave groups and individuals who have set out to reverse the damage."
- "The malign influence of the regime in China … was especially profound in 2020" with Beijing ramping up its "meddling in the domestic political discourse of foreign democracies …".

Observers who took close note of China's steady rise and the advent of Putinism in Russia are not likely to be surprised by Freedom House's discouraging findings. While European- and US-style democracies might have been the preferred model of governance for much of the world in the 1990s, a very appealing alternative presented itself in the 2000s, at least in the eyes of leaders with an affinity for repression and autocratic rule. Countries have discovered they can enjoy robust trade and generous assistance from the likes of China irrespective of their record on democracy and human rights. This has

---

3   Freedom House, *Freedom in the World 2021: Democracy under Siege*, https://freedomhouse.org/report/freedom-world/2021/democracy-under-siege.

weakened the West's ability to rely on the usual array of carrots and sticks, which it wielded to much greater effect before, say, China's ascendance. Why endure the pieties of the West and bend to its will when China, and sometimes Russia too, match or eclipse the largesse of the West, without making assistance contingent on adherence to international norms?

Those working in the democracy and rule of law field often are among the first to detect the stench of repression wafting from neighbouring countries. And so it was for those working in the former Soviet Union in the early 2000s; they quickly sensed the impact that Putin, in faraway Moscow, would have on the Central Asian republics and elsewhere in the former Soviet space. His impact would later be felt in former Soviet bloc countries that had already acceded to the European Union, most notably Hungary.[4]

As those in the rule of law promotion field can attest, bad habits and bad ideas generally enjoy speedier uptake than good ones. For example, when a repressive non-governmental organisation (NGO) law is passed in one country, in short order copycat versions can be found wending their way through parliaments in far-off countries that share a desire to hamstring civil society or suffocate it outright. Judges in formerly repressive countries, many of them timid to begin with, reflexively become more pliant and less independent when they sense a resurgent crackdown on civil society and the media is afoot.

Even setting aside the malign influence of China and Russia over the last 15 years in particular, rule of law promotion *always* will be the most slow-moving, painstaking and enigmatic undertaking within the entire democracy and governance field. For example, civil society organisations typically sprout up soon after the ousting of a repressive leader. The media can begin to thrive and operate freely in relatively short order, even after being tightly controlled for decades in formerly repressive countries. Democratic elections classified by impartial observers as 'free and fair' usually can be held within a few years – and almost certainly within a decade or two – after the fall of a dictator. On the other hand, progress in the rule of law is far more challenging. It is not susceptible to rapid progress. How many corrupt, tightly controlled judiciaries, previously under the thumb of a dictator, have become genuinely independent and transparent within 10 years or even 20 years after a dictator's fall? How many countries scoring poorly on corruption indices achieve marked progress within five or 10 years, or for that matter 15 to 20 years? One explanation is that, broadly speaking, a justice system and levels of corruption are a much

---

4   Eroding democracy and the rule of law in Hungary, an EU and NATO member, has been one of Russia's chief aims and singular achievements. In 2006, Hungary fared quite well in the World Bank's rule of law index, scoring in the 83rd percentile globally. By 2019, its score had dropped significantly, placing it in the 68th percentile. Freedom House's 2021 *Freedom in the World* report rated Hungary as "Partly Free", the *only* EU member state (among 27) to earn this designation. It is well-known that Hungary is teeming with Russian spies. In fact, it is an open secret that Budapest serves as Russia's base for conducting malign activities, not only in Hungary, but throughout Europe.

closer reflection of, and proxy for, a country's prevailing culture than, say, the media. For better or for worse, national cultures do not change quickly, and as a result neither does the state of the rule of law.

3. Donors: moving forward

Below are various challenges faced by rule of law donors, coupled with critiques and recommendations relevant to common donor practices.

3.1 Assessment of needs and host country buy-in

A long-time member of the donor community observed that, in the old days, rule of law donors did not know what they did not know. Today, they know what they do not know, more or less. The individual lamented that the main problem today is that donors too often ignore what they already do know. Thus, donors continue to issue multi-year, multi-million-dollar requests for proposals without first conducting a comprehensive rule of law assessment and without having secured assurances at the highest levels of the host country government that it will supply the political muscle needed to implement the top-down reforms being contemplated. In fact, politically sensitive, top-down reforms of this sort ideally should have been proposed by high-ranking members of the government to the donor in the first place. Without well-placed and committed host country champions at various layers in the government (and ideally civil society too), the chances of an ambitious reform project achieving hoped-for results are slim.[5]

3.2 Over-optimism, pet projects and political pressure

A seasoned rule of law practitioner noted that donors still suffer from 'development agency hubris', which leads donors to believe they can cure a decades-old rule of law problem with a few million dollars. The development road is littered with the project ideas of development professionals who thought their uncommonly good ideas could defy the odds and achieve success where others had failed. This phenomenon is far more common than many might imagine, resulting in individuals temporarily suspending their sworn allegiance to follow best practices in order to pursue a pet project. Every rule of law implementer can cite at least one current or past project that was launched by a donor in roughly this fashion.

Another troubling phenomenon is this: in their haste to 'move money out the door' in response to political pressure from the legislature or the president's/prime minister's office, donors sometimes undertake costly and ill-conceived rule of law programmes. Predictably, most flop. This was especially true in Afghanistan and

---

5   On a related note, commentators continue to urge donors to conduct sophisticated political economy analyses (PEA) as part of a broader assessment of the viability of a rule of law project. Especially in the last few years, donors such as USAID have heeded the call, with implementers following suit and including a PEA in their funding proposals and workplans. In her book, *Advancing the Rule of Law Abroad: Next Generation Reform*, Rachel Kleinfeld offers a helpful five-step methodology for devising a rule of law programme. See pp188–208 of that book.

Iraq, the rare case where there arguably was more money available than the host country legal communities could absorb and spend responsibly.

3.3 Rule of law gains are slow and require patience

Donors and *their* donors – namely, national legislatures – must resign themselves to the fact that it will take most developing countries multiple decades to transform themselves into rule of law states with outside assistance, and even longer without it. This is especially the case in countries emerging from conflict or a sustained period of authoritarian or colonial rule. Although foreign visitors arriving in a capital city may be impressed by new construction and vibrant street life, many countries receiving assistance are profoundly impaired in ways that are not immediately visible. Often, large swathes of the population, including people in decision-making roles, are deeply scarred and limited by their past experiences, such as living through a civil war, genocide, pervasive and sustained racial or ethnic discrimination, or an extended period of authoritarian rule. Others are constrained by cultural norms. For example, imagine a newly appointed, reformist justice minister who is genuinely persuaded that corruption and nepotism are harming her country. If a down-and-out family member seeks a ministry job for which they are not qualified, does the minister turn her back on the family member, flouting a centuries old code of 'looking after one's own'? Or does she just say "OK, just this one time"?

3.4 Fighting corruption and the status quo

Finding ways of promoting the rule of law and reducing corruption are among the most pressing challenges in the entire field of international development. Why? Because a weak rule of law impedes every facet of development. For example, failure of the legal system to accord women the rights enjoyed by men suppresses human development and economic growth throughout the developing world. This point was made by the United Nations' landmark Arab Human Development Report (2004), which identified the lack of women's rights as one of the single most debilitating problems plaguing the Arab world.[6] Corruption also undermines development efforts immeasurably. For example, as a result of widespread corruption, donor-supplied pharmaceuticals are frequently diverted and sold on the black market, depriving the poor of much-needed drug treatments and causing senseless deaths, sometimes as a result of taking counterfeit medications.

3.5 Top-down projects

Donors' waning fondness for top-down projects is a positive development, as

---

6   Nobody has spoken more eloquently and persuasively about the need to prioritise women's rights than Nobel Prize-winning economist Amartya Sen.

these projects are often costly and have a high failure rate. Top-down judicial reform and anti-corruption initiatives top the list of projects that are most likely to fail, usually due to a lack of sustained political will at the highest levels of government.[7] In this regard, donors would be wise to think like an economist. For example, let us assume that a $5 million judicial reform project will achieve 100 (hypothetical) 'impact points' if successful, but the project has a 10% chance of success. If one compares that to a $5 million legal education reform project that, if successful, will achieve 50 impact points but has a 40% chance of success, an economist would counsel the donor to pursue the legal education project, which offers double the likely return on investment.[8] Even today, donors tend to overstate the value of training judges and government officials, and to undervalue a more grassroots-oriented approach that includes, say, a robust and sustained civic education campaign directed at youth. This tendency is sometimes referred to as 'rule of law orthodoxy',[9] placing exaggerated emphasis on building the technical competence of justice sector actors, when more often than not, the root problem is a culture of corruption that permeates the judiciary, other key institutions and society as a whole. The likelihood that a handful of workshops will materially alter a corrupt 50-year-old judge's views on corruption – and more importantly, his or her habits – is fanciful thinking. But finding donors willing to invest in 50-year-old judges is far easier than finding donors willing to invest in moulding the views of young people or law students on the devastating impact of corruption on their countries.

3.6 More emphasis needed on bottom-up approaches

Donors need to continue embracing a more bottom-up, grassroots approach to rule of law promotion efforts. Academics and practitioners are nearly unanimous in recommending this shift. In fact, one would be hard-pressed to find a single

---

7   Training judges is of course essential. Helping to create a corps of competent judges is central to the rule of law. But training judges can be a comparatively costly endeavour and is often fraught with problems. Usually, political will at both the executive and judicial branch level is essential for an ambitious judicial training initiative to generate meaningful impact. Messrs Zurn, Nollkaemper and Peerenboom, citing a 2007 Transparency International study on corruption and the judiciary, note that "study after study demonstrates that giving more independence and authority to incompetent and corrupt judges does not produce just outcomes or enhance public trust in the judiciary in developing countries": Michael Zurn, Andre Nollkaemper and Randy Peerenboom (eds), *Rule of Law Dynamics* (Cambridge University Press, 2012), p313.

8   In this hypothetical case, the judicial project yields 10 points, since it has a 10% probability of yielding 100 rule of law impact points (0.1×100 points). On the other hand, the legal education project yields 20 points (0.4×50 points). Nothing should be read into the assignment of impact points in this example, as a case can be made that reforming the legal education system would be *more* consequential and would generate more impact points in the long run. In fact, given that most judges must graduate from law school in order to become a judge, the positive impact that a well-run, practice-based legal education system can have on an aspiring judge is immeasurable. It is worth noting that corruption at many law schools (eg, grade buying) in developing countries is deplorable and potentially nightmarish, especially for female students, who on a regular basis receive demands for sexual favours from professors and deans in return for good grades or letters of recommendation. Regardless of gender, these law schools are far from ideal environments for judges or lawyers to commence their legal careers.

9   See Steven Golub, *Beyond Rule of Law Orthodoxy: The Empowerment Alternative* (Carnegie Endowment of International Peace, Carnegie Paper No 43, October 2003).

voice advocating for a return to a greater emphasis on top-down reforms. Instead, donors need to focus far more attention on projects that directly affect people's everyday lives. Since a large percentage of the population in aid-intensive countries is poor, it follows that a large proportion of rule of law assistance should be directed at projects that improve the lives of the poor. Projects that focus on access to justice and legal empowerment of the poor appear to have a high success rate, although more hard evidence is needed to support this assertion. Further, projects that target the legal needs of the poor can often be implemented on a shoestring, at least compared to institutional reform projects, such as court automation projects. In fact, many such projects can be implemented through modest sub-grants to well-regarded local civil society organisations (CSOs), with comparatively modest levels of oversight by donors/implementers.

3.7 Focus on women's and environmental rights groups

Donors should consider focusing more bottom-up efforts in areas where CSO actors are especially energetic and intrinsically motivated. For several reasons, women's rights and environmental rights are two areas that tend to be particularly fruitful. First, CSOs working in these two areas often rise up on their own and do exemplary work, with or without donor assistance. Intrinsically motivated groups are precisely the type of groups donors should support, as they are more likely to continue their work after donor funds have dried up.

Secondly, promoting women's rights is crucial to development. There are numerous studies demonstrating that funds invested in advancing women's and girls' rights and their education provide a significant boost to economic development. Thirdly, women constitute more than half of the population of most countries, while fully 100% of the population is affected by a country's environment. In other words, women's and environmental rights are not niche or 'flavour of the day' issues that often stir up great interest for short periods, only to be forgotten by donors after, say, two to three years. Fourthly, and perhaps most importantly, even repressive countries are often willing to provide enough running room for women's and environmental rights advocates to operate effectively. Inattention or the absence of active meddling by government officials is often all that is needed for many projects to thrive.

3.8 Simplification of court and legal procedures

Several commentators have argued that one of the most important contributions that rule of law donors and assistance providers can make is helping to simplify court and legal procedures that the poor – and especially the illiterate poor – struggle to understand and follow. These confusing and intimidating procedures effectively exclude large swathes of the population from deriving any benefit or protection from the legal system.[10] Especially in the last, say, five years, a 'community-based justice' movement appears to have caught fire among both donors and implementers, perhaps in that order. The idea behind it is simple: try to improve the problem-solving capacity of local courts, the ones that average people, including the indigent, use to resolve problems they cannot resolve themselves. In many countries, judges and lawyers simply do not see themselves as public servants. Among other things, this movement seeks to change that unhelpful mindset.

3.9 Access to legal information

In a similar vein, numerous commentators have noted that increasing access to legal information is too often ignored by donors, despite the fact that it has an extremely high 'pay off' relative to donor funds spent. As one seasoned implementer noted: "These days, putting things online should be a given. But it's not." Providing the poor with access to usable legal information is especially important. Another seasoned implementer noted how little information is available about how the criminal justice system operates in a given country. If you are the parents of a child who has just been arrested, you should be able to find information about what your child's rights are, what procedures await them, how to find a lawyer, etc. Given the added challenges faced by those who are illiterate, this information also should be available as a video on a state-run website and on YouTube. This is not an especially costly project, but the dividends could be large; further, donors likely could identify a local bar association to help produce such online information with a very modest sub-grant.

3.10 The need for more indices that can help measure progress in certain key rule of law areas

Everyone loves a good index. Freedom House's Freedom in the World, Transparency International's Corruption Perception Index, and the World Justice Project's Rule of Law Index are all heavily relied upon, both by the international development community, but also by journalists. The problem is there are too few of them. Despite the strides donors and implementers have made with respect to monitoring and evaluation of rule of law projects, there are too few indices that can help with goal-setting at the outset of a project or to gauge progress at the midpoint or completion of the project. For example, one useful index that would reveal a great deal about the entire criminal justice system in a country is a pre-trial detention index. It could even start as a regional index (eg, Central America) and perhaps expand after being piloted

---

10   Justice Houses in Colombia and the relatively new small claims court system in the Philippines are worthy of further study and perhaps replication elsewhere.

there. In short, such an index could measure how long arrested persons spend in jail before being properly charged and accorded their basic rights, such as the right to speak to a lawyer, something that is enshrined in the laws of many countries, but which is regularly flouted. The broader point is that, to improve something, ideally one should obtain a baseline measurement and track progress or setback every year, or every two or three years if funding is limited. Reliable indices are critical to this endeavour.

3.11 Addressing cultural norms

Altering cultural norms (ie, rejecting bribery as a necessary evil in order to 'get things done') is absolutely essential. Yet most lawyers and donors are not well equipped to craft the most effective approach to achieving such changes. The rule of law community would be well served by enlisting non-legal experts (eg, sociologists, neuroscientists, anthropologists, media experts) to help devise better strategies for addressing cultural norms that prevent the rule of law from taking hold, such as widespread tolerance of corruption. To date, few if any donors or implementers have availed themselves of the added firepower that a multidisciplinary team could bring to the challenge of solving many rule of law problems.

Addressing 'cultural issues' can be tricky. In part, this is because many view it as impolitic to assert that this or that country is beset by a 'culture of corruption' or a 'culture of lawlessness'. But that is precisely the nub of the problem, that is, culture. Understanding the connection between culture on the one hand, and corruption and lawlessness on the other, is a critical starting point. The rather ingenious Diplomatic Parking Ticket study provides insights into the degree to which cultural norms and corruption are linked.[11] In "Corruption, Norms, and Legal Enforcement: Evidence from Diplomatic Parking Tickets", authors Fisman and Miguel tracked international diplomats in New York City to see which of them paid their parking tickets. Diplomats, as is well known, enjoy immunity and are therefore free to ignore parking tickets with impunity. The study found that diplomats from countries that scored well on Transparency International's Corruption Perceptions Index generally had the fewest unpaid tickets. Thus, 66 diplomats from Finland, Norway, Denmark, and Sweden collectively had only 12 unpaid tickets over the course of one year, despite the fact they were free to toss parking tickets in the nearest trash can without suffering any consequences. In contrast, diplomats from just two countries, Chad, and Bangladesh, together filled New York City's trash cans with over 2,500 unpaid tickets during this same period. As one might guess, Chad and Bangladesh consistently score near the bottom of anti-corruption indices.

---

11   Raymond Fisman and Edward Miguel, "Corruption, Norms, and Legal Enforcement: Evidence from Diplomatic Parking Tickets", 115 *Journal of Political Economy* 6 (December 2007) 1020–1048.

In short, the study found that individuals who tend to respect laws in their home country (eg, Scandinavians) also do so elsewhere, even when they are free to flout laws without penalty. They carry their respect for the law – ingrained in them by their home country's pervasive culture of lawfulness – everywhere they go.

A separate study found that one of the most reliable predictors of whether a country will be governed by a strong rule of law is the degree to which cultures emphasise 'embeddedness' or 'autonomy', which the authors described as follows:

> *Embeddedness refers to a cultural emphasis on the person as embedded in the group and committed to maintaining the status quo, propriety, and restraint of actions or inclinations that might disrupt group solidarity or the traditional order. The opposite pole of autonomy describes cultures in which the person is viewed as an autonomous, bounded entity who finds meaning in his or her own uniqueness.*[12]

Countries scoring high on embeddedness include Nepal, Indonesia and Ghana. Countries scoring high on autonomy include Austria, Switzerland and Germany. The authors further note that:

> *A rule-of-law norm is less likely to find support in societies whose culture emphasizes embeddedness. The key values in such cultures – respect for tradition, honoring elders, and obedience – encourage people to seek guidance in sources other than the law.*[13]

This finding will not be terribly surprising to seasoned rule of law implementers, but it can and should inform the choices made about which strategies might be most effective in changing mindsets in countries that emphasise embeddedness (eg, Afghanistan). Finally, perhaps the most important passage in this study is the following:

> *Cultural value[s] ... can promote or undermine law-abidingness ... through the personal values that members of society acquire. There is substantial evidence that* value acquisition occurs largely during childhood and early adolescence.[14] (emphasis added).

3.12 Focus on youth

If it is true that such value acquisition occurs largely in one's youth, and common sense suggests it does, why is such a tiny fraction of rule of law promotion resources directed at young people? Why don't donors invest more heavily in devising and implementing a youth strategy aimed at building a rule of law culture? Donors, and to a lesser degree implementers, are risk averse, one manifestation of which is a reluctance to invest in projects that cannot produce

---

12   Amir N Licht, Chanan Goldschmidt and Shalom H Schwartz, "Culture Rules: The Foundations of Rule of Law and Other Norms of Governance", *Journal of Comparative Economics* 35 (2007) 659–688.
13   *Ibid.*
14   *Ibid.*

demonstrable, short-term impact.[15] This is especially true today, given donors' emphasis on measuring results, coupled with impatient legislatures demanding evidence that taxpayer funds are generating tangible impact.

There are many compelling reasons to focus on youth. First, there are a lot of them. This is especially the case in poor countries that receive substantial aid, with the median age sometimes hovering around 20 years. Examples include Afghanistan (18.9 years), Ethiopia (17.9 years) and Tanzania (17.7 years). This is in stark contrast with the most developed and generous donor countries, such as Japan (47.3 years), Germany (47.1 years), Netherlands (42.6 years) and Canada (42.2 years). Secondly, based on the current state of knowledge, it is not implausible to suggest there may be a relatively brief window during which rule of law values can be acquired as a matter of 'second nature'. This critical internalisation window may be open until a person is 18, 20 or 25 years of age, but it seems highly unlikely that it extends into one's 40s, 50s and beyond, a demographic that receives a large share of overall rule of law assistance (eg, prosecutors, judges). Thirdly, it is cost effective. Training young people via in-school or after-school programmes costs a fraction of what it costs to train lawyers, prosecutors and judges. Training law students is also extremely cost effective.

When it comes to implementing democracy and governance programmes, including those focused on the rule of law and conflict mitigation, brain science and related principles of intellectual and moral development provide further support for intensified efforts directed at youth.[16] As Dr Bruce Wexler of Yale University writes:

> *Neurobiological research indicates that the human frontal lobes continue to actively develop until a person is 20–25 years old, and these are regions of the brain thought to be closely associated with values, morality, emotion, and other personality traits.*[17]

He also notes that:

> *During the first part of life, the brain and mind are highly plastic ... and shape themselves to the major recurring features of their environments. During these years, individuals have little ability to act on or alter the environment, but are easily altered by it.* By early adulthood, the mind and brain have elaborately developed structures and a diminished ability to change those structures.[18] (emphasis added).

---

15   In contrast to, say, a childhood vaccination programme, where progress can be measured month to month, changing the mindset of young people in a developing country can take years to show proof of progress.

16   As noted by Yona Teichman and Daniel Bar-Tal: "From pre-adolescence (age 10 and later) abstract and hypothetical thinking begin to develop, providing the ground for valuing justice, dignity, equality, and human rights. All of these contribute to the advance of social tolerance": Yona Teichman and Daniel Bar-Tal, *Handbook of Race, Racism, and the Developing Child: Acquisition and Development of a Shared Psychological Intergroup Repertoire in Context of Intractable Conflict* (John Wiley & Sons, 2008), pp460–461.

17   Bruce Wexler, *Brain and Culture: Neurobiology, Ideology, and Social Change* (MIT Press, 2006), p242.

18   *Ibid*, at p5.

Nepotism is one example of an especially difficult habit to break, especially for people weaned on the virtue of 'looking after one's own'. In fact, disavowing an age-old commitment to look after one's own in favour of a more meritocratic approach would be very disruptive to cultures with high degrees of 'embeddedness' (referenced above). Yet, young people are the ones most likely to accept the risks and tolerate the disruption needed to build a meritocratic, rule of law state.[19]

3.13   Crime

Crime and the lack of physical security is an especially acute problem for the poor in many countries. In fact, it is among the most debilitating rule of law challenges for people from all socio-economic levels. Addressing this issue typically requires a combination of bottom-up and top-down initiatives. Crime prevention efforts, especially at the local level (as opposed to the national level), have a reasonable success rate, particularly when the police are not actively involved in the underlying criminal activity.

The inability to address crime often is the undoing of progressive leaders who embrace democratic and rule of law values. A corollary to that is that high crime rates open the door for leaders for whom democracy and the rule of law are an afterthought or even clash with their core values. The Philippines comes to mind, with strongman President Duterte capitalising on the public's exasperation with rising crime to gain power and maintain it. The trade off, which many Filipinos were willing to accept, was a major erosion in the rule of law in return for a crackdown on crime, one that resulted in scores of extrajudicial killings, and left scores of innocent people dead.

3.14   Government donors

Government donors are often overly bureaucratised, and sometimes lack the stealth and risk-taking cultures needed to implement rule of law assistance programmes in challenging environments. Private foundations, on the other hand, tend to be more fleet-footed and less bureaucratic. Government donors and those who fund them (legislatures) should consider parcelling out a very modest portion of their rule of law funds to private foundations or NGOs with a proven track record in the rule of law field. These funds could be labelled 'innovation

---

19   Since donors and implementers who are part of the rule of law movement have tended to undervalue the importance of youth, perhaps there is value in examining how some of the most successful movements of the last century have employed youth strategies. For example, the Soviet Union's signature youth movement, Komsomol, had tens of millions of members at its height in the 1970s, including a now famous boy named Vladimir Putin. In fact, a significant percentage of Russia's adult population today are thought to have once been Komsomol members, perhaps explaining in part Russia's illiberal tendencies and the appeal, or at least tolerance of, the Kremlin's revanchist impulses. Similarly, in today's China there are thought to be well over 100 million members of the Young Pioneers, a mass youth organisation created by the Communist Party in 1949. More recently, Al Qaeda and ISIS have effectively advanced a call for global jihad in response to perceived anti-Muslim oppression, a message that especially appeals to the developmental needs of adolescent males, many of whom consume jihadist propaganda on their smartphones.

funds' – that is, funds designed to encourage experimentation with unconventional approaches to rule of law programmes, with no strings attached other than the usual accounting requirements associated with government grants.

3.15 Need for public opinion surveys

There is remarkably little data about what populations in aid-intensive countries feel they need or want from their justice system. Before embarking on an ambitious and costly effort to promote the rule of law in a country, donors should consider pooling funds to conduct extensive public opinion surveys about the justice system. These surveys, conducted face-to-face by teams of tablet-wielding interviewers, can reach 3,000 to 8,000 people in urban and remote areas in the least developed countries in the world (eg, Mali) for less than $475,000.[20] To be sure, this is a substantial sum; but this up-front investment will almost certainly pay for itself by increasing both the quality of assistance and the likelihood this assistance will be directed at reforms that enjoy widespread support. Finally, absent radical changes in the country, the findings of these surveys can help inform decisions about which projects to undertake for roughly three to four years, or perhaps longer.

3.16 Lack of coordination

The rule of law donor community must redouble its coordination efforts. The literature is replete with examples of donors tripping over themselves, and funding programmes with conflicting aims, even in the smallest countries where one would think it would be hard to avoid each other.[21] This is also an acute problem in capital cities, such as Washington DC, where major players in the rule of law arena, such as the Department of State, USAID, the Departments of Justice, Commerce and others, continue to struggle with coordination and the maximisation of limited resources. There are efforts afoot to address this, and reason to believe it will improve matters. But tribalism within agencies is notoriously difficult to extinguish.

3.17 Traditional justice

Donors' interest in 'traditional' or 'informal' justice has raised many questions about whether this is the area in which donors can make the most important

---

20   Such surveys have been conducted by the Hague Institute for the Internationalisation of Law with
        funding from the Dutch government.
21   One of the better examples of collaboration in the field can be found in eastern Democratic Republic of
        the Congo (DRC), where the United Nations, the US Department of State, private foundations, USAID
        and various other bilateral donors (ie, Netherlands, Norway) have collaborated in a mostly exemplary
        fashion to address the ongoing rape crisis in war-torn eastern DRC. There, donors have funded mobile
        courts to travel to remote villages, enabling survivors of rape perpetrated by military personnel and
        civilians to obtain justice that would have eluded them had they been forced to travel for several days
        to the nearest provincial courthouse. See Michael Maya, "Mobile Courts in the Democratic Republic of
        Congo: Complementarity in Action?" in *Innovations in the Rule of Law*, The Hague Institute for the
        Internationalisation of Law and the World Justice Project (2012), at www.hiil.org/data/sitemanagement/
        media/WJP&HiiL%20UN%20Report-UNGA%20Event(1).pdf.

investment. As one commentator noted, working in this area raises questions about both opportunity cost and donors' comparative advantage. Which rule of law programmes are donors not embarking on because of their focus on traditional justice? Also, what can donors do to materially alter an often murky dispute resolution system without disturbing the essence of the system and its attendant virtues (eg, the ability to deliver swift dispute resolution, with outcomes widely accepted by the local community)?

Several commentators have argued that donors' comparative advantage lies elsewhere, although it is true that donors have a mastery of international standards, especially regarding women's rights, the Achilles heel of many traditional systems. Finally, one of the most important questions is: Do people who are responsible for carrying out traditional justice in their city or village really want donor assistance? Or is this an example of donors wanting something that their intended beneficiaries have not asked for or are interested in? This deserves further study.

3.18   Lack of dialogue between donors and implementers

Donors need to provide more intellectual leadership in the rule of law field, including by harnessing the learning that implementers acquire in the course of carrying out donor-funded programmes. Donors should expect more from their implementers. For example, implementers have not been asked to share lessons learned with the broader rule of law community in any systematic fashion. Finding effective mechanisms for creating a more productive dialogue within the rule of law community is critical. At a minimum, thought should be given to requiring implementers to write brief, end-of-project reports that can be circulated within the donor agency and ideally more broadly. Finally, donors only infrequently sponsor public forums at which implementers and donors can share with the broader rule of law community useful information about projects or country conditions. Other than a few donors (eg, World Bank), this does not even occur on a semi-regular basis. With the advent of Zoom, Skype, cheap conference calling options and the like, or the use of old technology (eg, working lunches around a conference table), there is no reason why these exchanges should not occur more frequently.[22]

4.   Implementers: moving forward

Many of the challenges and critiques above also have relevance to implementers. For example, many implementers continue to find the prospect

---

22   Implementers are hungry for these exchanges. They want to get better at what they do, but the lack of regularised professional development opportunities for rule of law implementers is striking. Rule of law professionals working in developing countries are especially isolated, and might benefit the most from Zoom webinars, conference calls, etc in which their peers from other countries can share their experiences.

of implementing an ambitious, top-down programme irresistible, even when the requisite political will for it to succeed is shaky at best. Thus, donors and implementers often jump at the chance to work with a country's highest courts, even in the absence of adequate signals that the high court is prepared to institute meaningful reforms or has the political backing to do so. Implementers might achieve more impact and serve the public better by training trial court judges on recent changes to important laws (eg, a newly revised criminal code). The following are other challenges facing implementers as well as critiques of approaches common to some – but of course not all – implementers.

4.1   Implementers' hubris

Implementers are prone to 'implementers' hubris', just as donors are susceptible to development agency hubris. Too often, implementers fall in love with their own ideas and then try to sell them to sceptical local partners. Sometimes, the idea is based on something they have seen work well in another developing country, one that is superficially similar. Other times, the idea might be inspired by something they have seen work well in a country – often their own – with a robust rule of law that bears few similarities to the developing country under consideration. Not infrequently, the proponents of these ideas are managers of rule of law projects in Western capitals. To make matters worse, in the course of vetting these ideas, scepticism expressed by the field office is often discounted and perhaps attributed to the field office's lack of a can-do attitude. Almost every implementer with a decade or more of experience will confess to having seen a colleague (or perhaps themselves) fall into some variation of this self-made trap.

4.2   Bottom-up projects

Risk-taking is critical, and both donors and implementers should be willing to try new things, especially when it comes to the use of technology. But the majority of rule of law interventions should have a relatively strong track record of prior success. Commentators traditionally point to bottom-up projects as those most likely to generate impact and provide good value for donor funds expended. Some of these undertakings include: access to justice initiatives, especially those that increase the capacity of established NGOs to take on more needy clients; access to legal information, such as compiling laws and making them readily available online or through hard copies; simplifying court procedures and making a court environment less intimidating for users, especially the poor;[23] projects that tap into an issue of particular concern to a

---

23   Accessing legal services can be an unnecessarily unpleasant, nerve-jangling experience for average citizens. One commentator cited the example of a crowded notary office in a developing country where people regularly cut queues. Out of desperation, the notary office instituted a system whereby visitors took numbered tickets and waited for their number to be called. Daily scrums were eliminated, and order was achieved rapidly. People reported being very satisfied with the new system.

community (eg, land rights) and helping to mobilise CSOs to address these concerns; projects that increase the availability of legal counselling, especially in remote areas, including through the use of paralegals; projects that engage youth, such as Street Law, which train law students and others to educate the public about civic duties and rights, conflict mitigation techniques, international human rights principles, etc; projects that focus on law schools, including the opening of legal clinics that enable law students to assist indigent clients, and the training of law professors to use interactive, practice-based teaching methods as opposed to the traditional lecture format that deprives students of the opportunity to engage in dialogue and debate.

4.3 'Do no harm', especially in repressive regimes

In repressive countries, implementers should not delude themselves into thinking that they can help accelerate regime change. Further, they should not push CSOs to engage in risky projects that might achieve short-term gains but could undermine the CSO's ability to operate in the long term. This mindset is consistent with the 'do no harm' ethos that should inform all programming decisions. If a CSO already is engaged in a risky project, one commentator noted that providing additional donor funding or technical assistance is fair game, as CSOs should be allowed to accept certain risks as part of an organic bottom-up movement. The trick is not to lure a CSO into accepting undue risk, simply because money is being dangled in front of them.

4.4 Engaging host country professionals to lead programmes and redoubling professional development efforts

Historically, implementers were not sufficiently committed to building the capacity of host country professionals to serve as directors of rule of law programmes. Instead, they tended to rely on Western directors, who, while highly professional, often could not interact as effectively with host country partners as an equally professional host country national or a person from the region (eg, engaging a Cameroonian national to direct a programme in the Democratic Republic of Congo). This has changed in the last five years in particular, with donors often insisting that host country professionals assume greater responsibility. This is a very positive development but there is still room for donors and implementers to make the development of foreign nationals a higher priority when carrying out rule of law programmes. Foreign national staff persons are well positioned to eventually assume positions of responsibility with the government, CSOs, etc, long after donor funds dry up. Investing in their professional development is not costly and has the potential to pay significant dividends for the 30 or more years that remain in many of their working lives.

4.5   Access to lawyers

Implementers should explore ways to solve legal problems by bringing the law to the people, as opposed to waiting for people to seek out the law. An example of this is helping people to obtain health, educational or other benefits to which they are entitled under the law. This can be facilitated by providing access to a lawyer on the premises of, for example, a health clinic, an employment office, or a domestic violence clinic. One-stop legal services that provide legal counselling at, say, a hospital frequented by domestic violence or rape victims can greatly increase the likelihood that individuals will receive legal counselling and seek redress for wrongs committed against them. The work that the ABA Rule of Law Initiative (ABA ROLI) has done to address the rape crisis in war-torn Eastern DR Congo is one example of this approach in action, but there are many others.

4.6   Monitoring and evaluation

Most implementers are still struggling to monitor and evaluate their programmes effectively, but they have made great strides in the last 5–10 years. Lawyers have not traditionally excelled at data collection or analysis. Mostly because of donor pressure, they have been forced to improve, often by hiring dedicated monitoring and evaluation experts, a position that, with few exceptions, was unheard of, say, 20 years ago. Implementers need to ensure donors allocate sufficient resources to include a robust monitoring and evaluation component in programmes they fund. Implementers may also need to push back on donors who go overboard on monitoring and evaluation, especially with small grants. One commentator referred to it as the "tyranny of measurement", with implementers forced to spend an ever-larger percentage of the budget and brain time on monitoring and evaluation, but without commensurate returns.

4.7   Holding governments to account

Most developing countries in which rule of law implementers operate have ratified myriad UN human rights treaties. However, comparatively little effort has been expended in helping CSOs to hold their governments accountable for failing to meet their treaty-based obligations. This is a missed opportunity. Even something as simple as helping CSOs to write and submit shadow reports can be helpful.

4.8   Improving court services

Finding ways to promote a culture of professionalism within legal institutions, especially poorly funded government institutions, is challenging but important work. For example, a reformist chief judge can help turn around a court by challenging his or her team to better serve users of the court. One way to do that is to provide court users with a court satisfaction survey that invites them to identify ways in which their experience was positive or problematic. The court staff, in turn, can find creative ways to address problems that come to light, thereby reducing the number of complaints about poor or confusing service. Responding creatively and swiftly to problems raised by citizens can be a source of pride for court staff and can also serve as a model for nearby courts.

4.9 Engaging organisational development experts

Rule of law implementers should consider enlisting organisational development experts more frequently. In the best-case scenario, such experts would work part-time or full-time in a field office and be made available to various organisations, especially those receiving sub-grants from the implementer. CSOs could become more effective if they availed themselves of such organisational development assistance (ie, for tasks such as establishing hiring and employment protocols or devising office policy manuals). Most CSOs could also benefit from assistance with external relations, including dealing with the media, lobbying their government and fundraising. More generally, local CSOs should be taught to do virtually everything that implementers are able to do, including writing proposals and conducting high-level needs assessments.

4.10 'Best fit' solutions

Several commentators have implored implementers to stop trying to promote practices or create institutions that constitute best practice in Western countries. Instead, it is better to aim for 'best fit' solutions that help solve the unique problem in the country or locale in question even if they fall well short of international best practice. Incremental improvements can be built upon in future years. In the short term, modest improvements give the public something about which they can feel hopeful, spurring them to demand more such positive changes.[24]

5. Recipients of technical assistance: moving forward

Although the focus of this chapter is on donors and implementers, demanding greater accountability on the part of recipients of rule of law assistance constitutes both fair play and a good practice.

5.1 Coordinating projects

Host country governments sometimes struggle to maintain a firm grasp on all the rule of law projects underway in their country at any given time. Governments cannot assume that donors and implementers will always be

---

24   See Rachel Kleinfeld, *Advancing the Rule of Law Abroad: Next Generation Reform* (Carnegie Endowment for International Peace, 2012).

aware of each other's initiatives or that they will work in a coordinated, complementary fashion even if they are aware. It is ultimately the government's job to ensure that donors and implementers are not working at cross-purposes, either accidentally or by design. For example, better oversight might prevent a law being developed with European Commission assistance from inadvertently coming into conflict with legislation being developed with the help of US technical assistance.

5.2 The need for 'straight talk'

Recipients of rule of law assistance need to be more candid and assertive in conveying their concerns about the viability of programme ideas proposed by donors and implementers. Too often, they go along with a project that they feel has a questionable chance of succeeding. As one implementer noted, recipients have a hard time walking away from offers to collaborate, especially when the donor/implementer is prepared to procure equipment or other things valued by the recipient. Another implementer noted that recipients can also be fickle, agreeing to collaborate on a project and later changing their minds after donors/implementers have invested significant time and resources on the project. Sometimes, post-mortems reveal that the local partner for one reason or another never really intended to follow through on its stated commitment.

Recipients of assistance also need to be more forthcoming about their lack of capacity to take on certain projects. At any given time, they may be working with several donors/implementers and may simply lack the human resources to take on a single additional project. Also, recipients of assistance should be willing to engage in dialogue with donors/implementers about their capacity-building needs, such as improving project management skills or financial accounting capacity. This is one of the most important types of assistance needed by recipients, even though most people would not characterise this as rule of law assistance.

5.3 Awareness of needs in rural areas

Successful CSOs, especially those based in a capital city, can quickly lose touch with the sentiments and needs of citizens in provincial cities in their own country. In fact, the individuals employed by these CSOs are especially prone to this phenomenon, as they are often elites to begin with (eg, highly educated English speakers). Further, the salaries paid to locally hired CSO personnel, which are often supported or paid in full by grant funds, render them far wealthier than most of their fellow citizens, especially those in rural areas. CSO personnel need to take measures to ensure they are not providing advice to donors and implementers based largely on input they receive from the intelligentsia in the capital city. They need to maintain a network of reliable contacts outside the capital city who keep them updated on justice-related priorities (and frustrations) in rural areas.

## 6.	Future of rule of law assistance – trends and possibilities
Just as few people predicted the collapse of communism in Eastern Europe and the Soviet Union, there will be many other surprises in store for the rule of law community in the coming years. Here are some important developments to look out for in the coming decade and beyond.

### 6.1	Technology
There is little question that technology has the potential to advance the rule of law and increase access to information and justice. Even before the advent of Zoom, judges, without ever leaving their chambers, were using videoconferencing technology to conduct hearings that ensured jailed defendants were not being held unlawfully. Also, SMS texts have made it possible to alert authorities and lawyers in real time about election-related fraud or to inform the public about changes in legislation. In the future, every country's entire body of laws will be easily accessible online. Why is this so important? Even today one hears of judges and prosecutors who lack access to current laws, and determine cases based on legislation that was repealed years before because they never received a hard copy of the new law. Separately, online platforms may be able to help ever larger numbers of people solve disputes more effectively, including through online mediation and dispute resolution services. Finally, the next 10 years almost certainly will see major breakthroughs in the use of Artificial Intelligence in legal contexts. It is beyond the scope of this chapter to address this issue, but there is little doubt that AI will profoundly affect how law is practised in highly developed countries, and eventually less wealthy countries too. Rule of law implementers will need to study the good and the bad of AI and harness its power to good effect in developing countries.

### 6.2	Regional rule of law leaders
Regional leaders have the potential to be at least as effective as providers in the developed West when it comes to delivering rule of law assistance. At the moment, most of the countries that might have been suggested 10 years ago are no longer so attractive given their own struggles (eg, South Africa and even Chile). In the coming decade, we can only hope that some of these regional leaders will rebound, and possess the credibility to provide technical assistance in their backyard to countries with a decidedly weaker rule of law.

### 6.3	Neuroscience
The field of neuroscience will play a much more pronounced role in the delivery of rule of law assistance in the upcoming 10–20 years, just as it will in every facet of life. For example, how information is delivered to the citizenry will be heavily influenced by brain science, as we obtain a better understanding

of how people respond, for example, to certain concepts and words. This will help us craft more tailored rule of law and anti-corruption messages. As Frank Lutz and other political consultants know, finding which specific words in a campaign speech are able to excite people in a positive way and which elicit a negative response (sometimes subconsciously) is critical to transmitting a message effectively. For example, people respond very differently when an estate tax is referred to as a 'death tax'. Brain scans that demonstrate people's reactions to certain phrases make this possible but are too costly to use widely in the near term.

6.4   Epigenetics

Epigenetics may also help explain the difficulty that certain countries have in emerging from a period of sustained conflict or other trauma. Further study will be required, but it appears likely that, at least on a micro level, epigenetics can explain in part the behaviours observed in individuals in post-conflict or post-genocide societies.[25] Whether that negatively affects life in a country on a macro level, such as the country's adherence to the rule of law or the quality of governance, needs to be explored.

6.5   Demographics

Demographics will be increasingly factored into rule of law promotion efforts. The need to target youth more intensively, especially in countries with median ages in the high teens and low 20s, will become more obvious with the passage of time, with neuroscientists leading the way. Also, there will likely be an increased need to bolster the capacity of urban courts, especially in Africa and Asia. Why? Because we are currently witnessing the most dramatic migration to urban centres in the history of mankind. This trend is accelerating; but already for the first time ever, more people live in urban than non-urban areas. With people flocking to overcrowded cities, reliance on traditional justice

---

25   As psychobiologist Dr Inna Gaisler-Salomon noted: "it is undeniable that stress experienced during a person's lifetime is often correlated with stress-related problems in that person's offspring – and even in the offspring's offspring. Perhaps the best-studied example is that of the children and grandchildren of Holocaust survivors. Research shows that survivors' children have a greater-than-average chance of having stress-related psychiatric illnesses like post-traumatic stress disorder, even without being exposed to high levels of stress in their own lives. Similar correlations are found in other populations. Studies suggest that genocides in Rwanda, Nigeria, Cambodia, Armenia and the former Yugoslavia have brought about distinct psychopathological symptoms in the offspring of survivors." Inna Gaisler-Salomon, "Inheriting Stress", *New York Times* (7 March 2014), available at www.nytimes.com/2014/03/09/opinion/sunday/can-children-inherit-stress.html. See also Nader Perroud, Eugene Rutembesa, Ariane Paolini-Giacobino *et al*, "The Tutsi Genocide and Transgenerational Transmission of Maternal Stress: Epigenetics and Biology of the HPA Axis", 15 *The World Journal of Biological Psychiatry* 4 (2014) 334–345. Given the findings of this emerging field (epigenetics), it is sobering to consider the impact that Stalin's purges and gulags, World War II, and the Cultural Revolution (1966–1976) have had and might still be having on the people of Russia and China. Well over 70 million people perished in two generations in those two countries alone, much of it because of grotesque misrule. Further, more than 5 million Ukrainians are estimated to have died as a result of the Soviet famine in 1932–1933, which Stalin engineered in order to crush Ukraine's nationalism and its resistance to the forced collectivisation of farms.

mechanisms that are practised mostly outside major urban centres may diminish in importance over time. Also, as the general population ages in both the developed and developing world, there will be far more need to address elder abuse and criminal activity targeting the elderly, such as scams.

6.6   Specialised courts

Specialised courts may become more common, as they are efficient and may provide superior services to discrete populations (eg, small claims courts that deliver comparatively swift justice without any lawyer involvement, or family courts for matters relating to custody and divorce). Given the wave of migration to urban centres, there may be a greater need for specialised courts that deal with landlord–tenant disputes, as many who once owned tracts of land in rural areas are suddenly becoming renters.

6.7   Routinisation of law and legal services

Law will become increasingly routinised. This is already happening in the developed world through online templates that obviate the need for a lawyer's services in certain matters. This phenomenon will spread to developing countries as well. Further, just as the health sector relies on protocols for dealing with the most common medical conditions, the legal profession will do the same for routine legal issues. This routinisation phenomenon, which is closely related to technology and AI, bodes well for the poor and underserviced populations.

6.8   Direct grants to local CSOs

A larger percentage of donor funds will go directly to CSOs, bypassing traditional assistance providers (eg, Western NGOs and contractors) in many cases. There is a danger that CSOs will not be able to handle funds well at first and that this will generate second-guessing of this approach, but in the end this trend will continue, albeit with greater attention paid to building the capacity of local CSOs.

6.9   Empirical data and monitoring and evaluation

Greater reliance on empirical data and an emphasis on monitoring and evaluation is here to stay. It is unclear whether calls for more randomised controlled trials in the rule of law field will come to fruition. It is quite possible that they will not or that they will have only a limited effect on the field of technical legal assistance in the coming, say, 10 years.

6.10   Paralegals and hybrid problem solvers

There will be more hybrid problem solvers available in the future, namely paralegals or people with less legal training than fully qualified lawyers. They will almost certainly play a role equal to that of lawyers in helping to increase access to justice, especially in rural areas.

6.11 Correction of unrealistic expectations

The rule of law community will acquire an even better appreciation of just how many twists and turns there are on the road to reform, especially in post-conflict or post-autocratic countries. It should not be a surprise when countries that have experienced repression for decades (such as Iraq, Libya or Egypt) descend into chaos after an autocrat or dictator is toppled. Building the rule of law in those countries will require an extended, significant investment. There are no short-cuts. The 'easy' countries have all been welcomed into the world's rule of law community. All we are left with now are the hard cases, such as the Democratic Republic of the Congo, Myanmar, El Salvador, and a few cases that have yet to materialise, such as North Korea.

6.12 Indices

The sophistication of indices that measure the rule of law will continue to increase. Also, indices capable of promoting positive changes in the rule of law, such as Transparency International's Corruption Perceptions Index and the US State Department's Trafficking in Persons Report, will continue to be developed. For example, an index that measures compliance with the UN Guiding Principles on Business and Human Rights (the 'Ruggie Principles') could have an enormous impact on the behaviour of business enterprises who engage in questionable business practices in developing countries. This could take the form of a perceptions index, such as Transparency International's Corruption Perceptions Index, or a more research-based index that catalogues specific practices that violate the UN Guiding Principles. Persuading businesses to respect human rights and the rule of law, especially in developing countries, is one of the single most important advances that could be made in promoting the rule of law around the world. Fortunately, the rise of the Environment, Social and Governance (ESG) movement in the last few years makes this all the more likely, as capital already is beginning to flow toward good corporate citizens and away from bad ones.

6.13 Enabling environment for rule of law promotion, or lack thereof

The 1990s were, quite simply, a pleasant aberration. The overall enabling environment for rule of law promotion will continue to be extremely challenging for the foreseeable future, just as it has been since the beginning of this century. In large part, this can be attributed to the ascendance of China, and to Russia's very transparent effort to undermine Western institutions and Western democracies. Both countries can be counted on to continue providing cover for governments known to be routine rule of law violators, as well as leaders responsible for truly grave violations of international law, such as Syria and North Korea. One potential counterweight, however, is the United Nations' inclusion of goals relating to rule of law and governance in its post-2015 agenda, known as the UN's Sustainable Development Goals (SDGs). Of the 17 Goals, SDG 16 – 'Peace, Justice and Strong Institutions' – touches very directly on the rule of law. Progress in achieving the UN Millennium Development Goals (which expired in 2015) exceeded the expectations of most experts. It is of course possible that the UN's SDGs will be similarly successful, although improving health and education levels in a developing country is infinitely less challenging than improving governance and the rule of law. Also, achieving climate action (SDG 13) is almost certain to fall terribly short, and so too will efforts to achieve climate justice, especially for the world's poorest and most disadvantaged. Bolstering the capacity of CSOs to pursue climate justice at both the national and international level is an acute need.

6.14 Privacy

One of the singular challenges facing the entire world in the coming 5–10 years is fundamentally a rule of law problem: how we protect people's privacy from private actors, and more importantly, governmental actors. With the advent of cheap and ubiquitous CCTV, cheap and readily available digital storage banks that house vast troves of private data, and obsessive snooping aimed at ferreting out dissenters and perceived troublemakers, governments enjoy the upper hand and likely always will. The challenge, then, becomes one of containment, that is, establishing and enforcing clear boundaries of what are and what are not acceptable incursions on our privacy. Each country will draw that line differently. Europe has taken the lead on privacy issues. China also has taken the lead – as a violator of privacy. Other autocratic regimes, especially in the developing world, surely admire China's surveillance state, and will be eager to adopt their practices in the coming years.[26] How the rule of law community will deal with this challenge is deeply worrying, especially since it is unlikely that many of the worst violators of privacy would be willing to adopt an international convention on privacy or even 'guiding principles' akin to the UN Guiding Principles on Business and Human Rights. If there is a third edition of this book, we should not be surprised if one or more chapters is dedicated solely to the rule of law and privacy in the (post-) digital age.

7. Conclusion

As the preceding pages make clear, promoting the rule of law in the developing world is one of the great challenges of our day. Prior to the fall of the Berlin Wall

---

26 The United States, with its formidable National Security Agency, is no slouch when it comes to the dark art of electronic surveillance of its citizens, and also must be watched closely.

and the collapse of the Soviet Union, rule of law promotion efforts could be characterised as a series of stuttering steps. Not only was funding limited, but donors and implementers lacked a roadmap or academic literature to guide them. It was only after the collapse of communism in the Eastern bloc that the rule of law field truly came into its own; the contributions of rule of law assistance efforts in that region were far-reaching and, in many ways, remarkable.

With the benefit of hindsight, the Eastern bloc countries that transitioned from communism to rule-of-law-abiding democracies over the last 30 years were the comparatively easy cases. Those countries, even in the 1990s, bore little resemblance to today's Burundi, with its history of civil war, genocide, low literacy rates and crushing poverty. Nor did Eastern bloc countries much resemble today's Vietnam, Cambodia, Liberia, Iraq, DR Congo or Guatemala, all of which have been convulsed by civil war, genocide or other catastrophic events. These are just some of the countries that rule of law promoters are working in today, that is, the hard cases.

Much has been learned, especially in the last 30 years, about what does not work. An equal or greater amount has been learned about what *does* work. This is reflected in the sophistication and sensitivity demonstrated by today's implementers, as they craft and implement rule of law programmes around the world. But as this chapter points out, some of the most basic lessons are still being ignored, often due to hubris. Donors and implementers should hold themselves to higher standards and adhere to widely agreed upon best practices, such as avoiding the temptation to implement ambitious, costly, top-down projects without the political will necessary to make it viable, or without an adequate needs assessment and sober analysis of the likelihood of success.

Despite the accumulation of best practices and lessons learned over the last 60 years, significant gaps in our knowledge remain, most notably how to assist host country reformers to more effectively address destructive cultural norms and practices that undermine the rule of law and development generally. This and the previous chapter argue that the solution centres in part on identifying the right audience to whom messages about civic duty and the importance of the rule of law are transmitted.

For a variety of reasons, these chapters advance the argument that youth are the optimal audience. Young people possess the greatest drive to try new things and are uniquely open to rethinking generations-old habits and practices. Youth also possess the greatest aptitude for accepting new ideas and learning new concepts, owing to basic neuro-scientific principles. Also, demographics matter: the young constitute a large percentage of the population, especially in countries with the weakest rule of law.

As noted above, the median age in some of the world's most aid-intensive countries is roughly 19 years; in comparison, the median age in the United

States and Japan is 38 and 47 years, respectively. These statistics point to a need to devote greater resources to youth. It goes without saying that the poor also represent a significant percentage of the population in most aid-intensive countries. Thus, more rule of law resources should be directed at addressing their needs as well. Doing so would be in line with commentators' calls for a greater emphasis on bottom-up rather than top-down projects, and the laudable people-centred justice movement.

A recurrent theme in much of the best rule of law commentary is the need to adjust expectations about what can be accomplished by rule of law promotion efforts, irrespective of how much money is thrown at a problem. To take an extreme example, imagine spending $1 billion per year over the next decade in a handful of countries that score at the bottom of various rule of law indices. Is it conceivable that this prodigiously funded effort would bring about the rule of law, even if every best practice was adhered to by donors and implementers? The answer is assuredly 'no'. Countries with profoundly troubled and violent histories, such as Somalia, Libya, Afghanistan and Iraq are almost certainly two generations (or more) from enjoying a robust rule of law, no matter how much rule of law assistance they receive and how expertly it is carried out. Clearly, the stakes associated with a rule of law vacuum in these countries, but also in less extreme cases such as Nigeria, will remain high. Finding ways to advance the rule of law more effectively in these and other countries will surely remain one of the most urgent challenges faced by the international community in the coming decades.

In closing, the developed world needs to face the fact that we are well into a second decade of concerted efforts to undermine the rule of law and democracy around the world. If anything, we should expect even more vigorous efforts in the next 20 years, aided by the deft use of technology and social media. As Freedom House's *Freedom in the World* report makes clear, retrograde state actors have won the battle for 15 years straight; but it is foolhardy and even dangerous to point to China, Russia and others as the sole reason for this troubling, 15-year losing streak. A chaotic United States, for example, has done more to prove the points China and Russia are trying to make than one ever could have imagined possible. A chaotic United Kingdom has not helped matters, with other democratic and rule of law stalwarts also making many unforced errors. Returning to a central theme of these two chapters – that is, the centrality of youth in overseas rule of law promotion efforts – what's good for the goose is good for the gander. The best antidote against a further erosion of global democracy and the rule of law is by strengthening it in developed countries long admired by the developing world. Getting our own house in order is best done by focusing on our own youth, and teaching them the basics about the rule of law, democratic norms, civic duty, etc; in other words, investing in a fortified rule of law culture within our own borders. Perhaps this will give rise to a modest rule of law and democratic renaissance in the United States and elsewhere.[27] One thing is certain. The stakes are enormous if we do not reverse the present slide. It is, after all, unseemly to peddle a product to a sceptical buyer when it does not work all that well in the hands of a long-time user.

Finally, it is useful to remind ourselves that soft power won the first Cold War, and it is our best hope of winning the next one.

---

27   Gallup first polled Americans about their trust in government in the 1970s, and after a hiatus, resumed
      their polling in 1997. Confidence in government has gradually trended downward since 1997. Currently,
      43% of Americans say they have a great deal or fair amount of confidence in the executive branch.
      Americans' trust in the legislative branch is currently 33%, or five points higher than its all-time low of
      28% in 2014, a time of extreme partisan gridlock. Trust in the judicial branch has remained relatively
      high in the last 25 years, with 67% currently expressing a great deal or fair amount of trust in it.
      However, there is a troubling 24-point gap between Republicans and Democrats, with the latter
      expressing far less trust.

Chapter 13. Durability of the rule of law[1]

Homer E Moyer, Jr
Miller & Chevalier

The phrase 'the rule of law' is not new, but over the last 30 years it has become ubiquitous, in both the popular press and scholarly literature on law reform and democratisation. In the years following the fall of the Berlin Wall, it became a rallying cry for the American Bar Association's technical legal assistance projects (CEELI and ROLI, as described elsewhere in this book) and for similar governmental and commercial efforts that followed. In just the last generation, the term has been popularised, repeatedly and variously defined, widely translated, misappropriated by authoritarian regimes, critiqued, and discarded as hopelessly imprecise. Although sanctified by rule of law advocates, 'the rule of law' is still not a self-defining phrase.

We have made definitional progress. We have moved well beyond the simplistic notion that 'the rule of law' simply describes obeying the law, regardless of its content or how the laws are adopted, interpreted and applied. We are also well past the early 1990s when CEELI volunteers recognised rule of law issues principally by the absence of the rule of law, a useful, if incomplete, inside-out definition, albeit one which those who have lived in oppressive regimes understand and can describe passionately. Only later did there emerge a series of thoughtful efforts to define the rule of law affirmatively.

1. Closing in on the definition

Gradually, we have come to understand that the rule of law is a shorthand phrase. It and its paraphrase, 'government of laws, not of men', refer to systems in which everyone, including the government itself, is bound by the law, laws protect individual rights and liberties, and courts are independent and just. Governments that are respectful of, and accountable to, the rule of law stand in contrast to systems in which government authorities have unchecked discretion, courts are politically controlled or powerless, and individual rights and equal treatment are not guaranteed. Specifically, the term 'rule of law'

---

1   This chapter is a substantially unchanged version of the final chapter, by Homer E Moyer, in *Building the Rule of Law: Firsthand Accounts from a Thirty-Year Global Campaign*, edited by James R Silkenat and Gerold W Libby. © 2021 American Bar Association. All rights reserved. Reproduced with kind permission.

denotes a series of core principles of self-government, including that governmental power is limited through constitutional or other mechanisms and is itself not above the law, that its law-making processes are transparent and accessible, and that its courts are independent and impartial, protect basic individual rights and liberties, and treat all persons equally before the law.

The powers of government can be constrained in a variety of ways, including defined and circumscribed constitutional grants of authority, separation of governmental powers among different branches, 'checks and balances' for each branch *vis-à-vis* the others (including judicial power to review and correct overstepping by other branches of government), and, ultimately, free elections by a country's citizens. Also, a free press, which can serve as an independent watchdog against governmental corruption or overreach of its powers, is often considered an informal 'fourth branch' of government. And the absence of official corruption, financial or political, is commonly noted as a feature of the rule of law since corrupt officials or government agencies can broadly undermine other rule of law principles.

Thoughtful scholarly discourse has led to some elaborate definitions that include large numbers of indicators. In addition, beyond legal circles, academics might note that definitions of 'the rule of law' in many respects parallel or overlap with definitions of 'liberal democracy' and a 'republic'. And others, noting early European discussions of rule of law concepts, think of 'the rule of law' as a largely Western concept. While legal systems do differ in how they balance individual and community rights, rule of law values are found in virtually all legal systems, as is evident from the legal systems of many non-Western countries, including Japan, South Korea, Singapore, and a number of Middle Eastern and African countries.

Thus, notwithstanding progress in narrowing the definitional boundaries of the term 'rule of law', there is no standard, universally agreed definition. Descriptions range from short dictionary definitions, which can be cryptic and non-specific, to elaborate, detailed definitions with multiple parts and sub-parts, sometimes of quite unequal significance. And in the world of polarised politics, the phrase continues to be used casually by politicians and others as an all-purpose, rhetorical slogan or weapon.

Moreover, approaches to evaluating progress in implementing the rule of law are of at least two broad types: ones that focus on what a society fully committed to the rule of law would look like and ones that focus on what governmental mechanisms and safeguards are essential in order to build and sustain the rule of law. Result-focused definitions survey whether, in fact, laws are respected, government is transparent and accountable, political discourse is honest and respectful, and people are treated equally under the law. They measure reality against an aspirational standard. Means-focused definitions offer a guide for becoming a rule of law society by describing what constitutional protections and safeguards are necessary to limit governmental power, maintain independent courts, keep government operations open and accessible, guarantee freedom of the press, and treat all people equally under the law regardless of circumstance. One approach looks at how a society is doing, rule-of-law-wise; the other describes what constitutional and institutional tools are necessary to get there.

2.   A 30-year lookback

Given the definitional growth pains and multiplicity of interpretations of this four-word term – and countless other variables that affect how a country governs itself – it is no wonder that graphs tracking the success of countries in implementing 'the rule of law' show jagged, erratic lines reflecting progress, reversals, rebounds and frustrations. The 25+ countries that eagerly sought independence from the Soviet Bloc following the fall of the Berlin Wall make the point. Today, 30 years later, they range from progressive, peaceful Baltic states, to slow-to-change Central Asian Republics, to a host of Central and Eastern European countries transitioning unevenly to embrace and implement rule of law principles. The rule of law patchwork in the rest of the world is, today, not dissimilar.

Russia – where *glasnost* and *perestroika* brought down the Berlin Wall, triggered the creation of 25 independent states, and unleashed euphoria across two continents – has, under President Putin, doubled down on autocratic government and suppression of opposing voices advocating rule of law principles. Consequences of this choice have included unrest at home, a distressed economy, and the perpetuation of inequities common in prior decades of state-dominated, communist rule. Russia itself has adopted and implemented elements of the rule of law only partially or temporarily.

Similarly, China's authoritarian regime maintains increasingly strict control over its population, with the Communist Party expanding its use of technological tools to monitor and restrict the freedoms of its citizenry. In doing so, it flouts international human rights standards, most notably with respect to ethnic minorities, seeks to extend the geographical reach of its power and authority, and promotes a trade-off of individual freedom and accountable government with a promise of stability and economic advancement. Both China and Russia have had brief periods of liberalisation, but today rely on unforgiving force to repress calls for reform and the rule of law.

Recent years have also seen some backsliding by countries that transitioned to more democratic societies, countries that removed authoritarian regimes but failed to replace them with new governments committed to the rule of law, and, most conspicuously, countries that have been long-time champions of the rule of law, but which have failed to adhere fully to their own traditions and stated values, the United States among them. The cause of such regressions has often been characterised as an international 'populist' surge. The results have been tracked by annual *Freedom in the World* surveys published by Freedom House, which in 2021 reported that net declines in the number of 'free' countries in the world have continued uninterrupted since 2006. They show what Freedom House has characterised as a deepening "long democratic recession".[2]

In Central and Eastern Europe, Hungary and Poland are today prominent examples of backsliding. Belarus and some Central Asian republics have made little or no rule of law progress since gaining independence. In 2021, Freedom House also saw a dramatic decline in India, severe repression in countries such as Venezuela and the Philippines, and, in sub-Saharan Africa, little democratic reform. A decade ago, the Arab Spring saw a series of governments replaced, but only Tunisia sought to sustain significant rule of law reforms. In Western Europe, 'populism' undermined the rule of law in some countries, and the United States saw its greatest single year-to-year decline in the history of the Freedom House survey.

The overlay of a global, coronavirus pandemic in 2020 and 2021 further provided many countries with an occasion to shift to more autocratic measures, with rule of law safeguards and principles among the casualties. Overall, the 2021 *Freedom in the World* survey showed, at best, a mixed, unencouraging picture to advocates of the rule of law.

Although trends in the levels of freedom in countries as reported by Freedom House are an imperfect gauge of progress for the rule of law, they are fairly reliable bellwethers. Frequently, as national freedom and democratic government go, so goes the rule of law. It is also the case that democratic and economic reforms often flow from efforts to build the rule of law, albeit often with a delay in economic returns that is captured by what economists refer to as the 'J curve'. Moreover, the rule of law, individual freedom, and free-market economies can be mutually reinforcing or, if disconnected, can create societal stresses or potentially destabilising incongruities.

The messy picture of countries' efforts to articulate, establish, sustain and adhere to rule of law principles has generated frustration and scepticism about the stamina of rule of law reforms. It has even prompted concerned discussions examining the future of democracy.

3. Challenges in building and sustaining the rule of law

Why has the progress towards freer societies based on the rule of law been uneven and uncertain? Why was it incorrect to assume, as many did in the early 1990s, that the rush to establish democratic societies following the disintegration of the Soviet Union would be unstoppable and relatively quick? The reasons are undoubtedly many, ranging from repressive resistance by

---

2   https://freedomhouse.org/report/freedom-world/2021/democracy-under-siege.

privileged old guards that retained power, to nostalgia for aspects of a past autocratic regime that people knew and had adjusted to. Lessons learned over the last 30 years do highlight two prominent additional factors: the scope of the challenges inherent in a society's transitioning to a fundamentally new form of national government and the rigorous demands of fully implementing core principles of the rule of law.

First, experience has now made plain how profound and complex is the process of transitioning from longstanding authoritarian rule to a democratic societal structure based on the rule of law and to an economy no longer controlled by the state. The challenges are compounded if the transitioning country has no older generation that previously lived under democratic rule. In the 1990s in newly independent countries that had been part of the Soviet Union, no such older generation was still living; in satellite countries that had been part of the Soviet Bloc, an older generation had known different systems, albeit 30–40 years before.

Although we frequently used the term 'law reform', what was underway in the early 1990s was vastly more than law reform. It was not a matter, as some at the time assumed, of simply writing a new constitution. As important as new constitutions were – changing from constitutions that were aspirational to constitutions that guaranteed rights and protections – new constitutions were just a first step. Nor was transitioning just a matter of writing new laws. Necessary new laws included new laws in areas that had not been part of the legal or public culture, such as private property, securities laws, intellectual property, international trade and human rights.

Additional implications followed. Relatively early on came the realisation that implementing new constitutions and new laws also required new institutions. Many necessary institutions had simply not previously existed or required top-to-bottom reform. Institutions and their new officials needed to develop their own processes and safeguards, gain experience, establish institutional norms and traditions, etc. Later came an appreciation that official corruption, something not on most original reform agendas, could follow naturally from autocratic regimes in which privilege for ruling elites was endemic and seen as an entitlement. Fresh new governments, new individual freedoms, and privatisation of state-owned enterprises created new opportunities for corruption, which came to be recognised as an existential threat to democratic transitions.

Moreover, political reforms were inextricably tied to economic reforms or, as one insightful new Polish minister said to me early in the process, "without economic reforms, there will be no political reforms". Generating and managing economic progress in new, free-market environments dependent on privately owned businesses, entrepreneurship, market forces of supply and demand, stock markets to facilitate broad private ownership of companies, integration into the global economy, and nascent governmental regulation presented a daunting forest of issues for transitional countries.

Also underappreciated by both euphoric reformers and many of their advisers were the necessary transformations in public attitudes toward government, including an understanding of the roles of citizens in a democratic society and expectations of how a democratic government should function. Transparency in governmental entities was both new and imperfect. Interacting with governmental entities in new ways, including by participating in agency decision-making, and even contesting government decisions, was new territory for much of the public. And, most fundamentally, elections that were free, honest and in which all citizens could meaningfully participate raised a host of additional issues, ones with which many mature democracies continue to struggle.

The breadth and depth of the challenges of such societal pivots warrant, and continue to receive, thoughtful analysis, aided immeasurably by hindsight. The point here is not to try to summarise the many elements of transitioning from longstanding totalitarian states to new law-based, democratic societies. Rather, it is simply to note what has since become obvious, namely, that such transformations are inordinately complicated and require persistence, trial and error, insightful collaborators, and something of a public consensus. That not all countries which courageously took on these challenges have succeeded in the short run is not difficult to understand. The thought that the process could be prompt and irreversible – as many participants and observers did think – was naïvely hopeful, uninformed and perhaps a bit presumptuous. Now having a more complete appreciation of the hurdles in fundamental transitions of government helps explain the kaleidoscopic picture of the last 30 years.

A second factor, which we may still underappreciate, relates to the rule of law itself. A reality that both advocates of the rule of law and reformers must acknowledge is that living up to the core principles and values of the rule of law is not a modest undertaking. In practice, rule of law principles are aspirational and decidedly ambitious. In the United States, a country constitutionally founded on rule of law principles, it has taken our entire history to broaden and apply the sacred principle in the Declaration of Independence that "all men are created equal", to those who were slaves (approximately 90 years later), to women who did not have the right to vote (145 years), to minorities subjected to discrimination based on race or ethnicity (190 years), and to those with non-conventional sexual orientation (245 years). And we are, today, reminded on a daily basis of how much further we have yet to go to live up to the principles we espouse. In hindsight, the progress can look slow and halting; at the same time, it also shows that continuing pressure to embrace noble ideals can itself generate continual progress.

The challenges inherent in just the principle of equal treatment before the law are apparent in the prolonged record of the United States, a country that espoused at least a modified version of that principle from its very beginnings. Even more telling, perhaps, is the number of countries that have declined even to espouse that principle, let alone try to implement it. A common inclination in countries that emerged from the Soviet Bloc a generation ago was to seek to solve issues of multicultural societies by redrawing national borders or otherwise segregating themselves into homogenous ethnic, religious or racial groups. The ending of Apartheid in South Africa 27 years ago, an example of a bold and ambitious transition, is still a work in progress.

The persistence of religious, ethnic, racial and other group-based conflicts around the world reflects the slow progress. Such historical divisions often define the boundaries of political parties or groups as well as social and personal separations. They are perhaps forerunners of what today is termed 'identity politics' in which political interests correspond to some aspect of personal identity rather than to race-neutral, religion-neutral, gender-neutral political principles. If sufficiently deep, they can polarise a society and thwart efforts to implement the rule of law. History confirms that equal treatment can come much more easily in homogenous, like-minded groups than in diverse societies, which most countries are or will become.

Other rule of law principles are equally ambitious. It is a stringent job description that calls for judges to be knowledgeable, wise, independent, impartial, impervious to corruption and free of bias or outside influence. The same is true for elected or appointed public officials whose job is to make judgments on issues that present complex questions, hard trade-offs, competing public interests and occasional dilemmas. The United States is today an example of how the elected legislative body of a democracy committed to the rule of law can be hobbled or gridlocked on important national issues because of divisions and ideologies that are at war with democratic decision-making in a large, diverse country. And the simple term, a 'free and independent press', incorporates a panoply of issues of how media fairly and responsibly inform the public and impartially monitor the performance of the public's government.

Recent years have also highlighted other demands and challenges to implementing rule of law principles and sustaining democratic, law-based societies. In republican governments ultimate power remains with the people, and day-to-day governing is the responsibility of representatives of the people. The people are not expected to be masters of the intricacies of governing a large, diverse country. What is necessary, however, is that the public have a basic understanding of how a republican government with separate branches of government functions, an appreciation of the challenges it confronts in resolving often complex national issues, and buy-in to the country's social contract or compact, which guarantees the freedoms and benefits that democratic governments commit to deliver.

The decline in civic education and the resulting decline in civic literacy in the United States in recent years have focused attention and concern on this issue. A common level of public knowledge of our country's governing structure, objectives and operation provides a baseline for informed citizen participation in the self-governing, representative government that our national constitution established. The importance of this prerequisite for citizenship has generated a growing outcry for a return to, and enhancement of, civic education. A useful yardstick for measuring the extent to which US citizens meet an appropriate level of civic knowledge could be the test given to all immigrants seeking to become naturalised US citizens. Passing grades on this test for all Americans would be a not unreasonable standard.

A related risk for rule of law societies is the rise in deliberate, partisan misinformation. While democratic societies promote broad speech freedoms and robust public debate, widespread public circulation and acceptance of false information or accusations can be a social cancer in a democratic society. It brings to mind Senator Daniel Patrick Moynihan's oft-quoted admonition that "Everyone is entitled to his own opinion, but not to his own facts".[3] This issue, enlarged and made more complicated by pervasive social media, a multiplicity of information sources, and the blending of fact and opinion in public media can create a severe risk for democratic societies. On a personal level, dealing with these new dynamics requires not just civic literacy, but also an open but sceptical mind and good interpersonal communication skills.

Finally, also related, is the phenomenon of political or partisan polarisation. As we in the United States have witnessed and as foreign adversaries have noted, political polarisation can be damaging to a democratic, rule of law society and crippling to its legislative body. In her book, *After Repression*,[4] Elizabeth Nugent convincingly demonstrates how and why political polarisation can thwart a transition from authoritarian regimes to democratic ones. Using two countries from the Arab Spring as case studies, she not only identifies necessary steps for a successful transition, but also explains why political polarisation during and immediately following a transition opportunity can defeat a transition to democratic government.

Her insights and observations are relevant not just to governments in transition. Hardened political polarisation in established democracies can cripple a country's law-making body and, if persistent, result in recurring gridlock or abrupt pendular swings in national policies, either of which is destructive of republican, democratic government. At a time when societies are becoming increasingly multicultural and diverse, decision-making on national issues necessarily requires give-and-take and compromise (without which

---

3   https://en.wikiquote.org/wiki/Daniel_Patrick_Moynihan.
4   See www.amazon.co.uk/After-Repression-Polarization-Democratic-Transition/dp/0691203059.

today's US government could never have been formed or sustained). That compromise is disparaged by some today as weak and unprincipled and is indeed a threat to republican governments and, as a result, to the rule of law.

The truth is that high-minded rule of law principles set high standards. Implementing and abiding by noble, aspirational rule of law principles is not a light-hearted undertaking. It requires both patience and impatience. That reality applies to both countries committed to the rule of law and those simply entertaining the possibility.

4.   The irrepressibility of the rule of law

Notwithstanding a mixed record over the last 30 years and the foregoing risks, there is compelling evidence to suggest that the rule of law is, and will remain, irrepressible. History indicates that the rule of law and its core principles are powerfully appealing, resilient and durable, as future Freedom House surveys will undoubtedly demonstrate.

It should be noted first, perhaps, that 'populist' trends come in various shapes and sizes. Although in recent years the term 'populist' has been used to refer to nationalistic political swings that have undercut democratic norms and the rule of law, populist moods and movements can go in various political directions. A generation ago, it was populist sentiment that drove two dozen countries to flee from the authoritarian control of the Soviet Union. Populism does not come in a single political stripe, and tomorrow's populism may bear little resemblance to today's version.

Beyond that, as important and worrisome as the Freedom House scorecards are, they do not test the relative strength and depth of appeal – and thus the staying power – of rule of law societies compared to authoritarian or oppressive ones. It is obvious that aspirations for the rule of law and calls for reforms can be suppressed by despotic or autocratic regimes, even for extended periods of time. With few interruptions, Russia has done so for a century and China for more than 70 years. The same approach is present in a number of other countries today. However, even violent government repression does not extinguish the powerful attraction of rule of law principles. Nor does it end persistent popular calls for reform or expunge an understanding of the beneficial effects that the rule of law can bring.

The enduring magnetism of the rule of law is evident in even the most autocratic of governments. Beyond the historic rush of countries escaping autocratic Soviet control in the 1990s, massive demonstrations, held at great personal risk, continue to take place in authoritarian states such as Russia and Belarus. China, reneging on its international commitments, has resorted to harsh sanctions and crackdowns in Hong Kong in response to large, recurring public demonstrations protesting the rollback of individual freedoms. Citizens of Venezuela have voted with their feet, with massive numbers leaving the country. Authoritarian rule in Syria, Libya, Turkey, Myanmar and countries in Central America has sparked massive waves of immigration to countries more respectful of the rule of law. Consistent features of totalitarian regimes are their lack of self-confidence to allow those who have different views or who oppose existing policies to speak freely and their unwillingness to defend the status quo in their countries in an open marketplace of ideas.

In contrast to bold, widespread public demonstrations protesting the absence of the rule of law, the world has seen little public clamour for more autocratic governments. While complexities and obstacles to comprehensive reform of national governments can lead to backsliding, autocratic regimes are rarely buoyed by voluntary, grass roots public support. There are no public calls for courts to be controlled by powerful heads of state, biased, or populated by judges open to financial or political bribery. Judges who lack integrity, trade favourable judgments for bribes, or respond to political or partisan pressure are not requested by litigants seeking to right a wrong. One need only ask someone who has lived in a repressive society in which its judiciary fails to adhere to basic rule of law standards.

Governments whose heads of state and other officials are honest, committed to serving the public good, accountable, and have limited powers are preferable to the alternatives. For most populations, honest government is not a passing or momentary societal aspiration. Likewise, a free and open press that creates a truly free marketplace of ideas is a durably good thing for humankind. Perhaps most of all, equal treatment of all persons before the law, as written and as applied, is a noble and lasting aspiration in a multicultural world. The desire for individual freedom and dignity has continued to manifest itself for centuries.

Freedom House, in addition to its annual assessments of the levels of freedom in various countries, also documents the number of countries in which demonstrations against autocratic governments have taken place. In 2019, Freedom House counted major protests in 39 countries – a telling indicator of public dissatisfaction with governments indifferent to the rule of law.[5] If feasible and quantifiable, surveys and assessments of the levels of dissatisfaction of citizens living in countries with dictatorial or oppressive governments would be an interesting complement to assessment of actual levels of freedom or actual adherence to the rule of law.

In short, departures from the rule of law or its absence do not occur because the principles that the rule of law embodies are themselves flawed. Nor is the rule of law rejected because the alternatives of powerful, arbitrary, repressive governments have greater public support. In countries with repressive regimes, there is no opportunity for citizens to make a choice because the regime in

---

5   https://freedomhouse.org/report/freedom-world/2021/democracy-under-siege.

power is often willing to take whatever steps are necessary to suffocate calls for the rule of law. Repression frequently involves mass arrests, imprisonment, torture, or death for opposition forces. In other countries attempting to experiment with, adopt or reclaim rule of law practices, it is unsurprising that the complexities and challenges of the process have resulted in a variety of short-term outcomes.

The powerful appeal of the key tenets of the rule of law, however, is unlikely to dissipate. It persists in countries ranging from those in which the absence of the rule of law is intensely and personally felt to countries in which rule of law principles are national values, if sometimes taken for granted or compromised. Because they are durable and persistent, their worth will be measured, as Chinese philosophers remind us from time to time, in the long run.

In the United States, a recent election has redirected national government policies from paths that they were on during a previous 'populist' administration. Some support for that variety of populism persists, however, perpetuating the high risks of political polarisation and leaving open how these recent issues will ultimately play out.

As a result, there have probably been few times in recent history that so appropriately call to mind the occasion when Ben Franklin was asked whether the Constitutional Convention had created a monarchy or a republic, to which he replied, "a republic", but added, "if you can keep it". For us – citizens living 230 years later in a diverse, technological society – that challenge is neither flippant nor anachronistic. As we need to remind ourselves from time to time: whether we can preserve the rule of law and keep the remarkable nation we have collectively created is up to us.

Chapter 14. Prospects and challenges for the rule of law

Richard J Goldstone
Retired justice of the Constitutional Court of South Africa
Robert A Stein
University of Minnesota Law School

We conclude this publication by offering some observations about the prospects and challenges for the rule of law in the years to come, in both its domestic and international applications. It will be clear from the preceding chapters that efforts to improve the rule of law are not a straight line forward; there will be two steps forward, followed by a step back. These efforts are more of a marathon than a sprint.

1. The rule of law within nation states

It will have emerged from the earlier chapters that there is wide agreement between scholars, judges and practitioners from all continents that, whatever it might embrace, the rule of law is central to democracy. In particular, there is unanimity that for democratic government to succeed there must be respect for the law, all must be subject to the law and accountable to an independent judiciary.

The separation of powers is no less crucial to the rule of law. While there is no perfect formula to achieve that separation, the courts must be separate from and independent of the executive and the legislature. This separation is an important source of friction between the judiciary and the other two branches of government. The popularly elected legislature and the executive are habitually jealous of their own powers and not infrequently resent their will being thwarted by unelected judges. In constitutional democracies it is the constitution that is supreme and in some democracies, based on the English system, it is the legislature that is supreme. It is this resentment of the powers of the judiciary that makes the rule of law, and indeed democracy, so fragile.

In times of prosperity and peace, there is less friction between the three branches of government. However, in times of war and political tension, resentment of the judges often bubbles to the surface. It is, of course, precisely in those times that threats to minorities and marginalised groups make the rule of law essential as a bulwark against tyranny. This fragility of the rule of law is exacerbated by the absence of any enforcement power in the courts and the corresponding reliance of judges upon the executive branch to give effect to their orders.

It is the lack of respect for orders of courts that are the mark of undemocratic and oppressive states. Those states have no independent judges and the courts are expected to reflect in their decisions the wish of the government of the day. In this context one thinks of countries such as China, Zimbabwe and the Russian Federation among, unfortunately, too many others. Even in Hungary and Poland, democracies and members of the European Union, there has been overreach and weakening of judicial independence in recent years. In Hungary, a commanding majority of the ruling party enabled legislation that lowered the retirement age of judges and assured the government of support by quiescent members of the judiciary who were appointed by the current government.

The United States has not been immune from curtailing civil liberties in times of stress and fear. The infamous internment of Japanese Americans in the wake of the attack on Pearl Harbor in 1941 is one illustration. Fear caused even the liberal New Deal government of President Franklin Roosevelt to displace thousands of Americans without justification. These violations of the rule of law are bipartisan and not restricted to any one political party. Another illustration is the reaction of the American government in the aftermath of the terrorist attacks on New York and Washington DC, on 11 September 2001. That reaction surfaced with the publication of the 2014 United States Senate Report, which provided evidence of the use of torture by the Central Intelligence Agency. The United States failed to comply with its domestic and international obligations under the United Nations Convention against Torture and the domestic legislation that has given affect to it. Both the Convention and the domestic legislation require the United States to investigate and charge those who are suspected of having committed acts of torture. This has recently become a situation that is under investigation in the International Criminal Court and referred to below.

In the United Kingdom, not long ago, the British prime minister called for legislation to curtail incendiary speech by Islamic preachers and, as some described, "the overly careful treatment of religious minorities in Britain".[1] He called on internet and social media companies to do more to fight militants' propaganda and recruiting.[2] Overreach is again a distinct danger – especially where, as in Britain, the courts are powerless to strike down parliamentary legislation.

South Africa, since the presidency of Nelson Mandela, was to be Africa's model democracy. However, members of the former government of President Zuma attacked the judiciary, especially in the wake of a court order preventing President Omar al-Bashir of Sudan from leaving the country, where he was

---

1   See Steven Erlanger, "David Cameron Calls on Muslims in Britain to Help End Extremism", *NY Times* (20 July 2015), www.nytimes.com/2015/07/21/world/europe/david-cameron-calls-on-muslims-in-britain-to-help-end-extremism.html.
2   *Ibid.*

attending an African Union meeting of African heads of state. The order was made to allow the court time to determine whether South Africa should arrest al-Bashir under a warrant issued by the International Criminal Court on charges of genocide and crimes against humanity. South Africa has ratified the Rome Statute and also has domestic legislation obliging it to carry out orders of the International Criminal Court. The government allowed al-Bashir out of the country in violation of the court order. The government claimed that the head-of-state immunity enjoyed by al-Bashir trumped its obligations under the ICC Statute or the domestic legislation implementing it. More recently, former President Zuma was ordered by the Constitutional Court to appear before a state inquiry into corruption. He failed to do so and the chair of the inquiry has requested the Court to imprison Zuma for contempt of its order.

These are but a few instances of a legislature or executive criticising the judicial branch for interfering with what is perceived to be the will of the majority. We would emphasise that in any state it is not the majority that requires constitutional or legal protection but minorities and marginalised groups.

Ultimately, the protection of democracy from attacks by the majority depends upon whether society has developed a rule of law culture in which a majority of the people will contest overreach by their own government. This has certainly been the position in Britain where, as mentioned earlier, Parliament is supreme and there is no written constitution. There, the reverence expressed at Runnymede on the occasion of the 800th anniversary of Magna Carta reflects the value attached by the people of Britain to the rule of law.

The rule of law is not majoritarianism. Even in those countries where there is a supreme parliament, the majority cannot do whatever it pleases. Where there is a constitution and the power of judicial review, legislation that violates the constitution is subject to being struck down by the courts. In countries with a supreme parliament, it is the good sense of the legislators and, equally importantly, the fear of being voted out of office in the next election that together deter overreach and unfair or inappropriate legislative actions.

The prospect of upholding the rule of law in any democracy will ultimately depend upon the respect given to it by the branches of government and the people. It is for this reason that in any democracy the vigilance shown by civil society often plays a crucial role. It is essential that human rights organisations, the media and religious organisations call attention to infractions of the rule of law and demand that remedial action be taken. Modern technology and, in particular, social media have given added power to civil society. It is for this reason that authoritarian regimes frequently take steps to control that technology. Its growing reach is making it increasingly difficult to control, as events in China have demonstrated.

2. The rule of law internationally

Until recent years the sovereignty of nations held sway in international relations and international law. With the shrinking of our world in consequence of modern technology and travel, that strict application of sovereignty has been shrinking. Nations can no longer ignore events in their neighbourhood and even further afield. The genocide committed in Rwanda in 1994 brought untold human and material devastation to that country and moreover destabilised all of the Great Lakes region of Africa. The consequences of that human calamity are still with us today, more than 25 years later. In 2015, there was again bloodshed in Burundi that is directly linked to the earlier genocide in Rwanda. It was the recognition by the Security Council that the Rwanda genocide threatened international peace and security that enabled and empowered it to establish the International Criminal Tribunal for Rwanda (ICTR).

The volume and importance of international trade has convinced leading trading nations that their interests dictate subjecting their governments to the jurisdiction of the Appellate Body of the World Trade Organization. That Body was disabled by the Trump Administration which vetoed the appointment of new judges when the terms of existing judges ended. There are now talks to resuscitate it.

Prior to the establishment of the two United Nations *ad hoc* tribunals for the former Yugoslavia and Rwanda, there was no international criminal justice. The work of the Nuremberg and Tokyo Tribunals represented multinational justice rather than international justice. Those attempts at justice by the victorious nations after World War II led to the hope of establishing a permanent international criminal court. That hope is to be found in Article 6 of the 1948 Genocide Convention and Article 5 of the 1973 International Convention of the Suppression and Punishment of the Crime of Apartheid. However, the Cold War put that endeavour on hold, and it was not until 1993 that the Security Council established the first truly international criminal court for the former Yugoslavia (ICTY).

The successes of the ICTY and ICTR were sufficient to provide the momentum that led to the establishment of the ICC. Those successes were impossible to anticipate in the early years of the two UN tribunals. The early arrest warrants issued by the ICTY were not implemented and accused war criminals were allowed to roam the streets of the towns and villages where their notorious crimes were perpetrated. The political will then changed in the late 1990s, and by the end of 2013 every one of the 166 alleged criminals indicted by the ICTY was arrested and brought to stand trial in The Hague. In the case of the ICTR, all but three of those indicted were arrested and brought to stand trial in Arusha.

Some 123 nations have decided that if impunity for the worst war criminals is to be terminated, the International Criminal Court (ICC) should be supported. Only when that court began to issue arrest warrants for African heads of state did the African Union raise objections to the court and question why only African cases were before it. The real question they should have asked was whether serious war crimes were being committed in African states. They should also have been drawing more attention to the manner in which powerful states were protecting the most serious war crimes from coming before the court. The situations in Sri Lanka and Syria come to mind. The sanctions imposed on the ICC by the Trump Administration were reversed by the Biden Administration. The United States, however, remains opposed to the ICC opening investigations into Afghanistan that includes the alleged war crimes committed by the CIA referred to above. So, too, the investigation into the situation in Palestine/Israel.

The international rule of law will continue to develop and be implemented for as long as nations, and especially large nations, consider that it is in the interests of their own people. That is very much a political question. The implementation of justice and respect for the rule of law are dependent on political will. It is on civil society that the responsibility increasingly lies to ensure that their leaders act in ways and adopt policies that are calculated to safeguard and advance the rule of law.

Appendix A: Universal Declaration of Human Rights

Adopted 10 December 1948

Preamble

Whereas recognition of the inherent dignity and of the equal and inalienable rights of all members of the human family is the foundation of freedom, justice and peace in the world,

Whereas disregard and contempt for human rights have resulted in barbarous acts which have outraged the conscience of mankind, and the advent of a world in which human beings shall enjoy freedom of speech and belief and freedom from fear and want has been proclaimed as the highest aspiration of the common people,

Whereas it is essential, if man is not to be compelled to have recourse, as a last resort, to rebellion against tyranny and oppression, that human rights should be protected by the rule of law,

Whereas it is essential to promote the development of friendly relations between nations,

Whereas the peoples of the United Nations have in the [UN] Charter reaffirmed their faith in fundamental human rights, in the dignity and worth of the human person and in the equal rights of men and women and have determined to promote social progress and better standards of life in larger freedom,

Whereas Member States have pledged themselves to achieve, in co-operation with the United Nations, the promotion of universal respect for and observance of human rights and fundamental freedoms,

Whereas a common understanding of these rights and freedoms is of the greatest importance for the full realization of this pledge,

Now, Therefore THE GENERAL ASSEMBLY proclaims THIS UNIVERSAL DECLARATION OF HUMAN RIGHTS as a common standard of achievement for all peoples and all nations, to the end that every individual and every organ of society, keeping this Declaration constantly in mind, shall strive by teaching and education to promote respect for these rights and freedoms and by progressive measures, national and international, to secure their universal and effective recognition and observance, both among the peoples of Member States themselves and among the peoples of territories under their jurisdiction.

Article 1.

All human beings are born free and equal in dignity and rights. They are endowed with reason and conscience and should act towards one another in a spirit of brotherhood.

Article 2.

Everyone is entitled to all the rights and freedoms set forth in this Declaration, without distinction of any kind, such as race, colour, sex, language, religion, political or other opinion, national or social origin, property, birth or other status. Furthermore, no distinction shall be made on the basis of the political, jurisdictional or international status of the country or territory to which a person belongs, whether it be independent, trust, non-self-governing or under any other limitation of sovereignty.

Article 3.

Everyone has the right to life, liberty and security of person.

Article 4.

No one shall be held in slavery or servitude; slavery and the slave trade shall be prohibited in all their forms.

Article 5.

No one shall be subjected to torture or to cruel, inhuman or degrading treatment or punishment.

Article 6.

Everyone has the right to recognition everywhere as a person before the law.

Article 7.

All are equal before the law and are entitled without any discrimination to equal protection of the law. All are entitled to equal protection against any discrimination in violation of this Declaration and against any incitement to such discrimination.

Article 8.

Everyone has the right to an effective remedy by the competent national tribunals for acts violating the fundamental rights granted him by the constitution or by law.

Article 9.

No one shall be subjected to arbitrary arrest, detention or exile.

Article 10.

Everyone is entitled in full equality to a fair and public hearing by an independent and impartial tribunal, in the determination of his rights and obligations and of any criminal charge against him.

Article 11.

(1) Everyone charged with a penal offence has the right to be presumed innocent until proved guilty according to law in a public trial at which he has had all the guarantees necessary for his defence.

(2) No one shall be held guilty of any penal offence on account of any act or omission which did not constitute a penal offence, under national or international law, at the time when it was committed. Nor shall a heavier penalty be imposed than the one that was applicable at the time the penal offence was committed.

Article 12.

No one shall be subjected to arbitrary interference with his privacy, family, home or correspondence, nor to attacks upon his honour and reputation. Everyone has the right to the protection of the law against such interference or attacks.

Article 13.

(1) Everyone has the right to freedom of movement and residence within the borders of each state.

(2) Everyone has the right to leave any country, including his own, and to return to his country.

Article 14.

(1) Everyone has the right to seek and to enjoy in other countries asylum from persecution.

(2) This right may not be invoked in the case of prosecutions genuinely arising from non-political crimes or from acts contrary to the purposes and principles of the United Nations.

Article 15.

(1) Everyone has the right to a nationality.

(2) No one shall be arbitrarily deprived of his nationality nor denied the right to change his nationality.

Article 16.

(1) Men and women of full age, without any limitation due to race, nationality or religion, have the right to marry and to found a family. They are entitled to equal rights as to marriage, during marriage and at its dissolution.

(2) Marriage shall be entered into only with the free and full consent of the intending spouses.

(3) The family is the natural and fundamental group unit of society and is entitled to protection by society and the State.

Article 17.

(1) Everyone has the right to own property alone as well as in association with others.

(2) No one shall be arbitrarily deprived of his property.

Article 18.

Everyone has the right to freedom of thought, conscience and religion; this right includes freedom to change his religion or belief, and freedom, either alone or in community with others and in public or private, to manifest his religion or belief in teaching, practice, worship and observance.

Article 19.

Everyone has the right to freedom of opinion and expression; this right includes freedom to hold opinions without interference and to seek, receive and impart information and ideas through any media and regardless of frontiers.

Article 20.

(1) Everyone has the right to freedom of peaceful assembly and association.

(2) No one may be compelled to belong to an association.

Article 21.

(1) Everyone has the right to take part in the government of his country, directly or through freely chosen representatives.

(2) Everyone has the right of equal access to public service in his country.

(3) The will of the people shall be the basis of the authority of government; this will shall be expressed in periodic and genuine elections which shall be by universal and equal suffrage and shall be held by secret vote or by equivalent free voting procedures.

Article 22.

Everyone, as a member of society, has the right to social security and is entitled to realization, through national effort and international co-operation and in accordance with the organization and resources of each State, of the economic, social and cultural rights indispensable for his dignity and the free development of his personality.

Article 23.
(1) Everyone has the right to work, to free choice of employment, to just and favourable conditions of work and to protection against unemployment.
(2) Everyone, without any discrimination, has the right to equal pay for equal work.
(3) Everyone who works has the right to just and favourable remuneration ensuring for himself and his family an existence worthy of human dignity, and supplemented, if necessary, by other means of social protection.
(4) Everyone has the right to form and to join trade unions for the protection of his interests.

Article 24.
Everyone has the right to rest and leisure, including reasonable limitation of working hours and periodic holidays with pay.

Article 25.
(1) Everyone has the right to a standard of living adequate for the health and well-being of himself and of his family, including food, clothing, housing and medical care and necessary social services, and the right to security in the event of unemployment, sickness, disability, widowhood, old age or other lack of livelihood in circumstances beyond his control.
(2) Motherhood and childhood are entitled to special care and assistance. All children, whether born in or out of wedlock, shall enjoy the same social protection.

Article 26.
(1) Everyone has the right to education. Education shall be free, at least in the elementary and fundamental stages. Elementary education shall be compulsory. Technical and professional education shall be made generally available and higher education shall be equally accessible to all on the basis of merit.
(2) Education shall be directed to the full development of the human personality and to the strengthening of respect for human rights and fundamental freedoms. It shall promote understanding, tolerance and friendship among all nations, racial or religious groups, and shall further the activities of the United Nations for the maintenance of peace.
(3) Parents have a prior right to choose the kind of education that shall be given to their children.

Article 27.
(1) Everyone has the right freely to participate in the cultural life of the community, to enjoy the arts and to share in scientific advancement and its benefits.

(2) Everyone has the right to the protection of the moral and material interests resulting from any scientific, literary or artistic production of which he is the author.

Article 28.

Everyone is entitled to a social and international order in which the rights and freedoms set forth in this Declaration can be fully realized.

Article 29.

(1) Everyone has duties to the community in which alone the free and full development of his personality is possible.

(2) In the exercise of his rights and freedoms, everyone shall be subject only to such limitations as are determined by law solely for the purpose of securing due recognition and respect for the rights and freedoms of others and of meeting the just requirements of morality, public order and the general welfare in a democratic society.

(3) These rights and freedoms may in no case be exercised contrary to the purposes and principles of the United Nations.

Article 30.

Nothing in this Declaration may be interpreted as implying for any State, group or person any right to engage in any activity or to perform any act aimed at the destruction of any of the rights and freedoms set forth herein.

Appendix B: International Covenant on Civil and Political Rights

Adopted 16 December 1966

Preamble

The States Parties to the present Covenant,

Considering that, in accordance with the principles proclaimed in the Charter of the United Nations, recognition of the inherent dignity and of the equal and inalienable rights of all members of the human family is the foundation of freedom, justice and peace in the world,

Recognizing that these rights derive from the inherent dignity of the human person,

Recognizing that, in accordance with the Universal Declaration of Human Rights, the ideal of free human beings enjoying civil and political freedom and freedom from fear and want can only be achieved if conditions are created whereby everyone may enjoy his civil and political rights, as well as his economic, social and cultural rights,

Considering the obligation of States under the Charter of the United Nations to promote universal respect for, and observance of, human rights and freedoms,

Realizing that the individual, having duties to other individuals and to the community to which he belongs, is under a responsibility to strive for the promotion and observance of the rights recognized in the present Covenant,

Agree upon the following articles:

PART I

Article 1.

1. All peoples have the right of self-determination. By virtue of that right they freely determine their political status and freely pursue their economic, social and cultural development.
2. All peoples may, for their own ends, freely dispose of their natural wealth and resources without prejudice to any obligations arising out of international economic co-operation, based upon the principle of mutual benefit, and international law. In no case may a people be deprived of its own means of subsistence.

3. The States Parties to the present Covenant, including those having responsibility for the administration of Non-Self-Governing and Trust Territories, shall promote the realization of the right of self-determination, and shall respect that right, in conformity with the provisions of the Charter of the United Nations.

PART II

Article 2.

1. Each State Party to the present Covenant undertakes to respect and to ensure to all individuals within its territory and subject to its jurisdiction the rights recognized in the present Covenant, without distinction of any kind, such as race, colour, sex, language, religion, political or other opinion, national or social origin, property, birth or other status.
2. Where not already provided for by existing legislative or other measures, each State Party to the present Covenant undertakes to take the necessary steps, in accordance with its constitutional processes and with the provisions of the present Covenant, to adopt such laws or other measures as may be necessary to give effect to the rights recognized in the present Covenant.
3. Each State Party to the present Covenant undertakes:
    (a) To ensure that any person whose rights or freedoms as herein recognized are violated shall have an effective remedy, notwithstanding that the violation has been committed by persons acting in an official capacity;
    (b) To ensure that any person claiming such a remedy shall have his right thereto determined by competent judicial, administrative or legislative authorities, or by any other competent authority provided for by the legal system of the State, and to develop the possibilities of judicial remedy;
    (c) To ensure that the competent authorities shall enforce such remedies when granted.

Article 3.

The States Parties to the present Covenant undertake to ensure the equal right of men and women to the enjoyment of all civil and political rights set forth in the present Covenant.

Article 4.

1. In time of public emergency which threatens the life of the nation and the existence of which is officially proclaimed, the States Parties to the present Covenant may take measures derogating from their obligations under the present Covenant to the extent strictly required by the exigencies of the situation, provided that such measures are not inconsistent with their other

obligations under international law and do not involve discrimination solely on the ground of race, colour, sex, language, religion or social origin.

2. No derogation from articles 6, 7, 8 (paragraphs 1 and 2), 11, 15, 16 and 18 may be made under this provision.

3. Any State Party to the present Covenant availing itself of the right of derogation shall immediately inform the other States Parties to the present Covenant, through the intermediary of the Secretary-General of the United Nations, of the provisions from which it has derogated and of the reasons by which it was actuated. A further communication shall be made, through the same intermediary, on the date on which it terminates such derogation.

Article 5.

1. Nothing in the present Covenant may be interpreted as implying for any State, group or person any right to engage in any activity or perform any act aimed at the destruction of any of the rights and freedoms recognized herein or at their limitation to a greater extent than is provided for in the present Covenant.

2. There shall be no restriction upon or derogation from any of the fundamental human rights recognized or existing in any State Party to the present Covenant pursuant to law, conventions, regulations or custom on the pretext that the present Covenant does not recognize such rights or that it recognizes them to a lesser extent.

PART III

Article 6.

1. Every human being has the inherent right to life. This right shall be protected by law. No one shall be arbitrarily deprived of his life.

2. In countries which have not abolished the death penalty, sentence of death may be imposed only for the most serious crimes in accordance with the law in force at the time of the commission of the crime and not contrary to the provisions of the present Covenant and to the Convention on the Prevention and Punishment of the Crime of Genocide. This penalty can only be carried out pursuant to a final judgement rendered by a competent court.

3. When deprivation of life constitutes the crime of genocide, it is understood that nothing in this article shall authorize any State Party to the present Covenant to derogate in any way from any obligation assumed under the provisions of the Convention on the Prevention and Punishment of the Crime of Genocide.

4. Anyone sentenced to death shall have the right to seek pardon or commutation of the sentence. Amnesty, pardon or commutation of the sentence of death may be granted in all cases.

5. Sentence of death shall not be imposed for crimes committed by persons below eighteen years of age and shall not be carried out on pregnant women.

6. Nothing in this article shall be invoked to delay or to prevent the abolition of capital punishment by any State Party to the present Covenant.

Article 7.

No one shall be subjected to torture or to cruel, inhuman or degrading treatment or punishment. In particular, no one shall be subjected without his free consent to medical or scientific experimentation.

Article 8.

1. No one shall be held in slavery; slavery and the slave-trade in all their forms shall be prohibited.
2. No one shall be held in servitude.
3. (a) No one shall be required to perform forced or compulsory labour;
   (b) Paragraph 3 (a) shall not be held to preclude, in countries where imprisonment with hard labour may be imposed as a punishment for a crime, the performance of hard labour in pursuance of a sentence to such punishment by a competent court;
   (c) For the purpose of this paragraph the term "forced or compulsory labour" shall not include:
      (i) Any work or service, not referred to in subparagraph (b), normally required of a person who is under detention in consequence of a lawful order of a court, or of a person during conditional release from such detention;
      (ii) Any service of a military character and, in countries where conscientious objection is recognized, any national service required by law of conscientious objectors;
      (iii) Any service exacted in cases of emergency or calamity threatening the life or well-being of the community;
      (iv) Any work or service which forms part of normal civil obligations.

Article 9.

1. Everyone has the right to liberty and security of person. No one shall be subjected to arbitrary arrest or detention. No one shall be deprived of his liberty except on such grounds and in accordance with such procedure as are established by law.
2. Anyone who is arrested shall be informed, at the time of arrest, of the reasons for his arrest and shall be promptly informed of any charges against him.
3. Anyone arrested or detained on a criminal charge shall be brought promptly before a judge or other officer authorized by law to exercise judicial power and shall be entitled to trial within a reasonable time or to release. It shall not

be the general rule that persons awaiting trial shall be detained in custody, but release may be subject to guarantees to appear for trial, at any other stage of the judicial proceedings, and, should occasion arise, for execution of the judgement.

4. Anyone who is deprived of his liberty by arrest or detention shall be entitled to take proceedings before a court, in order that court may decide without delay on the lawfulness of his detention and order his release if the detention is not lawful.

5. Anyone who has been the victim of unlawful arrest or detention shall have an enforceable right to compensation.

Article 10.

1. All persons deprived of their liberty shall be treated with humanity and with respect for the inherent dignity of the human person.

2. (a) Accused persons shall, save in exceptional circumstances, be segregated from convicted persons and shall be subject to separate treatment appropriate to their status as unconvicted persons;

   (b) Accused juvenile persons shall be separated from adults and brought as speedily as possible for adjudication.

3. The penitentiary system shall comprise treatment of prisoners the essential aim of which shall be their reformation and social rehabilitation. Juvenile offenders shall be segregated from adults and be accorded treatment appropriate to their age and legal status.

Article 11.

No one shall be imprisoned merely on the ground of inability to fulfil a contractual obligation.

Article 12.

1. Everyone lawfully within the territory of a State shall, within that territory, have the right to liberty of movement and freedom to choose his residence.

2. Everyone shall be free to leave any country, including his own.

3. The above-mentioned rights shall not be subject to any restrictions except those which are provided by law, are necessary to protect national security, public order (*ordre public*), public health or morals or the rights and freedoms of others, and are consistent with the other rights recognized in the present Covenant.

4. No one shall be arbitrarily deprived of the right to enter his own country.

Article 13.

An alien lawfully in the territory of a State Party to the present Covenant may be expelled therefrom only in pursuance of a decision reached in accordance with law and shall, except where compelling reasons of national security otherwise require, be allowed to submit the reasons against his expulsion and to have his case reviewed by, and be represented for the purpose before, the competent authority or a person or persons especially designated by the competent authority.

Article 14.

1. All persons shall be equal before the courts and tribunals. In the determination of any criminal charge against him, or of his rights and obligations in a suit at law, everyone shall be entitled to a fair and public hearing by a competent, independent and impartial tribunal established by law. The press and the public may be excluded from all or part of a trial for reasons of morals, public order (*ordre public*) or national security in a democratic society, or when the interest of the private lives of the parties so requires, or to the extent strictly necessary in the opinion of the court in special circumstances where publicity would prejudice the interests of justice; but any judgement rendered in a criminal case or in a suit at law shall be made public except where the interest of juvenile persons otherwise requires or the proceedings concern matrimonial disputes or the guardianship of children.

2. Everyone charged with a criminal offence shall have the right to be presumed innocent until proved guilty according to law.

3. In the determination of any criminal charge against him, everyone shall be entitled to the following minimum guarantees, in full equality:
    (a) To be informed promptly and in detail in a language which he understands of the nature and cause of the charge against him;
    (b) To have adequate time and facilities for the preparation of his defence and to communicate with counsel of his own choosing;
    (c) To be tried without undue delay;
    (d) To be tried in his presence, and to defend himself in person or through legal assistance of his own choosing; to be informed, if he does not have legal assistance, of this right; and to have legal assistance assigned to him, in any case where the interests of justice so require, and without payment by him in any such case if he does not have sufficient means to pay for it;
    (e) To examine, or have examined, the witnesses against him and to obtain the attendance and examination of witnesses on his behalf under the same conditions as witnesses against him;
    (f) To have the free assistance of an interpreter if he cannot understand or speak the language used in court;
    (g) Not to be compelled to testify against himself or to confess guilt.

4. In the case of juvenile persons, the procedure shall be such as will take account of their age and the desirability of promoting their rehabilitation.
5. Everyone convicted of a crime shall have the right to his conviction and sentence being reviewed by a higher tribunal according to law.
6. When a person has by a final decision been convicted of a criminal offence and when subsequently his conviction has been reversed or he has been pardoned on the ground that a new or newly discovered fact shows conclusively that there has been a miscarriage of justice, the person who has suffered punishment as a result of such conviction shall be compensated according to law, unless it is proved that the non-disclosure of the unknown fact in time is wholly or partly attributable to him.
7. No one shall be liable to be tried or punished again for an offence for which he has already been finally convicted or acquitted in accordance with the law and penal procedure of each country.

Article 15.

1. No one shall be held guilty of any criminal offence on account of any act or omission which did not constitute a criminal offence, under national or international law, at the time when it was committed. Nor shall a heavier penalty be imposed than the one that was applicable at the time when the criminal offence was committed. If, subsequent to the commission of the offence, provision is made by law for the imposition of the lighter penalty, the offender shall benefit thereby.
2. Nothing in this article shall prejudice the trial and punishment of any person for any act or omission which, at the time when it was committed, was criminal according to the general principles of law recognized by the community of nations.

Article 16.

Everyone shall have the right to recognition everywhere as a person before the law.

Article 17.

1. No one shall be subjected to arbitrary or unlawful interference with his privacy, family, home or correspondence, nor to unlawful attacks on his honour and reputation.
2. Everyone has the right to the protection of the law against such interference or attacks.

Article 18.

1. Everyone shall have the right to freedom of thought, conscience and religion. This right shall include freedom to have or to adopt a religion or belief of his

choice, and freedom, either individually or in community with others and in public or private, to manifest his religion or belief in worship, observance, practice and teaching.

2. No one shall be subject to coercion which would impair his freedom to have or to adopt a religion or belief of his choice.

3. Freedom to manifest one's religion or beliefs may be subject only to such limitations as are prescribed by law and are necessary to protect public safety, order, health, or morals or the fundamental rights and freedoms of others.

4. The States Parties to the present Covenant undertake to have respect for the liberty of parents and, when applicable, legal guardians to ensure the religious and moral education of their children in conformity with their own convictions.

Article 19.

1. Everyone shall have the right to hold opinions without interference.

2. Everyone shall have the right to freedom of expression; this right shall include freedom to seek, receive and impart information and ideas of all kinds, regardless of frontiers, either orally, in writing or in print, in the form of art, or through any other media of his choice.

3. The exercise of the rights provided for in paragraph 2 of this article carries with it special duties and responsibilities. It may therefore be subject to certain restrictions, but these shall only be such as are provided by law and are necessary:

   (a) For respect of the rights or reputations of others;

   (b) For the protection of national security or of public order (*ordre public*), or of public health or morals.

Article 20.

1. Any propaganda for war shall be prohibited by law.

2. Any advocacy of national, racial or religious hatred that constitutes incitement to discrimination, hostility or violence shall be prohibited by law.

Article 21.

The right of peaceful assembly shall be recognized. No restrictions may be placed on the exercise of this right other than those imposed in conformity with the law and which are necessary in a democratic society in the interests of national security or public safety, public order (*ordre public*), the protection of public health or morals or the protection of the rights and freedoms of others.

Article 22.

1. Everyone shall have the right to freedom of association with others, including the right to form and join trade unions for the protection of his interests.

2. No restrictions may be placed on the exercise of this right other than those which are prescribed by law and which are necessary in a democratic society in the interests of national security or public safety, public order (*ordre public*), the protection of public health or morals or the protection of the rights and freedoms of others. This article shall not prevent the imposition of lawful restrictions on members of the armed forces and of the police in their exercise of this right.

3. Nothing in this article shall authorize States Parties to the International Labour Organisation Convention of 1948 concerning Freedom of Association and Protection of the Right to Organize to take legislative measures which would prejudice, or to apply the law in such a manner as to prejudice, the guarantees provided for in that Convention.

Article 23.

1. The family is the natural and fundamental group unit of society and is entitled to protection by society and the State.

2. The right of men and women of marriageable age to marry and to found a family shall be recognized.

3. No marriage shall be entered into without the free and full consent of the intending spouses.

4. States Parties to the present Covenant shall take appropriate steps to ensure equality of rights and responsibilities of spouses as to marriage, during marriage and at its dissolution. In the case of dissolution, provision shall be made for the necessary protection of any children.

Article 24.

1. Every child shall have, without any discrimination as to race, colour, sex, language, religion, national or social origin, property or birth, the right to such measures of protection as are required by his status as a minor, on the part of his family, society and the State.

2. Every child shall be registered immediately after birth and shall have a name.

3. Every child has the right to acquire a nationality.

Article 25.

Every citizen shall have the right and the opportunity, without any of the distinctions mentioned in article 2 and without unreasonable restrictions:

(a) To take part in the conduct of public affairs, directly or through freely chosen representatives;

(b) To vote and to be elected at genuine periodic elections which shall be by universal and equal suffrage and shall be held by secret ballot, guaranteeing the free expression of the will of the electors;

(c) To have access, on general terms of equality, to public service in his country.

Article 26.

All persons are equal before the law and are entitled without any discrimination to the equal protection of the law. In this respect, the law shall prohibit any discrimination and guarantee to all persons equal and effective protection against discrimination on any ground such as race, colour, sex, language, religion, political or other opinion, national or social origin, property, birth or other status.

Article 27.

In those States in which ethnic, religious or linguistic minorities exist, persons belonging to such minorities shall not be denied the right, in community with the other members of their group, to enjoy their own culture, to profess and practise their own religion, or to use their own language.

PART IV

Article 28.

1. There shall be established a Human Rights Committee (hereafter referred to in the present Covenant as the Committee). It shall consist of eighteen members and shall carry out the functions hereinafter provided.
2. The Committee shall be composed of nationals of the States Parties to the present Covenant who shall be persons of high moral character and recognized competence in the field of human rights, consideration being given to the usefulness of the participation of some persons having legal experience.
3. The members of the Committee shall be elected and shall serve in their personal capacity.

Article 29.

1. The members of the Committee shall be elected by secret ballot from a list of persons possessing the qualifications prescribed in article 28 and nominated for the purpose by the States Parties to the present Covenant.
2. Each State Party to the present Covenant may nominate not more than two persons. These persons shall be nationals of the nominating State.
3. A person shall be eligible for renomination.

Article 30.

1. The initial election shall be held no later than six months after the date of the entry into force of the present Covenant.
2. At least four months before the date of each election to the Committee, other than an election to fill a vacancy declared in accordance with article 34, the Secretary-General of the United Nations shall address a written invitation to

the States Parties to the present Covenant to submit their nominations for membership of the Committee within three months.

3. The Secretary-General of the United Nations shall prepare a list in alphabetical order of all the persons thus nominated, with an indication of the States Parties which have nominated them, and shall submit it to the States Parties to the present Covenant no later than one month before the date of each election.

4. Elections of the members of the Committee shall be held at a meeting of the States Parties to the present Covenant convened by the Secretary-General of the United Nations at the Headquarters of the United Nations. At that meeting, for which two-thirds of the States Parties to the present Covenant shall constitute a quorum, the persons elected to the Committee shall be those nominees who obtain the largest number of votes and an absolute majority of the votes of the representatives of States Parties present and voting.

Article 31.

1. The Committee may not include more than one national of the same State.
2. In the election of the Committee, consideration shall be given to equitable geographical distribution of membership and to the representation of the different forms of civilization and of the principal legal systems.

Article 32.

1. The members of the Committee shall be elected for a term of four years. They shall be eligible for re-election if renominated. However, the terms of nine of the members elected at the first election shall expire at the end of two years; immediately after the first election, the names of these nine members shall be chosen by lot by the Chairman of the meeting referred to in article 30, paragraph 4.

2. Elections at the expiry of office shall be held in accordance with the preceding articles of this part of the present Covenant.

Article 33.

1. If, in the unanimous opinion of the other members, a member of the Committee has ceased to carry out his functions for any cause other than absence of a temporary character, the Chairman of the Committee shall notify the Secretary-General of the United Nations, who shall then declare the seat of that member to be vacant.

2. In the event of the death or the resignation of a member of the Committee, the Chairman shall immediately notify the Secretary-General of the United Nations, who shall declare the seat vacant from the date of death or the date on which the resignation takes effect.

Article 34.

1. When a vacancy is declared in accordance with article 33 and if the term of office of the member to be replaced does not expire within six months of the declaration of the vacancy, the Secretary-General of the United Nations shall notify each of the States Parties to the present Covenant, which may within two months submit nominations in accordance with article 29 for the purpose of filling the vacancy.
2. The Secretary-General of the United Nations shall prepare a list in alphabetical order of the persons thus nominated and shall submit it to the States Parties to the present Covenant. The election to fill the vacancy shall then take place in accordance with the relevant provisions of this part of the present Covenant.
3. A member of the Committee elected to fill a vacancy declared in accordance with article 33 shall hold office for the remainder of the term of the member who vacated the seat on the Committee under the provisions of that article.

Article 35.

The members of the Committee shall, with the approval of the General Assembly of the United Nations, receive emoluments from United Nations resources on such terms and conditions as the General Assembly may decide, having regard to the importance of the Committee's responsibilities.

Article 36.

The Secretary-General of the United Nations shall provide the necessary staff and facilities for the effective performance of the functions of the Committee under the present Covenant.

Article 37.

1. The Secretary-General of the United Nations shall convene the initial meeting of the Committee at the Headquarters of the United Nations.
2. After its initial meeting, the Committee shall meet at such times as shall be provided in its rules of procedure.
3. The Committee shall normally meet at the Headquarters of the United Nations or at the United Nations Office at Geneva.

Article 38.

Every member of the Committee shall, before taking up his duties, make a solemn declaration in open committee that he will perform his functions impartially and conscientiously.

Article 39.
1. The Committee shall elect its officers for a term of two years. They may be re-elected.
2. The Committee shall establish its own rules of procedure, but these rules shall provide, *inter alia*, that:
    (a) Twelve members shall constitute a quorum;
    (b) Decisions of the Committee shall be made by a majority vote of the members present.

Article 40.
1. The States Parties to the present Covenant undertake to submit reports on the measures they have adopted which give effect to the rights recognized herein and on the progress made in the enjoyment of those rights:
    (a) Within one year of the entry into force of the present Covenant for the States Parties concerned;
    (b) Thereafter whenever the Committee so requests.
2. All reports shall be submitted to the Secretary-General of the United Nations, who shall transmit them to the Committee for consideration. Reports shall indicate the factors and difficulties, if any, affecting the implementation of the present Covenant.
3. The Secretary-General of the United Nations may, after consultation with the Committee, transmit to the specialized agencies concerned copies of such parts of the reports as may fall within their field of competence.
4. The Committee shall study the reports submitted by the States Parties to the present Covenant. It shall transmit its reports, and such general comments as it may consider appropriate, to the States Parties. The Committee may also transmit to the Economic and Social Council these comments along with the copies of the reports it has received from States Parties to the present Covenant.
5. The States Parties to the present Covenant may submit to the Committee observations on any comments that may be made in accordance with paragraph 4 of this article.

Article 41.
1. A State Party to the present Covenant may at any time declare under this article that it recognizes the competence of the Committee to receive and consider communications to the effect that a State Party claims that another State Party is not fulfilling its obligations under the present Covenant. Communications under this article may be received and considered only if submitted by a State Party which has made a declaration recognizing in regard to itself the competence of the Committee. No communication shall be received by the Committee if it concerns a State Party which has not made

such a declaration. Communications received under this article shall be dealt with in accordance with the following procedure:

(a) If a State Party to the present Covenant considers that another State Party is not giving effect to the provisions of the present Covenant, it may, by written communication, bring the matter to the attention of that State Party. Within three months after the receipt of the communication the receiving State shall afford the State which sent the communication an explanation, or any other statement in writing clarifying the matter which should include, to the extent possible and pertinent, reference to domestic procedures and remedies taken, pending, or available in the matter;

(b) If the matter is not adjusted to the satisfaction of both States Parties concerned within six months after the receipt by the receiving State of the initial communication, either State shall have the right to refer the matter to the Committee, by notice given to the Committee and to the other State;

(c) The Committee shall deal with a matter referred to it only after it has ascertained that all available domestic remedies have been invoked and exhausted in the matter, in conformity with the generally recognized principles of international law. This shall not be the rule where the application of the remedies is unreasonably prolonged;

(d) The Committee shall hold closed meetings when examining communications under this article;

(e) Subject to the provisions of subparagraph (c), the Committee shall make available its good offices to the States Parties concerned with a view to a friendly solution of the matter on the basis of respect for human rights and fundamental freedoms as recognized in the present Covenant;

(f) In any matter referred to it, the Committee may call upon the States Parties concerned, referred to in subparagraph (b), to supply any relevant information;

(g) The States Parties concerned, referred to in subparagraph (b), shall have the right to be represented when the matter is being considered in the Committee and to make submissions orally and/or in writing;

(h) The Committee shall, within twelve months after the date of receipt of notice under subparagraph (b), submit a report:

(i) If a solution within the terms of subparagraph (e) is reached, the Committee shall confine its report to a brief statement of the facts and of the solution reached;

(ii) If a solution within the terms of subparagraph (e) is not reached, the Committee shall confine its report to a brief statement of the facts; the written submissions and record of the oral submissions made by the States Parties concerned shall be attached to the report. In every matter, the report shall be communicated to the States Parties concerned.

2. The provisions of this article shall come into force when ten States Parties to the present Covenant have made declarations under paragraph I of this article. Such declarations shall be deposited by the States Parties with the Secretary-General of the United Nations, who shall transmit copies thereof to the other States Parties. A declaration may be withdrawn at any time by notification to the Secretary-General. Such a withdrawal shall not prejudice the consideration of any matter which is the subject of a communication already transmitted under this article; no further communication by any State Party shall be received after the notification of withdrawal of the declaration has been received by the Secretary-General, unless the State Party concerned has made a new declaration.

Article 42.

1. (a) If a matter referred to the Committee in accordance with article 41 is not resolved to the satisfaction of the States Parties concerned, the Committee may, with the prior consent of the States Parties concerned, appoint an *ad hoc* Conciliation Commission (hereinafter referred to as the Commission). The good offices of the Commission shall be made available to the States Parties concerned with a view to an amicable solution of the matter on the basis of respect for the present Covenant;

   (b) The Commission shall consist of five persons acceptable to the States Parties concerned. If the States Parties concerned fail to reach agreement within three months on all or part of the composition of the Commission, the members of the Commission concerning whom no agreement has been reached shall be elected by secret ballot by a two-thirds majority vote of the Committee from among its members.

2. The members of the Commission shall serve in their personal capacity. They shall not be nationals of the States Parties concerned, or of a State not Party to the present Covenant, or of a State Party which has not made a declaration under article 41.

3. The Commission shall elect its own Chairman and adopt its own rules of procedure.

4. The meetings of the Commission shall normally be held at the Headquarters of the United Nations or at the United Nations Office at Geneva. However, they may be held at such other convenient places as the Commission may determine in consultation with the Secretary-General of the United Nations and the States Parties concerned.

5. The secretariat provided in accordance with article 36 shall also service the commissions appointed under this article.

6. The information received and collated by the Committee shall be made

available to the Commission and the Commission may call upon the States Parties concerned to supply any other relevant information.

7. When the Commission has fully considered the matter, but in any event not later than twelve months after having been seized of the matter, it shall submit to the Chairman of the Committee a report for communication to the States Parties concerned:

    (a) If the Commission is unable to complete its consideration of the matter within twelve months, it shall confine its report to a brief statement of the status of its consideration of the matter;

    (b) If an amicable solution to the matter on the basis of respect for human rights as recognized in the present Covenant is reached, the Commission shall confine its report to a brief statement of the facts and of the solution reached;

    (c) If a solution within the terms of subparagraph (b) is not reached, the Commission's report shall embody its findings on all questions of fact relevant to the issues between the States Parties concerned, and its views on the possibilities of an amicable solution of the matter. This report shall also contain the written submissions and a record of the oral submissions made by the States Parties concerned;

    (d) If the Commission's report is submitted under subparagraph (c), the States Parties concerned shall, within three months of the receipt of the report, notify the Chairman of the Committee whether or not they accept the contents of the report of the Commission.

8. The provisions of this article are without prejudice to the responsibilities of the Committee under article 41.

9. The States Parties concerned shall share equally all the expenses of the members of the Commission in accordance with estimates to be provided by the Secretary-General of the United Nations.

10. The Secretary-General of the United Nations shall be empowered to pay the expenses of the members of the Commission, if necessary, before reimbursement by the States Parties concerned, in accordance with paragraph 9 of this article.

Article 43.

The members of the Committee, and of the *ad hoc* conciliation commissions which may be appointed under article 42, shall be entitled to the facilities, privileges and immunities of experts on mission for the United Nations as laid down in the relevant sections of the Convention on the Privileges and Immunities of the United Nations.

Article 44.

The provisions for the implementation of the present Covenant shall apply without prejudice to the procedures prescribed in the field of human rights by or under the constituent instruments and the conventions of the United Nations and of the specialized agencies and shall not prevent the States Parties to the present Covenant from having recourse to other procedures for settling a dispute in accordance with general or special international agreements in force between them.

Article 45.

The Committee shall submit to the General Assembly of the United Nations, through the Economic and Social Council, an annual report on its activities.

PART V

Article 46.

Nothing in the present Covenant shall be interpreted as impairing the provisions of the Charter of the United Nations and of the constitutions of the specialized agencies which define the respective responsibilities of the various organs of the United Nations and of the specialized agencies in regard to the matters dealt with in the present Covenant.

Article 47.

Nothing in the present Covenant shall be interpreted as impairing the inherent right of all peoples to enjoy and utilize fully and freely their natural wealth and resources.

PART VI

Article 48.

1. The present Covenant is open for signature by any State Member of the United Nations or member of any of its specialized agencies, by any State Party to the Statute of the International Court of Justice, and by any other State which has been invited by the General Assembly of the United Nations to become a Party to the present Covenant.
2. The present Covenant is subject to ratification. Instruments of ratification shall be deposited with the Secretary-General of the United Nations.
3. The present Covenant shall be open to accession by any State referred to in paragraph 1 of this article.
4. Accession shall be effected by the deposit of an instrument of accession with the Secretary-General of the United Nations.
5. The Secretary-General of the United Nations shall inform all States which have signed this Covenant or acceded to it of the deposit of each instrument of ratification or accession.

Article 49.

1. The present Covenant shall enter into force three months after the date of the deposit with the Secretary-General of the United Nations of the thirty-fifth instrument of ratification or instrument of accession.
2. For each State ratifying the present Covenant or acceding to it after the deposit of the thirty-fifth instrument of ratification or instrument of accession, the present Covenant shall enter into force three months after the date of the deposit of its own instrument of ratification or instrument of accession.

Article 50.

The provisions of the present Covenant shall extend to all parts of federal States without any limitations or exceptions.

Article 51.

1. Any State Party to the present Covenant may propose an amendment and file it with the Secretary-General of the United Nations. The Secretary-General of the United Nations shall thereupon communicate any proposed amendments to the States Parties to the present Covenant with a request that they notify him whether they favour a conference of States Parties for the purpose of considering and voting upon the proposals. In the event that at least one-third of the States Parties favours such a conference, the Secretary-General shall convene the conference under the auspices of the United Nations. Any amendment adopted by a majority of the States Parties present and voting at the conference shall be submitted to the General Assembly of the United Nations for approval.
2. Amendments shall come into force when they have been approved by the General Assembly of the United Nations and accepted by a two-thirds majority of the States Parties to the present Covenant in accordance with their respective constitutional processes.
3. When amendments come into force, they shall be binding on those States Parties which have accepted them, other States Parties still being bound by the provisions of the present Covenant and any earlier amendment which they have accepted.

Article 52.

Irrespective of the notifications made under article 48, paragraph 5, the Secretary-General of the United Nations shall inform all States referred to in paragraph 1 of the same article of the following particulars:

(a) Signatures, ratifications and accessions under article 48;
(b) The date of the entry into force of the present Covenant under article 49 and the date of the entry into force of any amendments under article 51.

Article 53.

1. The present Covenant, of which the Chinese, English, French, Russian and Spanish texts are equally authentic, shall be deposited in the archives of the United Nations.
2. The Secretary-General of the United Nations shall transmit certified copies of the present Covenant to all States referred to in article 48.

Appendix C: International Covenant on Economic, Social and Cultural Rights

Adopted and opened for signature, ratification and accession by
General Assembly resolution 2200A (XXI) of 16 December 1966
entry into force 3 January 1976, in accordance with article 27

Preamble

The States Parties to the present Covenant,

Considering that, in accordance with the principles proclaimed in the Charter of the United Nations, recognition of the inherent dignity and of the equal and inalienable rights of all members of the human family is the foundation of freedom, justice and peace in the world,

Recognizing that these rights derive from the inherent dignity of the human person,

Recognizing that, in accordance with the Universal Declaration of Human Rights, the ideal of free human beings enjoying freedom from fear and want can only be achieved if conditions are created whereby everyone may enjoy his economic, social and cultural rights, as well as his civil and political rights,

Considering the obligation of States under the Charter of the United Nations to promote universal respect for, and observance of, human rights and freedoms,

Realizing that the individual, having duties to other individuals and to the community to which he belongs, is under a responsibility to strive for the promotion and observance of the rights recognized in the present Covenant,

Agree upon the following articles:

PART I

Article 1

1. All peoples have the right of self-determination. By virtue of that right they freely determine their political status and freely pursue their economic, social and cultural development.

2. All peoples may, for their own ends, freely dispose of their natural wealth and resources without prejudice to any obligations arising out of international

economic co-operation, based upon the principle of mutual benefit, and international law. In no case may a people be deprived of its own means of subsistence.

3. The States Parties to the present Covenant, including those having responsibility for the administration of Non-Self-Governing and Trust Territories, shall promote the realization of the right of self-determination, and shall respect that right, in conformity with the provisions of the Charter of the United Nations.

PART II

Article 2
1. Each State Party to the present Covenant undertakes to take steps, individually and through international assistance and co-operation, especially economic and technical, to the maximum of its available resources, with a view to achieving progressively the full realization of the rights recognized in the present Covenant by all appropriate means, including particularly the adoption of legislative measures.

2. The States Parties to the present Covenant undertake to guarantee that the rights enunciated in the present Covenant will be exercised without discrimination of any kind as to race, colour, sex, language, religion, political or other opinion, national or social origin, property, birth or other status.

3. Developing countries, with due regard to human rights and their national economy, may determine to what extent they would guarantee the economic rights recognized in the present Covenant to non-nationals.

Article 3
The States Parties to the present Covenant undertake to ensure the equal right of men and women to the enjoyment of all economic, social and cultural rights set forth in the present Covenant.

Article 4
The States Parties to the present Covenant recognize that, in the enjoyment of those rights provided by the State in conformity with the present Covenant, the State may subject such rights only to such limitations as are determined by law only in so far as this may be compatible with the nature of these rights and solely for the purpose of promoting the general welfare in a democratic society.

Article 5

1. Nothing in the present Covenant may be interpreted as implying for any State, group or person any right to engage in any activity or to perform any act aimed at the destruction of any of the rights or freedoms recognized herein, or at their limitation to a greater extent than is provided for in the present Covenant.

2. No restriction upon or derogation from any of the fundamental human rights recognized or existing in any country in virtue of law, conventions, regulations or custom shall be admitted on the pretext that the present Covenant does not recognize such rights or that it recognizes them to a lesser extent.

PART III

Article 6

1. The States Parties to the present Covenant recognize the right to work, which includes the right of everyone to the opportunity to gain his living by work which he freely chooses or accepts, and will take appropriate steps to safeguard this right.

2. The steps to be taken by a State Party to the present Covenant to achieve the full realization of this right shall include technical and vocational guidance and training programmes, policies and techniques to achieve steady economic, social and cultural development and full and productive employment under conditions safeguarding fundamental political and economic freedoms to the individual.

Article 7

The States Parties to the present Covenant recognize the right of everyone to the enjoyment of just and favourable conditions of work which ensure, in particular:
  (a) Remuneration which provides all workers, as a minimum, with:
      (i) Fair wages and equal remuneration for work of equal value without distinction of any kind, in particular women being guaranteed conditions of work not inferior to those enjoyed by men, with equal pay for equal work;
      (ii) A decent living for themselves and their families in accordance with the provisions of the present Covenant;
  (b) Safe and healthy working conditions;
  (c) Equal opportunity for everyone to be promoted in his employment to an appropriate higher level, subject to no considerations other than those of seniority and competence;

(d) Rest, leisure and reasonable limitation of working hours and periodic holidays with pay, as well as remuneration for public holidays.

Article 8

1. The States Parties to the present Covenant undertake to ensure:
   (a) The right of everyone to form trade unions and join the trade union of his choice, subject only to the rules of the organization concerned, for the promotion and protection of his economic and social interests. No restrictions may be placed on the exercise of this right other than those prescribed by law and which are necessary in a democratic society in the interests of national security or public order or for the protection of the rights and freedoms of others;
   (b) The right of trade unions to establish national federations or confederations and the right of the latter to form or join international trade-union organizations;
   (c) The right of trade unions to function freely subject to no limitations other than those prescribed by law and which are necessary in a democratic society in the interests of national security or public order or for the protection of the rights and freedoms of others;
   (d) The right to strike, provided that it is exercised in conformity with the laws of the particular country.

2. This article shall not prevent the imposition of lawful restrictions on the exercise of these rights by members of the armed forces or of the police or of the administration of the State.

3. Nothing in this article shall authorize States Parties to the International Labour Organisation Convention of 1948 concerning Freedom of Association and Protection of the Right to Organize to take legislative measures which would prejudice, or apply the law in such a manner as would prejudice, the guarantees provided for in that Convention.

Article 9

The States Parties to the present Covenant recognize the right of everyone to social security, including social insurance.

Article 10

The States Parties to the present Covenant recognize that:

1. The widest possible protection and assistance should be accorded to the family, which is the natural and fundamental group unit of society, particularly for its establishment and while it is responsible for the care and education of

dependent children. Marriage must be entered into with the free consent of the intending spouses.

2. Special protection should be accorded to mothers during a reasonable period before and after childbirth. During such period working mothers should be accorded paid leave or leave with adequate social security benefits.

3. Special measures of protection and assistance should be taken on behalf of all children and young persons without any discrimination for reasons of parentage or other conditions. Children and young persons should be protected from economic and social exploitation. Their employment in work harmful to their morals or health or dangerous to life or likely to hamper their normal development should be punishable by law. States should also set age limits below which the paid employment of child labour should be prohibited and punishable by law.

Article 11
1. The States Parties to the present Covenant recognize the right of everyone to an adequate standard of living for himself and his family, including adequate food, clothing and housing, and to the continuous improvement of living conditions. The States Parties will take appropriate steps to ensure the realization of this right, recognizing to this effect the essential importance of international co-operation based on free consent.

2. The States Parties to the present Covenant, recognizing the fundamental right of everyone to be free from hunger, shall take, individually and through international co-operation, the measures, including specific programmes, which are needed:
   (a) To improve methods of production, conservation and distribution of food by making full use of technical and scientific knowledge, by disseminating knowledge of the principles of nutrition and by developing or reforming agrarian systems in such a way as to achieve the most efficient development and utilization of natural resources;
   (b) Taking into account the problems of both food-importing and food-exporting countries, to ensure an equitable distribution of world food supplies in relation to need.

Article 12
1. The States Parties to the present Covenant recognize the right of everyone to the enjoyment of the highest attainable standard of physical and mental health.

2. The steps to be taken by the States Parties to the present Covenant to achieve the full realization of this right shall include those necessary for:

(a) The provision for the reduction of the stillbirth-rate and of infant mortality and for the healthy development of the child;

(b) The improvement of all aspects of environmental and industrial hygiene;

(c) The prevention, treatment and control of epidemic, endemic, occupational and other diseases;

(d) The creation of conditions which would assure to all medical service and medical attention in the event of sickness.

Article 13

1. The States Parties to the present Covenant recognize the right of everyone to education. They agree that education shall be directed to the full development of the human personality and the sense of its dignity, and shall strengthen the respect for human rights and fundamental freedoms. They further agree that education shall enable all persons to participate effectively in a free society, promote understanding, tolerance and friendship among all nations and all racial, ethnic or religious groups, and further the activities of the United Nations for the maintenance of peace.

2. The States Parties to the present Covenant recognize that, with a view to achieving the full realization of this right:

(a) Primary education shall be compulsory and available free to all;

(b) Secondary education in its different forms, including technical and vocational secondary education, shall be made generally available and accessible to all by every appropriate means, and in particular by the progressive introduction of free education;

(c) Higher education shall be made equally accessible to all, on the basis of capacity, by every appropriate means, and in particular by the progressive introduction of free education;

(d) Fundamental education shall be encouraged or intensified as far as possible for those persons who have not received or completed the whole period of their primary education;

(e) The development of a system of schools at all levels shall be actively pursued, an adequate fellowship system shall be established, and the material conditions of teaching staff shall be continuously improved.

3. The States Parties to the present Covenant undertake to have respect for the liberty of parents and, when applicable, legal guardians to choose for their children schools, other than those established by the public authorities, which conform to such minimum educational standards as may be laid down or approved by the State and to ensure the religious and moral education of their children in conformity with their own convictions.

4. No part of this article shall be construed so as to interfere with the liberty of individuals and bodies to establish and direct educational institutions, subject always to the observance of the principles set forth in paragraph 1 of this article and to the requirement that the education given in such institutions shall conform to such minimum standards as may be laid down by the State.

Article 14

Each State Party to the present Covenant which, at the time of becoming a Party, has not been able to secure in its metropolitan territory or other territories under its jurisdiction compulsory primary education, free of charge, undertakes, within two years, to work out and adopt a detailed plan of action for the progressive implementation, within a reasonable number of years, to be fixed in the plan, of the principle of compulsory education free of charge for all.

Article 15

1. The States Parties to the present Covenant recognize the right of everyone:
    (a) To take part in cultural life;
    (b) To enjoy the benefits of scientific progress and its applications;
    (c) To benefit from the protection of the moral and material interests resulting from any scientific, literary or artistic production of which he is the author.

2. The steps to be taken by the States Parties to the present Covenant to achieve the full realization of this right shall include those necessary for the conservation, the development and the diffusion of science and culture.

3. The States Parties to the present Covenant undertake to respect the freedom indispensable for scientific research and creative activity.

4. The States Parties to the present Covenant recognize the benefits to be derived from the encouragement and development of international contacts and co-operation in the scientific and cultural fields.

PART IV

Article 16

1. The States Parties to the present Covenant undertake to submit in conformity with this part of the Covenant reports on the measures which they have adopted and the progress made in achieving the observance of the rights recognized herein.

2. (a) All reports shall be submitted to the Secretary-General of the United Nations, who shall transmit copies to the Economic and Social Council for consideration in accordance with the provisions of the present Covenant;
    (b) The Secretary-General of the United Nations shall also transmit to the specialized agencies copies of the reports, or any relevant parts therefrom, from States Parties to the present Covenant which are also members of these specialized agencies in so far as these reports, or parts therefrom, relate to any matters which fall within the responsibilities of the said agencies in accordance with their constitutional instruments.

Article 17

1. The States Parties to the present Covenant shall furnish their reports in stages, in accordance with a programme to be established by the Economic and Social Council within one year of the entry into force of the present Covenant after consultation with the States Parties and the specialized agencies concerned.

2. Reports may indicate factors and difficulties affecting the degree of fulfilment of obligations under the present Covenant.

3. Where relevant information has previously been furnished to the United Nations or to any specialized agency by any State Party to the present Covenant, it will not be necessary to reproduce that information, but a precise reference to the information so furnished will suffice.

Article 18

Pursuant to its responsibilities under the Charter of the United Nations in the field of human rights and fundamental freedoms, the Economic and Social Council may make arrangements with the specialized agencies in respect of their reporting to it on the progress made in achieving the observance of the provisions of the present Covenant falling within the scope of their activities. These reports may include particulars of decisions and recommendations on such implementation adopted by their competent organs.

Article 19

The Economic and Social Council may transmit to the Commission on Human Rights for study and general recommendation or, as appropriate, for information the reports concerning human rights submitted by States in accordance with articles 16 and 17, and those concerning human rights submitted by the specialized agencies in accordance with article 18.

Article 20

The States Parties to the present Covenant and the specialized agencies concerned may submit comments to the Economic and Social Council on any general recommendation under article 19 or reference to such general recommendation in any report of the Commission on Human Rights or any documentation referred to therein.

Article 21

The Economic and Social Council may submit from time to time to the General Assembly reports with recommendations of a general nature and a summary of the information received from the States Parties to the present Covenant and the specialized agencies on the measures taken and the progress made in achieving general observance of the rights recognized in the present Covenant.

Article 22

The Economic and Social Council may bring to the attention of other organs of the United Nations, their subsidiary organs and specialized agencies concerned with furnishing technical assistance any matters arising out of the reports referred to in this part of the present Covenant which may assist such bodies in deciding, each within its field of competence, on the advisability of international measures likely to contribute to the effective progressive implementation of the present Covenant.

Article 23

The States Parties to the present Covenant agree that international action for the achievement of the rights recognized in the present Covenant includes such methods as the conclusion of conventions, the adoption of recommendations, the furnishing of technical assistance and the holding of regional meetings and technical meetings for the purpose of consultation and study organized in conjunction with the Governments concerned.

Article 24

Nothing in the present Covenant shall be interpreted as impairing the provisions of the Charter of the United Nations and of the constitutions of the specialized agencies which define the respective responsibilities of the various organs of the United Nations and of the specialized agencies in regard to the matters dealt with in the present Covenant.

Article 25

Nothing in the present Covenant shall be interpreted as impairing the inherent right of all peoples to enjoy and utilize fully and freely their natural wealth and resources.

PART V

Article 26

1. The present Covenant is open for signature by any State Member of the United Nations or member of any of its specialized agencies, by any State Party to the Statute of the International Court of Justice, and by any other State which has been invited by the General Assembly of the United Nations to become a party to the present Covenant.

2. The present Covenant is subject to ratification. Instruments of ratification shall be deposited with the Secretary-General of the United Nations.

3. The present Covenant shall be open to accession by any State referred to in paragraph 1 of this article.

4. Accession shall be effected by the deposit of an instrument of accession with the Secretary-General of the United Nations.

5. The Secretary-General of the United Nations shall inform all States which have signed the present Covenant or acceded to it of the deposit of each instrument of ratification or accession.

Article 27

1. The present Covenant shall enter into force three months after the date of the deposit with the Secretary-General of the United Nations of the thirty-fifth instrument of ratification or instrument of accession.

2. For each State ratifying the present Covenant or acceding to it after the deposit of the thirty-fifth instrument of ratification or instrument of accession, the present Covenant shall enter into force three months after the date of the deposit of its own instrument of ratification or instrument of accession.

Article 28

The provisions of the present Covenant shall extend to all parts of federal States without any limitations or exceptions.

Article 29

1. Any State Party to the present Covenant may propose an amendment and file it with the Secretary-General of the United Nations. The Secretary-General shall thereupon communicate any proposed amendments to the States Parties to the present Covenant with a request that they notify him whether they favour a conference of States Parties for the purpose of considering and voting upon the proposals. In the event that at least one-third of the States Parties favours such a conference, the Secretary-General shall convene the conference under the auspices of the United Nations. Any amendment adopted by a majority of the States Parties present and voting at the conference shall be submitted to the General Assembly of the United Nations for approval.

2. Amendments shall come into force when they have been approved by the General Assembly of the United Nations and accepted by a two-thirds majority of the States Parties to the present Covenant in accordance with their respective constitutional processes.

3. When amendments come into force they shall be binding on those States Parties which have accepted them, other States Parties still being bound by the provisions of the present Covenant and any earlier amendment which they have accepted.

Article 30

Irrespective of the notifications made under article 26, paragraph 5, the Secretary-General of the United Nations shall inform all States referred to in paragraph 1 of the same article of the following particulars:
  (a) Signatures, ratifications and accessions under article 26;
  (b) The date of the entry into force of the present Covenant under article 27 and the date of the entry into force of any amendments under article 29.

Article 31

1. The present Covenant, of which the Chinese, English, French, Russian and Spanish texts are equally authentic, shall be deposited in the archives of the United Nations.

2. The Secretary-General of the United Nations shall transmit certified copies of the present Covenant to all States referred to in article 26.

Appendix D: The Constitution of the United States

We the People of the United States, in Order to form a more perfect Union, establish Justice, insure domestic Tranquility, provide for the common defence, promote the general Welfare, and secure the Blessings of Liberty to ourselves and our Posterity, do ordain and establish this Constitution for the United States of America.

Article I.
Section 1. All legislative Powers herein granted shall be vested in a Congress of the United States, which shall consist of a Senate and House of Representatives.

Section 2. The House of Representatives shall be composed of Members chosen every second Year by the People of the several States, and the Electors in each State shall have the Qualifications requisite for Electors of the most numerous Branch of the State Legislature.

No Person shall be a Representative who shall not have attained to the Age of twenty five Years, and been seven Years a Citizen of the United States, and who shall not, when elected, be an Inhabitant of that State in which he shall be chosen.

Representatives and direct Taxes shall be apportioned among the several States which may be included within this Union, according to their respective Numbers, which shall be determined by adding to the whole Number of free Persons, including those bound to Service for a Term of Years, and excluding Indians not taxed, three-fifths of all other Persons. The actual Enumeration shall be made within three Years after the first Meeting of the Congress of the United States, and within every subsequent Term of ten Years, in such Manner as they shall by Law direct. The Number of Representatives shall not exceed one for every thirty Thousand, but each State shall have at Least one Representative; and until such enumeration shall be made, the State of New Hampshire shall be entitled to chuse three, Massachusetts eight, Rhode Island and Providence Plantations one, Connecticut five, New York six, New Jersey four, Pennsylvania eight, Delaware one, Maryland six, Virginia ten, North Carolina five, South Carolina five, and Georgia three.

When vacancies happen in the Representation from any State, the Executive Authority thereof shall issue Writs of Election to fill such Vacancies.

The House of Representatives shall chuse their Speaker and other Officers; and shall have the sole Power of Impeachment.

Section 3. The Senate of the United States shall be composed of two Senators from each State, chosen by the Legislature thereof, for six Years; and each Senator shall have one Vote.

Immediately after they shall be assembled in Consequence of the first Election, they shall be divided as equally as may be into three Classes. The Seats of the Senators of the first Class shall be vacated at the Expiration of the second Year, of the second Class at the Expiration of the fourth Year, and of the third Class at the Expiration of the sixth Year, so that one-third may be chosen every second Year; and if Vacancies happen by Resignation, or otherwise, during the Recess of the Legislature of any State, the Executive thereof may make temporary Appointments until the next Meeting of the Legislature, which shall then fill such Vacancies.

No Person shall be a Senator who shall not have attained to the Age of thirty Years, and been nine Years a Citizen of the United States, and who shall not, when elected, be an Inhabitant of that State for which he shall be chosen.

The Vice President of the United States shall be President of the Senate, but shall have no Vote, unless they be equally divided.

The Senate shall chuse their other Officers, and also a President *pro tempore*, in the Absence of the Vice President, or when he shall exercise the Office of President of the United States.

The Senate shall have the sole Power to try all Impeachments. When sitting for that Purpose, they shall be on Oath or Affirmation. When the President of the United States is tried, the Chief Justice shall preside: And no Person shall be convicted without the Concurrence of two-thirds of the Members present.

Judgment in Cases of Impeachment shall not extend further than to removal from Office, and disqualification to hold and enjoy any Office of honor, Trust or Profit under the United States: but the Party convicted shall nevertheless be liable and subject to Indictment, Trial, Judgment and Punishment, according to Law.

Section 4. The Times, Places and Manner of holding Elections for Senators and Representatives, shall be prescribed in each State by the Legislature thereof; but the Congress may at any time by Law make or alter such Regulations, except as to the Places of chusing Senators.

The Congress shall assemble at least once in every Year, and such Meeting shall be on the first Monday in December [Modified by Amendment XX], unless they shall by Law appoint a different Day.

Section 5. Each House shall be the Judge of the Elections, Returns and Qualifications of its own Members, and a Majority of each shall constitute a Quorum to do Business; but a smaller Number may adjourn from day to day, and may be authorized to compel the Attendance of absent Members, in such Manner, and under such Penalties as each House may provide.

Each House may determine the Rules of its Proceedings, punish its Members for disorderly Behaviour, and, with the Concurrence of two-thirds, expel a Member.

Each House shall keep a Journal of its Proceedings, and from time to time publish the same, excepting such Parts as may in their Judgment require Secrecy; and the Yeas and Nays of the Members of either House on any question shall, at the Desire of one-fifth of those Present, be entered on the Journal.

Neither House, during the Session of Congress, shall, without the Consent of the other, adjourn for more than three days, nor to any other Place than that in which the two Houses shall be sitting.

Section 6. The Senators and Representatives shall receive a Compensation for their Services, to be ascertained by Law, and paid out of the Treasury of the United States. They shall in all Cases, except Treason, Felony and Breach of the Peace, be privileged from Arrest during their Attendance at the Session of their respective Houses, and in going to and returning from the same; and for any Speech or Debate in either House, they shall not be questioned in any other Place.

No Senator or Representative shall, during the Time for which he was elected, be appointed to any civil Office under the Authority of the United States, which shall have been created, or the Emoluments whereof shall have been encreased during such time; and no Person holding any Office under the United States, shall be a Member of either House during his Continuance in Office.

Section 7. All Bills for raising Revenue shall originate in the House of Representatives; but the Senate may propose or concur with Amendments as on other Bills.

Every Bill which shall have passed the House of Representatives and the Senate, shall, before it become a Law, be presented to the President of the United States; If he approve he shall sign it, but if not he shall return it, with his Objections to that House in which it shall have originated, who shall enter the Objections at large on their Journal, and proceed to reconsider it. If after such Reconsideration two-thirds of that House shall agree to pass the Bill, it shall be sent, together with the Objections, to the other House, by which it shall likewise be reconsidered, and if approved by two-thirds of that House, it shall become a Law. But in all such Cases the Votes of both Houses shall be determined by yeas and Nays, and the Names of the Persons voting for and against the Bill shall be entered on the Journal of each House respectively. If any Bill shall not be returned by the President within ten Days (Sundays excepted) after it shall have been presented to him, the Same shall be a Law, in like Manner as if he had signed it, unless the Congress by their Adjournment prevent its Return, in which Case it shall not be a Law.

Every Order, Resolution, or Vote to which the Concurrence of the Senate and House of Representatives may be necessary (except on a question of Adjournment) shall be presented to the President of the United States; and before the Same shall take Effect, shall be approved by him, or being disapproved by him, shall be repassed by two-thirds of the Senate and House of Representatives, according to the Rules and Limitations prescribed in the Case of a Bill.

Section 8. The Congress shall have Power To lay and collect Taxes, Duties, Imposts and Excises, to pay the Debts and provide for the common Defence and general Welfare of the United States; but all Duties, Imposts and Excises shall be uniform throughout the United States;

To borrow Money on the credit of the United States;

To regulate Commerce with foreign Nations, and among the several States, and with the Indian Tribes;

To establish an uniform Rule of Naturalization, and uniform Laws on the subject of Bankruptcies throughout the United States;

To coin Money, regulate the Value thereof, and of foreign Coin, and fix the Standard of Weights and Measures;

To provide for the Punishment of counterfeiting the Securities and current Coin of the United States;

To establish Post Offices and post Roads;

To promote the Progress of Science and useful Arts, by securing for limited Times to Authors and Inventors the exclusive Right to their respective Writings and Discoveries;

To constitute Tribunals inferior to the supreme Court;

To define and punish Piracies and Felonies committed on the high Seas, and Offences against the Law of Nations;

To declare War, grant Letters of Marque and Reprisal, and make Rules concerning Captures on Land and Water;

To raise and support Armies, but no Appropriation of Money to that Use shall be for a longer Term than two Years;

To provide and maintain a Navy;

To make Rules for the Government and Regulation of the land and naval Forces;

To provide for calling forth the Militia to execute the Laws of the Union, suppress Insurrections and repel Invasions;

To provide for organizing, arming, and disciplining, the Militia, and for governing such Part of them as may be employed in the Service of the United States, reserving to the States respectively, the Appointment of the Officers, and the Authority of training the Militia according to the discipline prescribed by Congress;

To exercise exclusive Legislation in all Cases whatsoever, over such District (not exceeding ten Miles square) as may, by Cession of particular States, and the Acceptance of Congress, become the Seat of the Government of the United States, and to exercise like Authority over all Places purchased by the Consent of the Legislature of the State in which the Same shall be, for the Erection of Forts, Magazines, Arsenals, dockYards, and other needful Buildings; –And

To make all Laws which shall be necessary and proper for carrying into Execution the foregoing Powers, and all other Powers vested by this Constitution in the Government of the United States, or in any Department or Officer thereof.

Section 9. The Migration or Importation of such Persons as any of the States now existing shall think proper to admit, shall not be prohibited by the Congress prior to the Year one thousand eight hundred and eight, but a Tax or duty may be imposed on such Importation, not exceeding ten dollars for each Person.

The Privilege of the Writ of Habeas Corpus shall not be suspended, unless when in Cases of Rebellion or Invasion the public Safety may require it.

No Bill of Attainder or *ex post facto* Law shall be passed.

No Capitation, or other direct, Tax shall be laid, unless in Proportion to the Census or Enumeration herein before directed to be taken.

No Tax or Duty shall be laid on Articles exported from any State.

No Preference shall be given by any Regulation of Commerce or Revenue to the Ports of one State over those of another; nor shall Vessels bound to, or from, one State, be obliged to enter, clear, or pay Duties in another.

No Money shall be drawn from the Treasury, but in Consequence of Appropriations made by Law; and a regular Statement and Account of the Receipts and Expenditures of all public Money shall be published from time to time.

No Title of Nobility shall be granted by the United States: And no Person holding any Office of Profit or Trust under them, shall, without the Consent of the Congress, accept of any present, Emolument, Office, or Title, of any kind whatever, from any King, Prince, or foreign State.

Section 10. No State shall enter into any Treaty, Alliance, or Confederation; grant Letters of Marque and Reprisal; coin Money; emit Bills of Credit; make any Thing but gold and silver Coin a Tender in Payment of Debts; pass any Bill of

Attainder, *ex post facto* Law, or Law impairing the Obligation of Contracts, or grant any Title of Nobility.

No State shall, without the Consent of the Congress, lay any Imposts or Duties on Imports or Exports, except what may be absolutely necessary for executing it's inspection Laws; and the net Produce of all Duties and Imposts, laid by any State on Imports or Exports, shall be for the Use of the Treasury of the United States; and all such Laws shall be subject to the Revision and Controul of the Congress.

No State shall, without the Consent of Congress, lay any Duty of Tonnage, keep Troops, or Ships of War in time of Peace, enter into any Agreement or Compact with another State, or with a foreign Power, or engage in War, unless actually invaded, or in such imminent Danger as will not admit of delay.

Article II.

Section 1. The executive Power shall be vested in a President of the United States of America. He shall hold his Office during the Term of four Years, and, together with the Vice President, chosen for the same Term, be elected, as follows:

Each State shall appoint, in such Manner as the Legislature thereof may direct, a Number of Electors, equal to the whole Number of Senators and Representatives to which the State may be entitled in the Congress: but no Senator or Representative, or Person holding an Office of Trust or Profit under the United States, shall be appointed an Elector.

The Electors shall meet in their respective States, and vote by Ballot for two Persons, of whom one at least shall not be an Inhabitant of the same State with themselves. And they shall make a List of all the Persons voted for, and of the Number of Votes for each; which List they shall sign and certify, and transmit sealed to the Seat of the Government of the United States, directed to the President of the Senate. The President of the Senate shall, in the Presence of the Senate and House of Representatives, open all the Certificates, and the Votes shall then be counted. The Person having the greatest Number of Votes shall be the President, if such Number be a Majority of the whole Number of Electors appointed; and if there be more than one who have such Majority, and have an equal Number of Votes, then the House of Representatives shall immediately chuse by Ballot one of them for President; and if no Person have a Majority, then from the five highest on the List the said House shall in like Manner chuse the President. But in chusing the President, the Votes shall be taken by States, the Representation from each State having one Vote; a quorum for this Purpose shall consist of a Member or Members from two-thirds of the States, and a Majority of all the States shall be necessary to a Choice. In every Case, after the Choice of the President, the Person having the greatest Number of Votes of the Electors shall be the Vice President. But if there should remain two or more who have equal Votes, the Senate shall chuse from them by Ballot the Vice President.

The Congress may determine the Time of chusing the Electors, and the Day on which they shall give their Votes; which Day shall be the same throughout the United States.

No Person except a natural born Citizen, or a Citizen of the United States, at the time of the Adoption of this Constitution, shall be eligible to the Office of President; neither shall any Person be eligible to that Office who shall not have attained to the Age of thirty five Years, and been fourteen Years a Resident within the United States.

In Case of the Removal of the President from Office, or of his Death, Resignation, or Inability to discharge the Powers and Duties of the said Office, the Same shall devolve on the Vice President, and the Congress may by Law provide for the Case of Removal, Death, Resignation or Inability, both of the President and Vice President, declaring what Officer shall then act as President, and such Officer shall act accordingly, until the Disability be removed, or a President shall be elected.

The President shall, at stated Times, receive for his Services, a Compensation, which shall neither be increased nor diminished during the Period for which he shall have been elected, and he shall not receive within that Period any other Emolument from the United States, or any of them.

Before he enter on the Execution of his Office, he shall take the following Oath or Affirmation: – "I do solemnly swear (or affirm) that I will faithfully execute the Office of President of the United States, and will to the best of my Ability, preserve, protect and defend the Constitution of the United States."

Section 2. The President shall be Commander in Chief of the Army and Navy of the United States, and of the Militia of the several States, when called into the actual Service of the United States; he may require the Opinion, in writing, of the principal Officer in each of the executive Departments, upon any Subject relating to the Duties of their respective Offices, and he shall have Power to grant Reprieves and Pardons for Offences against the United States, except in Cases of Impeachment.

He shall have Power, by and with the Advice and Consent of the Senate, to make Treaties, provided two-thirds of the Senators present concur; and he shall nominate, and by and with the Advice and Consent of the Senate, shall appoint Ambassadors, other public Ministers and Consuls, Judges of the supreme Court, and all other Officers of the United States, whose Appointments are not herein otherwise provided for, and which shall be established by Law: but the Congress may by Law vest the Appointment of such inferior Officers, as they think proper, in the President alone, in the Courts of Law, or in the Heads of Departments.

The President shall have Power to fill up all Vacancies that may happen during the Recess of the Senate, by granting Commissions which shall expire at the End of their next Session.

Section 3. He shall from time to time give to the Congress Information of the State of the Union, and recommend to their Consideration such Measures as he shall judge necessary and expedient; he may, on extraordinary Occasions, convene both Houses, or either of them, and in Case of Disagreement between them, with Respect to the Time of Adjournment, he may adjourn them to such Time as he shall think proper; he shall receive Ambassadors and other public Ministers; he shall take Care that the Laws be faithfully executed, and shall Commission all the Officers of the United States.

Section 4. The President, Vice President and all civil Officers of the United States, shall be removed from Office on Impeachment for, and Conviction of, Treason, Bribery, or other high Crimes and Misdemeanors.

Article III.
Section 1. The judicial Power of the United States shall be vested in one supreme Court, and in such inferior Courts as the Congress may from time to time ordain and establish. The Judges, both of the supreme and inferior Courts, shall hold their Offices during good Behaviour, and shall, at stated Times, receive for their Services a Compensation, which shall not be diminished during their Continuance in Office.

Section 2. The judicial Power shall extend to all Cases, in Law and Equity, arising under this Constitution, the Laws of the United States, and Treaties made, or which shall be made, under their Authority; – to all Cases affecting Ambassadors, other public Ministers and Consuls; – to all Cases of admiralty and maritime Jurisdiction; – to Controversies to which the United States shall be a Party; – to Controversies between two or more States; – between a State and Citizens of another State; – between Citizens of different States; – between Citizens of the same State claiming Lands under Grants of different States, and between a State, or the Citizens thereof, and foreign States, Citizens or Subjects.

In all Cases affecting Ambassadors, other public Ministers and Consuls, and those in which a State shall be Party, the supreme Court shall have original Jurisdiction. In all the other Cases before mentioned, the supreme Court shall have appellate Jurisdiction, both as to Law and Fact, with such Exceptions, and under such Regulations as the Congress shall make.

The Trial of all Crimes, except in Cases of Impeachment, shall be by Jury; and such Trial shall be held in the State where the said Crimes shall have been committed; but when not committed within any State, the Trial shall be at such Place or Places as the Congress may by Law have directed.
Section 3. Treason against the United States shall consist only in levying War against them, or in adhering to their Enemies, giving them Aid and Comfort.

No Person shall be convicted of Treason unless on the Testimony of two Witnesses to the same overt Act, or on Confession in open Court.

The Congress shall have Power to declare the Punishment of Treason, but no Attainder of Treason shall work Corruption of Blood, or Forfeiture except during the Life of the Person attainted.

Article IV.

Section 1. Full Faith and Credit shall be given in each State to the public Acts, Records, and judicial Proceedings of every other State. And the Congress may by general Laws prescribe the Manner in which such Acts, Records and Proceedings shall be proved, and the Effect thereof.

Section 2. The Citizens of each State shall be entitled to all Privileges and Immunities of Citizens in the several States.

A Person charged in any State with Treason, Felony, or other Crime, who shall flee from Justice, and be found in another State, shall on Demand of the executive Authority of the State from which he fled, be delivered up, to be removed to the State having Jurisdiction of the Crime.

No Person held to Service or Labour in one State, under the Laws thereof, escaping into another, shall, in Consequence of any Law or Regulation therein, be discharged from such Service or Labour, but shall be delivered up on Claim of the Party to whom such Service or Labour may be due.

Section 3. New States may be admitted by the Congress into this Union; but no new State shall be formed or erected within the Jurisdiction of any other State; nor any State be formed by the Junction of two or more States, or Parts of States, without the Consent of the Legislatures of the States concerned as well as of the Congress.

The Congress shall have Power to dispose of and make all needful Rules and Regulations respecting the Territory or other Property belonging to the United States; and nothing in this Constitution shall be so construed as to Prejudice any Claims of the United States, or of any particular State.

Section 4. The United States shall guarantee to every State in this Union a Republican Form of Government, and shall protect each of them against Invasion; and on Application of the Legislature, or of the Executive (when the Legislature cannot be convened), against domestic Violence.

Article V.

The Congress, whenever two-thirds of both Houses shall deem it necessary, shall propose Amendments to this Constitution, or, on the Application of the Legislatures of two-thirds of the several States, shall call a Convention for proposing Amendments, which, in either Case, shall be valid to all Intents and

Purposes, as Part of this Constitution, when ratified by the Legislatures of three-fourths of the several States, or by Conventions in three-fourths thereof, as the one or the other Mode of Ratification may be proposed by the Congress; Provided that no Amendment which may be made prior to the Year One thousand eight hundred and eight shall in any Manner affect the first and fourth Clauses in the Ninth Section of the first Article; and that no State, without its Consent, shall be deprived of its equal Suffrage in the Senate.

Article VI.

All Debts contracted and Engagements entered into, before the Adoption of this Constitution, shall be as valid against the United States under this Constitution, as under the Confederation.

This Constitution, and the Laws of the United States which shall be made in Pursuance thereof; and all Treaties made, or which shall be made, under the Authority of the United States, shall be the supreme Law of the Land; and the Judges in every State shall be bound thereby, any Thing in the Constitution or Laws of any State to the Contrary notwithstanding.

The Senators and Representatives before mentioned, and the Members of the several State Legislatures, and all executive and judicial Officers, both of the United States and of the several States, shall be bound by Oath or Affirmation, to support this Constitution; but no religious Test shall ever be required as a Qualification to any Office or public Trust under the United States.

Article VII.

The Ratification of the Conventions of nine States, shall be sufficient for the Establishment of this Constitution between the States so ratifying the Same.

Amendments

Amendment I (1791)

Congress shall make no law respecting an establishment of religion, or prohibiting the free exercise thereof; or abridging the freedom of speech, or of the press; or the right of the people peaceably to assemble, and to petition the Government for a redress of grievances.

Amendment II (1791)

A well regulated Militia, being necessary to the security of a free State, the right of the people to keep and bear Arms, shall not be infringed.

Amendment III (1791)

No Soldier shall, in time of peace be quartered in any house, without the consent of the Owner, nor in time of war, but in a manner to be prescribed by law.

Amendment IV (1791)

The right of the people to be secure in their persons, houses, papers, and effects, against unreasonable searches and seizures, shall not be violated, and no Warrants shall issue, but upon probable cause, supported by Oath or affirmation, and particularly describing the place to be searched, and the persons or things to be seized.

Amendment V (1791)

No person shall be held to answer for a capital, or otherwise infamous crime, unless on a presentment or indictment of a Grand Jury, except in cases arising in the land or naval forces, or in the Militia, when in actual service in time of War or public danger; nor shall any person be subject for the same offence to be twice put in jeopardy of life or limb; nor shall be compelled in any criminal case to be a witness against himself, nor be deprived of life, liberty, or property, without due process of law; nor shall private property be taken for public use, without just compensation.

Amendment VI (1791)

In all criminal prosecutions, the accused shall enjoy the right to a speedy and public trial, by an impartial jury of the State and district wherein the crime shall have been committed, which district shall have been previously ascertained by law, and to be informed of the nature and cause of the accusation; to be confronted with the witnesses against him; to have compulsory process for obtaining witnesses in his favor, and to have the Assistance of Counsel for his defence.

Amendment VII (1791)

In Suits at common law, where the value in controversy shall exceed twenty dollars, the right of trial by jury shall be preserved, and no fact tried by a jury, shall be otherwise reexamined in any Court of the United States, than according to the rules of the common law.

Amendment VIII (1791)

Excessive bail shall not be required, nor excessive fines imposed, nor cruel and unusual punishments inflicted.

Amendment IX (1791)

The enumeration in the Constitution, of certain rights, shall not be construed to deny or disparage others retained by the people.

Amendment X (1791)

The powers not delegated to the United States by the Constitution, nor prohibited by it to the States, are reserved to the States respectively, or to the people.

Amendment XI (1795)

The Judicial power of the United States shall not be construed to extend to any suit in law or equity, commenced or prosecuted against one of the United States by Citizens of another State, or by Citizens or Subjects of any Foreign State.

Amendment XII (1804)

The Electors shall meet in their respective states, and vote by ballot for President and Vice President, one of whom, at least, shall not be an inhabitant of the same state with themselves; they shall name in their ballots the person voted for as President, and in distinct ballots the person voted for as Vice President, and they shall make distinct lists of all persons voted for as President, and of all persons voted for as Vice President, and of the number of votes for each, which lists they shall sign and certify, and transmit sealed to the seat of the government of the United States, directed to the President of the Senate; – The President of the Senate shall, in the presence of the Senate and House of Representatives, open all the certificates and the votes shall then be counted; – The person having the greatest number of votes for President, shall be the President, if such number be a majority of the whole number of Electors appointed; and if no person have such majority, then from the persons having the highest numbers not exceeding three on the list of those voted for as President, the House of Representatives shall choose immediately, by ballot, the President. But in choosing the President, the votes shall be taken by states, the representation from each state having one vote; a quorum for this purpose shall consist of a member or members from two-thirds of the states, and a majority of all the states shall be necessary to a choice. And if the House of Representatives shall not choose a President whenever the right of choice shall devolve upon them, before the fourth day of March next following, then the Vice President shall act as President, as in the case of the death or other constitutional disability of the President. – The person having the greatest number of votes as Vice President, shall be the Vice President, if such number be a majority of the whole number of Electors appointed, and if no person have a majority, then from the two highest numbers on the list, the Senate shall choose the Vice President; a quorum for the purpose shall consist of two-thirds of the whole number of Senators, and a majority of the whole number shall be necessary to a choice. But no person constitutionally ineligible to the office of President shall be eligible to that of Vice President of the United States.

Amendment XIII (1865)

Section 1. Neither slavery nor involuntary servitude, except as a punishment for crime whereof the party shall have been duly convicted, shall exist within the United States, or any place subject to their jurisdiction.

Section 2. Congress shall have power to enforce this article by appropriate legislation.

Amendment XIV (1868)

Section 1. All persons born or naturalized in the United States, and subject to the jurisdiction thereof, are citizens of the United States and of the State wherein they reside. No State shall make or enforce any law which shall abridge the privileges or immunities of citizens of the United States; nor shall any State deprive any person of life, liberty, or property, without due process of law; nor deny to any person within its jurisdiction the equal protection of the laws.

Section 2. Representatives shall be apportioned among the several States according to their respective numbers, counting the whole number of persons in each State, excluding Indians not taxed. But when the right to vote at any election for the choice of electors for President and Vice President of the United States, Representatives in Congress, the Executive and Judicial officers of a State, or the members of the Legislature thereof, is denied to any of the male inhabitants of such State, being twenty-one years of age, and citizens of the United States, or in any way abridged, except for participation in rebellion, or other crime, the basis of representation therein shall be reduced in the proportion which the number of such male citizens shall bear to the whole number of male citizens twenty-one years of age in such State.

Section 3. No person shall be a Senator or Representative in Congress, or elector of President and Vice President, or hold any office, civil or military, under the United States, or under any State, who, having previously taken an oath, as a member of Congress, or as an officer of the United States, or as a member of any State legislature, or as an executive or judicial officer of any State, to support the Constitution of the United States, shall have engaged in insurrection or rebellion against the same, or given aid or comfort to the enemies thereof. But Congress may by a vote of two-thirds of each House, remove such disability.

Section 4. The validity of the public debt of the United States, authorized by law, including debts incurred for payment of pensions and bounties for services in suppressing insurrection or rebellion, shall not be questioned. But neither the United States nor any State shall assume or pay any debt or obligation incurred in aid of insurrection or rebellion against the United States, or any claim for the loss or emancipation of any slave; but all such debts, obligations and claims shall be held illegal and void.

Section 5. The Congress shall have power to enforce, by appropriate legislation, the provisions of this article.

Amendment XV (1870)

Section 1. The right of citizens of the United States to vote shall not be denied or abridged by the United States or by any State on account of race, color, or previous condition of servitude.

Section 2. The Congress shall have power to enforce this article by appropriate legislation.

Amendment XVI (1913)

The Congress shall have power to lay and collect taxes on incomes, from whatever source derived, without apportionment among the several States, and without regard to any census or enumeration.

Amendment XVII (1913)

The Senate of the United States shall be composed of two Senators from each State, elected by the people thereof, for six years; and each Senator shall have one vote. The electors in each State shall have the qualifications requisite for electors of the most numerous branch of the State legislatures.

When vacancies happen in the representation of any State in the Senate, the executive authority of such State shall issue writs of election to fill such vacancies: Provided, That the legislature of any State may empower the executive thereof to make temporary appointments until the people fill the vacancies by election as the legislature may direct.

This amendment shall not be so construed as to affect the election or term of any Senator chosen before it becomes valid as part of the Constitution.

Amendment XVIII (1919)

[Repealed by Amendment XXI.]

Section 1. After one year from the ratification of this article the manufacture, sale, or transportation of intoxicating liquors within, the importation thereof into, or the exportation thereof from the United States and all territory subject to the jurisdiction thereof for beverage purposes is hereby prohibited.

Section 2. The Congress and the several States shall have concurrent power to enforce this article by appropriate legislation.

Section 3. This article shall be inoperative unless it shall have been ratified as an amendment to the Constitution by the legislatures of the several States, as provided in the Constitution, within seven years from the date of the submission hereof to the States by the Congress.

Amendment XIX (1920)

The right of citizens of the United States to vote shall not be denied or abridged by the United States or by any State on account of sex.

Congress shall have power to enforce this article by appropriate legislation.

Amendment XX (1933)

Section 1. The terms of the President and Vice President shall end at noon on the 20th day of January, and the terms of Senators and Representatives at noon on the 3rd day of January, of the years in which such terms would have ended if this article had not been ratified; and the terms of their successors shall then begin.

Section 2. The Congress shall assemble at least once in every year, and such meeting shall begin at noon on the 3rd day of January, unless they shall by law appoint a different day.

Section 3. If, at the time fixed for the beginning of the term of the President, the President elect shall have died, the Vice President elect shall become President. If a President shall not have been chosen before the time fixed for the beginning of his term, or if the President elect shall have failed to qualify, then the Vice President elect shall act as President until a President shall have qualified; and the Congress may by law provide for the case wherein neither a President elect nor a Vice President elect shall have qualified, declaring who shall then act as President, or the manner in which one who is to act shall be selected, and such person shall act accordingly until a President or Vice President shall have qualified.

Section 4. The Congress may by law provide for the case of the death of any of the persons from whom the House of Representatives may choose a President whenever the right of choice shall have devolved upon them, and for the case of the death of any of the persons from whom the Senate may choose a Vice President whenever the right of choice shall have devolved upon them.

Section 5. Sections 1 and 2 shall take effect on the 15th day of October following the ratification of this article.

Section 6. This article shall be inoperative unless it shall have been ratified as an amendment to the Constitution by the legislatures of three-fourths of the several States within seven years from the date of its submission.

Amendment XXI (1933)

Section 1. The eighteenth article of amendment to the Constitution of the United States is hereby repealed.

Section 2. The transportation or importation into any State, Territory, or possession of the United States for delivery or use therein of intoxicating liquors, in violation of the laws thereof, is hereby prohibited.

Section 3. This article shall be inoperative unless it shall have been ratified as an amendment to the Constitution by conventions in the several States, as provided in the Constitution, within seven years from the date of the submission hereof to the States by the Congress.

Amendment XXII (1951)

Section 1. No person shall be elected to the office of the President more than twice, and no person who has held the office of President, or acted as President, for more than two years of a term to which some other person was elected President shall be elected to the office of the President more than once. But this Article shall not apply to any person holding the office of President when this Article was proposed by the Congress, and shall not prevent any person who may be holding the office of President, or acting as President, during the term within which this Article becomes operative from holding the office of President or acting as President during the remainder of such term.

Section 2. This article shall be inoperative unless it shall have been ratified as an amendment to the Constitution by the legislatures of three-fourths of the several States within seven years from the date of its submission to the States by the Congress.

Amendment XXIII (1961)

Section 1. The District constituting the seat of Government of the United States shall appoint in such manner as the Congress may direct:

A number of electors of President and Vice President equal to the whole number of Senators and Representatives in Congress to which the District would be entitled if it were a State, but in no event more than the least populous State; they shall be in addition to those appointed by the States, but they shall be considered, for the purposes of the election of President and Vice President, to be electors appointed by a State; and they shall meet in the District and perform such duties as provided by the twelfth article of amendment.

Section 2. The Congress shall have power to enforce this article by appropriate legislation.

Amendment XXIV (1964)

Section 1. The right of citizens of the United States to vote in any primary or other election for President or Vice President, for electors for President or Vice

President, or for Senator or Representative in Congress, shall not be denied or abridged by the United States or any State by reason of failure to pay any poll tax or other tax.

Section 2. The Congress shall have power to enforce this article by appropriate legislation.

Amendment XXV (1967)

Section 1. In case of the removal of the President from office or of his death or resignation, the Vice President shall become President.

Section 2. Whenever there is a vacancy in the office of the Vice President, the President shall nominate a Vice President who shall take office upon confirmation by a majority vote of both Houses of Congress.

Section 3. Whenever the President transmits to the President *pro tempore* of the Senate and the Speaker of the House of Representatives his written declaration that he is unable to discharge the powers and duties of his office, and until he transmits to them a written declaration to the contrary, such powers and duties shall be discharged by the Vice President as Acting President.

Section 4. Whenever the Vice President and a majority of either the principal officers of the executive departments or of such other body as Congress may by law provide, transmit to the President *pro tempore* of the Senate and the Speaker of the House of Representatives their written declaration that the President is unable to discharge the powers and duties of his office, the Vice President shall immediately assume the powers and duties of the office as Acting President.

Thereafter, when the President transmits to the President *pro tempore* of the Senate and the Speaker of the House of Representatives his written declaration that no inability exists, he shall resume the powers and duties of his office unless the Vice President and a majority of either the principal officers of the executive department or of such other body as Congress may by law provide, transmit within four days to the President *pro tempore* of the Senate and the Speaker of the House of Representatives their written declaration that the President is unable to discharge the powers and duties of his office. Thereupon Congress shall decide the issue, assembling within forty-eight hours for that purpose if not in session. If the Congress, within twenty-one days after receipt of the latter written declaration, or, if Congress is not in session, within twenty-one days after Congress is required to assemble, determines by two-thirds vote of both Houses that the President is unable to discharge the powers and duties of his office, the Vice President shall continue to discharge the same as Acting

President; otherwise, the President shall resume the powers and duties of his office.

Amendment XXVI (1971)

Section 1. The right of citizens of the United States, who are eighteen years of age or older, to vote shall not be denied or abridged by the United States or by any State on account of age.

Section 2. The Congress shall have power to enforce this article by appropriate legislation.

Amendment XXVII (1992)

No law, varying the compensation for the services of the Senators and Representatives, shall take effect, until an election of Representatives shall have intervened.

Appendix E: The South African Bill of Rights

Chapter 2 of the Constitution of South Africa

---

7. **Rights**
   (1) This Bill of Rights is a cornerstone of democracy in South Africa. It enshrines the rights of all people in our country and affirms the democratic values of human dignity, equality and freedom.
   (2) The state must respect, protect, promote and fulfil the rights in the Bill of Rights.
   (3) The rights in the Bill of Rights are subject to the limitations contained or referred to in section 36, or elsewhere in the Bill.

8. **Application**
   (1) The Bill of Rights applies to all law, and binds the legislature, the executive, the judiciary and all organs of state.
   (2) A provision of the Bill of Rights binds a natural or a juristic person if, and to the extent that, it is applicable, taking into account the nature of the right and the nature of any duty imposed by the right.
   (3) When applying a provision of the Bill of Rights to a natural or juristic person in terms of subsection (2), a court–
      (a) in order to give effect to a right in the Bill, must apply, or if necessary develop, the common law to the extent that legislation does not give effect to that right; and
      (b) may develop rules of the common law to limit the right, provided that the limitation is in accordance with section 36(1).
   (4) A juristic person is entitled to the rights in the Bill of Rights to the extent required by the nature of the rights and the nature of that juristic person.

9. **Equality**
   (1) Everyone is equal before the law and has the right to equal protection and benefit of the law.
   (2) Equality includes the full and equal enjoyment of all rights and freedoms. To promote the achievement of equality, legislative and other measures designed to protect or advance persons, or categories of persons, disadvantaged by unfair discrimination may be taken.

(3) The state may not unfairly discriminate directly or indirectly against anyone on one or more grounds, including race, gender, sex, pregnancy, marital status, ethnic or social origin, colour, sexual orientation, age, disability, religion, conscience, belief, culture, language and birth.

(4) No person may unfairly discriminate directly or indirectly against anyone on one or more grounds in terms of subsection (3). National legislation must be enacted to prevent or prohibit unfair discrimination.

(5) Discrimination on one or more of the grounds listed in subsection (3) is unfair unless it is established that the discrimination is fair.

10. Human dignity

Everyone has inherent dignity and the right to have their dignity respected and protected.

11. Life

Everyone has the right to life.

12. Freedom and security of the person

(1) Everyone has the right to freedom and security of the person, which includes the right–

(a) not to be deprived of freedom arbitrarily or without just cause;

(b) not to be detained without trial;

(c) to be free from all forms of violence from either public or private sources;

(d) not to be tortured in any way; and

(e) not to be treated or punished in a cruel, inhuman or degrading way.

(2) Everyone has the right to bodily and psychological integrity, which includes the right–

(a) to make decisions concerning reproduction;

(b) to security in and control over their body; and

(c) not to be subjected to medical or scientific experiments without their informed consent.

13. Slavery, servitude and forced labour

No one may be subjected to slavery, servitude or forced labour.

14. Privacy

Everyone has the right to privacy, which includes the right not to have–

(a) their person or home searched;

(b) their property searched;

(c) their possessions seized; or

(d) the privacy of their communications infringed.

15. **Freedom of religion, belief and opinion**
   (1) Everyone has the right to freedom of conscience, religion, thought, belief and opinion.
   (2) Religious observances may be conducted at state or state-aided institutions, provided that–
      (a) those observances follow rules made by the appropriate public authorities;
      (b) they are conducted on an equitable basis; and
      (c) attendance at them is free and voluntary.
   (3) (a) This section does not prevent legislation recognising–
         (i) marriages concluded under any tradition, or a system of religious, personal or family law; or
         (ii) systems of personal and family law under any tradition, or adhered to by persons professing a particular religion.
      (b) Recognition in terms of paragraph (a) must be consistent with this section and the other provisions of the Constitution.

16. **Freedom of expression**
   (1) Everyone has the right to freedom of expression, which includes–
      (a) freedom of the press and other media;
      (b) freedom to receive or impart information or ideas;
      (c) freedom of artistic creativity; and
      (d) academic freedom and freedom of scientific research.
   (2) The right in subsection (1) does not extend to–
      (a) propaganda for war;
      (b) incitement of imminent violence; or
      (c) advocacy of hatred that is based on race, ethnicity, gender or religion, and that constitutes incitement to cause harm.

17. **Assembly, demonstration, picket and petition**
   Everyone has the right, peacefully and unarmed, to assemble, to demonstrate, to picket and to present petitions.

18. **Freedom of association**
   Everyone has the right to freedom of association.

19. **Political rights**
   (1) Every citizen is free to make political choices, which includes the right–
      (a) to form a political party;
      (b) to participate in the activities of, or recruit members for, a political party; and
      (c) to campaign for a political party or cause.

(2) Every citizen has the right to free, fair and regular elections for any legislative body established in terms of the Constitution.

(3) Every adult citizen has the right–

    (a) to vote in elections for any legislative body established in terms of the Constitution, and to do so in secret; and

    (b) to stand for public office and, if elected, to hold office.

20.   **Citizenship**

No citizen may be deprived of citizenship.

21.   **Freedom of movement and residence**

(1) Everyone has the right to freedom of movement.

(2) Everyone has the right to leave the Republic.

(3) Every citizen has the right to enter, to remain in and to reside anywhere in, the Republic.

(4) Every citizen has the right to a passport.

22.   **Freedom of trade, occupation and profession**

Every citizen has the right to choose their trade, occupation or profession freely. The practice of a trade, occupation or profession may be regulated by law.

23.   **Labour relations**

(1) Everyone has the right to fair labour practices.

(2) Every worker has the right–

    (a) to form and join a trade union;

    (b) to participate in the activities and programmes of a trade union; and

    (c) to strike.

(3) Every employer has the right–

    (a) to form and join an employers' organisation; and

    (b) to participate in the activities and programmes of an employers' organisation.

(4) Every trade union and every employers' organisation has the right–

    (a) to determine its own administration, programmes and activities;

    (b) to organise; and

    (c) to form and join a federation.

(5) Every trade union, employers' organisation and employer has the right to engage in collective bargaining. National legislation may be enacted to regulate collective bargaining. To the extent that the legislation may limit a right in this Chapter, the limitation must comply with section 36(1).

(6) National legislation may recognise union security arrangements contained in collective agreements. To the extent that the legislation may limit a right in this Chapter, the limitation must comply with section 36(1).

24. **Environment**

Everyone has the right–

    (a) to an environment that is not harmful to their health or wellbeing; and

    (b) to have the environment protected, for the benefit of present and future generations, through reasonable legislative and other measures that–

        (i) prevent pollution and ecological degradation;

        (ii) promote conservation; and

        (iii) secure ecologically sustainable development and use of natural resources while promoting justifiable economic and social development.

25. **Property**

(1) No one may be deprived of property except in terms of law of general application, and no law may permit arbitrary deprivation of property.

(2) Property may be expropriated only in terms of law of general application–

    (a) for a public purpose or in the public interest; and

    (b) subject to compensation, the amount of which and the time and manner of payment of which have either been agreed to by those affected or decided or approved by a court.

(3) The amount of the compensation and the time and manner of payment must be just and equitable, reflecting an equitable balance between the public interest and the interests of those affected, having regard to all relevant circumstances, including–

    (a) the current use of the property;

    (b) the history of the acquisition and use of the property;

    (c) the market value of the property;

    (d) the extent of direct state investment and subsidy in the acquisition and beneficial capital improvement of the property; and

    (e) the purpose of the expropriation.

(4) For the purposes of this section–

    (a) the public interest includes the nation's commitment to land reform, and to reforms to bring about equitable access to all South Africa's natural resources; and

    (b) property is not limited to land.

(5) The state must take reasonable legislative and other measures, within its available resources, to foster conditions which enable citizens to gain access to land on an equitable basis.

(6) A person or community whose tenure of land is legally insecure as a result of past racially discriminatory laws or practices is entitled, to the extent provided by an Act of Parliament, either to tenure which is legally secure or to comparable redress.

(7) A person or community dispossessed of property after 19 June 1913 as a

result of past racially discriminatory laws or practices is entitled, to the extent provided by an Act of Parliament, either to restitution of that property or to equitable redress.

(8) No provision of this section may impede the state from taking legislative and other measures to achieve land, water and related reform, in order to redress the results of past racial discrimination, provided that any departure from the provisions of this section is in accordance with the provisions of section 36(1).

(9) Parliament must enact the legislation referred to in subsection (6).

26. Housing

(1) Everyone has the right to have access to adequate housing.

(2) The state must take reasonable legislative and other measures, within its available resources, to achieve the progressive realisation of this right.

(3) No one may be evicted from their home, or have their home demolished, without an order of court made after considering all the relevant circumstances. No legislation may permit arbitrary evictions.

27. Health care, food, water and social security

(1) Everyone has the right to have access to–
  (a) health care services, including reproductive health care;
  (b) sufficient food and water; and
  (c) social security, including, if they are unable to support themselves and their dependants, appropriate social assistance.

(2) The state must take reasonable legislative and other measures, within its available resources, to achieve the progressive realisation of each of these rights.

(3) No one may be refused emergency medical treatment.

28. Children

(1) Every child has the right–
  (a) to a name and a nationality from birth;
  (b) to family care or parental care, or to appropriate alternative care when removed from the family environment;
  (c) to basic nutrition, shelter, basic health care services and social services;
  (d) to be protected from maltreatment, neglect, abuse or degradation;
  (e) to be protected from exploitative labour practices;
  (f) not to be required or permitted to perform work or provide services that–
    (i) are inappropriate for a person of that child's age; or
    (ii) place at risk the child's well-being, education, physical or mental health or spiritual, moral or social development;
  (g) not to be detained except as a measure of last resort, in which case, in addition to the rights a child enjoys under sections 12 and 35, the child

may be detained only for the shortest appropriate period of time, and has the right to be–

    (i) kept separately from detained persons over the age of 18 years; and

    (ii) treated in a manner, and kept in conditions, that take account of the child's age;

(h) to have a legal practitioner assigned to the child by the state, and at state expense, in civil proceedings affecting the child, if substantial injustice would otherwise result; and

(i) not to be used directly in armed conflict, and to be protected in times of armed conflict.

(2) A child's best interests are of paramount importance in every matter concerning the child.

(3) In this section "child" means a person under the age of 18 years.

29. Education

(1) Everyone has the right–

    (a) to a basic education, including adult basic education; and

    (b) to further education, which the state, through reasonable measures, must make progressively available and accessible.

(2) Everyone has the right to receive education in the official language or languages of their choice in public educational institutions where that education is reasonably practicable. In order to ensure the effective access to, and implementation of, this right, the state must consider all reasonable educational alternatives, including single medium institutions, taking into account–

    (a) equity;

    (b) practicability; and

    (c) the need to redress the results of past racially discriminatory laws and practices.

(3) Everyone has the right to establish and maintain, at their own expense, independent educational institutions that–

    (a) do not discriminate on the basis of race;

    (b) are registered with the state; and

    (c) maintain standards that are not inferior to standards at comparable public educational institutions.

(4) Subsection (3) does not preclude state subsidies for independent educational institutions.

30. Language and culture

Everyone has the right to use the language and to participate in the cultural life of their choice, but no one exercising these rights may do so in a manner inconsistent with any provision of the Bill of Rights.

31. **Cultural, religious and linguistic communities**
    (1) Persons belonging to a cultural, religious or linguistic community may not be denied the right, with other members of that community–
        (a) to enjoy their culture, practise their religion and use their language; and
        (b) to form, join and maintain cultural, religious and linguistic associations and other organs of civil society.
    (2) The rights in subsection (1) may not be exercised in a manner inconsistent with any provision of the Bill of Rights.

32. **Access to information**
    (1) Everyone has the right of access to–
        (a) any information held by the state; and
        (b) any information that is held by another person and that is required for the exercise or protection of any rights.
    (2) National legislation must be enacted to give effect to this right, and may provide for reasonable measures to alleviate the administrative and financial burden on the state.

33. **Just administrative action**
    (1) Everyone has the right to administrative action that is lawful, reasonable and procedurally fair.
    (2) Everyone whose rights have been adversely affected by administrative action has the right to be given written reasons.
    (3) National legislation must be enacted to give effect to these rights, and must–
        (a) provide for the review of administrative action by a court or, where appropriate, an independent and impartial tribunal;
        (b) impose a duty on the state to give effect to the rights in subsections (1) and (2); and
        (c) promote an efficient administration.

34. **Access to courts**
    Everyone has the right to have any dispute that can be resolved by the application of law decided in a fair public hearing before a court or, where appropriate, another independent and impartial tribunal or forum.

35. **Arrested, detained and accused persons**
    (1) Everyone who is arrested for allegedly committing an offence has the right–
        (a) to remain silent;
        (b) to be informed promptly–
            (i) of the right to remain silent; and
            (ii) of the consequences of not remaining silent;

(c) not to be compelled to make any confession or admission that could be used in evidence against that person;

(d) to be brought before a court as soon as reasonably possible, but not later than–

(i) 48 hours after the arrest; or

(ii) the end of the first court day after the expiry of the 48 hours, if the 48 hours expire outside ordinary court hours or on a day which is not an ordinary court day;

(e) at the first court appearance after being arrested, to be charged or to be informed of the reason for the detention to continue, or to be released; and

(f) to be released from detention if the interests of justice permit, subject to reasonable conditions.

(2) Everyone who is detained, including every sentenced prisoner, has the right–

(a) to be informed promptly of the reason for being detained;

(b) to choose, and to consult with, a legal practitioner, and to be informed of this right promptly;

(c) to have a legal practitioner assigned to the detained person by the state and at state expense, if substantial injustice would otherwise result, and to be informed of this right promptly;

(d) to challenge the lawfulness of the detention in person before a court and, if the detention is unlawful, to be released;

(e) to conditions of detention that are consistent with human dignity, including at least exercise and the provision, at state expense, of adequate accommodation, nutrition, reading material and medical treatment; and

(f) to communicate with, and be visited by, that person's–

(i) spouse or partner;

(ii) next of kin;

(iii) chosen religious counsellor; and

(iv) chosen medical practitioner.

(3) Every accused person has a right to a fair trial, which includes the right–

(a) to be informed of the charge with sufficient detail to answer it;

(b) to have adequate time and facilities to prepare a defence;

(c) to a public trial before an ordinary court;

(d) to have their trial begin and conclude without unreasonable delay;

(e) to be present when being tried;

(f) to choose, and be represented by, a legal practitioner, and to be informed of this right promptly;

(g) to have a legal practitioner assigned to the accused person by the state and at state expense, if substantial injustice would otherwise result, and to be informed of this right promptly;

    (h) to be presumed innocent, to remain silent, and not to testify during the proceedings;

    (i) to adduce and challenge evidence;

    (j) not to be compelled to give self-incriminating evidence;

    (k) to be tried in a language that the accused person understands or, if that is not practicable, to have the proceedings interpreted in that language;

    (l) not to be convicted for an act or omission that was not an offence under either national or international law at the time it was committed or omitted;

    (m) not to be tried for an offence in respect of an act or omission for which that person has previously been either acquitted or convicted;

    (n) to the benefit of the least severe of the prescribed punishments if the prescribed punishment for the offence has been changed between the time that the offence was committed and the time of sentencing; and

    (o) of appeal to, or review by, a higher court.

(4) Whenever this section requires information to be given to a person, that information must be given in a language that the person understands.

(5) Evidence obtained in a manner that violates any right in the Bill of Rights must be excluded if the admission of that evidence would render the trial unfair or otherwise be detrimental to the administration of justice.

36. Limitation of rights

(1) The rights in the Bill of Rights may be limited only in terms of law of general application to the extent that the limitation is reasonable and justifiable in an open and democratic society based on human dignity, equality and freedom, taking into account all relevant factors, including–

    (a) the nature of the right;

    (b) the importance of the purpose of the limitation;

    (c) the nature and extent of the limitation;

    (d) the relation between the limitation and its purpose; and

    (e) less restrictive means to achieve the purpose.

(2) Except as provided in subsection (1) or in any other provision of the Constitution, no law may limit any right entrenched in the Bill of Rights.

37. States of emergency

(1) A state of emergency may be declared only in terms of an Act of Parliament, and only when–

    (a) the life of the nation is threatened by war, invasion, general insurrection, disorder, natural disaster or other public emergency; and

    (b) the declaration is necessary to restore peace and order.

(2) A declaration of a state of emergency, and any legislation enacted or other action taken in consequence of that declaration, may be effective only–

(a) prospectively; and

(b) for no more than 21 days from the date of the declaration, unless the National Assembly resolves to extend the declaration. The Assembly may extend a declaration of a state of emergency for no more than three months at a time. The first extension of the state of emergency must be by a resolution adopted with a supporting vote of a majority of the members of the Assembly. Any subsequent extension must be by a resolution adopted with a supporting vote of at least 60 per cent of the members of the Assembly. A resolution in terms of this paragraph may be adopted only following a public debate in the Assembly.

(3) Any competent court may decide on the validity of–

(a) a declaration of a state of emergency;

(b) any extension of a declaration of a state of emergency; or

(c) any legislation enacted, or other action taken, in consequence of a declaration of a state of emergency.

(4) Any legislation enacted in consequence of a declaration of a state of emergency may derogate from the Bill of Rights only to the extent that–

(a) the derogation is strictly required by the emergency; and

(b) the legislation–

(i) is consistent with the Republic's obligations under international law applicable to states of emergency;

(ii) conforms to subsection (5); and

(iii) is published in the national Government Gazette as soon as reasonably possible after being enacted.

(5) No Act of Parliament that authorises a declaration of a state of emergency, and no legislation enacted or other action taken in consequence of a declaration, may permit or authorize–

(a) indemnifying the state, or any person, in respect of any unlawful act;

(b) any derogation from this section; or

(c) any derogation from a section mentioned in column 1 of the Table of Non-Derogable Rights, to the extent indicated opposite that section in column 3 of the Table.

Table of Non-Derogable Rights

1 Section Number	2 Section Title	3 Extent to which the right is protected
9	Equality	With respect to unfair discrimination solely on the grounds of race, colour, ethnic or social origin, sex, religion, or language.
10	Human Dignity	Entirely
11	Life	Entirely
12	Freedom and Security of the person	With respect to subsections (1)(d) and (e) and 2(c).
13	Slavery, Servitude and forced labour	With respect to slavery and servitude.
28	Children	With respect to: • subsection (1)(d) and (e); • the rights in subparagraphs (i) and (ii) of subsection (1)(g); and • subsection 1(i) in respect of children of 15 years and younger.
35	Arrested, detained and accused persons	With respect to: • subsections (1)(a), (b) and (c) and (2)(d); • the rights in paragraphs (a) to (o) of subsection (3), excluding paragraph (d); • subsection (4); and • subsection (5) with respect to the exclusion of evidence if the admission of that evidence would render the trial unfair.

(6) Whenever anyone is detained without trial in consequence of a derogation of rights resulting from a declaration of a state of emergency, the following conditions must be observed:

(a) An adult family member or friend of the detainee must be contacted as soon as reasonably possible, and informed that the person has been detained.

(b) A notice must be published in the national Government Gazette within five days of the person being detained, stating the detainee's name and place of detention and referring to the emergency measure in terms of which that person has been detained.

(c) The detainee must be allowed to choose, and be visited at any reasonable time by, a medical practitioner.

(d) The detainee must be allowed to choose, and be visited at any reasonable time by, a legal representative.

(e) A court must review the detention as soon as reasonably possible, but no later than 10 days after the date the person was detained, and the court must release the detainee unless it is necessary to continue the detention to restore peace and order.

(f) A detainee who is not released in terms of a review under paragraph (e), or who is not released in terms of a review under this paragraph, may apply to a court for a further review of the detention at any time after 10 days have passed since the previous review, and the court must release the detainee unless it is still necessary to continue the detention to restore peace and order.

(g) The detainee must be allowed to appear in person before any court considering the detention, to be represented by a legal practitioner at those hearings, and to make representations against continued detention.

(h) The state must present written reasons to the court to justify the continued detention of the detainee, and must give a copy of those reasons to the detainee at least two days before the court reviews the detention.

(7) If a court releases a detainee, that person may not be detained again on the same grounds unless the state first shows a court good cause for re-detaining that person.

(8) Subsections (6) and (7) do not apply to persons who are not South African citizens and who are detained in consequence of an international armed conflict. Instead, the state must comply with the standards binding on the Republic under international humanitarian law in respect of the detention of such persons.

38. **Enforcement of rights**

Anyone listed in this section has the right to approach a competent court, alleging that a right in the Bill of Rights has been infringed or threatened, and the court may grant appropriate relief, including a declaration of rights. The persons who may approach a court are–

(a) anyone acting in their own interest;

(b) anyone acting on behalf of another person who cannot act in their own name;

(c) anyone acting as a member of, or in the interest of, a group or class of persons;

(d) anyone acting in the public interest; and

(e) an association acting in the interest of its members.

39. **Interpretation of Bill of Rights**

(1) When interpreting the Bill of Rights, a court, tribunal or forum–

(a) must promote the values that underlie an open and democratic society based on human dignity, equality and freedom;

(b) must consider international law; and

(c) may consider foreign law.

(2) When interpreting any legislation, and when developing the common law or customary law, every court, tribunal or forum must promote the spirit, purport and objects of the Bill of Rights.

(3) The Bill of Rights does not deny the existence of any other rights or freedoms that are recognised or conferred by common law, customary law or legislation, to the extent that they are consistent with the Bill.

About the authors

Essam Al Tamimi

Chairman, Al Tamimi & Company

e.tamimi@tamimi.com

Essam Al Tamimi established Al Tamimi & Company in 1989. As chairman of the firm, Essam has over 34 years' experience in litigation and arbitration in the UAE and the GCC countries, covering almost all fields of law, both private and public law.

Essam received the Lifetime Achievement Award for outstanding contribution to the Gulf Legal Market, as well as receiving the Lifetime Achievement Award from Chambers and Partners in 2019. He has assisted federal and local governments in drafting laws and regulations relating to the Telecommunications Law Authority, Dubai Internet and Media City. He supported the Dubai Chamber of Commerce & Industry in drafting the Federal Industrial Law and implanting regulations. He also contributed to drafting of the relevant laws for establishing several Free Zones in the UAE and assisted the Dubai International Financial Centre Authority in drafting a number of new laws and regulations. In addition to drafting laws, Essam is a regular speaker on Middle Eastern laws and regulations and an expert on the rule of law.

Al Tamimi & Company is now the largest law firm in the Middle East with 17 offices in nine countries and 810 employees. Essam is actively involved in the development of arbitration laws and the training and development of arbitration across the region.

Elizabeth A Andersen

Executive director, World Justice Project

eandersen@worldjusticeproject.org

Elizabeth A Andersen is executive director of the World Justice Project, leading its global efforts to advance the rule of law through data collection and analysis, research and support for a worldwide stakeholder network. She has more than 25 years of experience in the international legal arena, having served previously as director of the American Bar Association Rule of Law Initiative (ABA ROLI) and its Europe and Eurasia Division (previously known as the Central European and Eurasian Law Initiative or ABA CEELI), as executive director of the American Society of International Law (ASIL), and as executive director of Human Rights Watch's Europe and Central Asia Division. Elizabeth is an expert on international human rights law and rule of law development, she has published widely on topics in these fields, and her work has been recognised with a number of awards, including the ASIL Prominent Woman in International Law Award.

About the authors

Kathryn Cameron Atkinson
Member and chair, Miller & Chevalier
katkinson@milchev.com

Kathryn Cameron Atkinson is the chair of Miller
& Chevalier. Her practice focuses on international
corporate compliance and investigations, in
particular, the Foreign Corrupt Practices Act (FCPA)
and international anti-corruption and anti-money
laundering laws, and corporate governance. She
has twice been selected as a government-appointed
Independent Compliance Monitor pursuant to
FCPA-related Department of Justice and Securities
and Exchange Commission resolutions involving
KBR, Inc and ZimmerBiomet, Inc, and often
represents corporations investigating and
remediating compliance failures.

Recognised by *Chambers Global* (Band 1, USA)
as a "leading figure in the world of FCPA
compliance", Kathryn was named in *Global
Investigation Review*'s inaugural "Women in
Investigations" (2015) and "Top FCPA
Practitioners" lists (2021), and *Latinvex*'s "Latin
America's Top 100 Female Lawyers: FCPA and
Fraud" (2017–2021), among others. A frequent
speaker and author on anti-corruption and
compliance topics, she has served as faculty in the
CEELI Institute's Investigating and Prosecuting
Official Corruption training.

Mark S Ellis
Executive director, International Bar Association
mark.ellis@int-bar.org

As executive director of the International Bar
Association (IBA) Mark Ellis leads the foremost
international organisation of bar associations, law
firms and individual lawyers in the world. Prior
to joining the IBA, he spent 10 years as the first
executive director of the Central European and
Eurasian Law Initiative (CEELI), a project of the
American Bar Association (ABA).

Mark served as legal adviser to the
Independent International Commission on
Kosovo, chaired by Justice Richard J Goldstone
and was appointed by OSCE to advise on the
creation of Serbia's War Crimes Tribunal. He was
actively involved with the Iraqi High Tribunal.

In 2015, he was appointed as chair of the UN-
created Advisory Panel on Matters Relating to
Defence Counsel of the Mechanism for
International Criminal Tribunals (previously to
the ICTY and ICTR).

Twice a Fulbright Scholar at the Economic
Institute in Zagreb, Croatia, he earned his JD and BS
(Economics) degrees from Florida State University
and his PhD in Law from King's College, London.

A frequent speaker and media commentator
on international legal issues, Mark has published
extensively in the areas of international
humanitarian law, war crimes tribunals, and the
development of the rule of law.

Richard J Goldstone
Retired justice of the Constitutional Court of
South Africa
rjgoldstone38@gmail.com

Richard J Goldstone served as a Justice of the
South African Constitutional Court from 1994 to
2004. He was the first Chief Prosecutor of the UN
International Tribunals for the former Yugoslavia
and Rwanda. Since 2004 he has taught
international humanitarian law in a number of
leading law schools in the United States and
Europe. In 2020 he chaired the International
Expert Review of the International Criminal Court
appointed by the Assembly of States Parties. He
is an international honorary member of the
American Academy of Arts and Sciences and of
the New York City Bar. He is an honorary bencher
of the Inner Temple, London and an honorary
fellow of St John's College, Cambridge.

Mariah A Lindsay
PhD Candidate, Department of Sociology,
University of Wisconsin-Madison
mariahalindsay@gmail.com

Mariah A Lindsay is a doctoral candidate in the Department of Sociology at the University of Wisconsin-Madison and a Kemper Knapp Fellow. Formerly, Mariah served as the Senior Executive Policy Fellow and Coordinator of Programs for the Center for Biotechnology and Global Health Policy at the University of California, Irvine School of Law. She was also a producer on *Ms.* magazine's podcast, On the Issues with Michele Goodwin. As a Fellow, she co-taught UC Irvine's Reproductive Justice Law Clinic with Professor Michele Goodwin.

Previously, Mariah was a staff attorney at the California Women's Law Center, where she engaged in legal and policy work related to Title IX, reproductive health and rights, and landlord-tenant law. Mariah also served as an If/When/How Reproductive Justice Federal Fellow with the National Asian Pacific American Women's Forum in Washington DC.

Mariah earned her Juris Doctor from UC Irvine School of Law in 2018 and her Bachelor of Arts in Political Science, *summa cum laude*, from California State Polytechnic University, Pomona in 2015.

Michael Maya
Director, International Bar Association
michael.maya@int-bar.org

As the director of the International Bar Association's North America office in Washington DC, Michael Maya liaises with the legal profession, US government agencies and international organisations (ie, United Nations, World Bank). Public service initiatives in which he is active include projects on civic education on the rule of law, climate justice, business and human rights, and North Korean human rights.

Prior to joining the IBA, he worked with the ABA Central European and Eurasian Law Initiative in Uzbekistan and Russia before returning to the United States to serve as the director of CEELI's programmes in the former Soviet Union and later as CEELI's Deputy Director. In 2007, he helped spearhead the consolidation of the ABA's international development programmes, which together formed the American Bar Association Rule of Law Initiative. As ABA ROLI's deputy director, he helped oversee programmes in 60 countries. During his tenure at the ABA, Michael also played a role in the launch of the World Justice Project and the conception and development of the Rule of Law Index, working alongside its founder, William Neukom.

Michael earned a BS from Indiana University and a JD from Cornell University, after which he practised law in New York City.

Homer E Moyer, Jr
Senior counsel, Miller & Chevalier
hmoyer@milchev.com

Homer E Moyer is one of America's leading international lawyers and an expert in international anti-corruption law. A political appointee of both political parties, he served as Counsellor to the Secretary and General Counsel of the US Department of Commerce. Homer co-founded and chaired CEELI, a *pro bono* project in which more than 5,000 lawyers and judges provided technical legal assistance to newly independent, former communist countries. He founded and chairs the CEELI Institute, a rule of law institution and training centre in Prague. A past chair of the International Section of the ABA and Rule of Law Forum of the IBA, he has received GIR and ABA Lifetime Achievement Awards and the Chambers award for Contributions to the

Legal Profession. The author of *Justice and the Military*, a treatise on military law, and *The R.A.T. (Real-World Aptitude Test): Preparing Yourself for Leaving Home*, Homer is a graduate of Emory University and Yale Law School.

Robert A Stein

Professor of Law, University of
Minnesota Law School
stein@umn.edu

Robert A Stein is Everett Fraser Professor of Law at the University of Minnesota Law School. From 1994 to 2006, Professor Stein was the executive director and chief operating officer of the American Bar Association. Prior to that he was dean of the University of Minnesota Law School and William S Pattee Professor of Law.

Professor Stein has been chair of the International Bar Association Professional and Public Interest Division and co-chair of the IBA Rule of Law Action Group. He is a commissioner in the Uniform Law Commission and has served as President of the ULC. He is a member of the American Law Institute and has served on the ALI Council. He is an internationally recognised scholar in the areas of the rule of law and estate planning.

Allison M Whelan

Sharswood Fellow, University of Pennsylvania
Carey Law School; Associate fellow, Leonard
Davis Institute of Health Economics, University
of Pennsylvania
allisonmwhelan@gmail.com

Allison M Whelan is a Sharswood Fellow at the University of Pennsylvania Carey Law School and an associate fellow at the Leonard Davis Institute of Health Economics at the University of Pennsylvania. Allison's research and teaching encompass a broad set of medical, science and social policy issues at the intersection of administrative law, health and FDA law, constitutional law, bioethics, public health preparedness and social justice.

Previously, Allison was an associate at Covington & Burling LLP in Washington DC in the firm's Food, Drug, and Device Practice Group. Allison advised pharmaceutical companies on a variety of regulatory and compliance issues, developing a particular expertise in advising clients that research and develop medical countermeasures.

Allison clerked for the Honorable Guido Calabresi of the US Court of Appeals for the Second Circuit and the Honorable William J Kayatta, Jr of the US Court of Appeals for the First Circuit. She also served as the inaugural senior fellow for the Center for Biotechnology and Global Health Policy at the University of California, Irvine School of Law. Allison graduated from the University of Minnesota Law School, *summa cum laude* and Order of the Coif. She holds a Master of Arts in Bioethics from the University of Minnesota.